# MODERNITY BRITAIN

Opening the Box, 1957–59

# MODERNITY BRITAIN

## Opening the Box, 1957–59

David Kynaston

B L O O M S B U R Y

LONDON · NEW DELHI · NEW YORK · SYDNEY

First published in Great Britain 2013

Copyright © 2013 by David Kynaston

The moral right of the author has been asserted

No part of this book may be used or reproduced in any manner
whatsoever without written permission from the publisher except in the
case of brief quotations embodied in critical articles or reviews

Every reasonable effort has been made to trace copyright holders of material
reproduced in this book, but if any have been inadvertently overlooked the publishers
would be glad to hear from them. For legal purposes the Acknowledgements on page 397
and the Picture Credits on page 399 constitute extensions of the copyright page

Bloomsbury Publishing Plc
50 Bedford Square
London WC1B 3DP

www.bloomsbury.com

Bloomsbury Publishing, London, New Delhi, New York and Sydney

A CIP catalogue record for this book is available from the British Library

ISBN 978 0 7475 8893 1

10 9 8 7 6 5 4 3 2 1

Typeset by Hewer Text UK Ltd, Edinburgh
Printed and bound in Great Britain by CPI Group (UK) Ltd, Croydon CR0 4YY

MIX
Paper from
responsible sources
FSC
www.fsc.org   FSC® C020471

# Contents

# Author's Note

*Tales of a New Jerusalem* is a projected sequence of books about Britain between 1945 and 1979. The first two, *A World to Build* and *Smoke in the Valley*, are gathered together in the volume *Austerity Britain*; the next two, *The Certainties of Place* and *A Thicker Cut*, in the volume *Family Britain*. Accordingly, *Opening the Box* is the fifth book in the sequence, and in effect comprises the first half of the volume *Modernity Britain*, which is intended to cover the years 1957–62.

# OPENING THE BOX

This book is dedicated to Lucy

# PART ONE

# I

# Isn' 'e Smashin'?

'Council tenants and potential council tenants are today a much more typical section of the population at large than ever before,' declared a junior housing minister, Enoch Powell, to the annual conference of the Society of Housing Managers on Thursday, 10 January 1957 – at almost exactly the moment that Harold Macmillan was calling at the Palace to succeed Sir Anthony Eden as the new Conservative prime minister. Later that afternoon, discussion turned to the nonconformists. 'I find that, generally speaking, there is no cause for complaint about the standard of decoration of those tenants who "defy regulations" and do their own,' conceded Lambeth's director of housing, Mr C. C. Carter. 'They carry out the decorations to a standard which is usually very satisfactory. I am not sure whether the day has not arrived when you might well let tenants do their own internal decorations.' Next day's main address was given by Mrs E. Denington, vice-chairman of London County Council's Housing Committee. 'I think that the natural way for people to live is in houses,' she insisted. 'I should like to sound a word of warning to authorities which are thinking of building flats. I believe that no more than 5 per cent of the population want to live in flats. Do not build them unless you have to, and if you have to then do make provision for children, because if you do not you have no right to grumble if they are a nuisance.'

Judy Haines as usual was at home in Chingford on Saturday the 12th. 'Fed up,' she noted flatly. 'Girls went to pictures, John [her husband, earlier known as Abbé] to London, and here I am. Decided to please myself and blow housework. Therefore I enjoyed some needlework – Pamela's frock and curtains.' Another diarist, Allan Preston, the

25-year-old son of an English teacher, went to Burnden Park in the afternoon. 'The first half was very entertaining,' he recorded of the home team's First Division clash with Leeds. 'Both sides attacked crisply and at half time Bolton were winning 4–2. The second half was more dismal. Two goals only were scored and there were one or two unpleasant incidents.' Stay-at-homes could have watched Percy Thrower's *Gardening Club* and *The Lone Ranger* on BBC television, while 7.30 saw another favourite, *Dixon of Dock Green*, back for his third series. 'The whole family has been eagerly waiting for the return of Dixon,' reported a viewer, 'and judging by this edition [characteristically called 'Give a Dog a Good Name'] this series is going to be every bit as good as the last.' *Hancock's Half Hour* by this time was on both radio and television, and on Sunday evening the Light Programme broadcast 'Almost a Gentleman', episode 14 of the fourth radio series: overlooked once again in the New Year's Honours List, the anti-hero of 23 Railway Cuttings, East Cheam is persuaded he needs etiquette lessons, with predictably disastrous results. Perhaps revealingly, Philip Larkin seems never to have evinced any interest in, let alone enthusiasm for, Tony Hancock. 'An utterly lonely Sunday, spent indoors except for the usual excursion to the pillar box,' Larkin wrote from his flat in Hull later that evening to Monica Jones in Leicester. 'I have sat doing nothing since about 4 o' clock, & am now slightly drunk on rum and honey & hot water. The usual revolting insufficient meals – an awful tinned steak pudding, like eating a hot poultice, & sausages ... I can't ever remember being so dead since about 1947.'[1]

'Top People Take *The Times*' was a new poster from Monday the 14th, as the PM sought to finalise his administration. 'Many considerations had to be borne in mind,' the Old Etonian (like his predecessor) would reflect after a difficult process. 'The right, centre & left of the party; the extreme "Suez" group; the extreme opposition to Suez; the loyal centre – and last, but not least, U & non-U (to use the jargon that Nancy Mitford has popularised), that is, Eton, Winchester, etc. on the one hand; Board school & grammar school on the other.' Top people also had to face the cameras, and Macmillan on the 17th found himself on fraught terms with the new-fangled teleprompter as he gave a ministerial broadcast. Reactions were mixed. 'In its *extremely* clear intimation that we were neither a second-rate power nor a satellite [i.e. of the USA], it gave me a lift of the heart such as I had never hoped to experience again,' wrote the once-Marxist novelist Patrick Hamilton to his brother. But a 67-year-old housewife in Barrow, Nella Last, was appalled to read next morning in her *Daily Express* about Macmillan's apparent promise to move decisively towards what she called 'free trade with Europe': 'I'm not either clever or well read, I don't – can't – decide the issues of such a step, BUT I *do* disagree utterly with one man coming to a T.V. screen, & calmly announcing such a step . . . As I tidied round I thought that many cleverer heads than mine would feel the same sense of "shock"!' Labour's television guru Anthony Wedgwood Benn was abroad, but heard disturbingly favourable reports on his return. 'His television performance was evidently a very dramatic one,' Benn noted. 'His call for an "opportunity state" has created interest and discussion just when things looked so soggy in his own Party.' The Edwardian actor-manager was indeed not someone to underestimate, though Malcolm Muggeridge soon afterwards had a bit of fun in *Life*. 'The lean, sinewy neck pulsates,' he told his American readers, 'the tired grey features wear a smile; the voice, soft and sibilant, emerges from the drooping moustache. A publisher? No. A civil servant? No. A Prime Minister.'[2]

Modelled on the Parisian jazz club Le Caveau, the Cavern opened in Liverpool the evening before Macmillan's broadcast. Nearly 2,000 people queued outside, only 600 were able to get in, and (reported a local paper in a brief story about 'Liverpool's New Jazzy Club') 'dressed in jeans, skirts and sweaters, they filled every corner of the club, standing packed between the bricked arches', as they listened to 'various jazz bands' plus the Coney Island Skiffle Group. The foreign influence was spreading. 'The snack bar near Kew Gardens station was crowded out,' noted the solipsistic, emotionally impenetrable civil servant Henry St John on Saturday the 19th. 'There seem no times or seasons for anything now; people seem to fill cafés day and night, whereas they used to be almost deserted except at meal times.' The old insularity was also starting to go in football, with Manchester United the first English team to take part (in defiance of the football authorities) in the European Cup and soon afterwards – on 6 February – beating Bilbao 3–0 to reach the semi-finals. Next day's *Listener* reviewed Lawrence Durrell's novel *Justine*, the first volume of what would become an exotic literary phenomenon, *The Alexandria Quartet*. 'Less fiction than incantation,' reckoned Ronald Bryden, 'beautifully conceived, only too consciously beautiful in the writing.' Durrell himself lived in Provence and was fond of calling England 'Pudding Island', a view that in certain moods the young American poet Sylvia Plath (recently married to Ted Hughes) shared. 'It is often infuriating to read the trash published by the Old Guard, the flat, clever, colorless poets here,' she wrote back home a few days earlier. Little was as unashamedly English as *At the Drop of a Hat*, the musical revue by Michael Flanders and Donald Swann playing since 24 January to packed houses at the Fortune Theatre. 'None of their songs are very melodious and not all of them are really amusing,' grumbled Anthony Heap, local government officer in St Pancras and inveterate first-nighter, but Harold Hobson in the *Sunday Times* relished the 'kindly satire' and 'the crisp, neat, elegant, cultured jokes about gnus, bindweed, the monotonous lot of the umpire in the Ladies' Singles at Wimbledon, the very contemporary furniture of his flat, and the disastrous season of 1546 in the English theatre'. Flanders (bearded and in a wheelchair) had, Hobson added, 'an inner merriment which, when he is not speaking, communicates itself to the audience'.[3]

The day after Flanders and Swann opened in the West End, five shop stewards at Briggs Motor Bodies, the Ford Motor Company's bodymaking plant at Dagenham, were suspended – one of them, an extrovert, free-speaking Cockney from West Ham called Johnny McLoughlin, indefinitely. His offence was that, during working hours, he had defied the wishes of his foreman by ringing a handbell in order to call a meeting in his toolmaking 'shop' to discuss possible strike action, following the suspension of two fellow shop stewards for unauthorised absences. Within days the 'bellringer' incident had led to a walk-out by some 8,000 employees. 'The workers of Briggs know very well that the Company is trying to exploit the situation of unemployment and short time which exists in Dagenham at the present time,' declared the Strike Committee, in the larger context of continuing post-Suez petrol rationing causing problems for the motor industry as a whole. 'They are trying to force a return to the bad old days when "Fordism" was a by-word for non-trade unionism, low wages, and bad working conditions.' Talks to reinstate McLoughlin broke down, with the man himself declining to look for another billet. 'What chance would I have after all the publicity this has brought me?' he explained on 12 February to the

*Daily Mail.* 'Wherever I go I am known as "the man who tolled the bell".' That same day, the Tory MP for Hornchurch, Godfrey Lagden, told the Commons that Briggs had 'the most unfortunate collection, above-average collection, of shop stewards who are practically Communists', adding that generally for the workers there 'it is extremely dangerous not to come out when they ring the bell'. Dagenham's Labour MP, John Parker, spoke of how at Ford (including Briggs) 'no attempt is made to treat individuals as live men and women, but to just take them as industrial cogs'. Two days later, Amalgamated Engineering Union (AEU) members at Briggs voted decisively for further strike action, though leaving time for government intervention. Through it all, there had been something else on the collective Briggs mind: the home tie (on 9 February) for the company's football team against the Amateur Cup holders, mighty Bishop Auckland. At a packed Rush Green, the visitors squeaked home by the only goal – 'very lucky', according to the *Barking Advertiser*'s 'Onlooker', against 'the motor boys . . . firing smoothly on all eleven cylinders'.[4]

Almost everywhere, whether in Dagenham or County Durham, the shared daily reference points were shifting from sound to vision. 'Mrs Atkinson keeps asking when we are coming in to see the Television,' Nella Last noted on the last Wednesday of January about her persistent neighbour, '& I'd a rather difficult task of explaining how my husband would never stay up to see any play.' Radio that evening included a road-and-housing-development storyline in *Educating Archie* and some typical by-play in *Take It From Here*. Standing outside the house he shares with his father, Ron Glum is kissing his girlfriend Eth good-bye when he realises he is locked out. He rings the bell to wake up Mr Glum senior, who opens the door:

> *Mr Glum:* Eth? What you coming round this time of night for?
> *Eth:* I'm going.
> *Mr Glum:* You mean you got an old man like me out of a hot bed just to tell me you're going? Oh, I dunno what's come over this generation. It's all them Elvis Parsley records.

Most people's focus that Wednesday, though, was on *Double Your Money*, in particular whether Lynda Simpson, a 13-year-old schoolgirl from Sutton Coldfield, would take the £500 she'd already won through her spelling prowess or try to double it. 'It's your decision, my girl,' her father was reported in the *Daily Mirror* as having told her, while Lynda herself calmly announced at the start of the programme, 'I think I'll disregard everybody's advice and go on.' So she did, entering the see-through box and successfully spelling five words: *manoeuvre, connoisseur, reconnoitre, chlorophyll* and *hypochondriac*. 'What are you going to do with the money?' asked compère Hughie Green. 'I'm going to buy a tape recorder and put the rest in the bank,' Lynda replied. 'I hope to go to a university and it'll help to pay for that.'[5]

Lynda had presumably passed her 11-plus, but that was not the case for the majority of the nation's children. Two days later, on 1 February, the BBC showed a largely reassuring television documentary about the exam, presented by the Canadian political analyst Robert McKenzie and featuring a secondary modern in north London. A chemist noted disapprovingly that 'there appeared to be no expense spared in this school to buy every bit of modern equipment possible', but a teacher's wife preferred to accentuate the positive: 'How wonderfully the children behaved. There was no glancing at the cameras, etc, which is so apt to distract the viewer.' This proved a relatively uncontroversial programme – unlike the following Monday's *Panorama*, which included a clip from a film by Dr Grantly Dick-Read (whose work had inspired the recently founded Natural Childbirth Association, later National Childbirth Trust) showing a natural childbirth through relaxation. Only two people rang in to complain, but the headline in the right-wing tabloid *Daily Sketch* was 'REVOLTING', its columnist 'Candidus' condemning the film as 'part of the exhibitionism that is the growing weakness of our day and age'.[6]

Between those two programmes, on the evening of Sunday the 3rd, Britain's first rock 'n' roll star, Tommy Steele, and his band were giving two performances (each lasting barely 20 minutes) in Leicester. 'The act itself is simple enough,' wrote Trevor Philpott in *Picture Post*. 'It's ninety per cent youthful exuberance. There is not a trace of sex, real or implied. The Steelemen, bass, drums, saxophone and piano, all writhe around the stage with their instruments – even the pianist doesn't have a stool. All the antics they, as professionals, freely admit have nothing to do with music. As Tommy would put it: "We do it for laughs."' As for the audience, it was 'happy – hysterically so', reported the *Leicester Mercury*. 'They were saying (in rock 'n' roll jargon): "Isn' 'e smashin'?" "Isn' 'e a luvly colour?" "Isn' 'e berrer than that other feller?" and "Aren't you glad you came, Elsie?" Others didn't say a word. They just shouted.' In fact not everyone was entirely happy. 'I felt rather ashamed of my sex on Sunday night,' an 18-year-old from Kibworth wrote to the paper: 'I'm no square, but it was shocking. Silly girls go to make fools of themselves by screaming and shouting, the whole of the show through. I attended the show but have no idea what he sang. I'm a great fan of Tommy's, but I like to listen not scream.' An immediate riposte came from Diane, Judy and Pat of 212 Wigston Lane, Leicester: 'We think he is the mostest and the best recording artist Britain has ever produced. THE WAY HE DIGS ROCK 'N' ROLL SENDS US ALL SCREAMING WITH DELIGHT.'

In spite of the attendant noise and hysteria, there was little dangerous about the 20-year-old Steele – a former merchant seaman called Tommy Hicks who was, in Philpott's words, 'an ordinary, likeable British kid who obviously gets a kick out of life' – nor was there about the appreciably older, rather podgy Bill Haley, who arrived in England with his Comets two days later. Besieged by fans at Waterloo station, Haley remarked, 'I'd rather the kids would show more restraint.' Over the next few weeks, for all the audiences' jiving in the aisles, his underlying middle-of-the-roadness was epitomised by his regular, benign refrain to journalists that 'all young people have a certain amount of vim and vigour and they like to let off steam and I really don't see too much harm in that'. Still, especially with Steele, *something* – just for a moment – was going on. 'There was a croak in his voice like he meant the words,' recalled Ray Gosling about walking down East Street market in south London around this time, as his latest hit, 'Singing the Blues', sounded out from the record trestles on the market stalls, 'and there were photographs of him bulldog-clipped to the stalls and Tommy Steele looked like us – cheeky British youth with tousled hair and pouting lips and a cockney so-fucking-what look.'[7]

There would be all too few market stalls in the Stepney–Poplar Comprehensive Development Area (CDA). 'Poplar will have its 19-storey skyscraper' was the *East London Advertiser*'s main headline on 8 February, having learned that the Minister of Housing, Henry

Brooke, had just given his approval to the London County Council's scheme for Tidey Street – thereby overriding the wishes of the local council, whose leader had recently described the scheme as a 'monstrosity'. Indeed, the considered view of the council was that high blocks of flats were 'just a load of trouble'. The *Architects' Journal* in its next issue disagreed: 'Tidey Street is unlikely to prove the best advertisement for tower blocks: but it is a great deal the better for having one, and may even convince the Poplar Borough Council that some of the objections of their tenants to high blocks can be overcome by improved design.' Brooke's was not the only approval, for on the 8th the Secretary of State for Scotland signalled the green light for the Hutchesontown/ Gorbals CDA. 'That guarantees an end to the dingy squalor that is Gorbals' was the unambiguously welcoming response of the *Glasgow Herald*. Accompanying photographs showed on the one hand a model of the new Gorbals with its 'spacious layout' and on the other a squalid back court in Florence Street, 'an example of the conditions which will be eliminated by the Glasgow Corporation plan'.

Of the human aspect of what would be involved in 'comprehensive development', not a word. A few days later, Wilfred Pickles was in the East End to present a live edition of radio's still very popular *Have a Go!*. One contestant was Sam Ward, a council park attendant living in Dagenham: 'I'd sooner be back in old Poplar; you can't beat the neighbours.'[8] One can perhaps exaggerate the neighbourliness of those neighbours, but (as in the Gorbals and, in due course, many other rundown inner-city areas) they were about to be cast to the four winds, as their intimate, intensely human world disappeared for ever.

Other issues, reported the *New Statesman*'s Norman MacKenzie from the 'slightly dingy dormitory area' of North Lewisham, were on voters' minds ahead of the by-election there on Valentine's Day:

> I liked that Gaitskell until he started running down our boys [i.e. British troops during the Suez crisis]. It isn't right for Labour to do that. They should get on with doing something for the old people. That's their business. *(Housewife)*
>
> I thought Macmillan would be different. But he's giving in to the Yanks, too. He should go on and teach those Egyptians and Indians a lesson. *(Shopkeeper)*

I don't care about foreign policy. If anything I've always believed Eden. But I'm going to retire next year, and they tell me that this Rent Bill will put my rent bill up 15 shillings a week. I won't be able to afford it on my pension. I know it sounds selfish but I'm going to vote for myself. *(Teacher)*

The Blues have always come and fetched me, and I've put one in for them. But they can find someone else this time. The doctor told me it was Mr Butler who put that money on my medicine, and I don't see why I should go out and catch my death for him. *(Pensioner)*

I don't like what Labour did over Suez. But that isn't what the voting is about, is it? They're against the Tories, and so am I. *(Busman)*

Hugh Gaitskell's Labour Party duly took the seat from the Tories, the latter's 'most positive set-back since the 1945 General Election' according to the *Sunday Times*. The three most obvious reasons were the Suez debacle, inflation and the legislation under way to de-freeze private-sector rents, but for respectable 'middle England' people – natural Tory voters – something else was increasingly agitating them: excessive taxation and the unacceptably high cost of maintaining the welfare state. 'We have worked hard and saved all our lives, and the worry of modern conditions may yet drive us into a mental institution,' a couple in their sixties from West Bromwich wrote to the *Birmingham Mail* on the day of the by-election. 'Can't the Government, who do everything for the lazy and extravagant, do something for the thrifty and careful? They'll take most of what we have left when we die, anyhow.' So too in Barrow earlier in the week. 'Mrs Atkinson was in a "militant" mood,' recorded Nella Last. 'She said "Welfare State" – time it got working smoother & not throwing money about.' Mrs Atkinson then proceeded to tell Last about a woman 'in a nearby road' who was 'never economising', became widowed, and was now getting her rent and rates paid. 'It's a queer world,' the diarist reflected later. 'No wonder there's unrest & discontent, no one seems to have the idea of standing on their own! I hear grumbles from OAPs & mothers drawing allowances, as if they feel there's a bottomless purse for the Govt to draw on, & it's their *right* to have an increasing share!'[9]

Another matter of state was vexing Last that Monday the 11th. 'I often say nowadays, though with ever lessening frequency, "nothing would surprise me nowadays",' she noted, but the guarded hints on the front page of the *Express*, of differences between the Queen & Duke of Edinburgh, was a bombshell . . . I felt *sick* with pity for the Royal Family, with 'spies' & 'disloyalty' in those near to them. I hope there's no foundation in the rumour, but they don't have a *lot* of shared interests on the whole. The Queen has horse racing, & he the sea. They don't seem to 'give and take'.

With Philip in Gibraltar near the end of his four-month world tour, the couple not due to be reunited until the following Saturday (in Portugal at the start of a joint visit there), and stories in the American press leading to official denials of any 'rift', the *Daily Mirror* was especially strident. 'FLY HOME, PHILIP!' it demanded on Monday, followed on Tuesday by 'DUKE – WHY NO ACTION?'. The Palace remained unmoved, and briefly the focus switched to the Queen's younger sister. 'When is Princess Margaret going to be her age (which is 26) and behave like a member of the Royal Family instead of a half-baked jazz mad Teddy Girl?' another royal-watcher, Anthony Heap, asked himself on Friday. 'For what should be reported in this morning's papers but that last night she went to see the latest trashy "rock 'n' roll" film [*The Girl Can't Help It*] at the Carlton – she never goes to an intelligent play or film – and, taking off her shoes, put her feet up on the rail round the front of the circle and waved them in time with the "hot rhythm".' Next day the Queen duly flew out in a Viscount, the Duke (with hearts on his tie) went into the plane at Montijo airfield for some private minutes, and when they emerged together he had, the *Sunday Express* was able happily to report, 'a tiny smear of lipstick on his face'.[10]

The couple missed a notable few days on the small screen, not least the controversial end of the so-called 'Toddlers' Truce'. This was the government-enforced ban on television programmes between 6 and 7 in the evening, to make it easier for parents to get younger children to bed, a ban that the commercial television companies had found increasingly irksome. 'Keep the Toddlers' Truce!' insisted the *Sketch*'s 'Candidus' in December 1956. 'The most docile children who are taken away from a fascinating programme will be tearful and deprived, and will lie awake thinking of what they are missing.' But the Postmaster General, Dr Charles Hill, was adamant that 'it was the responsibility of parents, not the State, to put their children to bed at the right time', and

16 February was set as the date for the start of hostilities. The BBC's new Saturday programme to fill that slot would be, explained the *Radio Times*, 'designed for the young in spirit who like to keep abreast of topical trends in the world about them', with 'plenty of music in the modern manner'.[11]

On the 16th itself, following a news bulletin, the *Six-Five Special* came down the tracks right on time, with a catchy signature tune ('over the points, over the points') and two definitely non-teenage presenters, Pete Murray and Josephine Douglas, doing the honours:

> *Pete:* Hi there, welcome aboard the *Six-Five Special*. We've got almost a hundred cats jumping here, some real cool characters to give us a gas, so just get with it and have a ball.
> *Jo:* Well, I'm just a square it seems, but for all the other squares with us, roughly translated what Peter Murray just said was, we've got some lively musicians and personalities mingling with us here, so just relax and catch the mood from us.

What followed over the next 55 minutes included rock 'n' roll from the King Brothers, jazz from Kenny Baker and his Dozen, ballads from Michael Holliday, a group of youngsters from Whitechapel singing a couple of folk songs, an interview with the film actress Lisa Gastoni, an exercise demonstration by the former boxer Freddie Mills and two muscular Hungarian refugees, an extract from a Little Richard film – and, a gloriously Reithian touch, the concert pianist Leff Pouishnoff playing a movement from Beethoven's 'Pathétique' Sonata and then, 'just to show that we, too, can play fast and loud', Chopin's Prelude in B flat minor.

'There was plenty of evidence to show that the older the viewer the less he (or she) enjoyed this programme,' was the predictable conclusion of BBC audience research, adding that though some older viewers were tolerant ('Of course we must cater for youth,' said one), others found it 'utterly trashy' and 'quite intolerably noisy'. As for teenage viewers, there were two perhaps representative responses, the first by an apprentice panel beater: 'I am what is known as a "square" so how could I enjoy this? And why do we have to have so much Rock 'n' Roll lammed at us?' 'This is what many of us have wanted for a long time

and I just cannot say how much I enjoyed it. But my dad was grumbling all the time. He said it was "just a lot of noise".' The *News
Chronicle* critic tended to agree with Dad – 'a noisy, clanking special'
– while the *Daily Telegraph*'s L. Marsland Gander confirmed all the
instinctive prejudices of his readers: 'A hundred "cats" were let loose
on unsuspecting viewers. Grim-faced, many of them oddly dressed in
tight trousers, they jived and did their dervish dances to loud brassy
noises.' But it was arguably the shrewd, level-headed Peter Black, the
*Daily Mail*'s TV critic, who called it right: Murray was 'jaunty', Douglas
was 'arch', and 'the whole thing smelled fragrantly of bread and butter'.[12]

Next day, Sunday, BBC programmes were set out in the *Radio
Times* with television coming before radio, for the first time, while
Monday saw the arrival of lunchtime television in the shape of *Lunch
Box* on ITV. 'People now eat from trays,' presenter Noele Gordon
said in advance, 'so they can watch the show and pick up our catch
phrases.' The show itself, focusing on viewers' birthdays and wedding
anniversaries as well as plenty of baby snapshots sent in by mothers,
drew some predictable flak – 'the most folksy, matey, cuddly
programme yet', reckoned Maurice Wiggin in the *Sunday Times* – but
again Black was perceptive, describing Gordon as 'absolutely first-
class, an elegant chum who catches perfectly the desired blend of
charm and class-war neutrality'. Yet it was not for *Lunch Box* that 18
February 1957 has gone down in television history, but for the launch
of the BBC's weekday evening programme to replace the Toddlers'
Truce. '*Tonight*', promised the *Radio Times*, 'will be kaleidoscopic
but it will not be superficial; it will be entertaining but it will also be
intelligent.'[13]

The first edition of this current affairs magazine, presented by the
avuncular, unflappable Cliff Michelmore, featured 12 items over 40
minutes. These included the FA Cup draw, a survey of the morning's
papers, a topical calypso by Cy Grant ('Future sociologists may well
speculate/On the impact of *Tonight* on the welfare state'), a nude statue
of Aphrodite that was causing consternation in Richmond-upon-
Thames, an interview with the Dame of Sark, a humorous sketch by a
young Jonathan Miller about Charing Cross Road shops, an interview
by Derek Hart with the veteran American broadcaster Ed Murrow on
the subject of post-Suez Britain, footage of conductor Arturo Toscanini's

funeral in Milan earlier in the day, and Cy Grant again, this time singing 'Kisses Sweeter than Wine'. The critics were qualifiedly positive: 'kept on repeating itself', but 'I applaud the programme's attempt to develop a free-and-easy topical programme' (Raymond Bowers, *Mirror*); 'had variety, some spice and reasonable pace but lacked compelling interest and gaiety' (L. Marsland Gander); 'a promising start', though Miller's sketch 'invaded the territory that Johnny Morris has made his own and was duly slaughtered by the comparison' (Peter Black). Viewers themselves gave largely favourable feedback about the first week's editions as a whole, with Grant's up-to-the-minute calypsos (sometimes written by the journalist Bernard Levin) 'particularly enjoyed' and 'the "personality" interviews' holding 'pride of place in viewers' estimation'. For Michelmore as anchorman, praise was almost unanimous: 'Viewers on all sides commended him as "a good mixer", friendly and informal in his approach to participants in the programme, and a clear and relaxed speaker, with the ability to cope quickly (and effectively) with any contretemps.'

*Tonight* was a breakthrough moment. For almost a year and a half, since its launch in September 1955, commercial television had been trouncing BBC in the ratings and, more generally, exposing it as stuffy, unimaginative and deeply paternalistic. *Tonight* – the inspiration of a brilliant, difficult 33-year-old Welshman, Donald Baverstock – was different. 'The aim would be to get on to a level of conversation with the viewers which means that the presentation and the manner of the people appearing in the programme would be very informal and relaxed,' he had written in early January to a BBC superior (Grace Wyndham Goldie), and over the next few years that was what, working closing with Alasdair Milne (a future director-general), he drove through. The tone was deliberately light, even irreverent, news mixing seamlessly with entertainment. Pioneering use was made of vox pop material, and above all the programme consciously placed itself on the side of the citizen and the consumer rather than the minister or the official. 'A kind of national explosion of relief' was how Goldie herself would contextualise *Tonight*'s impact. 'It was not always necessary to be respectful; experts were not invariably right; the opinions of those in high places did not have to be accepted.'[14] None of this happened overnight, not least in the field of planning and architecture, but a broad, unstoppable process was under way, and *Tonight* – for all its preponderant middle-classness – was an indispensable outrider.

For truly mass audiences, however, television's future lay elsewhere, and Tuesday the 19th saw a final new programme in this rather breathless sequence. Originally entitled *Calling Nurse Roberts* and set in the fictitious hospital Oxbridge General, *Emergency–Ward 10* was ITV's first high-profile, twice-weekly soap opera. 'Should run for ever,' Maurice Wiggin confidently predicted, adding:

> It is bound to delight all who gulp in euphoric draughts of an atmosphere of iodoform and bedpans. It has just about everything: a flawless blonde probationer nurse, and a dedicated brunette one, and a rather sleazy doctor, and a martinet sister, and a crotchety 'character' patient with a heart of gold. All it needs is for Dan Archer to be wheeled in by Gran Grove and operated on by Dr Dale, and that's the millennium, folks.[15]

2

# A Lot of Mums

'It was reading Hoggart forty years ago,' recalled Alan Bennett in his preface to *The History Boys* (2004), 'that made me feel that my life, dull though it was, might be made the stuff of literature.' Or, as David Lodge characterised the impact of Richard Hoggart's *The Uses of Literacy* (published in February 1957, going into Pelican paperback in 1958 and reprinted four times in the next seven years), 'In those days it was a kind of Bible for first-generation university students and teachers who had been promoted by education from working-class and lower-middle-class backgrounds into the professional middle class.' From the start, the chorus of critics' adjectives revealed this to be the right book for a particular cultural moment – 'challenging' (*Daily Herald*), 'invigorating' (*Daily Telegraph*), 'urgent' (*Observer*), 'required reading' (*TLS*) – while the *Manchester Guardian* devoted an editorial to Hoggart's 'moving and thoughtful' work:

> The first part is an exquisitely drawn picture of the urban working-class life in which the author (now an extra-mural tutor at Hull University) grew up; hard, sometimes harsh, conventional, gregarious, mother-centred, with an outlook limited in range but realistic within its limits. The second part describes the erosion of some old landmarks by the irrupting new media of popular culture – the cheap magazine with its sex and 'bittiness', the cheap novel with its sex and violence, the juke-box, some radio, much television, all 'full of a corrupt brightness, of improper appeals and moral evasions', and all leading to a broad and shallow condition of mind, a hazy euphory, and an increasingly ready response to (a significant phrase) 'sensation without commitment'.

Hoggart himself (born in 1918) had grown up in the Hunslet district of
Leeds, the *locus classicus* of the book's wonderfully vivid, often very
autobiographical opening half. The cultural historian Richard Johnson
has offered perhaps the most acute assessment of why, over and above
those who identified with the 'scholarship boy' theme, *Uses* had such
appeal: 'It was surely the fact that working-class culture was described
intimately, from within, that made the book so powerful. For the
middle-class reader, it was a solvent of assumed cultural superiorities or
a lesson, at the very least, in cultural relativities.'[1]

Two months later in 1957, another, more explicitly sociological,
study (also in due course a best-selling Pelican) likewise hit the mark. 'I
suppose that, having in our various ways in our previous jobs been on
the fringes of the Establishment, we are in revolt against it,' Michael
Young had reflected the previous year about himself and his colleagues
at the recently founded Institute of Community Studies. 'We feel,' he
continued,

> that our former associates in the Cabinet's Ministries and Parties were in
> a strange way out of touch with the ordinary people whom they so confi-
> dently administered, and we feel that we want to put them right. For this
> purpose a mere first-hand description of what people's lives are like
> seems to us justified . . . We pin our faith on our powers of observation
> and our more or less literary skill in describing the results. Then too we
> are in protest against the contemptuous attitude which the intellectual
> department of the Establishment seems to have towards the working
> classes . . .

In the event, *Family and Kinship in East London*, co-written by Young
and Peter Willmott, had an even greater initial impact than Hoggart's
*Uses*. During the last eight days of April, the *Star* (one of London's
three evening papers) ran a five-part serialisation ('Londoners under
the microscope'); there were major stories on the book in the *Herald*,
the *Mirror*, the *News Chronicle* ('Strangers in a Council Paradise')
and the *Telegraph* ('East Enders Dislike Spacious New Estates: Family
Links Are Missed'). *The Times* had a long leader ('The Ties that
Matter') endorsing the housing aspect of the central argument that
most Bethnal Greeners preferred to stay in their familiar local

community rather than move out to the less friendly new LCC estate in 'Greenleigh' (in fact Debden), while the *Daily Mail* ran a big feature story ('The wife-beater doesn't live here any more') highlighting the claim that Bethnal Green husbands were becoming increasingly domesticated:

> It is a refreshing change from the deluge of treatises on problem families, Teddy Boys, juvenile delinquency, broken homes, and child neglect which have created an impression that working-class families are dis-united, unsocial, and unhappy.
>
> Mr Willmott lived in Bethnal Green for two years during the researches with his social-worker wife, Phyllis, and two young children. He enjoyed the rich, down-to-earth, companionable life so much that he left only because he wanted a garden for the children.

The reviews themselves were largely positive, typified by the conclusion of George Bull's in the *Financial Times*: 'This shrewd – and in places extremely amusing – book combines warmth of feeling with careful sociological method. It should make us look at the new towns and estates with a keener eye.'[2]

One avowedly left-wing critic (whose own Fabian pamphlet *Socialism and the Intellectuals* had made a mini-splash at the start of the year) took on both books. 'The main trouble with Mr Hoggart's diagnostics is that they are as thin in illustrations as his reminiscences are rich' was Kingsley Amis's negative reaction to the second half of *Uses*:

> He sees his 'mass publications and entertainments' from the outside. He tells us in a note that ballroom dancing is the second-largest entertainment industry in the country with its 500-odd ballrooms, but he might never have been in one of them for any sign he gives of understanding the part they play in their patrons' world. His account of modern popular songs is evidently based upon an exiguous, ill-chosen sample and is riddled with precarious intuitions about such imponderables as the kind and degree of self-consciousness displayed. He does not know what television programmes are like or how people behave while they watch them; he does not know that *Astounding Science Fiction* prints some of the best works in its genre despite its name and cover which are

doubtless all he has seen of it; he does not even know that there is more than one kind of comic strip.

Amis's final sentence was a disdainful flick of the wrist from someone who had himself come a long way in barely three years: 'It would be pleasant to say of the book written out of such obvious earnestness and decency of feeling that it represented an achievement, but it is only an attempt.' He was on the whole warmer towards *Family and Kinship*, praising Young and Willmott as 'observant, tactful, sympathetic, humorous – and able to write'. But he did wonder about the key element in their treatment of community in Bethnal Green:

> The central figures of this network are the mums, educators, providers of the family meeting-place, non-technical obstetric consultants, child-care advisers, regular lenders of that vital ten-bob note. I hope I can say without undue disrespect that if I were a working-class girl in Bethnal Green I should probably find somewhere like Holyhead or Wick a handy place to conduct my relationship with Mum after marriage, but then I am not, and on the evidence here presented I cannot doubt that my feelings are shared by few. Or I would not doubt it if I were certain that the authors never confused seeing Mum every day and liking it with seeing Mum every day and being too pious, too timid or too lazy to complain.

'Anyhow,' as he added with a certain weariness, 'a lot of Mums are seen a lot of the time.'

Other readers also had their reservations, with undoubtedly the spikiest intervention coming in May from Leonard Cottrell, a BBC producer who for several months had been researching the New Towns clustered around London (including Stevenage, Bracknell, Crawley and Hemel Hempstead). Declaring himself 'sick of middle-class reviewers and sociologists who persist in sentimentalising the working class', he continued in a riposte in the *Listener* to its recent favourable review (by an academic psychologist) of *Family and Kinship*:

> 'Mum' is a monster . . . In my investigations I have found, time and time again, that working-class wives are happy and relieved to put thirty miles between themselves and 'Mum'; that she is no longer there to interfere

with her aboriginal warmth, her glutinous, devouring affection. Young wives who had been dominated throughout childhood, adolescence, and marriage by these stupid, arrogant, self-pitying matriarchs have suddenly found that they can do without them, to the benefit of their own happiness and that of their husbands.

Strongly suspecting that the same was true in 'Greenleigh', and lamenting that Young and Willmott 'will not face up to the fact', Cottrell went on:

> In my experience a small minority of New Town residents long for the pubs, the fish-and-chip shops, the 'chumminess' of the crowded streets; perhaps three or four per cent, not more. The rest are extremely glad to have, for the first time in their lives, a home of their own, with fitted carpets, 'contemporary' furniture, and a washing-machine – all the middle-class trimmings over which middle-class social investigators shake their heads but which working-class people value, when they can get them.
>
> The trouble is that some middle-class people, such as authors and book-reviewers, will persist in romanticising aspects of working-class life of which they themselves have had no direct experience – 'neighbourliness', 'kinship', etc., and the stifling, claustrophobic intimacy of crowded tenements, which have been forced upon working people by sheer economic circumstance.

That autumn, in *Encounter*, Tosco Fyvel called 'surely too romantic' the authors' 'sweeping conclusion' that 'Bethnal Greeners should be rehoused on the spot so that their family ties could be kept intact', arguing from their own evidence that at 'Greenleigh' the 'significant answer was that given to the investigators even by discontented families: that they would not think of returning to Bethnal Green because of the undisputed advantage of the new Estate for their children'. Soon afterwards, a damning-with-faint-praise review in the *TLS* ('their field work was reasonably careful') took particular issue with how 'the authors deplore the fact that workers moved to Essex developed middle-class, particularly lower middle-class, ways':

The fact is that in Bethnal Green these families were isolated from those social patterns increasingly characteristic of Great Britain. It was rather in Essex that they encountered the current face of things for the first time. The authors regret the destruction of working-class traditions, but their own remedies will hardly alter the larger movement of British society.

Perhaps the most suggestive review was in the obscure pages of *Case Conference*, 'A Professional Journal for the Social Worker and Social Administrator'. Justifiably praising the book's many-sidedness, and Young and Willmott's 'ear for language', the young housing expert David Donnison thought aloud about whether 'Greenleigh' itself (depicted by the authors as cold, non-communal, materialistic, etc.) was *really* the prime culprit for the feeling of loss and helplessness among many Bethnal Greeners newly or recently settled there:

> Could the *old* community also be to blame – a community with so shel-tered a social life that its warm human relationships are all ready-made for children to grow into without ever consciously 'making' a friend? It may be that the cosy neighbourliness of our traditional, long-settled working-class areas has been achieved at the cost of a dangerous isolation from the outside world: people may feel surrounded with friends and relatives in neighbouring houses and streets, yet look with suspicion on those who live the other side of the main road, or in the next borough; people may achieve a warm sense of comradeship with other working men, and nurse an unreasoning hostility towards foremen, managers, clerks and professional workers.

'Communities such as Bethnal Green have many strengths which our society needs to preserve,' Donnison concluded, 'but in other ways they may be as unfitted to the modern world as the streets that are scheduled for clearance.'[3]

For Young himself – the driving force in what was a fruitful, comple-mentary partnership with Willmott – the appearance of *Family and Kinship* was the justification of his decision some six years earlier to move away from party politics and into sociology and social policy. 'Yours  is  a  study  of  *living*  people,  who  come  and  go,  all through, – rather like a novel, and at times like scenes from a play,' his benefactress and co-dedicatee Dorothy Elmhirst wrote to him from Dartington Hall after receiving her copy:

> I feel I know the individuals, – they seem to come right out to greet me. Surely this is a new method, – I mean the interweaving of charts, statistics, factual statements with the spontaneous, individual voices of human beings speaking their thoughts and feelings. The effect is vivid and exciting. And how well you bring out the contrasts between Bethnal Green and Greenleigh! The implications of migration are quite startling, aren't they? – the shift in the whole balance of family roles, the class distinctions that arise, the importance of possessions, and that dreadful competitive struggle to keep up with the neighbours. And yet surely the only answer can't be to improve conditions in Bethnal Green. Will you be challenged, I wonder, in that conclusion?
>
> Michael, – this is an important book – and it achieves something that Chekhov used to talk about – the art of saying serious and profound things in a light vein.

Essentially a shy, reserved man who had known relatively little love in his life, Young replied with a deeply revealing letter:

> It is certainly true that B. Green is somewhat idealised. Some days, walking through the streets, I see it all in a different way, cramped, grey, dirty, with all the beauty pressed out of it into the pitiless flag-stones; and that vision is perhaps as true as the one that I usually have, which is not of the place but of the people, who live with such gusto and humour, are earthy although there is little of it there, and who are admirable (& maybe have much character) just because they have imposed life upon such a terrible city environment. The people of an Indian village even, have more cultural resource in their surroundings. I hardly dare talk about the people, & tried not to make judgements on them in the book, except obliquely, because when I get away from the description, I become sentimental. My unconscious engages gear. The secret of why I am so attached to these working-class people lies buried there, and has remained inviolate even to the analysis.

'It is disconcerting, but somehow exciting (if one could bring it out),' he finished, 'to recognise that the book is not about Bethnal Green but Michael Young.'[4]

Whatever the psychodramas involved, the two books – *Uses* and *Family and Kinship* – bequeathed, taken together, three significant legacies.

The first was the way in which they decisively moved the working class into the centre of the cultural frame, after 12 post-war years of what seems in retrospect almost perverse marginalisation. In 1955, in his coruscating *Encounter* essay on British intellectuals, Young's American friend and colleague Edward Shils had forcefully made the point that the absence of the working class – at least two-thirds of the population – was the glaring, seldom-discussed elephant in the room of British intellectual life, whether in terms of treatment or of the personal backgrounds of the intellectuals themselves. From the late 1950s on, this would no longer be the case, at least as far as subject matter was concerned. There were, however, two problems, both owing at least something to *Uses* and *Family and Kinship*. One was that the working class now at last getting proper attention tended to be the *traditional* working class – just as that very class was starting to fragment, not least through the devastating impact of huge slum clearance programmes. The other problem was the implicit exaltation of working-class over middle-class ways of life and values – an exaltation that in time would influence not only the unnecessarily brutal destruction (irrespective of the underlying rights and wrongs) of the grammar and direct grant schools but also the disastrous emergence by the 1970s in the Labour Party (and on the left generally) of what the commentator David Marquand has helpfully called 'proletarianism'.

The second legacy also had political implications. This was the profound, puritanical mistrust of modern, commercial culture and American-style, TV-watching materialism – that 'Candy-floss World' vehemently denounced by Hoggart, that competitive acquisitiveness in 'Greenleigh' described by Young and Willmott with understanding but without warmth or approbation. By the late 1950s the Labour Party's relationship with affluence was becoming increasingly tortured – theoretical acceptance of its desirability combined with visceral dislike of its manifestations – and these two much-read, undeniably moralistic books (especially *Uses*) played their part in delaying for over three decades a resolution of this troubled relationship.

Finally, especially with *Family and Kinship*, there was the bittersweet (but for many years mainly bitter) 'urbanism' legacy. If the main thrust of 1940s-style planning had been towards dispersal, epitomised by the New Towns programme, by the late 1950s the prevailing mood – at least amongst the 'activator' intelligentsia – was the other way, and undoubtedly Young and Willmott, with their powerful, emotionally charged exposition of the virtues of community in traditional urban settings like Bethnal Green, helped to fuel it. Yet there were two fundamental ironies involved: not only did most Bethnal Greeners of the 1950s and after, especially younger ones, have a much greater desire to leave the area and move upmarket than *Family and Kinship* suggested (as the authors would explicitly concede in their introduction to the 1986 edition); but in the climate of the time, 'urbanism' inevitably meant the wholesale demolition of rundown (if often homely) Victorian terraced 'cottages' and, in their place, the large-scale erection of high-rise blocks of flats – this *despite* Young and Willmott's adamant insistence that such blocks were at best only a partial solution to the housing problem. 'One of the most extraordinary aspects of this sorry affair is that in practice the new flatted estates had little in their favour,' they would ruefully reflect in 1986, in relation to inner-city areas all over the country, not just Bethnal Green, during that fateful, transformative period between the late 1950s and early 1970s.[5] It was a sad legacy for an inspiriting, life-enhancing book.

---

Even if they underestimated its attraction, Young and Willmott were absolutely right to pinpoint the importance of 'Greenleigh', emblematic of many other dispersed estates and settlements that had been built since the war and mainly housed manual workers. Indeed, one commentator, Charles Curran, claimed in the *Spectator* in 1956 that, in the context of the full-employment welfare state, these estates had been responsible for creating a new class in the shape of those living there: 'They have been lifted out of poverty and also out of their old surroundings. Now they form the bulk of the inhabitants on the municipal housing estates that encircle London and every other urban centre. They are the New Estate of the realm.' The rest of his piece was mainly derogatory, especially about the culture of this 'New Estate' – 'a place of mass-production comfort, made easy by hire-purchase . . . ideas of furnishings are derived from the cinema and from women's magazines . . . books are rare, bookshelves rarer still' – as also was a radio talk given by June Franklin not long before the publication of *Family and Kinship*, about the experience of living in Crawley New Town with her family. Emphasising that they had given it every chance – 'we have joined local organisations, two of our children attend local schools, and last year my husband was a candidate in the parish council election' – she now admitted defeat: 'The social life is simply that of a village. I tried, but I found it difficult, to work up enthusiasm for an endless round of whist drives, beetle drives and jumble sales. It bored me. I feel my life shrinking. And I don't think it's really a good way to make friends, in spite of the official advice handed out to us to "join something".' Almost certainly middle class, Franklin was looking forward to moving to a place into which she could get her 'roots' – and 'bury the memories of five years in Subtopia'.[6]

Debden itself, aka 'Greenleigh', has not yet been the subject of a systematic historical study, but we do have contemporary surveys of comparable places. When Margot Jefferys in 1954–5 interviewed housewives at South Oxhey, an LCC out-county estate in Hertfordshire, she found three-quarters of those transplanted Londoners 'on the whole' glad to have made the move, with only one in twelve 'entirely sorry'. Perhaps predictably, those who had found the transition difficult, causing loneliness and even mental illness, tended to be older women. In the late summer of 1958 it was explicitly with the Young/Willmott findings in mind that Manchester University's J. B. Cullingworth conducted a detailed survey of 250 families who had moved to an overspill estate at Worsley, eight miles from the centre of Salford. A common pattern emerged: a six-month honeymoon (i.e. the vastly improved living conditions), a year of disenchantment (often relating to lack of external facilities) and then a pragmatic acceptance of the new environment, which did indeed tend to be less 'communal' (fewer pubs and clubs) and more home- and TV-centred. 'Although nearly half said that they had not wished to move to Worsley,' he reported, 'only 17 per cent wanted to return to Salford. The majority of families seemed to have settled down to their suburban way of life whether or not they wished to leave Salford.' The following summer, Cullingworth conducted a survey in Swindon – in other words of overspill from London – and found broadly similar results, with improved housing conditions again being the single most important criterion for most people.

A particularly judicious, well-informed overview of the whole question was provided by Hilary Clark, deputy housing manager at Wolverhampton, who in December 1958 gave a paper to the Royal Society for the Promotion of Health on 'Some Human Aspects of Overspill Housing'. Observing at the outset that building flats in central areas was not *the* answer – 'houses are preferred because they are more suitable for family life – people cannot be conditioned on a large scale to believe that flats are as good' – and that therefore overspill housing was necessary, she confronted the pessimistic 'Greenleigh' version: 'In my experience, a new estate is thought of as remote and unknown at first, but as it grows and brothers and sisters of potential residents move there, it becomes less forbidding to the families who are deciding whether to go.' Overall, she had found, 'a high proportion of local authority overspill tenants seem to settle down well after the first few years'.[7]

By this time four of the biggest concentrations of new or recent settlers from the inner city were Glasgow's peripheral estates: Pollok, Drumchapel, Easterhouse and Castlemilk. During 1957, the year of *Family and Kinship*, the sociologist Maurice Broady conducted a series of interviews with tenants on the huge Pollok estate, mainly members of tenants' associations. Their general, not necessarily representative, view was that things were improving and that such blights as vandalism and sectarianism were on the decrease, though more shops would be appreciated, as well as such facilities as children's playgrounds. Not everyone, though, was happy, among them Mrs Stewart, living in the Craigbank district:

She complained very sorely about the rough people on the buses and about the noise made by the people upstairs. There was invariably a rough family in each block. She was particularly concerned that her little boy, who goes to a private school, should not pick up bad habits by associating with the other children in the scheme. As the local children were coming out of school she took me to a window to show me what was apparently an every-day occurrence: several little boys standing urinating in a circle. Many of the local children also swore badly. If you went to see a mother to complain about the children stealing things, for instance, she would ask the children whether they had done it, and if they said no, would defend her children against you . . .

Mrs Stewart had been an active member of the Craigbank Tenants' Association since its start in 1951, but, as she was compelled to admit about those around her, being a law-abiding tenant was one thing, being an active citizen quite another:

Two complaints particularly were made: that South Pollok should be at the entrance to the scheme, giving the area as a whole a bad reputation, and secondly that the houses were noisy. One young couple whom Mrs Stewart knew, who had been badly troubled by the noise made by a neighbour, had been told by Paton, the local factor, that if they could produce a petition with six signatures complaining about this neighbour he would be prepared to take some action. In the event however, although many complained, only one signed.[8]

# 3

# Never Had It So Good

'The first-floor gallery, known to our regular visitors as "gadget gallery", is maintaining its high standard this year,' reported L.E.W. Stokes-Roberts, organiser of the *Daily Mail* Ideal Home Exhibition. 'But because gadgets and labour-saving notions are so popular we have also originated another section for them, called "That's a Good Idea".' Stokes-Roberts was writing in the *Mail* on 4 March 1957, the day the Queen and Prince Philip were due to visit Olympia for a special preview, and the exhibition was opening the following morning for four weeks, with visits scheduled from Princess Margaret, the Duchess of Kent and other house-proud royals. A highlight this year at the Village of Progress was 'The *Woman's Hour* House', furnished by Jeanne Heal according to the results of a *Radio Times* questionnaire relating to her 'Castle in the Air' broadcasts. 'The front has a pillared porch, wooden shutters, and a balcony reminiscent of an American colonial-style house,' noted the *Mail* about this expression of listeners' taste. 'But inside, the rooms are modern with doors which fold back to make an open-plan living area and an eating bar which seats seven between the dining-room and the kitchen.' The exhibition itself – some 600 stands across 14 acres as well as a range of display houses, flats and shops – was its usual roaring success, but Anthony Carson in the *New Statesman* could only sound a regretful note, comparing the whole thing to 'a sort of florid uncle with endearingly excruciating taste'. As for the thousands flocking there, 'Where do the Ideal people come from? They come from the smaller columns of the evening newspapers, from television competitions, from public libraries beyond Hither Green. They are the untroubled, the stolid backbone, the beloved floating voters.'

Forty-one per cent may in a recent Gallup poll have expressed the wish to emigrate if they could (the highest figure since 1948), the Bank of England's new £5 note may have been (in *Punch*'s words) 'rather like a Victorian sampler as seen in a nightmare by the Council of Industrial Design', but the Ideal Home Exhibition was the annual sign that spring was in the air, even in Glasgow. There, a huge municipal campaign began on 11 March, involving over the next five weeks the X-raying of 87 per cent of the city's population in order to identify carriers of TB. 'Wonderful new treatments have greatly improved the outlook for patients with tuberculosis,' declared the Medical Officer of Health in an advance letter to all households, adding reassuringly that 'there will be no undressing, and all results will be entirely confidential'. Poverty as well as disease existed in all sorts of pre-gentrified places. Later in March, the then unpublished writer John Fowles went with his wife-to-be Elizabeth to Kentish Town and Camden Town 'to scout round for old furniture' for their flat in Hampstead. 'Peeling, pitted, endlessly dirty houses; children playing in the streets,' he recorded. 'The people all poor, or flashy; junk-shops, cheap grocers. E remarked that when she asked for half a pound of cheese they cut it and cut it again till it weighed exactly what she wanted; not as here, where nobody minds paying for a two-ounce miscalculation.'[1]

A month later, the Wednesday after Easter, the 22-year-old Brian Epstein – a student at RADA and living alone – was not so far away, in Finchley Road, when he found himself being arrested for 'persistent importuning' earlier in the evening in the public lavatory at Swiss Cottage tube station. 'The damage, the lying criminal methods of the police in importuning *me* and consequently capturing me, leaves me cold, stunned and finished,' he wrote immediately afterwards. Next morning, however, on the advice of a detective, he pleaded guilty at Marylebone Magistrates' Court and was fined rather than being imprisoned.

For Manchester United's 'Busby Babes' it was the cruellest of springs: that same Thursday they went out of the European Cup, after a pulsating 2–2 draw against Real Madrid in front of a raucous, bellowing Old Trafford crowd, prompting the *Manchester Guardian*'s 'An Old International' (Don Davies) to reflect that 'Bedlam after this will hold no terrors.' Nine days later, on 4 May, the unfairest, most unreconstructed of Cup Finals saw United lose their goalkeeper Ray Wood to a cynical assault by Aston Villa's Peter McParland ('one of those things that can happen in football', the TV commentator Kenneth Wolstenholme reassured the nation), play most of the match with effectively ten men and eventually go down 2–1, with a brace for McParland. For one spectator, Harold Macmillan, 'the Cup-Tie Final' was the end of 'a particularly tiresome week', but 11 days later he welcomed petrol coming off the ration after five post-Suez months. Hull University's librarian could muster at best only two springtime cheers. 'This institution totters along, a cloister of mediocrities isolated by the bleak reaches of the East Riding, doomed to remain a small cottage-university of arts-and-science while the rest of the world zooms into the Age of Technology,' Philip Larkin wrote to a friend near the end of May. 'The corn waves, the sun shines on faded dusty streets, the level-crossings clank, bills are made out for 1957 under billheads designed in 1926.'[2]

'1926' indeed, for it was a spring of industrial troubles. 'When it's a question of capital and labour there's no such thing as impartiality' was the reaction of the 'bell-ringer' Johnny McLoughlin to the news in late February that the Minister of Labour, Iain Macleod, was appointing a court of inquiry under Lord Cameron to investigate the dispute at the Ford-owned Briggs plant in Dagenham. McLoughlin was talking to *The Economist*'s 'special correspondent', who also listened to some of the men as they had a smoke outside the factory gates. 'I reckon an inquiry's what we want,' said one. 'What this plant needs is a dose of salts, and not just for the management either.' Some six weeks later, Cameron came down almost wholly on the side of management: it had been justified in not reinstating McLoughlin, who was characterised as 'glib, quick-witted and evasive', with 'a considerable capacity' for 'agitation and propaganda'. More generally, the shop stewards at Briggs were described as a Communist-influenced 'private union within a union enjoying immediate and continuous contact with the men in the shop, answerable to no superiors and in no way officially or constitutionally linked with the union hierarchy'. Even so, if those were the headline findings – summed up by *The Times*'s ensuing castigation of the Briggs shop stewards as 'a cancer on the body of trade unionism'

– Cameron did also note 'a certain insensitivity in the mental attitude of the Company towards those whom they employ' and 'a desire to impose, rather than agree by negotiation'. The episode as a whole left at least one lasting legacy: McLoughlin was reputedly the ultimate inspiration for Fred Kite, the character so memorably played two years later by Peter Sellers in *I'm All Right, Jack*.[3]

That satirical film would accurately reflect the increasing national focus on the unions and labour relations, with the spring of 1957 seeing a palpable ratcheting-up. 'The *shipbuilding strike started*,' recorded Marian Raynham in Surbiton on 16 March. 'And there are 900 million pounds of orders at stake. I think it is wicked.' Anthony Heap agreed, and on the 20th, with the shipbuilders out and a national engineering strike imminent, he reflected that 'Union bosses have got too big for their boots. Meanwhile the more intelligent and industrious Germans and Japanese will continue to capture our world markets by competing with manufactured goods at much keener prices – and good luck to them!' At about the same time, Malcolm Muggeridge discussed the 'strike situation' with the radical journalist Claud Cockburn: 'Thinks, as I do, that we may now really be for it – strikes becoming general strike, possibly civil war. On the other hand, perhaps not. Anyway, sooner or later, crack-up inevitable.'

To gauge the mood among the strikers themselves, the journalist John Gale went to the Cammell Laird shipyard at Birkenhead, where 'a slim man with floppy brown hair, faint sidewhiskers and big eyes' told him: 'Myself, I'm dead against the strike. Honestly, 75 per cent don't want it, but they are behind the unions … A lie-in for two days is all right but I'll be definitely relieved when the strike is over. I don't like painting the house. I haven't got to wheeling the pram yet. My wife isn't very pleased. All the women blame the top union men.'

As for government, Macmillan talked a tough game to himself, expressing determination not to repeat the 'industrial appeasement' of 'the Churchill–Monckton regime'. But in practice, as events unfolded, he let Macleod have his head, and that highly capable minister was unwilling to fight a battle he was far from sure he could win, not least with sterling fragile and public opinion overall marginally more sympathetic to the strikers than the employers. 'The only possibility is some form of arbitration' had been his view from the outset, and over these weeks he applied considerable pressure on the employers, to ensure that by early April (with over six million working days already lost) it was possible to appoint a court of inquiry, to be chaired by Professor Daniel Jack. 'The news that the grave shipbuilding and engineering strikes had been called off caused an enormous wave of public relief here,' the writer Mollie Panter-Downes told her *New Yorker* readers on the 4th, adding however that 'most people seem to feel cautiously that the situation is not as yet anything better than a truce in the bitter industrial battle – a battle of which the country as a whole is heartily weary and critical'. Four weeks later, Jack gave the unions more or less what they wanted, leaving the employers (above all the Engineering Employers' Federation) bitterly frustrated and the government looking rather impotent. But as Macleod had already explained to Macmillan while awaiting the Jack findings, 'there is no short cut to the problem of making men get on better with each other and there is little we can do, either by government exhortation or by legislation'.[4]

Another vexed area, ripe for re-evaluation, was defence. On 4 April the *Evening Standard* covered the continuing trial at the Old Bailey of Dr John Bodkin Adams, the Eastbourne doctor accused (but eventually acquitted) of hastening rich old ladies on their way, and slipped in an item about the retirement of a stockbroker called Herbert Ballard, known for many years on the Stock Exchange as 'the Mayor of Tooting' even though he had never lived in Tooting and never been a mayor. The main story, though, made a particularly direct appeal to the nation's youth: 'Call-Up Planned To End By 1961'. The phasing out of National Service was part of *Defence: Outline of Future Policy*, a White Paper presented by Duncan Sandys, son-in-law of Winston Churchill and nicely evoked by Ferdinand Mount as 'that formidable slab of old red sandstone'. Other key elements included a general reduction in overseas forces, in the explicit context of Britain's reduced economic means, and a pivotal role for the nuclear deterrent, with the *Standard* quoting Sandys: 'Development of the hydrogen bomb and of rocket weapons with nuclear warheads has fundamentally altered the whole basis of military planning.' The White Paper was a cardinal document, and the historian Jim Tomlinson has helpfully elucidated the driving political-cum-economic motives: not only would a nuclear strategy 'free trained manpower for the civilian sector' but it would 'reduce the claims of conventional weapons development and production on economic resources which could better be used to raise the standard of living'. In short, 'nukes would replace guns to allow more resources for butter'.

For the British aircraft industry this was a major hit, leading to the cancellation of many projects and much downsizing, while more broadly the White Paper fitted into a post-Suez narrative of national decline. 'England is now too olde to have reason to be merrie' was the motion put before the Cambridge Union a month later, though the undergraduates voted defiantly against, 96 to 68. Not long afterwards, Churchill's physician, Lord Moran, asked Sir Oliver Franks, distinguished civil servant and now chairman of Lloyds Bank, whether he was gloomy about the future. 'I think the period 1945 to 1975 may be like 1815 to 1845,' Franks replied.

> We have a good many old men at the top living in the past. Macmillan tells how he was in Darlington in 1931 at the time of mass unemployment, and he was horrified by what he saw. There is a Labour leader [presumably Frank Cousins of the Transport and General Workers' Union], too, who says bitter things to the TUC because for ten years his father was out of employment, and tramped up and down the Great North Road, looking for a job. They think more about this than of the last war. Nothing much will happen until a new generation takes over; we need younger men who are not obsessed with the past, men who are thinking over where they want to go.[5]

Six days after the Sandys White Paper saw a notable opening night. It was a sell-out, so when (recalled Colin Clark, Alan's younger brother and PA to the star) Princess Margaret arrived late demanding the best seats in the house, 'some unfortunate couple had to be kicked out'. During the interval, 'a large red-headed actress' sat naked on the stage 'draped in a Union Jack, with a trident and a helmet, in the pose of Britannia on a penny coin' – of course 'not allowed to move a muscle, otherwise the theatre would be shut down' (i.e. by the Lord Chamberlain). Inevitably, Anthony Heap was there:

Those of us who went to the Royal Court tonight to scoff at John Osborne's successor to the excruciatingly boring and ridiculously over-rated 'Look Back in Anger' had, perforce, to rapidly revise our opinion of this controversial young actor-playwright and stay to bray as 'The Entertainer', with no less distinguished a play jockey than Sir Laurence Olivier up, romped home an easy winner . . . It has wit, irony, humour and pathos in plenty and, despite Tony Richardson's much too slow production, the acting to match. Olivier's vital virtuoso performance as the flashy, facetious, irrepressible and irresponsible music hall comic dazzles and delights at every turn.

'I shall, in sooth,' he concluded, 'be very surprised if "The Entertainer" doesn't prove to be the play of the year, and Olivier's the performance.'

The audience agreed, but most of the critics were less wholeheart-edly enthusiastic, with few bringing out the state-of-the-nation character of the play, above all the clapped-out music-hall comedian Archie Rice as symbol of the declining power that Suez had so starkly revealed. The partial exceptions were Kenneth Tynan and John Wain: the former, in the *Observer*, acclaimed Osborne's ambi-tion ('the big and brilliant notion of putting the whole of contempo-rary England on to one and the same stage'); the latter, in a review on the Third Programme, emphasised the play's theme of surrender to 'the transatlantic invasion', quoted Archie's vaudevillian father looking back on the great Edwardian days ('We were English – and we spoke English'), and noted that 'crudely daubed' on the 'hideous backcloth showing three blousy nudes', against which Archie performed, was 'not, as it used to be, the Eiffel Tower and the Seine but New York harbour'. Of course, *The Entertainer* was also nota-ble because of Olivier, the greatest living English actor, now so publicly embracing the theatrical new wave – an astonishing moment. Yet for Olivier himself it was *au fond* a marriage of convenience. Within two days of the opening he was demanding cuts to 'all that anti-Queen shit', and after Richardson demurred he successfully insisted, as part of his contract for the West End transfer, that the most offensive line ('the gloved hand waving at you from the golden coach') be taken out, along with some others. 'They didn't make that much difference to the play,' Richardson would reflect, 'but Larry felt he'd bravely defended the Queen.'[6]

The legacy of the previous autumn was Hungary as well as Suez, and at least one biographer has speculated that it was the Soviet invasion that helped give Kingsley Amis a significant rightwards push. 'I think the best and most trustworthy political motive is self-interest,' he had asserted soon afterwards in his Fabian pamphlet *Socialism and the Intellectuals*. 'I share a widespread suspicion of the professional espouser of causes, the do-gooder, the archetypal social worker who knows better than I do what is good for me.' Indeed, he claimed, one 'edge' that the Tories had over the socialists was that 'they at least are not out to do anybody any good except themselves'.

Amis would never be part of the post-Hungary New Left, starting to take firm shape by spring 1957. 'Those who feel that the values of a capitalist society are bankrupt, that the social inequalities upon which the system battens are an affront to the potentialities of the individual, have before them a problem, more intricate and more difficult than any which has previously been posed,' declared the editors in the first number of *Universities and Left Review*. 'That is the problem of how to change contemporary society so as to make it more democratic and more egalitarian, and yet how to prevent it degenerating into totalitarianism.' Their solution was 'the regeneration of the whole tradition of free, open, critical debate' – partly through the magazine itself, partly also through the Universities and Left Review Club, due to hold fortnightly discussion meetings in the 'comfortable and informal surroundings' of the Royal Hotel, Woburn Place. All four editors were in their twenties, three of them (including Stuart Hall, a West Indian Rhodes Scholar) were Oxford-based, and the fourth, Ralph (later Raphael) Samuel, was researching London dockers' history at the London School of Economics. A strong line-up in this spring issue included G.D.H. Cole, Eric Hobsbawm (still a member of the Communist Party), E. P. Thompson ('parts of Mr Amis's recent pamphlet bristle with inhibitions against the affirmation of positive, humanist values'), film critic and director Lindsay Anderson ('Commitment in cinema criticism') and David Marquand (then an Oxford undergraduate).

The *ULR*'s second issue (Summer 1957) featured a symposium (including a rather cagey Raymond Williams) on Hoggart's *Uses*, while by then the first issue of the *New Reasoner* had appeared, co-edited by Thompson and his fellow historian John Saville. 'We have no desire to break impetuously with the Marxist and Communist tradition in Britain,' they insisted – a rather different stance to the broader-based pluralism of the *ULR*. The longest piece, by Thompson himself, was characteristically called 'Socialist Humanism: An Epistle to the Philistines'. This was mainly an attack on Stalinism, accused of 'anti-intellectualism, moral nihilism, and the denial of the creative agency of human labour'. But in the last few pages Thompson turned specifically to the British situation, arguing that the working class had, following its considerable '1945' achievement with the establishment of the modern welfare state, 'got no further because, being pragmatic and hostile to theory, it does not know and feel its own strength, it has no sense of direction or revolutionary perspective, it tends to fall into moral lethargy, it accepts leaders with capitalist ideas'. And he had a pop at the Labour politician Anthony Crosland, quoting the 'more open-air cafés, brighter and gayer streets at night' passage from Crosland's recent *The Future of Socialism* and declaring it an inadequate vision:

> Men do not only want the list of *things* which Mr Crosland offers; they want also to change themselves as men. However fitfully and ineffectively, they want other and greater things: they want to stop killing one another; they want to stop this pollution of their spiritual life which runs through society as the rivers carried their sewage and refuse through our nineteenth-century industrial towns.[7]

The British Communist Party itself lost some 7,000 of its 33,000 members as a result of Hungary, but the Scottish poet Hugh MacDiarmid decided that this was the moment to rejoin. Even if all the accusations made by 'the enemies of Communism' were accurate, he declared in the *Daily Worker* in late March, 'the killings, starvings, frame-ups, unjust judgements and all the rest of it are a mere bagatelle to the utterly mercenary and unjustified wars, the ruthless exploitation, the preventable deaths due to slums, and other damnable consequences of the profit motive, which must be laid to the account of the so-called "free nations of the West".' A Party Congress held at Hammersmith Town

Hall over the Easter weekend overwhelmingly endorsed Soviet Russia's action and its own executive's unambiguous support. Among those speaking was a 19-year-old Yorkshire delegate, the miner Arthur Scargill, who told a spirited story of youthful industrial militancy in his own pit and accused the party of 'criminal neglect' of the Young Communist League, given that 'the young people of Britain alone can determine the future of socialism in this country'. A particularly key vote was the heavy defeat for a minority report on party democracy that sought to open up debate. 'There is an authoritarian tendency in the party, a tendency to distrust the rank and file and keep down discussion' insisted one of the report's authors, the historian Christopher Hill. 'We have been living in a world of illusions. That is why the 20th Congress and the Hungarian events came as a shock to so many party members. We have been living in a snug little world of our own invention.' Hill resigned from the party immediately afterwards, while a co-author, Malcolm MacEwen, was soon expelled. His offence was refusing to resign from the editorial board of the *New Reasoner*, high on the party's index of prohibited publications. 'The chairman of the panel that heard my case at a perfunctory but perfectly friendly hearing was Johnny Mahon,' recalled MacEwen about one of the party's leading apparatchiks and the driving force behind the closing-down-debate majority report. 'Had we been in a "people's democracy" I think he would have shaken my hand before firmly despatching me to the gallows.'[8]

It was about this time that L. Ely of Barnes had a Hoggartian letter in the *Daily Worker* castigating jazz, rock and skiffle as 'nearly the No. 1 bore in Great Britain', claiming that 'for everyone who finds relaxation and pleasure there are the many whose fostered interest is of a blasé, moronic character', and calling on the paper to 'make a stand against commercialism, against candy-floss and juke-box deterioration of our working-class culture'. In fact, at least two aspects of popular culture were now coming under serious threat, one in the long term, the other more immediately. The first was smoking, as a result of the Medical Research Council publishing in June a report that found a causal relationship between it and cancer, thereby cementing Richard Doll's groundbreaking study seven years earlier. Attitudes did not change overnight: the government kept a careful distance from the report, denying that it had a specific duty to warn the public; Chapman Pincher in the *Daily Express* inveighed against 'interfering' medics; and the *Manchester Guardian* cautioned that any anti-smoking legislation would 'run counter to British susceptibilities', adding that since there was 'no evidence that smokers harm anybody but themselves . . . an act forbidding smoking in public places would have no more moral validity than one prohibiting it altogether'.

The aspect of popular culture far more imminently endangered in 1957 was the cinema. 'The standard of films today is not big enough to merit more than one run,' lamented a cinema manager, Leonard Caton, in March. 'We have no answer to television.' Caton's cinema was the Olympia in Irlams o' th' Height, Salford, and it had just closed its doors, with the building sold to a local radio and TV dealer. 'I intend to open it as a showroom where people can come in to see sets working,' announced the new owner. 'The atmosphere is ideal for people to sit down and watch TV.' Elsewhere, cinemas under threat were resorting to all sorts of gimmicks and promotions to try to retain their once loyal audiences. 'During the three weeks that *The Curse of Frankenstein* played,' remembered the New Zealand writer Janet Frame about her 'tiring and depressing' month later this spring working as an usherette at the Regal in Streatham, 'vampires, stakes, silver bullets, a model of Frankenstein, all in a mixture of horror folklore, were displayed in the foyer' – as 'all the while the manager, a short middle-aged man with an upward gaze and sandy hair, looked increasingly anxious.' Still, the cinema kept its traditional uses: one Friday afternoon in May the weather in London was 'so horrid' that the middle-aged, highly respectable Madge Martin and her Oxford clergyman husband went to 'the small Cameo Royal' to see 'a naughty French film', namely *And God Created Woman* with 'the kitten-like Brigitte Bardot'.[9]

On the small screen, 14 March saw the launch of the most celebrated advertising magazine (or admag), *Jim's Inn*, with Jimmy Hanley as the genial landlord in the village of 'Wembleham' and everyday brands popping up in surprising places. Next day, the historian Hugh Trevor-Roper (shortly to pip the less establishment A.J.P. Taylor for the Regius Professorship at Oxford) appeared live on *Tonight* talking about the Ides of March. 'When that dreadful couple sang their lower-class

music-hall turn and ended in each others' arms before the camera, I felt
like walking out,' he complained afterwards. 'Nothing I could seriously
say on the subject of Julius Caesar, or indeed on any subject, could be
worth saying to the same audience as theirs . . . I felt that the whole
programme was simply a succession of knock-about turns in which I
would rather not take part . . . I cannot appear again.' Just over a fortnight later – on the same day that the *News Chronicle* reported that
homework standards had not been adversely affected by the end of the
Toddlers' Truce, with a grammar school head 'glad to say parents here
belong to the better classes and know how to control television' – came
a memorable *Panorama*. 'It isn't only in Britain that spring this year has
taken everyone by surprise,' was how Richard Dimbleby began the last
item, going on to deliver a deadpan commentary about the spaghetti
harvest in Switzerland, with accompanying footage apparently showing spaghetti cultivation in progress. 'And that,' he concluded, 'is all
from *Panorama* on this first day of April.' The BBC telephone exchange
in Lime Grove was inundated with calls – 'mainly', recalled Leonard
Miall, 'to settle family arguments: the husband knew it must be true
that spaghetti grew on a bush because Richard Dimbleby had said so
and the wife knew it was made with flour and water, but neither could
convince the other'.[10]

BBC executives needed something to smile about. '*Hey, Jeannie!* [a
benign sitcom] is surely a much better, more attractive and more
intelligent programme than *The Buccaneers* [a pirate series starring
Robert Shaw],' Cecil McGivern wrote in March to Robert Silvey,
head of audience research, about the respective BBC and ITV
programmes that had been up against each other on the early evening
of Saturday, 9 February. 'Yet its audience was only 9 [i.e. 9 per cent of
a panel of almost 500 with access to both channels] as against *The
Buccaneers* 29 . . . This really is discouraging!' To which Silvey replied:
'I am tempted to say that if you altered the word "yet" in your
comment to "hence" it might have been nearer the truth. Seriously,
what warrant have we for assuming that "the best" of a given kind of
material will assuredly draw the majority?' He went on: 'Surely ITV's
Saturday programme represents a single-minded pursuit of the
admass; whereas our schedule looks more like a BBC-type attempt to
entertain a wide spectrum.' Other BBC programmes that evening had

included *Dixon of Dock Green, Billy Smart's Circus, The Dave King Show, Twenty Questions* and a play called *Aunt Mary*, while among ITV's attractions were *Wyatt Earp, The 64,000 Question* (an American-style game show) and *Val Parnell's Saturday Spectacular*. As Silvey conceded about Saturday evenings, 'the ITV has the reputation now, so for many it's a case of switching on to ITV unless there is an overwhelming reason not to'.

Altogether, some 45 per cent of all households had a TV set by the end of May; just over half of those sets transmitted commercial television, so far available only in London, Birmingham and the North. In homes where both channels could be viewed, the audience share was roughly 35 per cent for the BBC and 65 per cent for ITV, with the latter doing even better among young people and the more prosperous part of the working class. Soon afterwards, on 19 June, ITV unveiled a big new comedy hit with Granada's *The Army Game* about duty-dodging conscripts. Barely a week later, the Corporation's troubled fortunes were epitomised by the sudden end after three years of its pioneering soap *The Grove Family*. 'This programme is going down and down,' the *Spectator* had recently grumbled. 'All the naturalism it once had has disappeared. Even Grandma seldom gets a good line.' Understandably, the father-and-son writing team of Roland and Michael Pertwee had asked for a break, and by the time they were ready to return, the jobbing builder Bob Grove and his north London family were a television memory.[11]

On unfashionable radio, a durable innovation was ball-by-ball commentary on the Test matches, starting at Edgbaston on 30 May. Commentators included John Arlott and Rex Alston, with magisterial summaries by E. W. Swanton. The contrast was stark with television (commentators Brian Johnston and Peter West), which that day covered less than an hour and a half's play, with intruders including *Mainly for Women, Watch with Mother* ('Rag, Tag and Bobtail') and *Champion the Wonder Horse*. The Test itself featured on the final two days an epic partnership of 411 between Peter May and Colin Cowdrey, leaving West Indies to scramble a draw at the death. 'Yes, wasn't the Test splendid,' Larkin wrote afterwards to Monica Jones. 'I heard of it only through periodic bulletins from the switchboard operator, but about 5 I could stand no more & cleared off home to listen to the last 1½ hours ball by ball. I revelled in the very *facts* of the score – the 500 plus for 4 wickets: it took me back to 1938 & 1934.' For all that resonance, the eight-hour partnership by the two amateur batsmen involved a huge amount of cynical pad play, tacitly supported by the home umpires, to counter the magical West Indian spinner Sonny Ramadhin. 'I could have wept for him,' remembered his fellow spinner Johnny Wardle, England's twelfth man. 'If he appealed 50 times, at least 30 were plumb out lbw even from the pavilion. It was a great partnership in its way, but an utter scandal really.'

Pad play was part of what was increasingly felt to be cricket's over-defensive, slow-scoring malaise. Three weeks later, the writer C.L.R. James – West Indian and Marxist – launched an assault on 'the long forward-defensive push, the negative bowling' as 'the techniques of specialized performers (professional or amateur) in a security-minded age', and called those cricketers 'functionaries in the Welfare State'. His piece in the *Cricketer* coincided with the second Test at Lord's, where among MCC members watching in the pavilion was a retired Eton teacher, George Lyttelton. 'Weekes was good; so was Cowdrey,' he reported to his old pupil and regular correspondent Rupert Hart-Davis. 'I passed him and Bailey as they went in on Friday morning. I murmured "Good luck". Cowdrey said "Thank you, sir"; Bailey said nothing. In five balls Bailey was out and in five hours Cowdrey had made 152.'[12]

The Edgbaston match was still in progress when soon after 9 a.m. on Saturday, 1 June at Lytham St Anne's, one Ernie (Ernest Marples, the energetic Postmaster General) set in motion a rather larger ERNIE (Electronic Random Number Indicator Equipment, a machine the size of a small van) to make the first Premium Bonds draw. Since November, the public had bought 49 million bonds; some 23,000 prizes were available, and there were 96 winners of the £1,000 top prize. Later that day, Harold Macmillan, godfather of Premium Bonds, was in his old constituency, Stockton-on-Tees. 'It was strange to drive down the old High St, now so modern & smart & prosperous, then so drab (but more beautiful),' he noted, adding that 'the old Georgian houses have had their fronts "Woolworthed"'. 1 June was also the date of the final issue – after 19 years – of *Picture Post*. 'What will the one-eyed monster devour next?' wondered Anthony Heap, and indeed television was doubtless the major cause of the magazine's demise, though as one of its journalists, Katherine Whitehorn, has pointed out, *Picture Post* by the end had 'completely lost its sense of who it was aiming at', with no coherent character running through its pages, quite unlike the great days. Still, its death was a blessing for *Tonight*, with Fyfe Robertson, Trevor Philpott and Kenneth Allsop all moving in due course on to Donald Baverstock's talented, diverse team.

Three days later, on Tuesday the 4th, the leaving students at the Central School of Speech and Drama, including Judi Dench and Vanessa Redgrave, gave the customary job-touting public matinee at Wyndham's. Among those watching was the wife of the manager of the Frinton Summer Theatre; later that day she wrote to Redgrave offering a summer engagement at Britain's most staid resort. There was also a surprise in the post for Kenneth Barrett, who ran the John Hilton Bureau, in effect a citizen's advice bureau subsidised by the *News of the World*. On Friday he received a typed letter, addressed to the bureau, that had been found – almost torn in two – in a gutter in Soho. The writer was a 17-year-old who had left school two years earlier and since worked 'as Comis waiter' in a London hotel (its name missing, as was the writer's name and address):

Every day when I was on time off I used to go over to Hyde Park for a walk etc because I did not want to stay indoors and as it was summer the Park was the best attraction. But constantly I was followed by men who kept on either sitting near me or trying to make up conversation. I did not realise what they wanted till one day one of these men asked me to go to his flat. I was so scared I got up and ran. This also happened at the tables I used to serve at. The men used to say such things as 'Come out with me when you have time off'. So I told my friend who I thought appeared to be my friend. But instead of helping me he said that I should go about with these men. These incidents were not only happening in the Park but in the Hotel. Staff rooms etc. So I left that job. I am scared at going to the pictures by myself because nine times out of ten a man always comes up next to me and I suppose you would call it assault me. I go about with a group of friends . . . one of these invited me to his house for a records evening. Well when I got there we played a few records and his mother and father went out to the pictures leaving us in the house. He then asked me to have a friendly wrestle and then after about five minutes fighting I realised that he was constantly pressing himself so close to me that I just could not help myself. You may say to yourself 'Well why didn't I try to stop him'. Well you see I like to think of sex doings but I would never let any man go that far. You see that is why I have always let these men and boys do this to me. In other words to put it point blank to you I would never go with a man or boy for money or otherwise. But only do the fairly harmless things. Please do not let my parents know or I would leave home for good. I have just had to let some one know. Please just advise me what to do.[13]

'Modernity' may have meant different things to different people, and the pace of change varied considerably from place to place, but by 1957 it was unmistakeably becoming the dominant (albeit top-down) zeitgeist – a spirit of the age epitomised by the desire in relation to the built environment to dump the past, get up to date and embrace a gleaming, functional, progressive future. This spring, in at least three major provincial cities, the modernity drive was under way.

In Birmingham, work began on the city's Inner Ring Road, for which the earliest plans dated back to 1917 but as it would now take shape very much the creation of the City Engineer, Sir Herbert Manzoni. Meanwhile in Sheffield, preliminary work also started on the streets-in-the-sky Park Hill development, destined to become emblematic, and in Bradford, reported the *Yorkshire Post*'s John Bland, 'bulldozers are creating miniature mountains of rubble, demolition squads are battering down rows of abandoned offices, and yawning potholes, worthy of Ingleborough, gape in the roadway'. The 'man of vision' behind Bradford's Development Plan was the City Engineer and Surveyor Stanley Wardley. Bland interviewed him in his office, where a scale model showed 'a modern centre spaciously laid out around the civic precincts', a centre in which 'few present-day buildings are recognisable except for the Town Hall, the Wool Exchange, Britannia House and a cinema or two'. Wardley was in confident mood – 'This is not just a plan that may happen. It is on its way' – while Bland, after noting that new blocks of flats had been built or were being built to replace slums, concluded: 'Bradford will certainly be one of the first cities in Britain to be not only worthy of the 20th century but also proud to look the 21st in the face.'

Elsewhere, the rhetoric was similarly being cranked up. In London's East End, the tenth anniversary of the inauguration of the Stepney–Poplar comprehensive development area not only came soon after the LCC's decision to press ahead with two new housing schemes (Clive Street and Mountmorres Road) involving four 17-storey blocks of flats but was the cue for 'an exhibition, a lantern lecture, and a bus tour' that, explained the *Architects' Journal*, 'made it possible in a morning to glimpse the "grand design" which is being put together piece by piece "to make the East End a very beautiful place," as the LCC Planning Committee's chairman put it'. In Liverpool, a strongly pro-modernity local journalist, George Eglin, had a three-part feature in the *Liverpool Daily Post* about the wonders of Rotterdam, an almost entirely rebuilt city that had 'banished the higgledy-piggledy development ideas of the old city, the conglomeration of dwellings, shops, offices and workshops that had grown up together', and was instead now becoming 'a city with room to breathe, where people can live, work and play in pleasant and efficient surroundings' – in stark contrast to Liverpool's 'archaic, stultified approach to post-war civic problems'. A youngish, idealistic architect-cum-planner, Graeme Shankland, was a fair representative of progressive opinion. 'One cannot avoid the impression that at present we are frightened of the new scale of the city,' he declared in the spring issue of *Universities and Left Review*. 'This fear, masquerading as "the avoidance of monotony", is false. The real danger is muddle – than which nothing is more monotonous.' And he insisted that because 'social demands' were now greater – whether of business or housing or education or traffic – so must 'the scale of the mid-twentieth-century city therefore be larger'. In short, it was time, more than time, to replace 'the present small-scale patchwork city pattern'.[14]

Did all this inevitably mean a substantial and increasing proportion of future new housing being in the form of flats and high-rises? Quite a strong pro-flats consensus had already emerged by the mid-1950s, but in 1957 itself – during which year there were almost 73,000 local authority approvals for new houses, compared with almost 32,000 for flats and just over 10,000 for high-rises – the debate was still surprisingly

lively, with the way led that spring by the resolutely individualist architectural journalist Ian Nairn. 'People are being driven from the centre
not by congestion but by the wrong sort of redevelopment,' he declared.
'Elizabeth Denby [a well-known, much-respected housing consultant]
has plenty of unpublished evidence to show that what working-class
families really wanted was the type of building they had before – a
house and garden, cosily planned and near their work . . . If you rehouse
entirely with flats, then naturally the big families will want to leave.'
Denby herself confirmed soon afterwards that 'the form of high-flat
redevelopment is unacceptable to many English families', calling it an
approach 'in which architects delight' even though 'I have still to find
one who lives in such a block himself!' Significantly, she added that her
analysis of 'four London squares' had shown that *family houses* with a
reasonably large common garden and good private gardens can be
grouped at the same density as *family flats*, costing less and giving
greater human satisfaction'.

Later in March there was a sharp squall in Birmingham: David
Eversley, a university lecturer, flatly stated in the local *Mail* that 'people
like their own front door and a garden', that in fact 'the whole social
tradition in the Midlands is against flats and tenements', and cited 'the
barracks on the cliffs at Rubery' as a prime example of 'cramped and
noisy and ill-ventilated' flats. To this Dennis Thomas, chairman of the
City Council's Planning sub-committee, replied that most flats were
much better than those at Rubery, adding: 'In a city of houses and
gardens, it is understandable that people cling to the old idea of things.
However, if we build flats with properly developed open spaces around,
we shall overcome this prejudice.' And in May, in the letters page of
*The Times*, Michael Young and Peter Willmott, fresh from the success
of *Family and Kinship*, noted that 'the overwhelming majority' of their
East End interviewees wanted 'a house rather than a flat', preferably in
a familiar location, and called on architects to 'apply their ingenuity to
designing decent terraced houses with small gardens at high densities'.

The sociologists, however, were divided. A riposte came from John
Westergaard, who on the basis of research at the recently built Lansbury
estate in Poplar argued that 'the antipathy towards flats, although
strong, is not immutable', and that indeed, more generally, 'the success
of the new tall blocks suggests that the traditional attitude is

not permanent'. As Patrick Dunleavy has observed, it would take the sociological profession as a whole until the 1960s to tackle 'the social dimensions of high-flat living' and, as a result, 'slowly come round to a better-founded and generally more critical appraisal of the implications of the high-rise boom'.[15]

Even so, the sense of it not being an open-and-shut question – or at least involving potentially awkward sensibilities – continued in the early summer. Analysing why Manchester had not tried to solve 'the overspill problem' by 'building so high that as many families are rehoused on the site [i.e. of slum clearance] as living on it before demolition', the *Manchester Guardian*'s local government correspondent noted (as if it was a given): 'There are, of course, social objections to compelling families with young children to live in high flats, and economic objections to a form of housing that costs over twice as much, in labour and materials, both to build and to maintain, as the two-storey dwelling which the vast majority of tenants prefer.' Later in June, Birmingham's City Architect A. G. Sheppard Fidler explained to the Housing Centre in London that it was his council's current policy to provide 30 per cent of new housing in tall blocks, with most of the rest in four-storey maisonettes. He showed slides demonstrating how, since his arrival in the city five years earlier, great care had been taken in deciding what buildings should be placed close to tall blocks in order 'to bring the scale down to the ground and humanise the whole scheme', as well as generally 'producing the feeling of enclosure so familiar and popular in Birmingham'. The Housing Minister was the solid, well-intentioned, cricket-loving Henry Brooke, who soon afterwards, at a slum clearance conference, felt compelled to defend the high-rise approach. 'High flats do not always lead to heaven,' he conceded, 'but they are certainly not the housing hell some of their opponents seem to think.'[16]

Even one of the most-publicised redevelopment schemes failed to generate unalloyed enthusiasm. 'A clean sweep' of the Hutchesontown/ Gorbals area was 'necessary', Ninian Johnston reckoned in 'Miracle in the Gorbals?' (published in the spring issue of a Scottish architectural magazine), 'not only because of the existing conditions, but also to achieve an integral plan which will not suffer intrusion and infiltration by through traffic and undesirable development'. However, Johnston could not help noting wistfully that 'many of the buildings have been substantially built to sound individual designs, and it appears that if they had not been neglected and allowed to fall into disrepair, some might have been incorporated in new planning proposals'. The *Architects' Journal* was somewhat more sceptical. Although 'in general the proposals would transform the area out of all recognition, and completely for the better', nevertheless 'it seems questionable whether the layout at the density adopted ... provides either the necessary community open space, or contrasting small-scale intimacy and large-scale openness, that one would like to see'.

A particularly informed, telling critique came from Glasgow University's Tom Brennan in the June issue of the *Scottish Journal of Political Economy*. Pointing out that 'during a survey of what were reputed to be the two worst blocks in the Comprehensive Development Area it was found that nine households out of ten had made fairly substantial improvements', so that 'less than five per cent were dirty or in a poor state of decoration', he dared to ask the fundamental question 'whether adaptations could not be made to improve conditions sufficiently in the present area at something less than the cost [an estimated £13 million] of tearing the whole place down'. And he pressed on:

> Is it really impossible to make these buildings fit at reasonable cost if the problem is examined simply as a technical one and restrictions which might be imposed by out-of-date bye-laws and regulations are ignored? To the layman it certainly looks as if the roofs could be repaired, not for a few pounds but well within the limits of cost of the alternative which has been put forward. Informal enquiry of one or two people with the right kind of technical experience suggests that it would also be possible to design a free-standing toilet cabinet with a shower bath and lavatory which could be installed easily ...

Bearing in mind these and other practical possibilities, and characterising the Gorbals as an area where 'a large proportion of the population' had already 'adapted themselves very well' in spite of overcrowding, Brennan nevertheless at the last implicitly accepted that the larger argument was likely to go the other way. 'If the planners still say that the property in the scheduled area is in such poor condition that it has to be pulled down now, that it has no useful life left and would fall down in any case, then that is the answer.'[17] And in truth, this particular debate was by that time effectively over, with perhaps the two most distinguished British architects of the time, Robert Matthew and Basil Spence, already appointed as consultants for the detailed designing work of the new Gorbals.

'For the Planned as well as the Planners' was by now the motto of the Town and Country Planning Association's magazine, and the historical challenge is to recover the often ignored views of the planned. At this stage they could as easily be positive as negative. When in March the *Star* ran a front-page story about the problems of damp on the LCC's high-rise Ackroydon estate on Wimbledon Common – 'The Shame of London: Woman grows cress on damp armchairs in flats that are the wonder of the world' – and even compared it to 'rat-ridden dockland', tenants quickly spoke up. 'I could not wish to live anywhere better,' one woman told the *Architects' Journal*, another that 'this is the finest estate in London, and anybody here will tell you so'. Or take (talking to a Liverpool paper around the same time) the tenants of Coronation Court, a ten-storey block on the East Lancashire Road:

It takes some getting used to at first, but once you've convinced yourself you are not dreaming, it is like being on a permanent holiday. The central-heating scheme is marvellous. We really wanted a house, but until we came here we didn't know how comfortable a flat could be. *(Mrs Joan Dutton, who with her husband had lived with her mother for the previous sixteen years)*

We don't want any publicity, we just want to say a very big thank you to the Corporation for bringing us together after seven terrible years apart. It's like starting married life all over again. *(Couple on seventh floor who had been living apart with their respective parents)*

I've no complaints at all. My wife and I waited 18 years for a place of our own. Now that we've got it, we're happy. What more can I say? I know the terrible conditions some unfortunate folk are living under . . . Yes, we are very lucky indeed. *(Middle-aged man on fourth floor)*

It was very different, reported the *Coventry Standard* not long afterwards, on Charter Avenue in the low-rise estate at Canley on the city's outskirts. Mrs E. Whitehead, a pensioner, complained that her flat was damp and cold and 'smells like a graveyard', while Mrs Beryl Stamper, living next door with two young children, was also suffering from the dampness, had nowhere nearby to hang her washing, was worried that the children had nowhere to play in safety and crisply announced that 'whoever told the planners to go ahead didn't look at it from a woman's point of view'. Meanwhile in Barking, the local council had announced 'Operation Clearance', a 15-year plan to demolish 2,000 houses in the middle of the town and replace them with modern homes. 'We have bought this house and kept it spic and span for 20 years or more,' a housewife in St Paul's Road told the local paper. 'I've worked hard to keep it in good condition. Why should they come and pull it down? This is our home.' Mr W. Garland, also living in St Paul's Road, was equally outraged: 'Go along London Road and look at the new Council flats. They look lovely from the front – but at the back the conditions are beyond description. There is more justification to call them "slums" than our homes. And that is what they want to build here.'[18]

It is not quite true that the planners never listened to the planned. The LCC, for example, employed a sociologist, Margaret Willis, who during these months produced two typically painstaking surveys: one on how tenants in flats and maisonettes used their balconies, which in practice usually depended on how privately they were situated; and one on the wishes of old people living in flats and bungalows on the council's estates, with the great majority expressing reluctance to live any higher (up to eight or ten storeys) even if there was a lift. Yet overall – and on the part of 'activators' generally, not just planners – it is hard not to feel that, in this whole area of urban development and the often rapidly changing built environment, there existed a yawning gulf between those making the pronouncements (on whichever side of the argument) and those being pronounced upon. An increasingly active activator was John Betjeman. 'I cannot believe,' he declared in the *Spectator* in May, 'that the London County Council decision to reconstruct the Albert Bridge, Chelsea, means that it is to be destroyed and that we will never see its graceful outline again. Shining with electric lights to show the way to Festival Gardens, or grey and airy against the London sky, it is one of the beauties of the London river.' In the event, the Albert Bridge was saved – aesthetically a happy outcome, but not necessarily what would have happened if, say, there had been a referendum on the matter in south-west London. Or, as an anonymous verse in *Punch* put it, parodying Macaulay:

> When the driver inches slowly
>     Through motor-darkened squares;
> When the traffic-cop stands helplessly
>     In trackless thoroughfares;
> With weeping and with gnashing
>     Still is the story told
> How Betjeman saved the Albert Bridge
>     In the brave days of old.[19]

'A sweltering day!' recorded Judy Haines in Chingford on 6 July. Elsewhere that Saturday, Florence Turtle in Wimbledon Park went with the Wandsworth History Circle on a coach trip to Blenheim, 'conducted round the ground floor rooms by an educated young man who spoke well'; Madge Martin in Oxford travelled the other way, to 'the last of the Light Festival Concerts' in the 'serene, cool atmosphere' of the Royal Festival Hall; Nella Last in Barrow accompanied her husband to Ulverston, where 'I *never* saw so much "dripping" ice cream'; and Philip Larkin in Hull 'yielded to the temptation of buying an antiperspiration atomiser, partly for the fun of squirting it about, but whether it will be of any use or not I don't know'. In Liverpool, 12-year-old Patricia Buckley of Bootle Grammar School for Girls was crowned Bootle's Carnival Queen; long queues formed at the pier head for boats to New Brighton and the Isle of Man; and, reported the *Liverpool Echo*, 'Corporation buses bound for Woolton, Aigburth Vale, and other outlying districts of the city were full, many people carrying picnic hampers.' Did some of those Woolton-bound passengers picnic on the field behind St Peter's Church? There, as part of the annual church fête ('tickets 2/-, refreshments at moderate prices') and standing on a makeshift stage, the Quarry Men Skiffle Group performed that afternoon, led by a tousled 16-year-old wearing a checked shirt and tight black jeans. 'Paul met me the first day I did "Be-Bop-a-Lula" live onstage,'

John Lennon would remember 23 years later, just hours before his death.

> A mutual friend brought him to see my group. And we met and we talked after the show and I saw he had talent and he was playing guitar backstage and doing 'Twenty Flight Rock' by Eddie Cochran and I turned round to him right then on first meeting and said do you want to join the group and he said um hmm you know hmm de hmm and I think he said yes the next day as I recall it.[20]

The heatwave was over by Thursday the 18th, the date of the next *Vauxhall Mirror*, monthly house magazine of Vauxhall Motors in Luton. 'One more Victor rolls off the track and then the family is off on holiday,' declared the caption to the front-page photo of the assembly line. 'It's good to be beside the seaside and it's good to know that the Victor – like all our products – is going swimmingly. And that is our insurance of happy holidays in the years ahead.' The monthly '20 Questions' slot featured C. Bradbury of Div 70, whose answers might have been those of any respectable, decently paid working man:

> What characteristic do you most dislike in other people? – *Unreliability.*
> What would you like to be other than yourself? – *Stanley Matthews, because he is my idea of a true sportsman.*
> If you had three wishes, what would you wish for? – *A little more money for the old folks, continued good health, peace in our time.*
> If you could meet anyone living today, whom would you choose? – *Her Majesty the Queen.*
> If you could do any job at all, other than the one you have now, what would you do? – *Pilot a jet airliner.*
> What is your secret ambition? – *To go on a world tour with my family.*
> If you could do something unconventional without let or hindrance, what would you do? – *Level off the hill I have to climb to get home to lunch.*
> Is Rock 'n' Roll a vice, a habit, a passing craze, a good expression of high spirits, a form of hysteria, or a mere racket? – *Not enough space allotted to express my opinion.*
> Which is the stronger sex? – *No doubt about it – man!*

The back page was an advertisement for Taylor Woodrow houses. 'IT'S YOUR WELCOME HOME – never before at so low a cost, has such streamlined home luxury been offered' (in this case at £2,175 freehold on the Skimpot Estate, Hayhurst Road, Luton). 'Many features have been incorporated to bring you new pleasure, new comfort. It has spacious rooms, an ultra-modern kitchen, including refrigerator, luxury bathroom, ample space for a garage, good sized garden and – above all – it is designed to a plan which makes for gracious living, and built to make the housewife's work easier and happier.'

That evening's performance at Frinton Summer Theatre was Gerald Savory's comedy *A Likely Tale*. 'The atmosphere of the play is brilliantly created by the two dear old sisters who talk of their past beaux over their crochet and tea cups,' appreciatively noted the *East Essex Gazette*'s critic of this latter-day *Cranford*. 'Pauline Murch and Vanessa Redgrave succeed in playing admirably these two characters.' Two days later, on Saturday the 20th, Stirling Moss at Aintree in a green Vanwall became the first British driver to win a world championship grand prix in a British car; Anthony Heap by contrast 'came nowhere in the fathers' eat-a-dog-biscuit-before-starting race' at his son's sports day in Great Missenden; Judy Haines's husband treated her and the children to a matinee at the Royal Ballet ('He bought us a pound box of Mackintosh's Week-End Assortment'); and miners and their families gathered for the annual Durham Miners' Gala. Poor weather and the start of a national bus strike badly depleted numbers, but, added the *Durham Chronicle*, 'the spirit of the gala was unimpaired', with boating 'as usual a popular pastime', while 'crowds spent liberally at the "fun of the fair" on the high ground'. Tellingly, 'while thousands listened to the speeches,' including one from the Labour leader Hugh Gaitskell, 'still more thousands spent their time in other ways.'[21]

By six o'clock much of the younger part of the TV public was settling down for *Six-Five Special* – Josephine Douglas and Pete Murray still in charge but the concert pianist long gone, with this evening's stars including the crooner Dennis Lotis and the up-and-coming British rock 'n' roller Terry Dene. In Bedford there was more serious business, however. Amidst rain, some 3,000 assembled at Bedford Town's football ground, the Eyrie, to listen to the Prime Minister. All seats were under cover at 10s and 2s, covered standing room was free, and most of the intermittent heckling came from League of Empire Loyalists, though right at the start as Macmillan rose to speak, there was a piercing yell of 'Up the Eagles!' Resting his notes on a locally made oak box presented to him for the occasion by four Bedfordshire Conservative Associations, the long-sighted speaker, too vain to wear glasses, was about halfway through his speech when, having listed some of the economic progress since 1951, he peered at his typewritten text and read the immortal passage:

> That is all to the good.
> Indeed,
>      let's be frank about it;
>      most of our people
>          have never had it so good.
> Go around the country,
>      go to the industrial towns,
>      go to the farms,
> and you will see a state of prosperity
>      such as we have never had
>          in my lifetime –
> nor indeed ever in the history
>      of this country.

Much of the rest of Macmillan's speech was about the dangers of inflation, but the five words 'never had it so good' would soon become inextricably linked with – even come to define – the main thrust of his premiership. For Macmillan himself, ultimately a moralist, this would prove understandably frustrating; and for a different, less materialistic gauge of satisfaction, he might have appreciated 'The Letter of the Week', from Mrs M. S. of Tayport, in the issue dated that day of the homeliest of magazines, the *People's Friend*:

> I love to read the letters page every week. How many interesting people write to you!
>     But isn't it a good thing that people aren't all alike and don't all do spectacular things?

I am just an ordinary housewife with a husband and family to look after. My day is a busy full one. I'm happy doing my work and knowing my family need me.

I think I have one of the most satisfying jobs in the world, and it's not everyone who can say that. I wouldn't change it for anything.[22]

# PART TWO

# 4

# Catch a Falling Sputnik

'The main change that has taken place in the last few years is that customers no longer seem as price-conscious as they were,' the *Financial Times* noted about Marks & Spencer some four months after Macmillan's speech. 'Ninety-five-shilling dresses are found to sell better than 65s models.' Yet none of M&S's 237 stores had fitting rooms, and, more generally, in terms of the apparently inexorable shift into a shiny new consumerist world, there were by 1957 at least three significant areas of continuity.

Starting with consumer durables, ownership figures for the second half of the year showed that their penetration was far from total: 56 per cent of adults owned a TV set, 26 per cent a washing machine and only 12 per cent a refrigerator (the figure for the working class specifically being just 5 per cent). In addition, only 21 per cent of adults had a telephone, while even in Colin Shindler's home in Prestwich, Manchester, where his businessman father kept a Humber Hawk in the drive and a Hotpoint washing machine had recently arrived, they still used a mangle on wash day.

Nor, a further continuity, were supermarkets anything like ubiquitous. The *Liverpool Echo*'s 'Onlooker' reckoned in September that they 'seem to have made much more of a mark in the South of England than so far they have in the North. Motoring in London and the Thames Valley, I was surprised to find them in quite small towns and suburbs.' Would they spread? 'I suspect,' added Onlooker, 'that in the North we may be more reluctant than the Southerners to forgo our cross-the-counter courtesies.' In fact, there was a total of almost 4,000 self-service shops in Britain, but the great majority were relatively small, at around

1,000 square feet. And although supermarkets were undoubtedly on the rise – Sainsbury's with nine so far, Fine Fare (part of the Allied Bakeries Group) with 15 and planning to open another 15 in the next 12 months – these were still, in the long sweep of things, the Dark Ages. 'The out-of-town supermarket, based on the North American pattern of the out-of-town shopping centre in the open country, has not yet been attempted,' the *FT* pointed out around the time of Onlooker's southern tour. 'The obvious reason is the comparatively small number of cars owned in Britain [only 24 per cent of the population had a car].' Moreover, existing high-street supermarkets 'as yet provide no parking accommodation' – and thereby 'probably miss much potential trade which goes to the neighbourhood grocer, the shop at the corner, the grocer who still delivers (which supermarkets do not) and the grocer who brings his shop to the house'.

The third continuity, helped by a shopping environment in which only 2 per cent of all food products sold were pre-packed, was thrift. Radio and television repairs; the hire and repair of gas appliances; matches, soap and cleaning materials – all featured strongly in 1957's pioneer annual household expenditure survey. 'A really tasty dish, and economical too!' was the headline in *Woman's Own*, two days before Macmillan's speech, for Philip Harben's recipe for cold pigeon pie, while Mrs H. had revealed earlier in the summer in the same magazine that 'I cut my loofah into slices – some for cleaning pans, others for bases to hold flowers steady in a vase.'[1] Economical hints from readers remained a staple of many popular publications.

Even so, there was plenty new on the market in 1957, often being aggressively pushed through the recently available medium of television advertising. Fry's Turkish Delight, the scientifically devised (by Lyons) instant porridge known as Ready Brek, 'the new, exciting taste of Gibbs SR', the original aftershave (Old Spice), the Hoovermatic twin tub, Wash and Spin Dry machine – all were fresh entrants, while in general two trends stood out. One was towards home-centredness, epitomised by the rapid growth of sales of canned beer, up from 1.5 million cans in 1954–5 to 70 million by 1957–8. 'It's nice to watch television but it's even nicer when you've got a drink in your hand,' Gregory Ratcliffe, a Birmingham shopkeeper, told *Reynolds News*. 'Makes it more intimate somehow. Gives you the feeling that you're in a posh cabaret.' The outspoken textile manufacturer Cyril Lord was already plugged in to the home, manufacturing and selling tufted carpets that made use of new man-made fibres and were aimed squarely at the mass market, often replacing linoleum in working-class homes. Soon there would be a TV jingle – 'This is luxury you can afford by Cyril Lord', a jungle accurately described by his biographer as 'relentless' – and his carpets were set to become a byword for the gathering consumer boom. The other trend, though far from invariable, was towards going upmarket. The launch of Camay soap involved a series of mildly risqué Norman Parkinson photographs in the more superior women's magazines, with Parkinson himself claiming elsewhere that he used Camay for shaving in the bath. In the autumn Van den Berghs heavily promoted a new soft-blend luxury margarine, Blue Band, with distinctive gold-coloured packaging. And about the same time, faced by a falling market share, the British Patent Perforated Paper Company decided that it needed a new approach if its cheap, traditional, notoriously non-absorbent toilet paper, Bronco, was to thrive against more yielding competitors like Andrex.[2]

Inevitably, the pleasure and excitement of new possessions could come tinged with regret, as when shortly before Christmas the parents of 13-year-old Subrata Dasgupta, living in Derby, 'bought a Bush electric record player'. Admittedly he could now buy records (LPs and EPs) that he had 'only handled wistfully in Dixons', but it was still 'with a great deal of sadness I put away our mechanical, wind-up gramophone', whose 'thick, metal-shiny playing arm which held the needle, curled up like a contented kitten, looked clumsy and prehistoric, compared to the lightweight "pick-up" arm on the new player'. The older teen, though, was probably melancholy-free if he or she acquired a Dansette: brightly coloured (usually a mixture of blues, creams, reds and turquoises) and unashamedly lo-fi, it still had the volume to get partygoers dancing.[3]

How to choose between competing goods and services? The first *Egon Ronay Guide* to restaurants appeared in 1957, but the event making greater waves came in October with the first issue of *Which?*, the magazine of the Consumers' Association. The CA itself had been started the previous year by a young American graduate, Dorothy Goodman, who on returning to the States had passed it over to Michael

Young. For Young, as he recalled some 20 years later, there was a direct, potentially fruitful link with the work he had been doing for *Family and Kinship*:

> In Bethnal Green we were able to reconstruct what was happening in the 19th century. It was clear that men's lives were very much centred on their work; they kept a large proportion of the family income for themselves and spent it quite separately from their wives in pubs and gambling and smoking. Partly they did it because the home was such a bloody uncomfortable place to be.
>
> What we saw was the beginning of a change. The younger men, although interested in their work, were giving more interest to their homes, having something more like a partnership with their wives in building up their homes. And this was symbolised by the material goods that people bought.
>
> They had a terrific pride, an emotional investment in these material goods, and it seemed that they would be more satisfied if they could feel that the things they were buying were efficient and functional. Anything, we thought, that could tell them that, would strike a chord. It struck much more of a chord with the middle classes than it did with the working classes.

The unfortunate class differential was no doubt inevitable, but perhaps less so was the dramatic whoosh of *Which?*'s early life. 'At 10 a.m. on Tuesday morning,' Young wrote on Friday the 10th to his benefactors the Elmhirsts, 'when we opened the doors of this office which we have rented for 10s a week, a special messenger arrived from Sir Simon Marks [chairman of M&S] with a standing order for 20 copies; and ever since then the letters have been pouring in.'[4]

Press response was initially cautious – no doubt on account of anxiety about advertising boycotts by upset manufacturers – but a favourable article and editorial in *The Times* helped ignite interest, as did an item by Marghanita Laski on the 11th in *Woman's Hour*, and within a month there would be some 10,000 members of the CA, few agreeing with the electrical retailer who told the *Electrical Times* that 'all these well-meaning but voluntary unofficial watchdogs are making much ado about nothing'. Among those do-gooders, the key editorial figure from early on was the hugely capable, clear-sighted Eirlys Roberts, fairly described on her death in 2008 as 'the mother of the modern British consumer movement'. Meanwhile *Which?* itself focused in its first issue – after a bold declaration that its mission was to supply 'the information, impartial, accurate and thorough, which will enable people to get better value for their money' – on electric kettles (the Russell-Hobbs failing one of the insulation tests), sunglasses, aspirin, cake mixes, scouring powders and pastes (Mirro, Vim and Ajax as the top-rated three, followed by Chemico and Gumption), and no-iron cottons, with additionally the results of Swedish tests of two popular British cars, the Austin 35 and the Standard 10 Saloon. 'Somehow it seems to belong quite well to a "classless middle-class" society,' Young wrote a week after the launch to the anthropologist Geoffrey Gorer, thanking him for his subscription. 'From now on everyone can have the same article, "the best".'

Sadly, what one does not get in the pages of *Which?* – undeniably imbued, for all its sterling work, with a whiff of paternalistic puritanism – are the voices of the consumers themselves. For those one can still turn occasionally to Mass-Observation (albeit by now an organisation devoted to market research rather than sociological enquiry), specifically to its Detergent Survey of late 1957 and early 1958. Among 40 housewives interviewed in London, Liverpool and Manchester, a headmistress said she would 'rather pay for a good all-rounder' and was 'old-fashioned enough to want to see the bubbles'; a part-time shop assistant declared herself 'very sensitive to smell' and thought 'they scent them too much, especially Daz'; and a Liverpool docker's wife, who went 'to the wash house to do the big wash', explained how 'I used to use Persil quite a lot' but had 'changed to Fairy Snow' because 'Persil is very hard on the hands'. One of the interviewees, in a small, untidy Paddington flat, was a childless 38-year-old who worked as a part-time researcher and was married to an *Encyclopaedia Britannica* sales rep. Not exactly a bright, bushy-eyed consumer, she described her washing routine:

Always on Sunday morning after I read the Sunday papers. It has to be very much of an emergency to wash any other time. I often find my husband's things on my chair or my ashtray, for me to wash up, if my husband wants anything done he'll follow me about with them, put them on my bed, my pillow and so on till I wash them. I can't wash things while I'm running the bath, because the bath looks too tempting. My terylene curtains, it's essential to wash them once a fortnight – I go on with mine till people mention it, but I don't care personally if they're black, and if my dog could speak, he'd ask for his bedding washed. In other words you can gather I don't like washing.[5]

'Some of the methods used to prevent coaches not involved in the stoppage from carrying on were far removed from the peaceful picketing allowed by law,' reported the *Manchester Guardian* on Tuesday, 23 July (three days after Macmillan's Bedford speech), about the ongoing national (outside London) busmen's strike. 'Drivers were attacked and beaten, tyres were slashed and windows broken – sometimes to the danger of passengers as well as crew.' Later that week at Headingley the West Indies were again on the rack, with the England fast bowler Peter Loader celebrating his hat-trick by dancing a fandango, very different to cricket's still customary low-key displays of emotion. But Philip Larkin on the Friday was more interested in *The Archers*. 'Don't you adore Carol Grey's voice when Toby S. [Toby Stobeman] is making love to her?' he asked Monica Jones. 'It quite broke me up over my leathery tinned tongue tonight: she goes all small & unconfident. She's the only woman on the programme I've ever liked. I'm getting to the point where I want to bang a skillet on Prue's [Pru Harris, later Forrest] head.' A less inveterate grumbler, Florence Turtle, spent the weekend in Suffolk, and on the train back to London 'a passenger remarked that he thought Liverpool St Station must be the dirtiest station in the world, a remark that I must agree with'. Harold Macmillan was more satisfied when his Monday audience with the Queen turned to the question of where the eight-year-old Prince Charles was to go to boarding school next term: 'She has chosen Cheam – a good preparatory school, solid but not smart.'[6]

In fact the royals and those around them were in for a tricky few months. 'A pain in the neck' was young Lord Altrincham's memorable description of the Queen's voice, in a trenchant article on the monarchy in the August issue of the *National & English Review*; he added that the unfortunate impression she gave in her speeches was of 'a priggish schoolgirl, captain of the hockey team, a prefect and a recent candidate for Confirmation'. Altrincham (the future John Grigg) largely blamed the monarch's 'tweedy' entourage – a 'tight little enclave of English ladies and gentlemen' – rather than Elizabeth herself, but that did not stop a torrent of abuse. The *Daily Express* inevitably led the way; in the *Daily Mail* the political commentator Henry Fairlie accused the peer of 'daring to put his infinitely tiny and temporary mind against the accumulated experience of the centuries'; Altrincham received some 2,000 letters of complaint and a punch in the face from a member of the League of Empire Loyalists; and Macmillan noted his luncheon guest Churchill as 'splendidly indignant'. Even so, a poll of *Daily Mail* readers found that as many as 35 per cent agreed with Altrincham, compared to 52 per cent disagreeing – and that among younger readers the split was actually 47–39 in his favour. Summing up 'this unofficial national debate' later in August, Mollie Panter-Downes wrote in the *New Yorker* that there were indeed 'many loyal and thoughtful English' who would be 'glad to see a bit of fresh air blown into the stuffier recesses of palace protocol'; she pinned her hopes on the 'forceful ventilating influence' of the Duke of Edinburgh, 'whose breezy common sense and intelligence make short work of red-tape trimmings'. The Queen's first minister was less convinced. 'After luncheon, a sharp little discussion with Prince Philip,' recorded Macmillan at Balmoral on 1 September. 'He is *against* our having a nuclear power. The tone of his talk confirms me in the view that he will try to play up to the Left. He may honestly think this to be in the Queen's interest. But I don't altogether like the tone of his talk. It is too like that of a clever undergraduate, who has just discovered Socialism.'[7]

One month later, and the controversy was still alive. 'Mr [Geoffrey] Howe is the chairman of the Bow Group, and as impertinent a young whipper-snapper as ever needed his breeks dusting,' was how the *Spectator*'s new Westminster correspondent 'Taper' (Bernard Levin) described the launch of that Tory pressure group's magazine *Crossbow*. 'He spent a good deal of his speech insulting Lord Altrincham in a particularly offensive, ham-fisted and naive manner.' A *Sunday Dispatch* photo caption a few days later about Princess Alexandra was a reminder of the royals' increasingly fish-bowl world – 'a princess plays tennis

– in slacks' – before news broke that, to coincide with the Queen's North American tour, New York's *Saturday Evening Post* was publishing a critical piece on the royals and their great cheerleader, Richard Dimbleby. The *Sunday Express* headline provided a pithy if not a balanced summary – 'MALCOLM MUGGERIDGE RIDICULES ROYAL FAMILY IN USA. ASTOUNDING ATTACK ON THE QUEEN. SHE IS CALLED DOWDY, FRUMPISH, BANAL' – and one of its readers, Nella Last in Barrow, reflected that 'after listening to his prim, waspish voice on "Any Questions"' she had pictured Muggeridge as an 'ageing Peke'. The *People* also weighed in, a front-page piece calling his article 'ruthless' and 'tasteless'. Next day he was banned from appearing on that evening's *Panorama*, and later in October the BBC's board of governors not only disinvited Altrincham from *Any Questions?* but decided not to renew Muggeridge's contract. 'This chap will never go on the air as long as I am director-general,' declared Lieutenant General Sir Ian Jacob, and, as a military man, he was as good as his word.[8]

'You go too flamin' far when you criticise our Queen, who does more good than you if you lived to be 5,000 . . . signed, Eight (loyal to the Queen) Teddy Boys.' So read one of the many patriotic letters to Altrincham back in August, but not everyone felt reassured by the nation's youth. 'We did not enjoy the horrid crowds of Leicester Square, Coventry Street and Piccadilly Circus,' recorded Madge Martin that month after an evening in London to see Anna Neagle in *No Time for Tears*. 'Surely these were exciting, gay places to be in at night, but now filled with the lowest type – Teddy boys with their friends of both sexes, etc. We had a cup of tea at Fortes – once the dear old Criterion – feeling tired and disgusted with this side of our dear London.' In September a series run by the *Liverpool Echo* about widespread vandalism on Merseyside culminated with readers expressing their views. Mrs M. Green of 10 Bower Road, Huyton blamed working mothers – 'when her day is spent largely outside her home, the pivot is removed and the family, as such, just disintegrates' – but for most there was a single, unambiguous line of thought:

We won't get anywhere until the punishment fits the crime. It is scandalous that if one catches a delinquent in the act and cuffs his ear, one is liable to be hauled up for assaulting a juvenile. *(M. Temple, 10 Abergele Road, Stanley, Liverpool 13)*

They ought to bring the cat in again: a few strokes with that would soon put an end to it. Teachers should be able to use the cane again to show children which is right or wrong. *(Mrs White, Parkgate Road, Neston)*

Why not bring back the birch like the Isle of Man? *('Disgusted' (OAP))*

Mrs K. E. Lee of 32 Barnsbury Road, Liverpool 4 also had a question, or rather two: 'What sort of homes do these little vultures come from and what kind of citizens are they going to be?'[9]

The young themselves were bothered by neither issue. On 7 August, a month and a day after the Woolton church fête, the Quarry Men (not yet with McCartney) played for the first time at the Cavern in Liverpool. 'We did some skiffle numbers to start off with but we also did rock 'n' roll,' recalled the drummer Colin Hanton. 'John Lennon was passed a note and, very pleased, he said to the audience, "We've had a request." He opened it up and it was from Alan Sytner [the club's cantankerous owner] saying, "Cut out the bloody rock 'n' roll."' Elsewhere these summer holidays, the 11-year-old Helen Shapiro first met the 10-year-old Mark Feld (later Marc Bolan), 'this chubby kid' whose 'quiff would cover his face when he combed it forward'. Another 11-year-old, Bob Harris, was on holiday with his parents in Cromer when he passed an amusement arcade and heard the American singer Paul Anka's 'Diana' coming from the jukebox ('There was a magic to it that made me want to be a part of the world it came from'), while the 14-year-old Lorna Stockton (later Sage) went with a friend to Southport:

Gail and I spent all our time and pocket money dashing from one juke-box to another to make sure that Pat Boone's chaste hit 'Love Letters in the Sand' would be drowned out all over the windswept town by 'All Shook Up'. The one was sweetness and light, the other inarticulate, insidious bump-and-grind . . . All the Elvises groaned and whimpered at once, and the waves rushed in and obliterated Pat Boone. And we clung to each other in a shelter smelling of orange peel and piss on the promenade, and shrieked with glee, like the Bacchae who dismembered Orpheus.

Skiffle was by now at its apogee, with the catchy (especially for this six-year-old boy) 'Last Train to San Fernando' by Johnny Duncan and the Blue Grass Boys steaming through the charts. But a curmudgeonly Welshman, Frank Lewis, was less enamoured when on 2 September he saw 'the Mountaineering Skiffle group' play at the Globe pub in Barry: 'The skiffle place was jammed with young people. Too many tunes all in one key. It begins to boredom [sic] after a while.'[10]

Two days later, HMSO published a blue paper-bound volume, 155 pages long and priced at five shillings. This was the Wolfenden Report – or *Report of the Committee on Homosexual Offences and Prostitution* – and its initial 5,000 print run sold out within hours. 'It is a fine, thorough, dispassionate piece of work, which uses words more clearly than many best-sellers do,' found Mollie Panter-Downes. Its two key recommendations were that prostitutes should be punished much more severely for accosting and that, more controversially, private homosexual relations between consenting adults should be decriminalised. 'It is not, in our view, the function of law to intervene in private lives of citizens, or to seek to enforce any particular pattern of behaviour,' declared the report about the latter aspect. 'It follows that we do not believe it to be a function of the law to attempt to cover all the fields of sexual behaviour.' Importantly, Wolfenden made clear that 'this limited modification of the law should not be interpreted as indicating that the law can be indifferent to other forms of homosexual behaviour, or as a general licence to homosexuals to behave as they please'. The following evening on ITV, a programme on the report – preceded by a warning to viewers that it was unsuitable for children and might distress some adults – featured an anonymous doctor (his back to camera), who was asked by the interviewer, 'Would you prefer to be normal?' 'Oh yes,' he replied, 'I would – if there was a guaranteed cure – a hope – that I could become an ordinary normal person I would certainly welcome it. I think all homosexuals would like to be cured and marry and have children.'[11]

Press reaction to the decriminalisation proposal was predictably mixed. Only two national dailies came out unambiguously against, namely the *Daily Mail* ('leaving perverts free to spread corruption') and the *Daily Express* ('cumbersome nonsense'); *The Times*, the *Manchester Guardian* and the *News Chronicle* were almost wholly supportive; the

*Daily Telegraph* worried that legalised homosexuality might spread like an infection; and the *Daily Mirror* initially sat on the fence, but eventually backed Wolfenden. Among the Sundays, the *Observer* was positive, but the *Sunday Times* warned against the undermining of the 'basic national moral standard', while in the *Sunday Express* the resolutely homophobic John Gordon wrote about 'degraded men' with 'bestial habits' and called the report 'The Pansies' Charter'. As for the weeklies, the *Spectator* asserted that 'whatever feelings of revulsion homosexual actions may arouse, the law on this point is utterly irrational and illogical'. Most provincial papers were hostile, and the *Scotsman* declared flatly that it was 'no solution to any public problem to legitimise a bestial offence'.

The *Mirror* took a poll of its largely working-class readers. Within a week there were nearly 7,000 votes in, overwhelmingly wanting prostitutes cleared off the streets but narrowly against decriminalisation of private homosexual behaviour. As further votes came in, those overall preferences stayed constant, while it became apparent that there were significant regional variations: roughly 1 in 2 in the south of England wanting decriminalisation, compared to 3 in 7 in the north and only 1 in 6 in Scotland. A more authoritative opinion poll (though broadly in line) was Gallup's, published later in September. This revealed that 81 per cent had heard about the report; that 42 per cent saw homosexuality as 'a serious problem', compared with 27 per cent 'not very' and 31 per cent 'don't knows'; and that 38 per cent agreed with decriminalisation, as against 47 per cent disagreeing. 'Considering all things,' commented Panter-Downes on Gallup's figures, 'this hardly represents the wave of scandalized indignation that many people thought would follow.'[12]

The issue rumbled on through the autumn, with one Oxford undergraduate, Dennis Potter, reflecting in *Isis* that 'inevitably the natural reaction of all of us who find the thought of homosexual behaviour repulsive or difficult to comprehend will be a troubled one'. Politically, the Home Secretary, Rab Butler, was inclined initially to legislate for decriminalisation, but soon found that he was out of line with mainstream Tory opinion and pushed the issue into the longish grass. The House of Lords did debate the question in December, with Lord Denning speaking for many when he condemned unnatural vices and insisted that the law should continue to punish homosexual conduct, albeit 'discreetly'. Meanwhile, for homosexuals themselves, the secrecy and gnawing anxiety continued – perhaps typified this autumn by how Brian Abel-Smith, arguably the most gifted social scientist of his generation, felt unable to apply for a safe Labour seat (the retiring Hugh Dalton's, in Bishop Auckland) for fear of public humiliation if his homosexuality was discovered. Earlier in the year there had been a sign of the Victorian permafrost starting to melt (with the Homicide Act, which restricted the use of the death penalty for murder), but for the moment this remained a right little, tight little island.[13]

———

'What the British people are waiting for,' Macmillan reflected privately on 17 September with an alert reference to an ITV game show, 'is the answer to the 64,000 question – how to stop rising prices & fall in value of money. They will (perhaps) accept measures to deal with these problems.' In the context of sterling under severe pressure, he went on: 'But they regard an exchange crisis (which they do *not* understand) as some kind of a swindle organised by foreigners.' Two days later the *Evening Standard* included a review of *Hamlet* at the Old Vic: 'Ophelia is played by a girl called Judi Dench, whose first professional performance this only too obviously is. But she goes mad quite nicely and has talent which will be shown to better advantage when she acquires some technique to go with it.' Homeward-bound commuters, though, could not avoid the front-page headline: 'Bank Rate Shock – Up To 7 per cent: Thorneycroft's H-bomb shakes the City'. Peter Thorneycroft was Chancellor, and he had gone for a 2-per-cent hike heavily under the influence of the Governor of the Bank of England, Cameron (Kim) Cobbold, whose spokesman was quoted in strikingly robust language: 'There has recently been a good deal of speculative pressure against the pound. People have been selling sterling. This will show them "where they get off".' The démarche temporarily did its job, confounding the instant, apocalyptic prediction of the cerebral merchant banker Siegmund Warburg (made privately to the Shadow Chancellor Harold Wilson and recorded in the diary of Wilson's colleague Richard Crossman) that 'it was a gamble which would not come off and we were in for a 1931 crisis, but this time with rising unemployment and rising prices simultaneously', yet it still generated plenty of scepticism.

The *Spectator*'s Keynesian economic commentator Nicholas Davenport was appalled, calling the move 'the crowning folly', while the more measured *FT* argued that unless there was real 'determination in extending restraint to wages', which in practice meant the government standing up to the unions, then 'nothing will have been gained, and much will have been lost'.[14]

There were two piquant consequences of this sharp tightening of policy. 'It is alleged that there was a "leak" about the intention of the Government to raise the Bank Rate,' Macmillan noted the following week, adding that 'careful enquiries' had found 'no trace of any irregularity'. The ambitious Wilson, however, was on the case, and by October he was publicly demanding a formal inquiry – a request eventually acceded to by a very reluctant Macmillan. The other consequence, barely noticed at the time, concerned the implications of an accompanying measure, the temporary forbidding of London banks to use sterling to finance third-party trade. Dollar deposits had already been mounting in Paris and London – in part reflecting the Cold War reluctance of Soviet and East European banks to trust their dollars to New York – and it was these dollars that some of London's banks now sought to use in order to go on doing their business of financing international trade. Such were the origins of what would become known as the Eurodollar market. One of its pioneers was the visionary Sir George Bolton, a former Bank of England man but now chairman of the Bank of London and South America (BOLSA). In his pitch for the job earlier in 1957 he had asserted, 'London has barely succeeded in maintaining its international banking system following the loss of political influence by the UK, the weakened position of sterling and the incapacity of the London Market to increase its foreign investment net.' Accordingly, those London banks, like BOLSA, 'whose main business is to maintain and develop a position in the foreign field will have to adapt their structure to meet the needs of the time'.[15] The Euromarkets, starting with the Eurodollar market, would be the means of that adaptation – and a first, long step towards London returning to its pre-1914 glories as an international financial centre.

Judi Dench's was not the only debut that autumn. 'Mr Ted Hughes is clearly a remarkable poet, and seems to be quite outside the currents of his time,' wrote the august critic Edwin Muir in the *New Statesman*, reviewing *The Hawk in the Rain*. 'His distinguishing power is sensuous, verbal and imaginative; at his best the three are fused together. His images have an admirable violence.' The very different poet Robert Conquest generously agreed in the *Spectator* – 'not just promising but very promising' – though his friend Kingsley Amis held his counsel, perhaps mulling instead over the tepid critical response to the just-released Boulting brothers' version of *Lucky Jim*. 'The film has taken what was farcical in the book and turned it into a rowdy, slap-happy, knockabout comedy in which all that was social, significant, representative, etc., etc., is kept firmly out,' reckoned Isabel Quigly, while Lindsay Anderson was even less forgiving: 'The characters have been flattened, simplified and vulgarised. The temptations of realist shooting have been consciously resisted, and the story has been wholly abstracted from reality.'

Elsewhere, Florence Turtle went to the Ambassadors to see *The Mousetrap* (almost six years in) and recorded that 'it was a Comedy Thriller, somewhat tripey but quite entertaining'; Anthony Heap 'walked down to Drury Lane Theatre and back in early evening to make enquiries about First Night seats for "My Fair Lady" seven months hence', discovering that 'booking for the first year commences next Tuesday!'; and the third series of *Hancock's Half Hour* on the small screen began at the end of September. 'I can't remember when I laughed so much at a comedy show on television,' declared a viewer. One cultural phenomenon largely passing under the radar was that of the cartoon character Andy Capp getting into his work-shy, beer-swilling, cigarette-dangling groove. Created by a Hartlepool man, Reg Smythe, he had first appeared in August in northern editions of the *Daily Mirror* and would soon go national, becoming an emblematic, wholly unreconstructed working-class figure. 'Look at it this way, honey,' Andy says in one of the early strips, leaning nonchalantly against the wall as his wife Florrie sits battered on the floor, 'I'm a man of few pleasures and one of them 'appens to be knockin' yer about!'[16]

'Forward with the People' was the slogan on the *Mirror*'s masthead, and on Thursday, 3 October the people's party, gathered on the south coast, experienced a day of high drama. Some six months after Muggeridge had noted Gaitskell telling him that the Labour Party was 'hopelessly split' over the H-bomb issue and that it was 'impossible to have sensible or coherent policy', and some five months after a British nuclear test in the Pacific, this was the day of decision – played out, recorded Panter-Downes with her novelist's eye, 'on the boarded-over ice rink of Brighton's Sports Stadium in a haze of cigarette smoke and Asian flu heated to the combustion point by strong television lights'. The pivotal figure was Aneurin Bevan: the rebel of 1951, by now shadow Foreign Secretary and in increasingly visible, if ultimately uneasy, partnership with Gaitskell. 'Already every inch a statesman in his dark suit, with his distinguished silvery thatch of hair,' noted Panter-Downes, 'he sat on the platform frowning over horn-rimmed spectacles at the *Times*, as though lifted intact from the bow window of a St James's Street club.' The quondam unilateralist also spoke, with that compelling oratory which few if any politicians of the era came close to matching:

> If you carry this [unilateralist] resolution and follow out all its implications and do not run away from it you will send a Foreign Secretary, whoever he may be, naked into the conference chamber. Able to preach sermons, of course; he could make good sermons. But action of that sort is not necessarily the way in which you can take away the menace of this bomb from the world.

A minute or two later, being heckled from the floor, he was provoked into dismissing unilateralism as 'an emotional spasm' – at which words, reported James Cameron next day in the *News Chronicle*, 'something like an emotional spasm did indeed go through that stark, crowded arena'. For Bevan's disciple and future biographer Michael Foot, and for others on the Labour left, it was a moment of deepest betrayal. Yet, Foot would insist in later years, the widely bruited idea that Bevan had 'entered into a cynical compact' – in other words, that his speech was the price of becoming Foreign Secretary in a future Labour government – 'was not merely deeply repugnant to his nature, but is utterly confounded by any study of the facts'.

At the conference itself, the unilateralist motion was crushingly defeated, with the leader of the Transport and General Workers' Union, Frank Cousins, unable to persuade his block-voting delegation to support it. Bevan's stance was no doubt electorally necessary, but arguably this was the fateful post-1945 moment when Labour and radical sentiment as a whole started to become increasingly detached from each other. 'People like himself had lost interest in the Party after Nye's Brighton speech,' Crossman (in 1961) would record the playwright Wolf Mankowitz telling him. 'That was the turning point. Since then they couldn't care less about the Parliamentary leadership or see any great distinction, indeed, between Gaitskell, Wilson and Crossman intriguing against each other.'[17]

In any case, another event – also science-related – quickly stole Bevan's thunder. 'Russians first to launch satellite,' noted Judy Haines on Friday the 4th, in an increasingly rare mention of current affairs. 'It is circling the earth at a fast rate and emitting signals.' This was Sputnik, the world's first man-made satellite and, amidst considerable popular enthusiasm, tracked from Britain by the new Jodrell Bank observatory. As early as the 5th the *FT* placed a dot by the globe on its normally staid front-page news summary; that same day Frances Partridge on behalf of 'Bloomsbury' welcomed the satellite as a news story for once 'something purely interesting and pleasant'; and Doris Lessing was one of many staying up all night hoping 'to catch a glimpse of it bowling past overhead'. On the 7th the *Evening Standard*'s headline was 'Thousands See The Blip', which had passed over London that morning at just after 7.07 a.m., and by the 11th the *FT*'s dot had transmuted into a satellite-like shape.

What were Sputnik's implications? 'The satellite is not an isolated breakthrough on a narrow front,' claimed the *New Statesman*. 'It merely crowns the growing pyramid of evidence that over a wide sector of scientific knowledge the Russians are advancing further and faster than the West.' Bevan agreed, asserting in *Tribune* that the satellite was evidence of Russia's 'technically dynamic society'. For Churchill 'the disconcerting thing', as he told his wife, was not 'the satellite itself' but 'the proof of the forwardness of Soviet Sciences compared to the Americans'. Gallup duly sounded public opinion: 36 per cent felt an increased respect for the Russians, 27 per cent could not understand why the Americans had been beaten to it, and only 14 per cent said that Sputnik had made them more frightened of Russia. Inevitably, the fascination eventually abated. 'As the week progressed and the satellite continued, after a panicky interval of doubt and speculation, to transmit its signals, the BBC allowed a note of boredom to creep into its bulletins,' Bernard Hollowood was recording in *Punch* by the 23rd.

'The satellite became "it". "Well," the announcer began, "it's still up there and going strong." The thing was proving rather a disappointment: it hadn't burned itself out, it hadn't landed on Washington, it wasn't quite playing the game. It was threatening to clash with the royal visit to Canada.'[18]

Six days into Sputnik's flight – and seven months after the announcement by the Paymaster-General, Reginald Maudling, of the tripling of the civil nuclear power programme – it was discovered that one of the nuclear reactors at Windscale (later renamed Sellafield) was on fire. That was early on Thursday the 10th. Over the next two days, as makeshift hoses delivered water into the reactor, enormous bravery was displayed, above all by the deputy works manager Tom Tuohy. 'I went up to check several times until I was satisfied that the fire was out,' he recalled. 'I did stand to one side, sort of hopefully, but if you're staring straight up the core of a shut-down reactor you're going to get quite a bit of radiation.' Or, as he also put it, 'I'm glad I was there, but I'd rather not do it again.' From the start the official line was to downplay the seriousness of the situation and its potential dangers: the BBC's six o'clock radio news bulletin on the 11th stressed that no public hazard was being caused because the wind was blowing from the east and carrying radioactivity out to sea, while next day the ban on the sale of locally produced milk covered only 14 square miles. Nevertheless, reflected Nella Last that Saturday after reading about the fire, 'I often have wondered about "fall" of atomic tainted dust from Windscale, or Calder'; she called the prospect of it being blown down the coast to Barrow '*not* a happy thought'.

Monday saw the ban being significantly extended – to 200 square miles, thereby including a further 500 farms – but the Atomic Energy Authority was adamant that 'people in the new area need have no apprehension about milk they have already drunk'. As for the undrunk milk, thousands of gallons were now being tipped into the sea, but it was too late to prevent what Panter-Downes soon afterwards described as 'a wave of national disquiet' not only about the 'alarming leak of radioactive iodine' into west Cumberland's milk supplies but, more generally, about 'what went wrong, why the Atomic Energy Authority was so slow in saying that anything had gone wrong, why the safety measures were fumbled – and slow off the mark, too'. This was probably an accurate assessment, to judge by Nella Last's chat on the 17th with her friend Mrs Higham. 'Like myself she has had "qualms" about these big atomic works,' Last noted, adding they were both agreed that 'there's bound to be downright ignorance of effects & results, with something so utterly new'. In fact the government had already commissioned an inquiry by the AEA's Sir William Penney, but on its completion later in the month Macmillan – deeply concerned not to endanger Anglo-American nuclear collaboration – was willing to release only a relatively anodyne version. 'On the whole, reassuring,' was the *News Chronicle*'s response to the ensuing White Paper on the accident, though in regard to Britain's ambitious atomic energy programme, the paper highlighted the 'radiation risks about which we still know far too little', plausibly asserting that 'it is this mystery, this sense of vague and ill-understood menace, which worries the public'.

And the locals? 'As an inhabitant of West Cumberland, the accident at Windscale has naturally been an unpleasant shock,' a woman wrote to a local paper in the almost immediate aftermath. 'The fact, however, that heightens the shock is that we were given no warning until the situation was under control. Why not? Suppose the situation had "run away"? What then? Surely people have a right to be given enough warning either to move their children out of the vicinity, or, at least, to keep them indoors if any severe accident is expected.' Accordingly, 'until we can rely on a more immediate warning of irradiation or even a threatened explosion, we shall remain dissatisfied and anxious'. Even so, the most authoritative historian of the episode, Lorna Arnold, reckons that 'Cumberland remained remarkably calm', and she points to the fact that Windscale, since the start of its construction ten years earlier, 'had brought employment and considerable prosperity to a severely depressed area'.

Jenny Crowther (later Uglow) was at school next to the plant and lived three miles up the coast at St Bees. 'People were told not to eat anything from their allotments,' she remembers. 'But the allotments were their pride and joy, and as the word "fallout" was used they assumed the ban only applied to vegetables above ground, as if rain had fallen on them, not radiation. They just ate the carrots and beetroot and potatoes without giving it a thought.'[19]

'I have discovered another August pleasure in London, and that is to walk in the evening light around the new council estates,' John Betjeman announced in his *Spectator* column a few weeks after Macmillan's Bedford speech.

> Some of the latest are magnificent, and when one compares their openness, lightness, grass and trees, and carefully related changes of scale from tall blocks to small blocks, with the prison-like courts of artisans' dwellings of earlier ages, one realises that some things are better than they were. 'The awful equality of it all is frightening,' a friend said to me. And that is true. If you are lucky enough to have one of these new workers' flats, there is not much chance of showing individuality . . . But there are compensations. There are light and air, and the shrieks of children, instead of echoing against brick walls, are dispersed in open space.

Betjeman singled out for praise Brixton's Loughborough estate ('tall concrete and glass blocks turn out to be two-storey houses built on top of one another'), the Cremorne estate near World's End ('provides a quiet walk among grass and houses which are of pleasant texture and to human scale') and in particular the vast Churchill Gardens estate by the river. 'It is hygienic, egalitarian and frightening, but it has a beauty and can never deteriorate into the squalor of the parts of Pimlico it has replaced,' he declared. 'Maybe it has no place for someone like me, but it gives one hope for modern architecture.'

Increasingly, though, Betjeman was in embattled mode about the forces of modernity. In October, soon after he had lamented how 'the majority of building projects today in Britain are ones of vast bulk' (as typified by the City of London's Bucklersbury House, 'that monster now dwarfing everything between the Monument and St Paul's'), he was campaigning vigorously to save John Nash's Regent's Park terraces from the wrecking ball. And in December, responding to an MP who wanted to see Tower Bridge demolished, he argued in his column that 'the reason why people dislike the word "planning" and those connected with it is not because they object to new towns or to flowering cherries and civic centres, but because in their minds planning is associated with destruction'. 'Bombing we can take,' he went on. 'It is part of the fortunes of war. Fire may be carelessness. But the deliberate pulling down of a familiar street or building with associations, the felling of timber in a village and the destruction of old cottages is really playing about with part of ourselves. They are roots and home to somebody.' He ended with a caustic personal observation: 'I have always noticed that progressive architects and planners and, no doubt, the chief share-holders in those sinister development trusts which are buying up London and ruining it with oblong-ended packing cases, live in old houses and go to a good deal of trouble to protect their views.'[20]

Yet for the planners themselves – but *not* the architects or developers – the unpalatable truth in 1957 was that their high tide had already passed. 'One of the expressions of bewilderment that is most commonly heard in the profession,' the once highly influential town planner Thomas Sharp told his peers that spring, 'is that to most people plan-ning has now become just a colossal bore and that to many others it is something actually to dislike with an active hostility.' He added, not implausibly, that 'what is most disliked about us, I think, is that control which we exercise over other people's activities with so little obvious and acceptable result'. Peter Self of the Town and Country Planning Association tended to agree: 'Town planning questions … seldom figure in party manifestos or wireless debates, and they arouse hardly any political controversy – more as a result of indifference than agree-ment. Planning controls are coming to be viewed as necessary evils, rather than as instruments for forging lasting benefits. A dead hand grips the spirit of planning.'

In late July the Institute of Contemporary Arts staged a highly charged meeting on the subject of 'planning controls' in London. Among architects speaking, Lionel Brett insisted that the case for control was ultimately to prevent 'the spivs' (i.e. presumably the devel-opers) from wrecking the environment; the ultra-modernist Peter Smithson was for complete abolition of aesthetic controls; and the equally modernist Ernö Goldfinger concurred. For the planners, Hertfordshire's County Planning Officer E. H. Doubleday spoke in unashamedly paternalistic vein about the value of planning control for 'arrogant young architects'. In a subsequent Third Programme talk, Brett astutely identified how on the part of younger architects there existed an increasing feeling that the post-war planners are out of touch with the real world of 1957, that our New Towns, neighbourhood centres, shopping precincts, national parks, etc, are not what is wanted and lack some essential thing that our old towns and neglected counties had, presumably spontaneity, so that nobody would ever want to paint a picture in Harlow or Bracknell . . . planners waste their time controlling elevations in Watford and Redhill when they should be concentrating their minds on Liverpool and Glasgow.

1960s-style urbanism, in short, was where the exciting future action lay, not 1940s-style planned dispersion. Brett added that, at the recent ICA meeting, 'the people on the platform in favour of planning control wore suits and ties and the people against it wore open shirts or turtle-necked jerseys'.[21]

In Liverpool itself, as in other major cities, the key players by this time were neither planners nor architects, nor yet developers or construction companies, but instead local politicians. 'It is already apparent that the eleven-storey blocks now going up are really insignificant when considered against their backgrounds and we are investigating very closely the possibility of going much higher,' stated Alderman David Nickson, Labour chairman of the Housing Committee, in early September, in the context of tower blocks rising on Everton Heights. 'This form of development is obviously the only answer to sprawl.' Later in the month he continued to insist that 'the Housing Committee take the view that there is no reason why the 20-storey mark should not be passed', adding that 'we regard this as important a step in the construction of domestic dwellings as was the breaking of the sound barrier in the world of aeronautics'. Soon afterwards the *Liverpool Echo*'s Municipal Correspondent wrote suitably portentously of time and the city:

Slowly but surely the face of Liverpool is changing and its terraced skyline, so familiar to travellers by sea arriving in or leaving the Mersey, is gradually taking on new features. Already Everton Brow is crowned with a mammoth block of flats [i.e. the ten-storey Cresswell Mount, opened in 1956], the symbol of the new Liverpool, and just below it, on the sweeping seaward slope, new twin blocks [i.e. The Braddocks], with the skeleton fingers of mammoth cranes reaching for the sky in close attendance, are fitting themselves into the landscape.

Just in case there were any doubters, he emphasised that the two new blocks were 'rising on a site that not so long ago was occupied by count-less mean cottages of uniform drab brick separated by narrow ditches of streets'.

Even so, when Nickson at the end of September reported on the Housing Committee's annual inspection of building developments, and set out again its aspirations for new blocks of up to 21 storeys, he was revealingly anxious about working-class families being housed high: 'They have always been used to the more ordinary type of dwelling, and we shall have to convince them of the advantages of this type of construction. If we can persuade the people to accept this type of build-ing as a reasonable type of home, then we will have achieved something worthwhile.'

At a City Council meeting in early October, the Tory councillor J. Maxwell Entwistle declared himself as supportive as the Labour group of high-rise blocks, and as opposed to unnecessary future over-spill to such places as Skelmersdale, Ellesmere Port or Widnes. 'Dislike flats as they might, the people of Liverpool would sooner stay, even in multi-storey buildings, than go to outlandish areas where there was little industry and the cost of getting back to the city was great.' Was that in fact a fair reflection of the wishes of Liverpudlians living in decaying inner-city areas? Easily the best evidence we have is the 1956 survey of residents of the Crown Street district: on the one hand, 61 per cent did indeed want to stay where they were, whether or not they were rehoused; on the other hand, in terms of those specifically living in houses *already* scheduled for slum-clearance demolition, almost half wished to move away entirely. Or, put another way, the survey's Liverpool University authors helpfully noted, 'variety, confusion and conflict prevailed both in the district as a whole and its sub-areas'.[22]

Across the Pennines, November 1957 saw the opening of a ten-storey block of flats about three-quarters of a mile from the centre of Leeds. This was the start of the Saxton Gardens development – hailed by the *Yorkshire Post* as 'one of the biggest post-war housing schemes of its kind in the Provinces' – with six further blocks, between five and nine storeys each, to be completed over the next year, altogether housing some 1,460 people on land that had been cleared of slums just before the war. That was when the nearby Quarry Hill estate had been opened, and its office now took on the additional management of Saxton Gardens. Indeed, with almost 4,000 people to be rehoused in due course in the York Road redevelopment scheme, which Saxton Gardens overlooked to the east, and a further 6,000 or so also to be rehoused in the Burmantofts area east of York Road, this meant, declared the *Post*, that 'Saxton Gardens will form part of a new central township with a population of more than 15,000 people.' On the day of the opening ceremony, the *Yorkshire Evening News* trumpeted loud and hard: 'With its central heating and domestic hot water in all dwellings, its gas or electric wash boiler with clothes drying cabinet in each flat; its 30 lifts and Garchey system of refuse disposal, Saxton Gardens reaches the heights of modern amenities.' At the ceremony itself, the major reported speech was given by Alderman F. H. O'Donnell, who had spent his boyhood on the Saxton Gardens site, then known as The Bank. 'To the people outside, The Bank was a place where policemen walked about in pairs. But, he pointed out, the people there 50 years ago worked hard for long hours and were as industrious, intelligent, and respectable as any in the country.' And O'Donnell ended by looking ahead: 'He hoped that the people of Saxton Gardens would be as good as the people of the old Bank, and that there would be not only 448 units of accommodation but 448 homes.'

Even the politicians of Bognor Regis had their dreams, as this autumn the possibility emerged of an apparently attractive deal with Billy Butlin, by means of which he would be permitted to build a holiday camp close to the town in return for knocking down his tatty funfair on the Esplanade and giving the land to the council. 'Not often does opportunity knock in so decisive a manner as it does in Bognor Regis today,' declared its chairman J. C. Earle.

Facing, as they do, the finest sandy beach on the South Coast, the opportunities for really bold and imaginative architecture are immense. Tall, modern buildings in the style of Basil Spence, Corbusier or the many other gifted architects practising today are what I hope to see. Nothing pseudo, nothing shoddy, we must not tolerate drab brick boxes. This is

our chance to have beautiful architecture reflecting our day and age, and
we must seize it with firm hands. Fine hotels, luxury flats, a solarium,
shops, theatres and conference halls, and civic buildings can and should
arise, fronted by a broad, impressive seaway.

With only one dissenter, who argued that a Butlin's holiday camp would
be disastrous for Bognor's image, the deal was overwhelmingly
approved.[23]

Almost everywhere, but above all in the major conurbations, the
greatest engine of physical change was of course the slum-clearance
programme. Slum clearance in 'the atomic age' was the theme of an
address by Dr Ronald Bradbury (Liverpool's City Architect) to a
national housing conference in September, which included the estimate
that almost two-thirds of the 850,000 unfit dwellings in England and
Wales were concentrated in about one hundred industrial towns, headed
by Liverpool itself (88,233), followed by Manchester, Birmingham,
Leeds, London, Hull, Sheffield, Salford, Stoke-on-Trent, Oldham,
Bradford and Bristol – 'all of which', noted Bradbury, 'have very
considerable slum problems'.

In third-placed Birmingham, it was around this time that demolition
began in the Ladywood district, a process of slum clearance that from
the start seems to have been carried out in a horribly flawed way, at
least to judge by the subsequent *cri de coeur* of Canon Norman Power
of St John's, Ladywood – *not* an opponent of slum clearance in principle. 'In all this redevelopment, during which I saw a living community
torn to pieces by the bulldozers and scattered to the four corners of the
city,' he recalled in 1965 in his short, devastating book *The Forgotten
People*, 'there was no consultation with the people most affected and
concerned. Neither was any opinion sought from local teachers, social
workers, organisation-leaders or clergy.' Crucially, Ladywood's demolition started not with the worst housing, but instead with some of the
better; Power surmised that 'probably the need to clear a space for the
new Inner Circle Road was one motive'. Overall, he went on, 'The
heart of our community was destroyed. A living, corporate personality
was crushed by the bulldozers. There were some extraordinary and
inexplicable side-effects. The new Waste Land was left waste for seven
years. But it was not cleared. It was left a wilderness of brick-ends, tin

cans, broken bottles and even half-demolished buildings.' In short, 'It was the best school of vandalism I have ever seen.'

Elsewhere, the *Salford City Reporter* announced towards the end of 1957 that '"HANKY PARK" AREA WILL SOON DISAPPEAR' – the district which, back in the 1930s, 'gained notoriety in Walter Greenwood's *Love on the Dole*' – while in Bristol some 10,000 houses were identified as needing to be cleared in the next five years, including among the steeply sloping Georgian terraces of Kingsdown, thus leading to protests from Betjeman downwards. In London the ongoing development of Notting Hill Gate (already involving considerable demolition ahead of planned road-widening, the replacement of the two existing underground stations on opposite sides of the road by a single station under it, and the construction of two tall slab blocks of flats as well as many new shops and offices) was likewise a source of unhappiness. 'The Village Behind The "Gate"' was the title of some verses that J. F. Adams of Bulmer Place sent in November to the local paper:

> Once we were happy the whole day through,
> With neat gardens where our flowers grew;
> There's not many left, sad to relate,
> In the Village behind the 'Gate' . . .
>
> We'll dig up our roots and home ties,
> Remember those welcomes and final goodbyes
> Of loved ones passed on early and late
> In the Village behind the 'Gate'.
>
> But there will be no friendship in skyscraper flats
> Or leaning on garden fence for chats,
> And help your neighbour in this new estate,
> Like we did in the Village behind the 'Gate'.

As it happened, it was not so far away, in the Kensington drawing room of the Victorian artist Linley Sambourne, that (a few days earlier) the Countess of Rosse had acted as hostess at a meeting to form the preservationist Victorian Group (later Society). Betjeman was present, as was the leading architectural journalist of the day, that qualified modernist (and suburb-loving, but New Town-hating) J. M. Richards. 'On the whole,' Richards suggested in vain soon afterwards, 'it had better avoid calling itself "Victorian" – the word now has overtones of funniness.'[24]

The Victorian era seemed remote enough when in due course the *Architects' Journal* ran its feature 'Buildings of the Year: 1957'. Presenting 'the uncensored opinions' of the users of a dozen or more newly completed buildings, the tone was largely positive. 'Smashing!' declared James Loft, a 52-year-old worker who had spent ten years in the dust of a cement factory before coming to the Bowater-Scott Tissue Mill, producing Andrex toilet rolls, at Northfleet, Kent. 'You don't know what the weather's like outside: it's practically always the same temperature in here.' Generally there,

> The workers, when asked what they like, find it difficult to put in words. Sally Donoghue, the shop steward in the converting department, said the girls liked the press button machinery. 'It's very modern, isn't it?' she said. Could she suggest any improvements? The answer was a simple, 'No.' Beryl Duff, a pretty Irish girl who was packing, said 'It's a good place to work in: it's modern, isn't it?' And pressed to say what she means by 'modern', she says it's light, airy and colourful. The very high quality of the toilet accommodation was mentioned by everybody who was interviewed, and Mr Morley [assistant manager] has found that it is appreciated by the staff and properly treated.

Elsewhere, Sir Vincent Tewson, General Secretary of the TUC, praised its new headquarters in Great Russell Street as 'a piece of contemporary architecture our eight million members can be proud of'; recently married Daphne Jones on the 14th floor of Great Arthur House, on the Golden Lane estate just north of the City of London, loved the 'feeling of being out in the open', with the balcony being 'like sitting in a garden', while in Basterfield House, one of the estate's four maisonette blocks, Angela Hobday, a nurse at Bart's, found it all 'exciting, so new and different, and such fun to be living in'; at Dunn's in Bromley (specialists in selling modern furniture), the managing director Geoffrey Dunn was almost entirely happy with his quasi-brutalist new premises, noting that he had had 'letters from perfect strangers, and not from such high falutin' addresses either, congratulating us on adding this shop to the town'; and at a primary school in Amersham, two small boys with caps askew, Geoffrey Magee and Garry Livemore, offered a spontaneous volley of praise – 'Super!' 'Smashing!' 'Supersonic!' – with the magazine reckoning that 'what appeals to the children most is the colour, the glass, the wallpapers, the lighting, in a word the bright modernity of the interior, as much as the practical arrangements'. The feature, though, did include a couple of grumblers. On the Claremont estate in West Ham, Mrs Nellie Richardson (living with her bus-conductor husband and four small children) was adamant that a flat 'isn't really a place for a family', adding that 'most of the time you have to say to the children, "keep it down a bit"'. And at the factory-like Churchfields Comprehensive (845 pupils in six completely isolated blocks) in West Bromwich, the headmaster Mr Hobart not only found the use of glass 'quite excessive', especially in south-facing rooms like his own study, but called the sound insulation 'downright disgusting'.

There were mixed feelings, too, in a vox pop survey late in 1957 of Britain's most emblematic city of post-war reconstruction. 'Generally, it is the older Coventrians who are least happy,' found the *Sunday Times*. '"Horrible ugly boxes!" they rail, as the new blocks go up. But the youngsters, with no nostalgic memories of the old town, are delighted. "The new cathedral," exclaimed a young typist with real fervour, "is going to be *beautiful* – lovely and bright, you know, not a gloomy old place like they usually are."' Even so, it was probably not all that aged a waitress who, in the Civic Restaurant, 'gazed wistfully across the new Broadgate at an isolated block of pseudo-Tudor beyond', and said, 'I'd have liked little black-and-white buildings really, but the foreign visitors all say this is wonderful.' The piece's accompanying photographs (including of the vast, glass-sided Owen Owen's depart-ment store) provoked a cross letter from a reader in the south-east. 'I see nothing admirable in the new Coventry,' he asserted. 'The large buildings illustrated last week might do for a prison or a boot factory, but I don't think they would do for the patrons of Nash and Wren. The style is ungentlemanly.' To which John Hewitt, the Ulster poet who had recently become curator of Coventry's new Herbert Art Gallery and Museum, replied a week later that the new centre of Coventry is built to a human scale . . . Coventry is not a capital city with the necessity for State architecture, impressive to visitor and reassuring to citizen. It does not belong either to the age of Wren or Nash. It is an industrial city, where motor-cars and aeroplanes and machine tools are manufactured. Having lived here for six months any other industrial town depresses me with the heavy pomposity and grimy insincerity of its architecture.

Meanwhile, one footloose, hard-to-please Londoner was finding everything disagreeable. 'On the whole a dull, disappointing tramp,' recorded Anthony Heap in November after a Sunday inspection of Denmark Hill, Herne Hill and Camberwell. 'Pleasantly picturesque this hilly part of South London may have been fifty years ago. Today it's just a dreary wilderness of uniform blocks of drab new council flats, and dilapidated old Victorian villas. And I'm not sure which look the most depressing.'[25]

---

'John went to football,' noted Judy Haines in Chingford on Saturday, 12 October, the day after the Windscale fire had been put out. 'I mowed the lawn. So much to do.' That same day the Tory conference (in Brighton, like Labour's) ended, with the party's new chairman, Lord Hailsham, the undoubted star and doing much to boost flagging, mid-term, post-Suez morale. Early each morning he appeared on the seafront in a blue dressing gown, bathing trunks and bedroom slippers, ready to take a chilly dip; his oration one evening to the Conservative Political Centre, containing a fierce, uninhibited attack on the conduct of the trade unions, was, according to Mollie Panter-Downes, 'rapturously hailed next day, over the conference coffee cups and cocktail glasses, as being "as good as one of Winston's wartime speeches"'. On the Saturday morning itself, winding up the conference, 'that stocky, rumpled figure' with a 'cherubic, aggressive face' (as she described Hailsham) found a prop and let himself go. 'At the end of his speech,' reported the *Sunday Times*,

he stretched out his hand and gripped the large handbell which Mrs Walter Elliot, the chairman, had used during the conference. Holding it above his head and ringing it with enthusiasm he said: 'Let it ring more loudly. Let it ring for victory.' As the delegates rose to their feet and cheered and stamped, Lord Hailsham shouted: 'Let us say to the Labour Party "Seek not to inquire for whom the bell tolls. It tolls for thee."'

At least one commentator, Francis Williams, was viewing the 50-year-old Hailsham by the end of the week as 'a potential prime minister', but Hailsham himself was quick to reassure Macmillan of his 'unqualified loyalty and support', adding, 'I am not quite such an ass as I seem.' Macmillan himself, just before the conference, had privately pondered his government's position. 'At the moment, the whole thing is swinging *away* from us,' he readily conceded. 'If we cannot bring back the traditional strength of the Party to the fold – small shopkeepers, middle class, etc., – we have no chance. But we also need at least three million trade union votes. We have a war on two flanks.' Over and above such tactical considerations was the increasingly asked question of what was to be done about national decline, relative though it may have been. Or, as a youngish *Daily Express* journalist with misplaced political ambitions, the future historian Maurice Cowling, put it from a particular perspective in a letter to the *Listener* later in October,

> Many people in Britain – not only tories, not only tories of the right, and not only members of the middle-class – fear that an infernal conjunction of inflation, excessive taxation, trade-union irresponsibility, governmental interference and governmental timidity have in the recent past been undermining Britain's social stability and may in the future destroy her economic prosperity.[26]

It was a different kind of decline that the contributors to *Declaration*, published the same month, mostly addressed. Edited by an ambitious 24-year-old publisher, Tom Maschler, the book was a gathering-up of those more or less connected with the 'Angry Young Men' (AYM) phenomenon, his only two refuseniks being Kingsley Amis and Iris Murdoch. Among the eight essayists, Doris Lessing (at 37 the oldest contributor and only woman) expressed her frustration at the 'kindly, pleasant, tolerant' British people, 'apparently content to sink into ever-greater depths of genteel poverty because of the insistence of our rulers on spending so much of the wealth we produce on preparations for a war against communism'; Colin Wilson went 'beyond the Outsider'; John Osborne, writing late and furiously, took scattergun aim, including at the Royal Family – 'the gold filling in a mouthful of decay'; Kenneth Tynan observed that 'the trouble with most Socialist drama, and with much Socialist thinking, is its joylessness'; and Lindsay Anderson coined the phrase 'chips with everything' (about the culinary ordeal of returning to Britain from abroad), called the absence of working-class characters from British films 'characteristic of a flight from contemporary reality', and claimed that Amis would 'rather pose as a Philistine than run the risk of being despised as an intellectual'.

Critical reaction was largely negative. J. W. Lambert in the *Sunday Times* was particularly hard on Anderson, not least his 'curiously old-fashioned worship of what he calls the "working-classes"', having failed to 'notice that the very nature of this stratum of society is changing'. So too Angus Wilson, at 44 possibly not unjealous of the AYM. 'We have rhetoric, exhortation, apocalyptic spine-chilling, smart-aleckry – each and all rather earnest and repetitive – but the total content is trivial,' he asserted in the *Observer*. And soon after, on the Third Programme, the middle-aged critic Alan Pryce-Jones frankly accused the eight of contempt for the public: 'They dislike it for one set of reasons if they are materialists. In that case, other people seem dull, gullible, and snobbish. If on the other hand they are transcendentalists, they accuse the public of lack of purpose, torpidity, unawareness.' Still, *Declaration* sold some 20,000 copies, made a lot of noise and put Maschler firmly on the map.[27]

Also in October, on Saturday the 19th, an undeniably authentic working man, Billy McPhail, scored three second-half headed goals in Celtic's 7–1 trouncing of Rangers in the Scottish League Cup Final, which was played with the usual heavy, laced ball. A third of a century later, long after the end of his professional career, McPhail would lose his claim in the courts for compensation, even though he had been suffering from pre-senile dementia since his thirties. Twelve days after his hat-trick, another Scottish working man, Lawrence Daly, attended a meeting at Glencraig Colliery, Fife – where there had been a plethora of unofficial stoppages over the past year – between National Coal Board management (including G. Mullin, Area General Manager) and

National Union of Mineworkers' officials (including Daly himself as local branch delegate). 'The position at Glencraig is very serious,' insisted Mullin. 'We spent money on this pit and the output should improve. Unless there is improvement, I may be compelled by circumstances to recommend to the Divisional Board to consider whether it is worthwhile carrying this pit on or not.' To which Daly riposted, 'You have refused to listen to the complaints from Glencraig for 15 years.' But Mullin was adamant: 'I would say to you people here, let a man examine himself – and you Mr Daly are talking about a manager being to blame – I think you are just as much to be blamed for the atmosphere at this pit. That is the impression I get from your manner and demeanour at this meeting.'

Towards the end, after Mullin had referred to an under-official being recently threatened by a miner, Daly baldly asserted that 'if men are treated as human beings that is not likely to happen'. Daly – an articulate, even charismatic man in his early 40s – had left the Communist Party the previous year and was starting to become the New Left's emblematic working-class representative. 'I can see how to carry on our cultural and intellectual work all right, and perhaps how to deepen and extend it,' E. P. Thompson wrote to Daly earlier in the month after staying at Glencraig with him and his wife Renée. 'But in the practical organisational side I am puzzled and depressed. I think there is a 50/50 chance that a new left party may in the end get formed, because I don't see how the broader labour movement will be transformed without an electoral threat being presented on the left of the official LP.'[28]

Daly, with a fine tenor voice, enjoyed singing Scottish and Irish folk songs, but like many in the New Left had little enthusiasm for commercial pop music. Top of the charts at the start of November were the Crickets with 'That'll Be The Day' – the vocal style as well as spectacles of their leader, Buddy Holly, an inspiration to the short-sighted John Lennon, by now at art college, while on Saturday the 16th, *Six-Five Special* was broadcast live from the 2i's coffee bar in Soho. The line-up included the pink-haired rocker Wee Willie Harris, seen calling Gilbert Harding (an improbable presence) 'daddy-o'; comedians Mike and Bernie Winters; and the Worried Men, whose Terry Nelhams would go on to become Adam Faith. The 2i's' most famous alumnus, Tommy Steele, was also present in a co-hosting role, just 48 hours before topping the bill at the Palladium's Royal Variety performance, a bill that featured (among others) Gracie Fields, Judy Garland, Tommy Cooper, Vera Lynn and Alma Cogan. That night, the week after his ninth birthday – marked by an unprecedentedly informal, hand-in-the-pocket official photograph by Cecil Beaton's usurper, the more modern-minded Antony Armstrong-Jones – there was no place in the royal box for Prince Charles, confined to quarters at prep school; but the Crazy Gang, lining up to meet the Queen, wore blue Cheam blazers and caps, with a large 'C' badge. Steele himself, reported the *News Chronicle*, initially struggled:

> His first number, 'Rock With The Caveman', ended in dull silence from an icy audience. The young Rock and Roll King started on 'Hound Dog'. Still the audience did not respond.
>
> Then, from the Royal Box high up on the right, somebody was heard clapping in rhythm. It was the Queen Mother.
>
> Once she turned to her daughter as if to say: 'Come on, dear,' but the Queen refrained. After a little, the Duke of Edinburgh started, rather half-heartedly, and off-beat.

Within weeks 'The Pied Piper from Bermondsey' was the subject of an *Encounter* profile by Colin MacInnes, who saw in Steele ('every nice young girl's boy, every kid's favourite elder brother, every mother's cherished adolescent son') the harbinger of a possible English challenge to the dominance of American songs and performers. Coming from whichever side of the herring pond, all this youth culture largely passed Gladys Langford by. In poor health in her late 60s, living alone in a room in Highbury Barn, she kept her diary going despite severe bouts of depression. 'Waiting to cross Highbury New Park,' she recorded on the last Thursday of November, 'I was amazed by the chivalry of the lorry-driver's mate, a handsome Teddy boy who leapt from the cabin and led me across the road like a courtly knight errant.'[29]

Other diarists this month focused on the unfolding Space Age. 'The 2nd Russian Satellite launched with a dog on board,' noted Gladys Hague, living with her sister in Keighley, on 3 November. 'Protests voiced from all over the world.' Or, as Macmillan wryly put it two days later, 'The English people, with characteristic frivolity, are much more exercised about the "little dawg" than about the terrifying nature of these new developments in "rocketry."' The dog, popularly known as Laika, 'obsessed the public imagination', wrote Mollie Panter-Downes. And when she was officially pronounced dead, recorded Frances Partridge on the 15th, 'the *Daily Mirror* came out with a wide border of black, and a great deal about soft noses and velvety eyes up there in the stratosphere'.

As for the satellite itself, degrees of excitement took several forms. 'It is far more momentous than the invention of the wheel, the discovery of the sail, the circumnavigation of the globe, or the wonders of the industrial revolution,' Anthony Wedgwood Benn reckoned in his diary on the 5th; at a Church Assembly meeting in London on the 12th, one speaker declared the Church should send a Sputnik into outer space with a bishop inside it, given that 'the present generation, founded on technology and science, is more interested in the "bleep, bleep" of the satellite than the "bleep, bleep" of the preacher'; and for almost a fortnight satellite-like shapes could again be spotted on the front page of the *FT*.

The canine aspect apart, perhaps the most striking thing about the episode was, a year after the USA had brutally pulled the plug on Eden's war against Nasser, the extent of the pleasure taken in America's technological humiliation – or what Panter-Downes tactfully described to her *New Yorker* readers as 'the slight chuckle with which a man might note the discomfiture of the rich neighbor across the way whose Cadillac has suddenly refused to start'. A few weeks later, the failure of an American rocket provoked some almost gleeful headlines from Fleet Street ('US calls it Kaputnik', 'Ike's Phutnik', 'Oh, What a Flopnik!'), while by the following spring schoolchildren were chanting the rhyme

> Catch a falling sputnik,
> Put it in a matchbox,
> Send it to the USA
> They'll be glad to get it,
> Very glad to get it,
> Send it to the USA

to the tune of Perry Como's 'Catch a Falling Star'.[30]

On Monday the 11th, Armistice Day, John Sandoe opened his

high-class bookshop in Chelsea, despite his grandmother's shock about the absence of shutters to cover the windows on Sundays. Next day, Sir Robert Fraser, director general of the Independent Television Authority (ITA), gave a press conference robustly criticising the BBC and defending commercial television, while *Woman's Hour* had at least one irritated listener. 'That wretched "know all" Ruth Drew took part in telling us "how",' noted Judy Haines. 'Another was telling us "how" in regard to fish, and another "how" in regard to washing, but Ruth *loves* housework. She takes a duster in *each* hand so that she doesn't waste time with the odd hand! Of course, I only hate her because she's not good for my conscience.' That same day, the Post Office's announcement of plans to introduce postal codes was neatly balanced by the Advisory County Cricket Committee's decision at Lord's to shelve yet again a proposed knockout competition. Arguably, though, the overall mood was for change, for two days later Buckingham Palace let it be known that after 1958 debutantes would no longer be presented at court, a decision effectively ending 'the Season' and perhaps reflecting Princess Margaret's reputed disgust that 'every tart in London can get in'.[31]

'The conventional characters of "good BBC" and "bad ITA" belong to the land of myth and fable,' Fraser had asserted at his press conference, responding to disparaging remarks by the head of BBC television. 'We are often told we have audiences of morons: we think we have an audience of men and women . . . What some regard as the herd, we respect as the human family.' Fraser was certainly talking from a continuing position of strength, having the day before given the key facts to Wedgwood Benn. 'In 4.5 million homes with choice, 75 per cent prefer ITA, 25 per cent preferring BBC if you include children,' the Labour MP duly noted. 'Excluding children the figures are 70/30.' Later in the week he lunched with the BBC's Mary Adams: 'She said they were absolutely defeated and in a complete dither.'

Still, the original television channel had its undoubted glories, not least the scriptwriters Ray Galton and Alan Simpson. 'There's a bite to *Hancock's Half Hour*,' observed the critic John Metcalf soon afterwards, 'a willingness to accept the worst in all of us, to make social and human observations that belong to the satirist rather than the clown.'

So too *Tonight*, soon to move to a 6.45 start and increasingly addictive to members of the Viewers' Panel:

> The whole programme is good from beginning to end. It also has the essence of surprise – you don't know what to expect next (which is the very thing that makes it hold you, I believe).
>
>   I would sooner miss my evening meal than miss this harmonious three (Cliff Michelmore, Derek Hart and Geoffrey Johnson Smith).

There had also been a sharpening-up in a key area. 'The BBC, inspired by ITV News, has improved the manner of its news presentation,' reckoned the *Spectator*'s John Cowburn in his end-of-year TV review, 'so that it is no longer the voice of the Establishment talking to the poor gammas.' Even so, for the medium as a whole, paternalism remained the order of the day: not only did the Postmaster General, Ernest Marples, refuse in December to allow an extension of viewing hours ('It is not only quantity but general quality and balance which has to be borne in mind') but many among the progressive intelligentsia disdained to acquire a set, so that, as Doris Lessing recalled, 'One could more or less work out someone's political bias by the attitude he took towards television.' Of course, there were variations. At the end of January, Michael Young was informing the anthropologist Geoffrey Gorer that his co-author Peter Willmott had become 'a real television addict': 'He says that he has not been to a cinema since December 16th when he acquired his new set.'[32]

Young passed on this titbit in the context of Gorer having been engaged since the autumn on a detailed investigation of television-watching habits. Adults were surveyed in November, leading to some suggestive statistics: 59 per cent of the upper middle class never had the set switched on while they were eating, compared to an overall average of 46 per cent; 22 per cent, mainly from the working class, always had the set on during meals; and, in answer to the question 'How important is television in your daily conversation?', 52 per cent overall replied, 'not at all important' (66 per cent in the case of the upper middle class). One of Gorer's 'greatest surprises' from the study was 'the apparent almost complete absence of emotional involvement of the viewers with "TV personalities"', while in general he reckoned that 'although TV will help somewhat to identify people who appear on the screen fairly

frequently its influence as a form of political education and enlightenment is practically non-existent'.

Two months later it was the turn of children to give their views:

> I would rather go out really; go down to the coffee bar or stay with a
> friend, we have the records on. Yes, records are more important. *(Jean
> Milner, 14, girls' grammar, Stoke-on-Trent)*
>
> Everyone sits down and watches it; you don't talk as much as you used
> to. If anyone came in, you used to talk – now you watch the television.
> *(Elaine Bate, 14, girls' grammar, Stoke-on-Trent)*
>
> I don't think some programmes it is a timewaster but with others it is.
> Such as these cowboy Westerns – I can't see what use you get from them
> but I watch them just the same. *(Peter Sockett, 14, secondary modern,
> Sheffield)*
>
> I ask if we can have it on and if my brother wants the BBC, there is
> always a row going on. *(Janet Slack, 10, primary, Sheffield)*
>
> I think I have learned a lot from it – Panorama and Tonight, these
> specially I like. Some of the comedy programmes haven't taught me
> much. *(D. J. Bettany, 15, boys' grammar, Newcastle-under-Lyme)*
>
> Westerns – you get sick of them. *(David Wise, 14, secondary modern,
> Crawley)*

Gorer's conclusion was that television had only two major effects on
young people: it made them stay at home more, and it made them go to
bed later. The *Manchester Guardian*'s television critic, in a swingeing
attack just before Christmas on ITV's fare for children, was much less
inclined to ignore the moral dimension. 'There is a certain amount of
crime and violence in these programmes,' he complained, 'but almost as
disturbing is the tawdry and trashy character of the incessant films and
series.' And he instanced *The Buccaneers* – 'a sort of pseudo-Stevenson
tale, in which, as in all ITV serials, neither character nor dialogue matter
one jot; action, crude, abrupt, and almost mechanical, is all that matters'.
Even *Robin Hood*, 'which I had thought passable when commercial
television began, now seems to have deteriorated into the same perfunctory, empty bustle as all the rest of the film serials'. In fact, the only
saving grace was *Rin-Tin-Tin*, 'the most humane of these affairs,
perhaps because this handsome dog can neither talk nor shoot'.

Radio's principal innovation this autumn was the coming of *Today* on the Home Service, in effect as the sound equivalent of *Tonight*. It began as two 20-minute strands, either side of *Lift Up Your Hearts* and the eight o'clock news; its debut on 28 October featured Petula Clark, interviews with a pilot and plane passenger, record reviews, Robert Morley on a first night, Eamonn Andrews on boxing, and an item about an auction of Napoleon's letters – a miscellany with not a hint of politics, let alone a bruising interview. It was not until the following summer that the raffish Jack de Manio, with his gin-and-tonic voice, became the main presenter, and another five years before *Today* more systematically focused on news and current affairs. *The Archers* remained the favourite radio programme, with some 18 million listeners. In late November a survey was conducted, and many fans 'paid tribute to the authentic atmosphere of the Ambridge community', as in the words of a police sergeant's wife: 'The characters – foolish, kind, wise and occasionally spiteful – make a very realistic programme.' A salesman's wife, however, found the female characters less plausible. 'Why are all the women rather crudely drawn? They whine, they nag, they grumble, they are usually very silly and demanding; and when they *are* good, they are very, very dull.'³³

———

The run-up to Christmas began for Judy Haines on the last day of November. 'Had an enjoyable but exhausting time in Gamage's,' she recorded. 'Girls got pencil cases from Father Christmas and enjoyed the Animal Show. I ordered four articles to be sent home.' The following Wednesday afternoon, in dense fog near Lewisham, the 4.56 steam express from Cannon Street to Ramsgate crashed into a stationary electric train, bringing down a bridge carrying a loop line over the track path and altogether killing 90 people. 'Bodies shrouded in blankets and coats lay in a long row beside the track,' reported the *Manchester Guardian*. 'Alongside were strewn handbags, gloves, shoes, and gaily wrapped Christmas parcels.' That was a disaster, down to human error as well as the weather, but later in the month three scandals began to unfold. On the 7th, in Thurso, a police officer was provoked by a foul-mouthed 15-year-old grocer's boy ('you think you're a smart fucker') into hitting him, leading to complaints which the police dismissed

before the local MP eventually forced a public inquiry, amidst considerable parliamentary disquiet about a cover-up. On the 9th, the former
and future right-wing Labour MP Woodrow Wyatt exposed on
*Panorama* the gerrymandering practices of the Communist-led
Electrical Trades Union, most recently its cynical blackballing of Les
Cannon, the union's gifted Education Officer who had resigned from
the CP over Hungary. And on the 19th, the Commons debated the
recently exposed abuses at Rampton Mental Hospital near Retford,
Nottinghamshire, where the mentally ill rubbed shoulders with violent
criminals. Amidst all this, the critic Hilary Corke (in the *Listener* on the
12th) ferociously attacked Doris Lessing (a writer 'of absolutely no
importance'); the 14-year-old future critic, Lorna Stockton, went to her
first, dismal school dance in Whitchurch, Shropshire and met Vic Sage
('temples glistening with sweat and Brylcreem'); and on the 16th, in a
live TV transmission of *Hancock's Half Hour*, much of the scenery fell
prematurely apart, leaving Hancock to play an entire scene holding up
a table. But at least the audience was laughing – unlike for the most part
at *Barnacle Bill*, the final Ealing comedy, released just before Christmas
to a critical panning summed up by Isabel Quigly's three words, 'a big
flop'. It was comic cuts, though, at a cold, wet Valley on Saturday the
21st, as ten-man Charlton Athletic came from 5-1 down to beat the
visitors Huddersfield Town 7-6, leaving their manager, Bill Shankly, for
once speechless until the train back reached Peterborough.[34]

A running subplot during December was the 'Bank Rate Tribunal'.
Reluctantly granted by Macmillan under political pressure, and sitting
at Church House, Westminster under Lord Justice Parker, its brief was
to determine whether there had been a 'leak' that accounted for the
heavy selling of gilt-edged stocks just before the 2-per-cent rise in the
Bank Rate on 19 September. The individuals under most suspicion were
two of the Bank of England's non-executive directors, Lord Kindersley
of Lazards and W. J. ('Tony') Keswick of Mathesons. Keswick's cross-
examination on the 6th, conducted by the Attorney General, Sir
Reginald Manningham-Buller, included the question of what he and his
brother had discussed five days before the rise. 'It is difficult for me,' he
observed in a memorable phrase that would be much cited, 'to remember the exact timing of conversation on a grouse moor.' Overall,
Macmillan was privately reflecting by the second week that the evidence

to the tribunal, 'tho' not really damaging, does the Capitalist system as a whole no particular good', while the following week the City establishment's increasing vexation with the proceedings was encapsulated by Kindersley's angry missive to the banker George Bolton about Manningham-Buller's 'offensive' winding-up speech: 'If he was the next gun to me tomorrow I would certainly use my cartridges in a different direction to the pheasants!!!' Even so, for outsiders it was a fascinating spectacle, watching (as Panter-Downes put it) 'a succession of spruce, pink-joweled City gentlemen easing themselves and their briefcases into the witness chair' and speaking a 'totally different language' about '"comparatively small"' deals of a million or so pounds. 'It has all been a revealing glimpse into a special, jealously guarded world,' she added, and 'many Conservatives are wondering what the average hard-up voter is going to make of it'.[35]

Christmas Day was marked by the Queen's first Christmas television broadcast, live from the Long Library at Sandringham. 'That it is possible for some of you to see me today is just another example of the speed at which things are changing all round us,' she observed. 'Because of these changes, I am not surprised that many people feel lost and unable to decide what to hold on to and what to discard, how to take advantage of the new life without losing the best of the old.' Viewers were predictably delighted:

> Her Majesty was so natural and her message must surely have moved and inspired many viewers. The innovation of TV in the Queen's home made us feel, as she herself said, that she is really our friend and not a removed figure.
>
> Her Majesty's relaxed, sincere and charming approach was captivating. It seemed in contrast to her former style of speaking, which always struck me as slightly aloof.
>
> A real thrill to see the Queen so clearly and so close.

It was a prosperous-feeling Christmas in Chingford. 'Had a picnic lunch in the lounge, which was most enjoyable,' Judy Haines noted two days later. 'Now we have electric fires in both dining and lounge we can use both rooms at a moment's notice.' Another diarist, Dennis Dee, was just starting out. A farm worker and horse breaker turning himself into a horse, pig and poultry breeder, he was 31 and had recently acquired a smallholding in the East Riding village of Winestead. A countryman of few words, he began his journal at the start of 1958 as economically as he intended to go on:

> *1 January.* Keen frost today. W [his wife Wendy] went to Hedon to see her mother. I am working for Mr Patchett at 'Westlands Farm', Winestead.
> *2 January.* More frost. I punctured George's car today.
> *3 January.* Frosty again today. Mowing the big ditches out at Westlands.
> *4 January.* Milder weather. Started to cut the large rough hedge round the paddock. A big job and a hard one.

That same day, Saturday the 4th, fellow diarist Madge Martin went to the Old Vic to see *A Midsummer Night's Dream*, in which 'Frankie Howerd, the comedian from the music-halls and radio, was a good, but quiet Bottom', playing alongside (she did not mention) Ronald Fraser as Flute and Judi Dench as First Fairy; next day, Anthony Heap visited his mentally unstable wife Marjorie at Friern Barnet, to which she had recently returned and where the doctors were going to try 'electric shock treatment' again. The weekend also saw, amidst stirring scenes, the last passenger train run between Abergavenny and Merthyr Tydfil. 'I have lived in a house where the back garden adjoins the line,' Graham Jones of 36 Rhyd-y-cae, Rassau wrote soon afterwards to the *Merthyr Express*.

> The trains passing by have formed part of our lives. Last Monday was so quiet and then we realised that no longer would those grand ladies of the steam track pass by again. To many on-lookers we may seem perhaps sentimental and a little foolish, but that sad last train with its even sadder whistles as it graced the track for the last time was to me and many others the end of something in our lives which will never be replaced.[36]

# 5

# Not a Matter of Popularity

On Monday, 6 January 1958 a disgruntled housewife in Paddington gave her Detergent Survey interview to Mass-Observation; Dennis Dee in Winestead did 'hedging and ditching at the farm' amidst 'heavy rain nearly all the day'; Madge Martin in Oxford went to *Barnacle Bill* at the Ritz ('amusing enough, but a little too farcical'); Judy Haines in Chingford took her daughters as a pre-school treat to Norman Wisdom's *Just My Luck* at the Odeon ('no indication as to where queues should form until opening time and there was a great reshuffle in the wind and rain'); the Queen took Charles and Anne to the Bertram Mills Circus at Olympia ('both the Royal children bounced up and down in their seats with excitement');[1] and all three Treasury ministers resigned – a unique event in twentieth-century British political history.[2]

The story had begun a year earlier when Macmillan, as the new prime minister, had chosen his Treasury team: Peter Thorneycroft as Chancellor of the Exchequer, Enoch Powell as Financial Secretary and Nigel Birch as Economic Secretary. The 47-year-old Thorneycroft, president of the Board of Trade since 1951, was a capable, seasoned politician whose main quirk was dropping into fashionable 1930s' Cockney twang at the end of sentences, and Macmillan had deployed him as campaign manager in the post-Eden succession battle with Rab Butler. Few doubted Thorneycroft's free-market instincts. 'No system of social security, no schemes of unemployment insurance,' he had written ten years earlier, 'are a substitute for enterprise, hard work, modern methods and up-to-date machinery,' adding that Keynesian 'remedies for unemployment still remain in the realm of theory'. And at the Board of Trade, his implacable opposition to import controls to protect the Lancashire textile industry had earned him the sobriquet 'the hangman of Lancashire' from Cyril Lord. Thorneycroft's instincts were shared by his two junior ministers: Powell, fresh from steering through legislation to de-control rents in the private housing sector, and Birch, an acerbic operator who had made his fortune as a stockbroker. In Powell's case, though, there was a paradox, namely the juxtaposition of a classical free-market approach (including, later in 1957, pushing fruitlessly for an extensive denationalisation programme) with a deep-dyed English nationalism. As William Rees-Mogg would put it after Powell's death, 'his two big ideas were not entirely compatible with each other'. For Powell himself in 1957, his new post – requiring uncompromising Gladstonian parsimony resting upon unbending willpower and unassailable grasp of detail – felt like destiny calling. 'As frigid as any spell woven by some ice maiden of a Nordic saga', noted one parliamentary sketch writer of his performance in May. 'Under his chilling touch the Finance Bill was laid out like a fish on a slab.'[3]

Within weeks of his appointment in January 1957, Thorneycroft was taking a hard, unyielding, non-Keynesian line. The government, he told his Cabinet colleagues at the end of the month, 'spends too much, drifts into inflation, then seeks to cure the situation by fiscal and budgetary measures'. And in case anyone misunderstood, he reiterated: 'We shrink from the measures necessary to cut expenditure, and inflation starts again.' His Budget in April was avowedly 'disinflationary', emphasising the indispensable 'maintenance of a satisfactory budget balance'; the next month he wrote to Macmillan insisting that government not 'spend more than we are spending already', asking for his support to help counter the inevitable pressure from spending ministers, and claiming there was a 'real danger' of 'an economic crash – or at any rate a sufficient stumble to throw the Conservatives out of office for quite a considerable time'.

During July, Thorneycroft's analysis of what needed to be done to slay the inflationary dragon developed significantly. On the 17th (three days before Macmillan's Bedford speech sought to highlight the dangers of inflation) he told the Cabinet that 'we should lose no opportunity of making it clear in public that the source of our inflationary disease is wages increasing out of all proportion to increases in production' – an understandable enough approach in the wake of the unions' victory in the engineering and shipbuilding strikes that spring. But by the 30th, his line to Macmillan was that 'the only resolute action which is really within the power of the Government' was 'to restrict the supply of money to the point where cost and price increases were checked by severe unemployment' – a strategy, he accepted, that 'would involve cuts in public investment and checking private investment by a savage credit squeeze'. In short, it was an embryonic form of monetarism, though the term itself had yet to be coined, and almost certainly, more-over, monetarism of a less full-blooded kind than that embraced by either Powell or Birch.

Then came September's sterling crisis, largely caused by 'hot money' speculators. A Keynesian economist, J.C.R. Dow, subsequently reflected that what was 'remarkable' about Thorneycroft's view of the crisis was 'the way in which he accepted rising prices at home as the cause of the run on the reserves'. Or, as the historian Ewen Green has suggested, it was an emergency that – for all Thorneycroft's undoubted, deeply sincere wish to protect the currency – also provided him 'with one more stick to belabour his colleagues into accepting his deflation-ary strategy'. Accordingly, the measures announced on 19 September included not only a 2-per-cent rise in the Bank Rate but also a two-year standstill in public-sector investment, and in his statement Thorneycroft stressed that, given his determination 'to maintain the internal and external value of the pound', there could be 'no remedy for inflation' that was 'not founded upon a control of the money supply'. Soon after-wards, at the IMF's annual conference in Washington, he loudly banged the same drum, prompting *The Economist* to observe that a British politician had, for the first time since 1945, 'openly offered to face unemployment, should that be the price of beating inflation and defend-ing the pound'.[4]

There was another, highly symbolic aspect to the economic debate this autumn. Back in April, in his Budget speech, Thorneycroft had pointed out that the British economy was facing particular problems as a result of what he called 'our function as banker for a large part of the world', i.e. the sterling area. That in itself was a breakthrough, bringing the issue out into the open. Siegmund Warburg would recall that when he told people soon after the war that sterling's reserve currency status no longer made sense for what had become a debtor country, he had been chastised by the governor of the Bank of England for breaking ranks from the general view, while when – in the immediate aftermath of the Suez crisis – Eden and Macmillan swapped notes on the burden of being bankers for the sterling area (with the latter noting laconically that 'we must either carry on the business with all its risks, or wind it up and pay 5s in the £'), it was very much a private exchange of views. But now, in the autumn of 1957, following the September measures that had placed in sharp focus the domestic implications of sterling's international role, the issue definitively broke cover. Two left-inclining figures, the economist A.C.L. Day and the economic journalist Andrew Shonfield, led the way in November. 'What Price the Sterling Area?' was the title of Day's Third Programme talk in which he asserted that 'the only sensible policy for the United Kingdom is to withdraw from our over-extended commitments to the sterling area', adding that it was 'extremely easy to exaggerate the importance of the financial services [i.e. invisible earnings] provided by the City'. As for Shonfield, a trenchant *News Chronicle* piece ('We should stop playing fairy godmother') claimed that the sterling area contributed nothing 'except a warm feeling that we still count for something pretty important in the world of international finance', accused it of 'taking away British capital for investment abroad, which we badly need to build more factories at home', and argued that internationally it put Britain 'in the position of a kind of buffer at the end of a long line of trucks'.

The orthodoxy, though, remained firmly the other way, and Shonfield quoted Thorneycroft himself stating recently in the Commons that the sterling area 'brings us a great deal in the way of wealth, strength and prestige'. Such was also the line, in a lengthy analysis entitled 'What Is At Stake', taken by *The Economist* shortly before Christmas: 'A major retreat from sterling's present responsibilities, whether on capital account or on current account, cannot possibly be represented as an unequivocal advantage to this country. It would create a new set of troubles.' Either way, the issue was live – much to the displeasure of the Bank of England's deputy governor, Humphrey Mynors, who soon afterwards privately referred to the wartime gunner and intelligence officer in the British Army as 'Andrew Shönfeld'.[5]

Meanwhile, a political crisis was coming to a head. On 22 December, after a long talk with Thorneycroft, Macmillan noted that 'the

Chancellor wants some swingeing cuts in the Welfare State expenditure – more, I fear, than is feasible politically'. The timing of the denouement was determined by Macmillan's long-planned departure on Tuesday, 7 January on a lengthy Commonwealth tour. At Cabinet on Friday the 3rd, Thorneycroft found himself isolated over his demand that, in addition to an agreed £100 million of cuts in estimated civil and defence expenditure for 1958–9, a further £50 million of savings be found, including through abolishing family allowances for the second child. An aggrieved Macmillan wrote next day, 'Thorneycroft behaved in such a rude & "cassant" way that I had difficulty in preventing some of the Cabinet bursting out in their indignation.' Increasingly over the weekend he came to the view that 'Nigel Birch & especially Enoch Powell' were 'egging him on', with the former appraised by Macmillan as 'a cynic', the latter as 'a fanatic'. By the end of Sunday's lengthy Cabinet meeting, Thorneycroft was still refusing to give significant ground, while Macmillan for his part was adamant that the abolition of the second child's allowance was 'neither politically nor socially desirable – it would be contrary to the tradition of the Conservative Party'. It is tempting but probably mistaken to accept Macmillan's picture of Thorneycroft as a pawn of Powell and Birch. Not only was Thorneycroft a substantial politician in his own right, with firm convictions, but Powell himself was insistent in later years that he and Birch were only 'minor partners' in the Chancellor's decision. Tellingly, once Thorneycroft had taken the decision to resign, he told Powell and Birch, 'that doesn't mean you have to go too'.[6] Both men, however, were just as determined to draw an unequivocal line in the sand.

In his resignation letter of the 6th, Thorneycroft flatly stated that 'the Government itself must in my view accept the same measure of financial discipline as it seeks to impose on others' and referred to the need for 'politically unpopular courses' – an implicit accusation that provoked Macmillan into replying: 'This is not a matter of popularity. We have never shrunk from unpopular measures. This is a matter of good judgement.' Birch's resignation letter to the PM stressed even more emphatically than Thorneycroft's that government expenditure must be reduced. 'These reductions are certainly painful and distasteful,' he declared, 'but the electorate is more likely to forgive us for taking painful and distasteful measures which they will know in their heart are right than for lacking in courage and clear thinking.' Macmillan himself, on a busy Monday, not only fulfilled the constitutional requirement of one Old Etonian (Thorneycroft) at No. 11 being replaced by another (Derick Heathcoat Amory), but found time to rehearse what he would say at London Airport the next day. Practice paid off. 'I said a few words to the BBC, TV etc.,' he duly noted, 'about the Commonwealth trip and "our little local difficulties". This will annoy a lot of people, but I think it will give them a sense of proportion.'[7] 'A little local difficulty' passed into political folklore, a triumph of style over substance.

In its reaction to this almost wholly unanticipated turn of events, the Tory-supporting press was largely disinclined to add to the government's troubles. The *Telegraph* argued that there had been 'a touch of the prima donna' about Thorneycroft's wish 'to dictate Government policy', that under Macmillan there would be 'no taking of the hand from the anti-inflationary plough', and that overall the episode was 'no economic Munich'; the *FT* criticised Thorneycroft's stance as unduly 'rigid'; for the *Express*, he was a 'stiff-necked' finance minister 'carrying fiscal purity to excessive lengths'; and for 'Candidus' (on behalf of the *Sketch*), not only was there 'not the least suggestion that the Government is wavering in its resolve to strengthen the value of the pound', but the crux of the 'disagreement' was 'whether rigid doctrine should prevail over common sense and flexibility'. With the *Mail* and the *Spectator* sitting it out, and the *Sunday Times* slightly pro-Macmillan ('the Government is not like a business'), support for Thorneycroft came only from *The Economist* and *The Times*. Even then, the former's backing was qualified – describing Thorneycroft as two-thirds 'a man of rare resolution', but one-third 'of peculiar punctilio' – so it was left to 'The Thunderer' (under the moralising editorship of Sir William Haley) to provide the heavy guns. 'Flinching' was the unambiguous title of its leader on the 7th, beginning: 'So Mr Macmillan has not, in the end, supported his courageous Chancellor of the Exchequer. All those who have felt that the battle for Britain's economic security is still in the balance must have hoped that that support would be forthcoming.' Next day saw a follow-up editorial on 'A Principle', that of keeping a lid on government expenditure: 'If, as we believe, a principle is at stake, the smallness of the amount involved becomes an argument for strict observance of the principle, not an argument that it does not really matter anyway.'[8]

Elsewhere, the provincial press was more instinctively inclined than the nationals to support the resigning trio – they 'have set an example in resolute adherence to the principle of an all-out economy drive and a standstill in Government expenditure which wholly commends itself to all who are honestly realistic in regard to the future', acclaimed the *Kent & Sussex Courier* – but there was still a widespread reluctance to follow those instincts through, especially if it meant rocking the Tory boat. 'To insist upon drastic Governmental economies, even to the extent of striking at the structure of the social services which Conservatives and Socialists alike have helped to build up, might seem an heroic policy, well attuned to the necessities of the times,' declared the *Yorkshire Post*. 'But,' it went on less than heroically, 'would it serve the national interest if it set the trades union movement by the ears?'

One commentator had no doubts about the merits of Thorneycroft's case or its importance in the big post-war picture. This was Harold Wincott, editor of the *Investors Chronicle* and contributor each Tuesday to the *FT*, with a defiantly homely, non-Oxbridge column that enjoyed a considerable following in the City and even beyond. 'I have yet to discover what the modern Conservative really believes in,' he wrote on the 14th.

> At least, stupid as I am, I have yet to discover that he believes in the things I expect him to believe in as a member of the party which is in opposition to Socialism. I expect the Socialists to introduce Excess Profits Taxes, to break records in the number of council houses they build, to perpetuate a profits tax which discriminates against distributed profits, to do nothing to foster the property and share-owning democracy which they know will destroy them if it really gets rolling, to go on depreciating the currency. I don't expect Conservatives to do these things.

Wincott then applauded Thorneycroft for having publicly thrown overboard at least 'one aspect of the Keynesian doctrine', namely that 'internal policies take precedence over the external value of the currency'. After a reference to 'the realities of our position in 1958', he

concluded: 'In the ultimate resort, if Mr Amory is not to be as expendable as Mr Thorneycroft was, it is the attitude of mind in the Conservative
Party which has got to change. For over six years now, that attitude has
been the "Dear-Mother-I-am-going-to-save-7s 6d-but-not-this-week"
attitude. It still is. But the supply of weeks is running out.'⁹

From the other end of the political spectrum, the *New Statesman* had
little sympathy for what it called 'The Silliest Chancellor', but did fore-
see that he would receive significant rank-and-file Tory support, given
that 'the political mood of the suburban middle-class Tory, who forms
the backbone of the local Associations, is a characteristic expression of
social and economic insecurity: angry, reckless and greedy'. One
provincial middle-class Tory sympathiser, Kenneth Preston in Keighley,
was certainly on Thorneycroft's side. 'A new Chancellor has been
appointed,' he noted on the 7th, 'and presumably now all these wage
claims that have been refused will be granted. Politics are a sad business.' When Gallup in due course produced its opinion-poll findings,
they showed that 42 per cent of all voters sided with Thorneycroft, 20
per cent with Macmillan, and the rest a mixture of 'neither' and 'unde-
cided'. As for specifically Tory voters, 36 per cent plumped for
Macmillan, compared to 33 per cent for Thorneycroft. Yet among those
same voters, confronted by the proposition that government expenditure, including defence and social services, should be cut back in order
to fulfil the government's first duty of fighting inflation and preserving
the value of the pound, 69 per cent agreed and only 13 per cent disa-
greed.¹⁰ How to explain the difference between the two Tory sets of
figures? Perhaps it was a combination of personal faith in Macmillan,
tribal loyalty to the party leadership and a certain innate reluctance to
think things through.

An important subset of Tory support was broadly in Thorneycroft's
camp. Oscar Hobson, doyen of City journalists, early on detected in
the Square Mile 'very strong support for, and sympathy with' the
former Chancellor, while soon afterwards the *Spectator* noted that the
resignations had been regarded in the City as 'a loss of nerve by the
Government at a particularly vital moment', as the 'disinflationary
policies were just beginning to be successful'. Even so, the probability
was that many practical City men did not quite see it as a black-and-
white issue. Rab Butler, temporarily in charge of the government,

reported to his absent master what a leading broker had told him: 'I would like to see the Government cutting every penny off expenditure. But if it is a matter of political judgement I would prefer to trust Macmillan rather than Thorneycroft.'[11] And of course, peculiarly important in the City, there was also the unquantifiable tribal factor.

Predictably, the Tory MPs closed ranks. So far from 'Flinching', one outraged backbencher, Robert Cary, wrote to *The Times*, 'the Prime Minister has faced courageously the issue of not only maintaining the stability of sterling, but, equally important, of sustaining social peace at home'. The same day his letter appeared, the 8th, the *Daily Express* published its poll of 58 Tory MPs, revealing only 6 open (if unnamed) supporters of Thorneycroft, 30 supporters of Macmillan and the rest of the Cabinet, 11 hedgers and another 11 refusing to comment. By the following week, the Tory chief whip Edward Heath was able to report reassuringly to Macmillan in Pakistan: 'Our members now seem to have settled down again and are waiting until the House resumes before passing final judgement. The party as a whole remains loyal to the Government but is still somewhat perplexed about the reasons for the resignations.' Parliament was due to reassemble on the 21st, and 'from all the signs', as Mollie Panter-Downes had already perceptively noted, 'Mr Thorneycroft will not receive much support in public in the House of Commons, whatever it may say in private'. She was in a crowded press gallery for the politically crucial economic debate on the 23rd, which, prior to a vote of confidence on the government's declared policy of keeping the pound strong and controlling inflation, included Thorneycroft's resignation speech:

> The Government, displaying some anxiety over possible abstentions on the Tory benches when it came time to vote, had reportedly drummed up Conservative absentees who were on holiday or away convalescing, and had got them to come along – sunburnt or wan or in any shape at all – to make the result look really heartening for home-and-abroad consumption. As it turned out, the Government need hardly have bothered, since there were no recriminations from Mr Thorneycroft, and the Party, cheering him to the echo, voted solid [i.e. for the government], in a glow of enthusiasm for the principles on which he had apparently insisted to the point of resignation. If this sounds bewildering, that was just about the way it seemed.

Or as Panter-Downes also put it, this 'demonstration of the gentle-manly oddities of the British political system' was 'enough to baffle foreign observers and make lots of Britons, too, feel somewhat confused as to who was hitting whom among all the congratulatory Conservative handshakes'.

In fact, the content of Thorneycroft's gravely delivered, 11-minute speech – a 'personal triumph', according to the *FT* – was far from anodyne. Since the war, he asserted, Britain had sought to combine a full-scale welfare state with a large defence programme, not to mention discharging its onerous responsibilities to the sterling area. He went on to offer his analysis of the consequences and implications of this not ignoble attempt: 'It has meant that for twelve years we have slithered from one crisis to another. Sometimes it has been a balance of payments crisis and sometimes of exchange but always it has been a crisis. It has meant the pound sinking from 20s to 12s. It is a picture of a nation in full retreat from its responsibilities. It is the road to ruin.' And he went on: 'The simple truth is that we have been spending more money than we should . . . It is not the sluice gate which is at fault. It is the plain fact that the water is coming over the top of the dam.' His conclusion was stirring: 'I believe there is an England that would prefer to face these facts and make the necessary decisions now. I believe that living within our resources is neither unfair nor unjust, nor perhaps, in the long run, even unpopular.'[12]

---

In the fullness of time, Thorneycroft and his co-resigners would be portrayed as proto-Thatcherite martyrs. And so in an obvious sense they were – despite the temptation to exaggerate the Macmillan of the mid-1950s (whether at No. 11 or No. 10) as a Keynesian spendthrift, and despite Edward Heath's characteristic insistence three decades later, in a radio interview about the episode, that 'the only way in which it was historic was that it showed that some people who wanted to get rid of Harold Macmillan as Prime Minister failed to do so'. Yet in truth, by 1958 itself, not only had the small-state free-marketeers barely joined battle, let alone started to win it, but the assumptions of a rising genera-tion of 'activators' were almost wholly pointing the other way. 'In economics he was, like the rest of our generation, under the influence of the Keynesian revolution,' William Rees-Mogg would recall about a fellow bright young graduate on the *FT*'s staff, Nigel Lawson. 'We looked on the neo-classical Treasury mandarins as dangerous old fuddy-duddies.'

Even so, the small but purposeful organisation that would do much to lay the intellectual ground for Thatcherism was by now in existence: the Institute of Economic Affairs, under the leadership of the extrovert Ralph Harris and the more cerebral Arthur Seldon, both from working-class backgrounds. The latter's first publication for the IEA, *Pensions in a Free Society*, had recently appeared. 'The philosophy underlying this paper is that most of us are now adult enough to be left, or to be helped, to live our own lives according to our own lights,' Seldon wrote. 'The transition from dependence to independence must be gradual; that is all the more reason for beginning soon.'[13] As long as collective memories remained strong of the slump of the 1930s, and of the appalling human misery that had accompanied it, it was a message that would struggle to win either emotional support or political traction.

# 6

# A Worried Song

On Saturday, 11 January, five days after Thorneycroft's resignation, the BBC experimented by televising two race meetings, at Newbury and Haydock Park, on the same afternoon. Most viewers thought it 'a very good idea', saving 'a lot of boring twaddle about the horses that are to appear in the next race', but 11 per cent found it 'unsettling' and 'hard to keep up with'. That evening Florence Turtle went to the Wimbledon Theatre to see Elsie and Doris Waters in *Cinderella* – 'it was good fun & especially for the many children' – while the Youngs and the Willmotts travelled to Little Cox Pond Farm, outside Hemel Hempstead. 'We dined in the usual baronial Fienburgh manner,' recorded Peter Willmott's wife Phyllis, by now keeping a regular diary. Their host Wilfred Fienburgh was 38, a Labour backbencher, intelligent, amusing, somewhat louche, with 'good looks and big brown eyes' that (recalled Denis Healey) 'often led him astray'. He told his guests 'the Parliamentary gossip: that Macmillan's youngest daughter is really Robert Boothby's; that Princess Margaret still carries a torch for Peter Townsend; that the Cabinet want Elizabeth to have another child; that Philip has a Wren officer for a mistress'. The guests stayed on after dinner. 'Michael [Young] is deaf to the sound and the pull of modern, popular music,' continued Phyllis. 'He looked almost uncomfortable as we listened to Wilf's records. Disconcerted, unsure.' The Youngs left at about midnight. 'The rest of us went on rousting until 2 a.m. We played records and ended up dancing and jiving. Wilfred pretends to be very up to date on it all. He probably is more than we are. I can't help feeling that it is more dignified to sit back and watch the youngsters caper.'[1]

Next day another perceptive woman living in north London, Jill Craigie, had a question or two for the film producer Michael Balcon. 'Can you honestly say that any of our directors gets under the skins of their women characters?' she asked him. 'Has your wife or daughter said anything to you about British films – I mean in the last six or seven years – "that is me, that is how I would have felt under those circum-stances"?' Judy Haines in Chingford was more concerned about her daughters' moral and educational well-being. 'I suggested they both pay as much attention to "Children's Newspaper" as to "School Friend" and "Girl",' she wrote on the 16th. 'Pamela said oh she most certainly did read C.N.; she knows *all* about Tommy Steele. I roared. She meant to be funny.' As it happened, the first issue of *Bunty* was just hitting the newsagents ('Ladybird Ring Free Inside!' announced the front page), with *Roxy* shortly on the way for Steele fans ('Tommy's Lucky Little Guitar Brought Marcie Luck In Love'). But arguably the most signal publishing event of early 1958 was the coming of *Woman's Realm*, launched by Odhams in February with a blizzard of advertising, includ-ing a four-page inset in *Radio Times*. 'On this, our birthday, we greet Her Gracious Majesty, the Queen, and with her all our readers,' began the editor's message in the first issue. 'We promise to serve them both loyally, and with all our hearts.' And she went on:

> Our country today *is* literally a woman's realm – ruled over by our young and beautiful sovereign and containing in itself those other realms in which all women are supreme.
>
> In the home and in the heart of her husband and her family, every woman finds happiness and fulfilment, as well as duty. This need never be a narrow domain, bounded though it often is by kitchen, nursery and household chores. Indeed, if she chooses to make it so, it can be the widest and most wonderful and the most rewarding realm in the whole world.

Items on later pages included Susan King's 'Favourite Family Puddings' (cherry apple flan, golden peach tart, magic mousse, topsy-turvy pine-apple, chocolate chiffon, butterscotch pie), a pull-out booklet of 'NEW knitting patterns', a special offer for 2/6 of 'Four Lovely Lipsticks for You!', a report called 'Can a husband want too much love?' by a founder of the Marriage Guidance Council, stories with titles like 'The Waiting Game' – and, almost throughout, a relentless domestic-cum-family focus. The editor was Joyce Ward, and she had a conscious aim, brilliantly realised, of seeking to increase the enjoyment of home life for women who did not go out to work and were often rather older than the readers of the two market leaders, *Woman* and *Woman's Own*. 'From the very first issue the magazine "went like a bomb" and has achieved considerable popularity in the North of England,' noted the historian of women's magazines Cynthia White a decade later. 'Judging by its correspondence, it draws the bulk of its readers from amongst home-bound housewives, as well as attracting a large number of lonely women in bedsitters.'[2]

One elderly woman living alone in a bedsitter was Gladys Langford. 'Depression deepening,' she wrote on the very Tuesday that the first *Woman's Realm* came out. 'Conversation nil.' By this time there was compelling testimony available in Peter Townsend's *The Family Life of Old People*, the offshoot of Young and Willmott's *Family and Kinship* that was likewise a study of Bethnal Green and also widely reviewed. 'Those who are afraid of an isolated old age will find no consolation in these pages,' noted an already apprehensive Kingsley Amis. But although Townsend pointed to serious deficiencies in provision for the elderly, it was not (with perhaps the exception of pensions) an area high on the political agenda. This same year in Glasgow, in a chronic ward of what had been a Poor Law hospital, the future geriatrician Bernard Isaacs encountered an utterly grim, twilight world:

> The dayroom was not a large room, perhaps six metres square. Its main item of furniture was a great grimy black stove, which stood in the centre of the room. It emitted very little heat, but evil-smelling wisps of smoke escaped from cracks and seams in its structure, blackened the walls and ceiling, and set the inhabitants of the room coughing and spluttering.
>
> Bunched around this stove, sitting on rickety wooden kitchen chairs, were some thirty or forty old men of terrifying appearance. Their countenances expressed a kind of dying rage, a wrath that had been replaced by despair, now become lifeless, unmoving, as though carved out of cold, grey stone.
>
> The bunch of cracked, unmoving bodies, silent apart from the occasional wracking cough or the switch of spittle into the stove, were dressed

in what answered for blue jackets and blue trousers . . . The jackets were shrunken, crumpled, shapeless, devoid of all buttons, thickly stained with dried soup, saliva, caked tobacco. The trousers, unsupported by belt or braces, devoid of all fly buttons, remained in position only by virtue of a chance fit between the circumference of the garment and that of the wearer's waist. This piece of good fortune was rare . . . The blue jacket and trousers were virtually all that the patients wore. There were no vests, no shirts, no ties, no underpants, no pullovers and cardigans.

Many of these neglected, ill-treated elderly people had, Isaacs in time came to realise, grown up in appalling, brutalising slums and then gone on to ill-treat their own children. Accordingly, 'the result was that when the parents reached old age, the children did not feel the reciprocal bond expected of them'.[3]

It was a world away from the money men in the City of London. 'There is no justification for allegations that information about the raising of the Bank Rate was improperly disclosed to any person,' roundly asserted Lord Justice Parker's Tribunal report, published on 21 January, about the rumoured 'leak' the previous September. As for those in receipt of advance warning of the rise, 'in every case the information disclosed was treated by the recipient as confidential and . . . no use of such information was made for the purpose of private gain'. For the government, the Bank of the England and the City, the dominant reaction was relief – the *FT* declaring the report had 'utterly vindicated the reputation of the City of London for financial integrity' – though considerable indignation persisted that the Labour opposition, and specifically Harold Wilson as Shadow Chancellor, had foisted the inquiry on them in the first place. In early February there followed, again at Labour's request, a two-day Commons debate on the episode, with Wilson himself giving an unabashed, virtuoso performance, not least with his cricket analogy for the City, where 'merchant bankers are treated as the gentlemen and the clearing bankers as the players using the professionals' gate out of the pavilion'. Left unspoken, and thereafter hanging in the air for many years, was the question of whether the two main suspects, Keswick and Kindersley, had got away with it. The

Bank of England's most recent historian, Forrest Capie, suggests that the latter anyway may have done so, pointing to how the British Match Company (on whose board he sat) had for several years faithfully held around £250,000 of gilts – until it abruptly got rid of them the day before the Bank Rate hike was announced. 'They sold that stock,' a leading gilts broker, Sir Nigel Althaus, would recall almost half a century later, 'and that seemed to me the absolute clincher, and I think Lord Kindersley was very lucky.'[4]

On Saturday, 1 February, two days before the Commons debate got under way, London witnessed two resonant sporting moments: at Highbury a crowd of over 60,000 watched the 'Busby Babes' beat Arsenal 5–4 in a pulsating encounter on a mud heap, among them a 15-year-old Spurs supporter, Terry Venables, there specially to see the Manchester United powerhouse left-half Duncan Edwards, only six years older. At Twickenham there was rare booing when Australia had one England rugby player carried off and another concussed, before at the death Coventry's Peter Jackson scored a memorable jinking, sway- ing try to clinch the match 9–6. The following evening saw the launch of BBC TV's arts programme *Monitor*, fronted by Huw Wheldon, its very name indicative of the Reithian paternalism that still permeated the Corporation's culture. 'Lean, eager, sardonic and compelling,' was one critic's view of Wheldon, who would later be heard to remark off- screen, 'We can't have someone who's overtly queer on the programme.' As for viewers, 'upstage', 'highbrow' and generally 'stodgy' was the early, unenthusiastic verdict. Next day, Monday the 3rd, the trial began at the Old Bailey of three senior Brighton police officers on charges of conspiracy – a trial that eventually led to the town's Watch Committee dismissing the chief constable – while that evening Wilfred Fienburgh died after his car had collided on Saturday night with a lamp post at Mill Hill. Tuesday featured the first nudity on British television (an excerpt on ITV from the Windmill Theatre's current non-stop revue), while on Wednesday a 3–3 draw at Red Star Belgrade saw Manchester United through to the semi-finals of the European Cup shortly before Anthony Heap went to the first night of Graham Greene's *The Potting Shed* at the Globe ('more of a parable than a play, and a pretty prepos- terous one at that'). And on Thursday the 6th, Dennis Dee encoun- tered 'keen frosts and winds' on his East Riding smallholding as he spent the day 'riddling spuds'; 14-year-old George Harrison met the Quarry Men; and Captain James Thain's twin-engined Elizabethan-class plane, chartered by Manchester United and having refuelled on the way back from Belgrade, failed to get full lift-off on the slushy runway at Munich airport.[5]

The news started to come through late that chilly afternoon: some 21 feared dead, including seven players, with both Duncan Edwards and the manager Matt Busby gravely injured, and the 20-year-old Bobby Charlton among the survivors. One of the eight journalists killed was the *Manchester Guardian*'s Don Davies. The sports editor had origi-nally assigned John Arlott to cover the match, but in the event 'An Old International', as Davies was invariably bylined, had taken Arlott's place. That evening much of the nation was in a state of disbelieving grief, but a Keighley diarist focused on the practicalities. 'Manchester United were to have played Wolverhampton on Saturday,' noted Kenneth Preston. 'That match has had to be cancelled. That will throw the League games out of gear. Then Manchester were in the running for some sort of European Cup. That will be upset.' He drew two lessons: 'If the aeroplane had been carrying troops we should not have heard as much about it. These accidents only go to show that man has not mastered the forces he thought he had mastered.'

Next day, Nella Last in Barrow 'thought with sadness of the Manchester people who died in the plane crash', reflecting how 'this time yesterday, wives would be shopping & planning a "welcome" meal', while in Manchester itself a young teacher, Vincent Walmsley, recorded in his diary that 'going through town this morning the one topic on the buses, in the streets, where people queued for papers, was yesterday's tragedy which has, because of its unique character, shocked the world; and Manchester to the core'. Brian Redhead, at the time a youthful journalist in Manchester, would remember people 'frozen' in the streets on learning the news, and generally it seems to have been stoicism – the legacy of two world wars – that marked the next few days. If so, that was little thanks to the press. 'One of the most distress-ing consequences of a catastrophe like the recent aeroplane accident in Munich,' complained Malcolm Muggeridge soon afterwards, 'is the manner in which the newspapers play it so hard that it is soon drained of all emotion, and even becomes positively repugnant.'

The bodies were flown back to Manchester on the evening of Tuesday the 11th and taken in solemn procession to Old Trafford. In cold and rain, thousands lined the 11-mile route – many, according to a local paper, with 'a bewildered look about them'. Eight days later a patched-up United, including emergency signings, played Sheffield Wednesday in the FA Cup and won 3-0; but although Busby was starting to pull through, the man who had been expected to captain England for much of the 1960s, Duncan Edwards, died in the early hours of the 21st.[6]

Just up the road from Manchester, a historic by-election campaign had been taking place either side of the crash. 'We do not intend to depart from our usual practice in by-elections that we do not influence voters nor report the campaigns in news bulletins,' ran the BBC's pompous announcement ahead of the Rochdale contest, with polling set for Wednesday the 12th, but the local commercial television station, Granada, boldly broke ranks. For the first time on British screens, it (together with ITN's bulletins) offered something approximating full-bodied political coverage. The seat was a Tory marginal, under threat from a Labour candidate whose agent was a young local councillor, Cyril Smith, while the Liberals' (now led by Jo Grimond) candidate was the articulate, not unglamorous Ludovic Kennedy, until recently an ITN newscaster. Granada's first election broadcast, on the 5th, was watched by over a third of the local electorate, with Kennedy coming out best in the eyes of those viewers. 'We shall lose Rochdale, I fear, by a lot,' privately predicted Macmillan (in Australia) on the 10th. 'The Liberal intervention in all these by-elections is very annoying.' Next day, eve of polling, Richard Crossman paid a visit. 'Though the centre of Rochdale is rather fine,' he noted, 'the rest of it is the usual ghastly Lancashire town, with its slummy streets running up and down the hills.' As for Granada's big debate that evening, with 'three journalists interrogating the three candidates' live in the Council Chamber, he reckoned Labour's Jack McCann was 'easily the best', followed by Kennedy.

'I'd have liked to sit up & hear the Rochdale Election results,' Nella Last wrote on the Wednesday evening itself before reluctantly going to bed. 'I don't share my husband's optimism that the Tories will hold the seat – the Liberal will *very* much split the votes.' She was right: the Tories lost to Labour, and were pushed into a bad third place, with many of their votes going to the Liberals, who enjoyed their biggest by-election vote for over 20 years. Macmillan landed at London Airport on Friday, and was soon being defended by Gerald Nabarro on *Any Questions?* ('he's an experienced tactician, an able politician, an outstanding statesman, and he'll handle the situation, and the Tory Party will still win the next election, and by a good majority ... LAUGHTER'), but the real story lay elsewhere. 'The televoter is born,' declared Kenneth Allsop that day in the *Daily Mail*. 'Rochdale has changed the nature of democratic politics. Theorizing may now end. Television is established as the new hub of the hustings.'[7]

Macmillan and the fellow Conservative whom he had vanquished for the keys to No. 10 were about to have a weekend of contrasting fortunes. 'As Mr Butler entered the hall, he was welcomed by a jazz band, the bangs of exploding squibs, shouting and singing,' reported the *Evening Standard* about a lively occasion on Friday the 21st at Glasgow University, where Rab Butler was due to be installed as rector and address the students. Whereupon:

> The first missiles began to fly. A tomato hit him square in the back. A flour bomb hit him full in the face.
>
> The barrage of missiles and noise continued throughout the ceremony and during Mr Butler's speech. Often he stood silent, waiting a rare chance to make himself heard.
>
> Finally the platform party stood and bravely sang 'God Save the Queen'. As they departed, fire extinguishers and water showered all over them.

The Home Secretary was already being strongly criticised by many Tories for his apparent softness towards crime, and it did not help his cause when the next day's papers featured photos of him covered in flour and soaked in foam. 'I understand youth,' Butler vainly protested. 'I have children of my own and I like to feel I haven't lost touch.'

Macmillan meanwhile was preparing to take his chance, on Sunday the 23rd, with the first live, one-on-one television interview with a prime minister. 'As the cameras were being lined up he derived considerable amusement from the seating arrangement,' recalled his inquisitor, ITN's Robin Day. 'He complained that whereas he was sitting on a hard upright seat, I was enthroned behind the table in a comfortable swivel chair with well-padded arms. This, said the Prime Minister, seemed to symbolize the new relationship between politician and TV interviewer. He felt as if he were on the mat.' In the 13-minute interview, Macmillan was at his relaxed, confident best, offering early on the characteristic post-Rochdale reflection that 'at home you are a politician, abroad you are a statesman' and later giving a calm, effective reply when Day asked him about the position of the Foreign Secretary, Selwyn Lloyd, who was facing even more Tory criticism than Butler: 'I do not intend to make a change simply as a result of pressure. I don't believe that that is wise. It is not in accordance with my idea of loyalty.' Should Day, though, have had the nerve even to raise the issue? The *Telegraph* ('Who is to draw the line at which the effort to entertain stops?') and the *Manchester Guardian* ('This may be judged a good or a bad development, according to taste, but it is certainly new') were unsure, but the *Mirror*'s 'Cassandra' had no doubts: 'The Idiot's Lantern is getting too big for its ugly gleam.' As for Macmillan, his private verdict later that evening was eloquent enough: 'I think it went well, altho' the questions were of the *Daily Mirror* type – brash & impertinent.'[8]

The Liberal revival would continue in late March with Mark Bonham Carter's dramatic by-election gain from the Tories at Torrington in north Devon. 'A splendid meeting in a kind of barn lit by paraffin lamps,' recorded his mother Lady Violet during a strongly rural campaign, 'full of enthusiastic horny-handed supporters.' Given the negative effects of the credit squeeze following the September measures, rising unemployment and the USA slipping into recession, any mid-term government was likely to be unpopular. For Macmillan, with the recalcitrant Thorneycroft gone and Heathcoat Amory likely to prove somewhat more malleable, the question was not whether to reflate but when to do so. This was certainly the case after 13 March. 'Roy Harrod to luncheon (alone),' the PM noted after a visit from his favourite – and loyally Keynesian – economist. 'He is very keen that we should start to take "anti-deflationist" measures. According to him, the slump is now the enemy, not the boom. I rather share his view.' For the moment, though, Macmillan was prepared to be cautious, knowing he had at least one pre-election budget up his sleeve.

Nor perhaps would he have been surprised if he had been present a few weeks earlier at a small dinner at the Garrick Club that included Gaitskell and an inveterate diarist. 'Hugh listed the reasons why those disillusioned with Toryism are not voting Labour,' recorded Richard Crossman.

> Labour is a high taxation party, Labour is a trade union party, Labour is a nationalization party and Labour is not as sound as the Tories on the foreign issues. When asked what he would do to change this hostility to Labour, he said there was a very limited amount one could do. He himself would play down the nationalization of steel but, after all, we are a trade union party, with these views.

Macmillan might also this spring have noted the first-quarter figures for the sales of domestic fridges: 57,000, up from 34,000 for the same period in 1957. A fridge, observed *The Times*, was increasingly viewed 'as a necessity rather than a luxury', but only one of the two main parties was psychically conditioned to be the white-goods party, the party of acquisitive consumerism, and that was not the still puritanical, producer-oriented people's party.[9]

On Friday, 14 March, the day after Harrod's lunch at No. 10, a viscerally non-Keynesian was at Maidstone, making her third attempt since returning to the political fray – after a phase of serious disenchantment in the mid-1950s – to land a winnable Tory seat. 'Mrs Thatcher went straight into politics, leaving only a very short time at the end of her talk for her tactics in nursing the seat,' reported the Area Agent to Central Office. 'She was asked about her ability to cope as a Member, having in mind the fact that she had a husband and a small family, and I do not think her reply did her a lot of good. She spoke of having an excellent nanny.' The twins' mother duly lost out to a 'very pleasant, ebullient' Old Etonian, John Wells – and, as Thatcher's biographer John Campbell nicely puts it, 'naturally the fact that Wells had four children under ten was not an issue'. That evening at the Woolwich Granada featured two performances by a touring package that had been on the road for the past fortnight: Buddy Holly and the Crickets; an English crooner, Gary Miller, who before the tour had been entertaining the troops in Cyprus; the Tanner Sisters, in effect the poor woman's

Beverley Sisters; the 13-piece Ronnie Keene Orchestra; and, supplying the gags and linking the acts, the relatively unknown Des O'Connor (billed as 'Comedian with the Modern Style'). Among those at the 6.45 show was a 14-year-old from Dartford, attending his first concert, still known as 'Mike' and accompanied by a classmate, Dick Taylor. 'Finally the Crickets appeared,' records his biographer Christopher Sandford.

> They plugged in; they tuned up. Jagger at this stage gave one of his world-weary sighs. What, he seemed to ask, was all the fuss about? Just then Holly announced 'That'll Be The Day', followed by 'Peggy Sue' and 'Rave On'. By the last Jagger was clapping along. During 'Not Fade Away' he was out of his seat, hair puffing over his eyes, miming the lyrics, showing incredible levity for one whose precept was at all times to 'stay cool'. Leaving the cinema he went as far as to announce to Taylor, 'That was a gas.'[10]

Thatcher and Jagger: their destinies would be linked far more closely than either ever imagined.

———

The package tour had ended the previous Tuesday at the Hammersmith Gaumont when on Saturday the 29th, Dennis Dee's diary made its first reference of the year to an external event. 'Grand National day,' he noted. 'Won by "Mister What" ridden by Freeman.' Two days later Philip Larkin, back from a London trip and starting work again on 'The Whitsun Weddings', told Monica Jones how he had been 'impressed afresh by the enormous cleanliness & efficiency of Southern region trains'. And on Tuesday the 1st the BBC's Radiophonic Workshop began at Maida Vale, the brainchild of Daphne Oram, who however would soon leave in protest at the Corporation rule that people could stay there for only three months, lest working with experimental sound lead to brain disturbances or even madness. Later that same day, *Hancock's Half Hour* on the radio included Hancock responding to a policeman's commonplace pronunciation of 'garage' by giving his own, posher version, with the second 'a' drawn out.[11]

Two notable new books were around at the start of April. 'This deadly analysis of managerial humbug in modern society', was Eric

Keown's approving summary of *Parkinson's Law* by C. Northcote Parkinson, with his *Punch* review calling it 'a book to make the ordinary down-trodden citizen hug himself with pleasure'. The other was Ian Fleming's *Dr No*, a year after *From Russia With Love* had catapulted him into the commercial big time. His latest provoked some severe criticism, above all from a young left-wing journalist, Paul Johnson. 'I have just finished what is, without doubt, the nastiest book I have ever read,' began Johnson's *New Statesman* piece, which argued that *Dr No*'s three basic ingredients, 'all unhealthy' and 'all thoroughly English', were 'the sadism of a schoolboy bully, the mechanized, two-dimensional sex-longings of a frustrated adolescent, and the crude, snob-cravings of a suburban adult'. *Dr No* was expected to sell half a million copies, prompting Johnson to reflect that 'our curious post-war society, with its obsessive interest in debutantes [their last season just beginning], its cult of U and non-U, its working-class graduates educated into snobbery by the welfare state, is a soft model for Mr Fleming's poison'. He might have added that a fourth key element in Fleming's thrillers by this time was the sharp sense of regret about – and defiance against – British decline, especially following Suez. 'At home and abroad,' lamented 007 in *From Russia With Love*, 'we don't show any teeth anymore, only gums.' Rapid decolonisation, moreover, was looming, and as Simon Winder puts it with pardonable exaggeration in his study of James Bond, *The Man Who Saved Britain*, 'as a large part of the planet slipped from Britain's grasp one man silently maintained the country's reputation'.[12]

For some, there was a different route to restoring national greatness.[13] 'The British of these times, so frequently hiding behind masks of sour, cheap cynicism, often seem to be waiting for something better than party squabbles and appeals to their narrow self-interest, something great and noble in its intention that would make them feel good again,' wrote J. B. Priestley on 'Britain and the Nuclear Bombs' in the *New Statesman* in November 1957. 'Alone, we defied Hitler; and alone we can defy this nuclear madness into which the spirit of Hitler seems to have passed, to poison the world.' The nuclear issue had had increasing salience since the Defence Review the previous April, followed soon after by Britain's H-bomb test at Christmas Island ('*OUR H-BANG!*', *Daily Express*) and then, in October, by Bevan's renunciation of unilateralism, the direct provocation for Priestley's much-read article. Private meetings ensued, before (on 17 February 1958) a public one took place at the Methodist Central Hall in Westminster, proving so popular that five overflow meetings had to be arranged. Priestley, Bertrand Russell, Michael Foot, A.J.P. Taylor and Alex Comfort were among the speakers; the rhetoric was fierce and inspiring, epitomised by Taylor's shouted claim that 'Any man who can prepare to use those weapons should be denounced as a murderer!' Thus the Campaign for Nuclear Disarmament (CND) was born as a new political and social reality – though a reader of the next morning's *Times* would not have been aware of the fact.

'What difference to the deterrent does our contribution make?' Robin Day asked Macmillan the following Sunday. 'Well, I think the independent contribution is a help,' he replied. 'It gives us a better position in the world, it gives us a better position in the United States, and it puts us where we ought to be, in a position of a great power.' Soon afterwards Anthony Wedgwood Benn resigned from the Labour front bench – not a unilateralist, yet morally unable to endorse the potential use of nuclear weapons – while Priestley by the end of March was complaining of how over the past few weeks the anti-CND establishment had been 'hurling wild accusations, making a personal issue of it from the word Go', with 'emotional' and 'hysterical' the two most favoured derogatory epithets. Among CND's many well-known supporters was John Arlott. 'So long as atomic weapons are competitive everybody is going to want them,' he told the *Any Questions?* audience at Bournemouth Town Hall on 4 April. 'I reckon in the end everybody will get them and sooner or later if that happens, one hot-headed maniac will drop one and that will be the end.'[14]

The programme went out on Good Friday, and that morning some 4,000 had gathered in Trafalgar Square for the start of a four-day, 45-mile protest march (organised from the offices of *Peace News*) to the Atomic Weapons Research Establishment at Aldermaston in Berkshire. 'This can be the greatest march in English history,' declared Michael Foot from the plinth on Nelson's Column, while among those on the first stage was Kenneth Tynan, 'cigarette authoritatively held at the ready' according to the *Manchester Guardian*, which went on to quote Mrs Anne Collins of Gillingham, pushing her small daughter in a pushchair: '"I've been thinking about this for ten years," she said, a humble yet fixed light in her eyes. "If I become a grandmother I don't want a bomb to drop on her and her children – I don't want to drop bombs on the Russians, either. I'd rather let the Communists take over." A trifle falteringly she walked on.' There were still 2,000 marching by the end of the day, but numbers thinned to 700 or fewer during a miserably cold, wet, even snowy Saturday. 'We came down the Bath Road to London Airport in the rain under the dripping skeletons of trees,' reported John Gale in the *Observer*. 'But we were mighty cheerful' as 'a scratch band played "It Takes a Worried Man to sing a Worried Song," and the notes of the clarinet floated clearly'. Among those at the front were the Rev. Donald Soper, the march's organiser Pat Arrowsmith ('astonishingly young, with black hair, a bright face, a pack on her back, a pale mauve raincoat and red luminous socks'), and 'a spruce-bearded figure with grey hair, cap and a fur-lined tank jacket, a master from Tonbridge School'. Generally, noted Gale, there were 'a lot of girls with long hair and earnest expressions'.

Two days later, on Easter Monday, the numerically reinforced marchers – still singing 'Don't you hear the H-bomb's thunder/Echo like the crack of doom?', the opening lines of a song for the march by the young science-fiction writer John Brunner – were met on a field outside the research station by a large band of waiting supporters. Tynan had been an early drop-out, but he now arrived by taxi, joining Christopher Logue and Doris Lessing for an impromptu picnic, while in the background a loudspeaker proclaimed the march's message: 'Lift up your heads and be proud. The lead has been given to the English people. Britain must take up that lead in the world. "England arise! The long, long night is over."' Inspiriting, patriotic words (quoting Edward Carpenter), but soon afterwards a rival megaphone, manned by the right-wing twins Norris and Ross McWhirter, boomed out an alternative message from the roof of their Mercedes: 'Each one of you is increasing the risk of nuclear war. You are playing Khrushchev's game. Moscow is making use of you.' Enraged marchers attacked the car, causing £150 worth of damage before they were forcibly removed by stewards.[15]

The emergence of CND did nothing for Labour unity. 'At sixes and sevens', was Wedgwood Benn's post-Aldermaston assessment of where the party stood over the nuclear issue, while Aneurin Bevan as shadow Foreign Secretary – his head and his heart facing in opposite directions – now had to perform (as Denis Healey later put it) 'prodigious acrobatics in a vain attempt to straddle the divide between unilateralist and multilateralist'. Constituency parties were far from unanimous in following Gaitskell's firmly multilateralist lead: in Greenwich one ambitious would-be MP, Richard Marsh, secured the nomination through wearing a prominent CND badge at his selection meeting. Either way, many CNDers were instinctively reluctant to have their cause identified too closely with Labour, let alone taken over – even though, realistically, unilateralism could only become British policy if Labour was converted to it. There was a telling moment when the march stopped in Reading: after a collection had been taken, a local party official announced that the proceeds would be divided between CND and Labour, but this produced such outrage that instead all the money went to CND. This attitude reflected in part the movement's strongly youthful composition, certainly in terms of marchers (one of whom was a cloth-capped student from Bradford College of Art, 22-year-old David Hockney). Indeed, the grass-roots membership as a whole would never be susceptible to central control, but was instead, as Stephen Woodhams has illuminatingly argued, 'the expression of individual desires and beliefs' – an individuality that 'might be seen to parallel the drive toward personal expression in wider social patterns ranging from consumer capitalism to modes of school learning'. CND was, in short, a precursor to the counterculture of the 1960s, with all of that phenomenon's diverse political implications and legacies.

'"Nuclear Disarmament" seems to be a purely middle-class show,' commented one observer of the pre-march gathering in Trafalgar Square, observing that banners came from districts like Hampstead or Finchley, while 'the only banner from a less bourgeois area – Woolwich – was borne by the local National Union of Teacher's. A.J.P. Taylor came reluctantly to agree. 'The Campaign is a movement of eggheads for eggheads,' he reflected in June, after several weeks of addressing crowded meetings around the country. 'We get a few trade union leaders, themselves crypto-eggheads. We get no industrial workers.' It was somehow emblematic that Pat Arrowsmith herself was a product of Cheltenham Ladies College, albeit a serial rule-breaker while there. Moreover, even within the progressive middle class (and not just the Labour Party), there were divided views. 'They would take what loot they wanted, set up their bases and leave the population to rot,' was Kingsley Amis's prediction about what the Russians would do if there was no nuclear deterrent, adding that 'they would simply suppress the BBC and the Press, not to mention shooting half a million chaps out of hand', while in north London during the march, recorded Phyllis Willmott, Michael Young 'went on Good Friday and Saturday, coming back each night to sleep in his bed'. But she and Peter 'could not decide whether his protest was good or useful or not'.

How did people at large view the unilateralist cause? 'All recent Gallup Polls seem to show,' noted Mollie Panter-Downes a fortnight after the march, 'that while the British public's heart may have its reasons for sympathizing with the Aldermaston marchers, solid British reason has not forgotten the lesson of the disarmament of the thirties.' Generally, the evidence was of around three opponents of unilateralism to every supporter. 'Interested silence' was, according to John Gale, the main characteristic of people watching the march, and he ended his report with a haunting question: 'People mainly watched and thought and wondered at the children in the rain. "Look at them there, those little children. But it won't make any difference. There'll be a war if there's going to be one." But will there?'[16]

---

'You can hear people banging doors – it is like guns going off,' declared Mrs Grace to the *Coventry Standard* in its January 1958 profile of Bell Green, one of the recently built council housing estates on the city's outskirts. Complaining about theft and inadequate drying facilities, and predicting that the estate would become 'another slum area', she announced that she and her husband were 'saving up to move as soon as we can'. Next week it was the turn of the Willenhall estate, where, as in Bell Green, the blocks of flats, mainly four storeys, prompted considerable dissatisfaction:

> I have a small baby. I can't get her outside at all unless I push her right round the back of the flats, where I can leave the pram under the window.
> (*Mrs M. Lennon*)

> I can't do any washing – there is no boiler at all. It's awful to have to pay so much money for a place like this. I would sooner be in a little cottage than this place. *(Mrs Amy Spencer)*

Among the well-intentioned activators, Michael Young continued to insist that the problems on such relatively low-density estates, mainly peopled by tenants transplanted from high-density inner-city areas, went far beyond an absence of physical amenities, even if the housing itself was satisfactory. 'Migration of this particular kind gives rise to great problems of mental health,' he had recently told a conference, adding that 'it would be almost fair to talk of a new disease – housing estate neurosis – because it is in some parts of the country assuming such dimensions that it is worthy of a name of its own'. In May 1958, his Home Service radio programme with Peter Willmott, 'Families on the Move', so starkly contrasted warm, tight-knit Bethnal Green with cold, atomised Debden that, as the *Observer* put it, 'the narrator's conclusion, that resettlement is a great thing but not at the expense of the old neighbourliness, sounded powerful and incontrovertible after the recordings'.

Three months later, in August, the first families moved on to a new estate on Oxford's eastern outskirts, Blackbird Leys. Many tenants came from areas of the city lately cleared of slums, notably St Ebbe's, to the vexation of those tenants who had come to Oxford to work at Cowley's prosperous, expanding car plants. 'I don't like it up here getting all the tail end,' insisted one. 'It's a disgusting place. Putting all the backend up here won't give people like us a chance to make this a decent place to live.' Stigmatised from the start, and utterly remote from the dreaming spires, Blackbird Leys would suffer acutely from vandalism while it was being completed. 'For four years,' recorded a local paper in 1962, 'acres of unlit buildings sites, inadequate police supervision, parental apathy and the provision of a public house catering mainly for young people, has provided a perfect setting for the idle, the mischievous, and the more sinister night people.'[17]

For those who, unlike Young, were pushing hard for dispersal and low density, the jewels in the crown were of course the New Towns – which, by 1958, were starting to change significantly. Take Stevenage, becoming not only more urban (with the first shops around the belatedly developed Town Square opening in June) but also more individualistic. The AGM of the Stevenage Residents' Federation attracted only 30 people, representing 0.1 per cent of the town's population; the *Stevenage Echo*, a seemingly well-established campaigning forum, closed; campaigns themselves became increasingly social rather than political, typified by the start of the Stevenage Nursery Association; and it was reported that 'gossip fences (or anti-gossip fences) six-feet high are being erected [by the Development Corporation] at the request of tenants who want privacy', with these fences 'being built around all the gardens'. There was also the thorny question of class. In Crawley the Development Corporation reluctantly accepted that it had no alternative but to give developers a freer hand if professionals, wanting appropriate private housing, were to be permanently attracted – an acceptance that in effect led to the town being divided into separate zones of public and private housing, as opposed to the previous policy of 'pepper-potting' private, unsubsidised houses through the estates. Much the same was happening in Harlow. 'When the town began they had this idea of mixing the executive-cum-business-man type of houses with those of the workers,' the *Harlow Citizen*'s editor explained to the *Daily Mail*. 'Human nature being what it is, the policy hasn't really succeeded. Now the house-building trend is towards segregation.' Or, as Mrs Ferguson, the wife of a local security officer, put it, 'In our neighbourhood, one side of the road is working-class and the other is rather middle-class. When the children come out to play you find they keep to their own sides of the street, as if a line were drawn down the centre.'

At this stage the only second-generation New Town in the offing was Cumbernauld, near Glasgow. Preliminary planning proposals appeared in May, and tellingly all the major facilities were to be concentrated in the central, hilltop area – an implicit abandonment of the neighbourhood planning, with its socially balanced neighbourhood units, that had dominated the idealistic thinking behind the first-generation New Towns.[18]

More generally in the built environment, 1958 was the year when modernism indisputably entered the mainstream. '"Modern" architecture of second and lower degrees of originality is now so universally accepted that even planning officers approve it,' rather sardonically

noted the *Architects' Journal* in March, before asserting flatly that
'"Modern" architecture is now the accepted style.' Over the next few
months, three new buildings helped to validate this claim: Coventry's
Belgrade Theatre, a municipal venture hailed by Kenneth Tynan as 'a
beautiful box of steel and glass and timber'; Gatwick Airport's steel-
and-glass terminal building, according to the ultra-modernist Reyner
Banham 'so up-to-date it shames the tatty old BEA Dakotas on the
tarmac'; and, at fusty Lord's, the gently modern, nicely curving Warner
Stand, which according to Sir Pelham Warner himself avoided being
one of those 'huge skyscraping stands which would turn the ground
into something approaching a cockpit'. An increasingly ripe modernist
target was the expanding world of higher education. In April the
*Architects' Journal* found it 'encouraging' that the design for a new
lecture block at Manchester College of Science and Technology was
'uncompromisingly modern', but not long afterwards lamented how
the almost completed Nuffield College in Oxford would 'stand as lasting evidence of a great industrialist's fear of progress in architecture'.
And from June the process was under way of drawing up a shortlist of
potential architects for the massive rebuilding of Leeds University, with
only modernists being seriously considered.[19]

The pursuit of modernity was quickening everywhere, it seemed. In
Westminster a pilot scheme for parking meters was trialled, 23 years
after they had first been used in America; near Luton the M1 began to
be built, eventually by some 7,000 workers, mainly from Ireland; in
Nottingham the city began to 'inflict on itself', in Simon Jenkins's
words, 'the absurd Maid Marian Way, cutting the old centre from the
castle mound and destroying, among a warren of streets, an exquisite
set of Queen Anne almshouses'; in Ilford there was the first move
towards a comprehensive redevelopment of the central area, above all
to upgrade the shopping facilities; on Tyneside a local paper applauded
how 'out of the jumble of small shops and Arab-owned coffee bars, the
new and ultra-modern South Shields Market Place has begun to emerge',
with 'the hotch-potch of buildings along the north-west corner' being
'swept away to make room for a concrete and glass office block'; in
Birmingham the decision to demolish the Market Hall, splendid and
Victorian, opened the way for an ambitious redevelopment of the city
centre; across England and Wales over 55,000 houses were demolished

in slum clearance areas, often in northern cities; in Edinburgh three young local architects won the competition for a major housing development at the Port of Leith, where the two resulting 21-storey towers (Cairngorm and Grampian Houses) would dominate the huge Leith Fort estate; and in Bethnal Green the new, high-rise Dorset estate, the borough's largest, was named after the Tolpuddle Martyrs. Bethnal Green was also host to Denys Lasdun's pioneering, controversial 'cluster' blocks: an 8-storey one in Usk Street and a 16-storey one (Keeling House) in Claredale Street, with the latter being topped out in August, as the Union Jack was flown, the mayor and mayoress looked on benignly, and the 200 workers celebrated with a pint. 'The thing was radically broken up, this building, into four discrete connected towers, each semi-d on a floor, each a maisonette, so that they were moving into homes not so very different from what they were used to, updated on sanitary stuff,' Lasdun would recall about his explicitly social purpose. 'It was an attempt to get some of the quality of life retained as distinct from being treated like a statistical pawn in a great prism.'[20]

By 1958 London was in the relatively early stages of a phenomenal office boom – one that would soon spread into the provinces. It had begun in the City with three buildings that went up in the mid-1950s: the Bank of England's New Change (just to the east of St Paul's), condemned by Pevsner in 1957 as a 'vast pile' that was 'shockingly lifeless and reactionary', but half a century later defended by Gavin Stamp as 'a stodgy but well-made classical design which made no attempt to upstage Wren', in contrast to the 'arrogant, irrational, vulgar' One New Change shopping centre that was replacing it; the more modern, 14-storey Bucklersbury House, which according to Ian Nairn had 'no virtues and no vices . . . it is the null point of architecture'; and Fountain House in Fenchurch Street, a 12-storey tower (on a low horizontal podium) that had an all-glass curtain wall and which became the prototype for what the architectural historian Nicholas Bullock has called 'commercial modernism'. Whatever the architectural style, the conditions were propitious by the late 1950s for a speculative property boom, not only in offices but also in shops and other development schemes. The Conservative government in November 1954 had abandoned the building controls of the previous 15 years; resourceful, clear-eyed property developers like Charles Clore, Jack Cotton and Max Rayne were fully aware of the potential financial jackpot; and the local authorities (whether in London or elsewhere) were usually no match for their ambitions, even if they did want to thwart them, by no means always the case.[21]

One architect above all – in every sense – was switched on to the possibilities. The planners 'feared me more than I feared them', the shrewd, unassuming, pipe-smoking Colonel Richard Seifert would accurately recall about his remarkable skill in exploiting loopholes in planning laws, thereby enabling the maximum lettable space from a site. Seifert ran his architectural practice (motto: 'Prestige Without Vulgarity') with all the focus and discipline of a military operation, befitting his army past. The imposing Woolworth House on Marylebone Road (1955) was his first major London building, and several hundred office blocks lay ahead as well as hotels and high-rise housing. 'Seifert was the antithesis of the image of the architect as bohemian artist,' noted an obituary. 'His solid businessman-like approach won him few friends in the architectural Establishment, which tended to dismiss his work as "development architecture".'[22]

During 1958 it became almost a cliché that London's skyline was changing dramatically. 'Skyscraper London' was the title in March of an enthusiastic piece in the *Star*, and soon afterwards Barbara Hooper painted a word picture on *Radio Newsreel*. After describing the visual effect of the tall blocks that had gone up, and were going up, in the City, she went on:

> Look north along Fleet Street, for instance. Not long ago the only square-topped white building was the *Daily Telegraph* office; now there is also Hulton House, eight storeys high, and St Bride's House, much the same height. Stand on the banks of the Serpentine in Hyde Park: a few months ago you could not see a building above the treetops, and now at least four storeys of the central tower on a huge building rear high above the trees. In and around Oxford Street at least two new shopping blocks are going up, some eight storeys high. If you go up the tower of Westminster Cathedral, as I have done, the view over that part of the West End is changing, too. Above the cluster of old dark roofs and chimneys you can pick out new office buildings in Whitehall, an engineering

block behind Buckingham Palace, twelve- and fourteen-storey blocks of flats near Paddington Station, and others down in Pimlico, and the tower of the massive London Transport headquarters by St James's Park. Soon, if you walk through St James's Park towards The Mall, 200 feet and more of the not-yet-built New Zealand House will partly block the view up Haymarket.

'If planning permission is given,' she concluded, 'there may be hotels in Park Lane and Lancaster Gate that are more than 300 feet high, and over on the South Bank of the Thames work has already begun on an office block [the Shell Building] 330 feet high – nearly as high as St Paul's.'

Not everyone was thrilled by London's new skyline. The same week in April that Hooper's evocation appeared in the *Listener*, a letter to the *New Statesman* from a professed layman, Arthur Kemsley of 106 Finchley Road, disparaged the 'infinite number of up-ended match-boxes' that now littered the London scene. 'The reason, it seems, is that a cube is the most economical structure to build . . . Every square inch of floor space is financially productive. And to hell with what it looks like.' His letter was probably read by John Fowles, who the following Sunday took a walk round a new estate in St Pancras:

The Regent Square area is now a postwar development scheme – gaunt blocks, cheap, shoddy. They reminded me of the Dartmoor prison blocks. High, rectangular, imprisoning. One great slab pitted like a cliff with red and mauve and blue square balcony-caves. Nearby were flats of a slightly earlier period – with ribbed corners, tired balconies and windows. None of them look as if they will last; the horror is that they will.

For the architectural historian Alec Clifton-Taylor, responding to Hooper in the following week's *Listener*, the time had arrived when 'we have got to decide, once for all, whether we are going to abandon the human values which are to the fore in London and launch out towards the creation of another megapolis, or not'; he hoped 'fervently' that the LCC would refuse permission for 'skyscraper hotels' in Park Lane and Lancaster Gate. Frainy Heap was probably on the other side of the argument. 'Every evening,' recorded Anthony in June about his nine-year-old son, 'he wanders across to trespass in the new 11 storeys high block of council flats over in Regent Square, ride up and down in its lift, and look over London from its roof.'

Soon afterwards, J. M. Richards in the *Architectural Review* offered his overview on the prospects for 'High London'. Although pleased that the very tall office block planned for Millbank had just received planning consent – 'it will provide the London landscape with a vertical punctuation mark just where it is needed' – his larger case was that 'it is unfortunate in the extreme that, with a few honourable exceptions, the new high buildings planned for London fall far below the best of what our architects are capable'. His explanation might have been written with Colonel Seifert in mind: 'The average property developer is not in touch with the best architectural advice, the kind of architect he favours, understandably from his point of view, being the kind with most experience of extracting the greatest profitable floor area from a given plot-ratio and of circumventing most speedily the rules and regulations that stand in his way.' Richards, a moderate modernist and a man of huge common sense, was disinclined to underestimate the significance of this historical moment:

> In accepting high buildings we are accepting nothing less than a revolution in the visual character of London, which has always been a horizontal city. But are we also aware of another revolution that follows? There were vertical elements in the old horizontal London, but these deserved their place because of their symbolic significance. They were the spires of churches and the towers of imperial institutions and the like; they were among the dignified furnishings proper to a capital city. The new vertical elements, dominant in the skyline, will instead be anonymous commercial blocks with no civic significance . . .

'How', he asked, 'are we going to reconcile the civic pride of a city confident in its ability to control its own future with the fact of its most conspicuous monuments being where they are simply because it was to some individual's profit to put them there?'[23]

Redevelopment generally remained a perhaps surprisingly contested process. In January it was reported that 'more than 14,000 council house tenants have decided to stay where they are rather than accept the offer of moving into luxury flats in an eight-storey block being built at Wolverhampton', with 'only 40 willing to change'. On the refuseniks being quizzed by housing officials, it emerged that their main objections to moving were that 'flats lack privacy, they have no gardens, children have to be penned in or sent into busy streets to play, and rents are higher', while 'some tenants think that noise would carry too easily in the flats and a few just don't like anything new'. In February in a talk in Bristol on that city's post-war planning and architecture, Ian Nairn castigated the apparent willingness to allow Kingsdown's demolition as 'frightening', observed of the Kingsmead shopping centre that he could not 'imagine so many buildings designed by so many different architects with the same level of mediocrity', and called the new Prudential building in the insensitively developed Lime Street area a 'monster'. Writing to the *Salford City Reporter* in March, 'Disgusted Citizen' implicitly questioned the very rationale of slum clearance: 'Having had the opportunity over many years of visiting people in their homes week after week, in every part of Salford and Manchester, I have arrived at the firm conclusion that slums are caused by the people themselves, not by the state of the buildings in which they live.' And soon afterwards, in a lecture to the Royal Institution of Chartered Surveyors, the architectural historian John Summerson almost as daringly wondered whether the current 'wave of curiosity and expanding interest' in old buildings, a nod perhaps to the recently formed Victorian Society, had 'something to do with our lack of success in producing a contemporary architecture which is warmly and instinctively loved'.[24]

Nairn was back in the fray in early April, one of some 700 people attending on a cold night another meeting at Kensington Town Hall to discuss the Notting Hill Gate scheme. 'Why was not the public asked their opinion at an earlier stage?' he asked, and a motion expressing dissatisfaction with the scheme was passed by a large majority. Back in Salford, local elections in early May highlighted the issue, according to a local journalist, of 'the general unsightliness of our clearance areas, extending over months and in some cases years', so that 'there never seems to be a clean sweep anywhere', while in Surbiton in June, the rumour that a block of flats was to go up near her brother's house prompted grim reflections from Marian Raynham: 'Awful things for families to live in. Every available space is being built on, & the planners *never* do anything to make a neighbourhood look prettier.' July saw Nairn commenting balefully on changes, partly in the context of road-widening, in a Cambridgeshire town – 'Wisbech is settling down, with complacent phrases all round, to a bit of self-destruction just as effective as the H-bomb' – and Lady Morris, retiring president of the National Federation of Community Associations, bemoaning how housing estates were still being built without adequate amenities, so that 'the people for whom they are intended are forced to choose between a home without a neighbourhood and a neighbourhood without a home'. The next month in Coventry, the councillor most responsible for that city's remarkable post-war reconstruction, George Hodgkinson, reluctantly conceded in an interview that retrenchment was becoming unavoidable, given that it was now increasingly difficult to receive public support 'for schemes which seem remote from their point of view'. But Hodgkinson himself was one of four Coventry councillors (including the chairman of the Housing Committee) who that August, according to a local MP soon afterwards, 'spent a week at the Edinburgh Festival at the cost of Wimpeys', which 'had so far done £8,000,000-worth of housing at Coventry, most of it without tenders'. Richard Crossman added that Wimpeys had also 'thrown some tremendous parties'.[25]

Ultimately, though, a combination of the spirit of the age and seemingly inescapable practical necessity was irresistible. '15-storey Flats Next?' ran a Salford headline in March, followed by news about plans for St Matthias No. 2 Clearance Area, where demolition was proceeding apace. 'As we go on,' explained the Housing Committee's Councillor N. Wright, 'we find that, because many people are loath to go from slum clearance areas into the overspill districts at Little Hulton and in Cheshire, we are more or less tied down to the high-flats type of density housing.' A week later another Salfordian, Mrs K. Mountney of Ewart Street, itself in a proposed clearance area, stoutly insisted that 'every available piece of land in this hemmed-in city must be used to its fullest advantage and if that means eight-storey flats on one's doorstep that's just one of the hazards of living in Salford'. Just along the road, Manchester had long been known for its scepticism about high rises, but that spring a delegation of councillors visited blocks of flats in

Berlin, Hamburg and Amsterdam. 'The Germans and the Dutch have learned to live in flats,' stated their admiring report in due course. The lesson for Manchester was that, provided 'great care' was 'exercised in the selection of tenants to occupy multi-storey development', then such development could 'provide good housing and a colourful and interesting development worthy of our city'. For most progress-minded activators, clearance and redevelopment was a black-and-white issue. 'We still have too many slums – both to live in and to work in,' declared T. Yates, chairman of the General Council of the TUC, when he formally opened the Dorset estate. 'To be rid of them we need more than bricks and mortar; more than men and women. We need courage and vision. In Bethnal Green, in their social development scheme, I believe they have shown this courage.'

So too with reconstruction more generally – with Coventry still a compelling emblem of modernity at its best. 'So much more like a city of the world than many other four or five times its size,' declared Stanley Baron in April in the first of his *Reynolds News* series on 'The Changing Face of Britain'. Soon afterwards, Coventry was also the obligatory first stop for the *News Chronicle*'s Sarah Jenkins in her 'So This Is England' series, as she praised its 'air of looking forward and not back'. An architect certainly not looking back was Peter Smithson. At about this time, in his capacity as a tutor at the Architectural Association, he received an essay from a fourth-year student on the current work of the Italian architect Ernesto. 'The essay spoke warmly of this new, softened modernism,' records the biographer of Richard Rogers, 'but it was anathema to Smithson who dismissed it all as romantic nonsense and demanded that the essay be rewritten. Similarly, a housing scheme by Rogers for Richmond Park, which displayed the same romantic tendencies and which derived in part from the neo-liberty revival in Italy, received the same response. It even had bow windows.'[26]

Back in the early 1950s, an unsuccessful entry by Smithson and his forceful wife Alison in the City of London's competition to design new housing at Golden Lane had done much to launch the concept of 'streets-in-the-air', usually known later as 'streets-in-the-sky' – in effect, an attempt to recreate, off the ground, the communal aspect of the working-class street. The first place where it came into being, rapidly attracting huge international attention, was the new Park Hill estate in Sheffield, on

a hillside overlooking the railway station and city centre, designed by
Jack Lynn and Ivor Smith for the go-ahead City Architect, Lewis
Womersley. 'Out of ugliness we are to create something of beauty and
utility,' declared the lord mayor on the last Friday of April 1958, as –
amidst the rubble of 800 condemned houses in the process of being
demolished – two veteran councillors (one Labour, one Tory) were
handed a souvenir trowel and laid the foundation stone. Soon afterwards,
ahead of the local elections, Labour's party political broadcast featured
the area's MP, George Darling, telling a housewife that Park Hill would
be 'a quiet, self-contained community, with its own shops and schools,
and other amenities'. Later in the broadcast, Councillor Harold Lambert,
vice-chairman of the Housing Committee and the driving force in pushing through Sheffield's new housing developments (not only Park Hill),
explained to Darling how while smaller children would be able to play,
under their mother's eye, on the 'large sheltered balcony' that each flat
would have, for older children there would be playgrounds at ground
level. 'The type of equipment we have in mind,' he added, 'is not only
entertaining, it is of an educational value for the kiddies, too.'[27]

Womersley himself was adamant, as he told a housing conference
two months later at London's County Hall, that 'the opportunities
which were missed for comprehensive redevelopment prewar are not to
be allowed to escape again'. By this time a similar spirit was starting to
imbue many of Glasgow's activators, especially in relation to the
Gorbals. There, the biggest redevelopment commission had been given
to the Scottish architect Basil Spence, best known for the new Coventry
Cathedral that was rising up and who was now acclaimed by the
*Architects' Journal* (in July 1958) as 'The Popular President', i.e. of the
Royal Institute of British Architects. 'Brilliance describes the man,'
declared the magazine's admiring profile. 'He designs fluently, speaks
fluently, is capable, sincere and almost too tender-hearted.' Following
his commission from Glasgow Corporation, Spence had visited Le
Corbusier's famous, hard-modernist *Unité d'Habitation* in Marseille
and been much impressed, not least by its nautical flavour; this summer,
on presenting to the Housing Committee his plans for ten 20-storey
blocks raised on stilts and with inset communal balconies, he enthusi-
astically claimed that 'on Tuesdays, when all the washing's out, it'll be
like a great ship in full sail!'

The Housing Committee itself, on giving its approval in late August to not only the blocks but also the whole layout for the development area (including shops, restaurants and much else), called Spence's scheme 'a new method of living in cities at high densities without loss of humanity', while the *Glasgow Herald* had no qualms about what would become 'the Queenies': 'The special feature is the provision of small garden or patio for each house, no matter at what height . . . By this perpetuation of the familiar tenement "green", it is hoped to create a community spirit.' A few days later, in a piece on 'The Hanging Gardens of the Gorbals', the *Architects' Journal* expressed the hope that Spence 'succeeds in his enterprising attempt to civilize the tenement'. In the words soon afterwards of the almost legendary journalist Hannen Swaffer (who back in 1950 had written powerfully in 'I have Ascended into Hell' about the overcrowded, rat-ridden tenements of the Gorbals) this was a scheme to ensure that in five years' time the Gorbals would have 'one of the finest community centres in the world'.

Swaffer was writing, in his column in the *People*, the week after claiming that London was 'gradually becoming a monstrosity of utilitarian architecture', typified by how the first sight on coming out of Paddington station was 'a beehive of offices – one block is almost 20 storeys high! – which is ugly beyond belief'. He added that he had recently expressed his views 'to Authority' (unnamed) and been blandly informed: 'That is the modern style.' Swaffer's attack on modern architects provoked a riposte, printed in the paper. 'They are not the inhuman, callous Big Brothers that Mr Swaffer would have us believe,' declared a young architect from Hull. 'The majority are working thoughtfully and sincerely, in face of complex and difficult problems. Many are succeeding.' Calling them 'the envy of the world', Alan Plater cited the LCC housing estates: 'They have brought fresh air and light to people who previously knew only backyards and smoky squalor. All great architecture was once "modern".'[28]

# 7

## Stone Me

On Friday, 11 April – four days after the end of the Aldermaston march and just as *Balthazar*, the second instalment of Lawrence Durrell's projected 'four-decker novel', left the literary critic Walter Allen 'eagerly awaiting the next shake of the kaleidoscope' – Accrington Stanley's vice-chairman, Charles Kilby, heard about the imminent sale, at an army depot in Aldershot, of the double-decker stand previously used for the Aldershot Military Tattoo. It seated 4,700, was on offer at a give-away £1,450 and seemed the heaven-sent answer to the perceived need to increase Peel Park's meagre seating capacity of 800. On Monday he and the chairman, Bob Moore, inspected the stand, and by Tuesday the club had successfully bid for it. Even allowing for the £10,000 cost of dismantling, conveyance and re-erection, Stanley were on course, reported an enthusiastic *Accrington Observer*, to save something like £25,000. Moore explained his rationale: 'The whole future of football is in the melting pot. There is a possibility in seasons to come of a super-European League, and with Stanley's ambitions as high as the sky we wish to be "in" on the ground floor and make Accrington one of the centres of football.' Sadly, there were three snags. Spending even £11,450 would push an already financially troubled club into further debt; it was completely the wrong type of stand for a football ground; and the notion of Stanley, never yet in one of England's two top divisions, as part of a European super-league was, to put it mildly, a stretch. 'We'll never fill it,' the cash-strapped, departing manager Walter Galbraith commented bluntly to a supporter, 'and I could have had three new players with the money.' As it happened, the Football League itself was about to be restructured, with Divisions Three and Four as national divisions replacing Third Divisions North and South. Stanley would be in Division Three, so a touch of nobility characterised the club's veteran director Sam Pilkington successfully pleading in May at a Football League meeting that there should be four-down and four-up between the two new divisions. 'Remember the Fourth Division clubs,' he urged. 'Give them a chance to rise again.'[1]

The week after Stanley sealed the fateful deal, Tony Hancock explored the infinite boredom of 'Sunday Afternoon at Home'. The opening lines, with their unscripted pauses and sighs, took a full 48 seconds to deliver:

> Tony: (Yawns) Oh dear! Oh dear, oh dear. Cor dear me. Stone me, what a life. What's the time?
> Bill [Kerr]: Two o'clock.
> Tony: Is that all? Cor dear, oh dear, oh dear me. I don't know. (Yawns) Oh, I'm fed up.

A few lines further on, Sid James put the Sunday feeling into global perspective: 'Look, so am I fed up, and so is Bill fed up. We're all fed up, so shut up moaning and make the best of it.' Making the best of it . . . Sundays were still Sundays, the Victorian age was still alive, and for children especially it could be an endurance test.

Even so, for all the ennui, a Gallup poll a few weeks after Hancock's radio episode revealed almost two-fifths of people not wanting places of entertainment to open on Sundays as on weekdays, 41 per cent disapproving of the idea of professional sport on Sundays, and 44 per cent favouring the existing shorter opening hours for pubs on Sundays. To each of those questions there were about 15 per cent of 'don't knows', so overall it was hard to discern an overwhelming desire for change.[2]

The 32-year-old Paul Raymond, hitherto best known for his nude touring revues, was probably not a sabbatarian. Raymond's Revuebar, opening on 21 April in Soho, had a conscious strategy: being a members' only club would get round censorship problems; the striptease would be appreciably more sexually explicit and 'Continental' than at the nearby, by now rather old-hat, Windmill Theatre; and altogether it would, as the historian Frank Mort puts it, 'evoke a world of contemporary metropolitan leisure'. This child of affluence was a success from the start. 'Already he has enrolled 10,000 half-guinea members,' recorded the *People*'s roving reporter Arthur Helliwell on the first Sunday after opening, 'and all last week they were queuing up in the bright afternoon sunshine for tables around the raised floor on which 20 beautiful girls appear in various degrees of nudity.' Raymond himself reassured Helliwell: 'I have never put on an indecent show in my life. In fact, I won't engage any girl with a bigger than 36 bust because I wouldn't like to embarrass my customers.'

Raymond's Revuebar had its first police raid on the evening of Friday, 2 May. The clientele found there included military men, impeccably middle-class gentlemen from the Home Counties, foreign tourists – and, noted the police statement, a party that had 'come down' from Stockport 'with their pals' for next day's Cup Final and had, via a local tour operator, booked tickets for Soho as well as Wembley. They were probably supporting Manchester United, as indeed was most of the country, only three months after Munich. Their opponents were Bolton Wanderers. 'We went down to London three days before the game,' remembered Bolton's captain Nat Lofthouse, 'and we all got a suit from Burtons, two pounds ten shillings – we all looked well.' Matt Busby was present, frail and with a walking stick, but an emotionally drained United were never really in it. The defining moment, with Bolton one-up, occurred not long after half-time. 'This shot came across,' Lofthouse recalled in 1992, 'and their goalie palmed it up, and before he caught it I went in and shoulder-charged him, and the ball, Harry Gregg and me finished in the back of the net, and the referee gave a goal. If that had've happened now I would have been sent off.' But in 1958 it was still a self-consciously man's game and there were no hard feelings from the United players, though next day, as the Bolton coach travelled through Salford on the way home with the cup, 'there were Manchester United supporters waiting with flour bombs in little packets, and they bombarded us'.[3]

The following evening, the middle-aged Labour frontbencher Richard Crossman encountered the youthful New Left, in the form of a Universities and Left Review Club meeting at a hotel in Monmouth Street, where 'a certain Raymond Williams' was giving a lecture on which Crossman had been asked to comment afterwards. 'I found it absolutely packed with some 300 young people, mostly under 30 and mostly, I fear, open-necked, swarthy and ugly,' he recorded. 'I noticed it was a bit of a dumpy atmosphere and I was slightly surprised when nobody, on an appallingly hot evening, welcomed me or offered me a drink at the bar.' The 50-minute lecture by Williams, an adult education tutor, was 'very competent, not at all stupid, but read in a dull, competent, dreary voice'; its theme was that 'there was not a good, high-class press and a bad, popular press, but various presses appealing to various audiences and catering for various tastes'. Crossman in response explained the difference between writing for the *New Statesman* and the *Daily Mirror*, before his evening then deteriorated: during the interval barely anyone spoke to him, while afterwards in the discussion an 'entirely humourless' attack on him 'consisted of disagreeing with things I had written in the [*Mirror*] column'. Watching was the tyro playwright Arnold Wesker. 'Boy!' he wrote next day to his future wife Dusty (about to do a stint as a waitress at Butlin's holiday camp in Skegness),

He just did not know where he had come. He thought he could toss a few humorous crumbs to the crowd and a couple of observations and they would be satisfied. He didn't even prepare anything. Beside Williams he was a loud showman. And when the discussion came – Jesus! he didn't know what hit him. The boys stood up and lambasted him in clear, precise terms. How could he, as a socialist, support a paper [i.e. the *Mirror*] which, for its vulgarity, was an insult to the mind of the working class; a paper which painted a glossy, film-star world. The smugness left his face, he evaded every direct question and even in winding up said nothing except 'Well, you high-class people are just as easily led up the garden path in your papers!' Which may be true – but that does not justify him leading the working class up the garden path in their papers!

Crossman's own take on the evening was rather different. These 'ex-Communists who broke away during the Hungarian crisis' were now, he concluded, 'creating a Chapel for themselves with an even more sectarian atmosphere'.

There was undeniably a cultural turn to the New Left. 'A reportage and critique of the "culture" of post-Welfare Britain' was one of the *ULR*'s central aims, stated an editorial soon afterwards, adding that 'we want to break with the view that cultural or family life is an entertaining sideshow, a secondary expression of human creativity or fulfilment'; while later in the summer David Marquand, still an undergraduate at Oxford, stated in the *Manchester Guardian* that Oxford's socialist intelligentsia were far more concerned with 'culture' than 'politics as usually understood', and he quoted one prominent university left-winger as having shouted at him recently, '*Look Back in Anger* is a more important political document than anything the Labour Party has said since 1951.'[4] Arguably, moreover, this was not just true of Osborne's play. For by the summer of 1958 the British theatre was in the middle of an extraordinary year, among other things taking the '1956' revolution to a whole new place and level, if not necessarily always immediately appreciated.

Ann Jellicoe's uninhibited *The Sport of My Mad Mother* at the Royal Court in February had set the ball rolling – Anthony Heap dismissing it as 'putrid piffle', but Kenneth Tynan acclaiming 'a play of spectacular promise and inspiring imperfection' and especially enjoying the 'raucous and lissom' Wendy Craig as 'the gang's symbolic mother' – before an intense theatrical sequence, lasting barely two and a half months, began at the Saville on 23 April with the musical *Expresso Bongo*. Principally the creation of Wolf Mankowitz (who via a scholarship had journeyed from East Ham Grammar School to being taught at Cambridge by the literary critic F. R. Leavis), and essentially a Steele-inspired satire on callow youths being discovered in Soho coffee bars and turned into pop stars by ruthless managers, it was warmly greeted as a latter-day *Beggar's Opera*. Heap was among the first-night admirers, praising 'a caustic and devastating wit that is no less effective for being essentially good-humoured', finding the songs 'engagingly bright and lively', and singling out Millicent Martin's 'excellent performance'.

Then, a week later, three days before the Cup Final, came the long-awaited *My Fair Lady* at Drury Lane, with Heap present again. 'Handsomely and colourfully staged,' he conceded, and 'ambles agreeably through a variety of scenes', but overall 'far from being the wonderful show we'd been led to expect, and what all the fuss was about in New York I can't imagine'. The paid critics were on the whole kinder: 'perfectly delicious' declared Derek Granger in the *Financial Times*, while Harold Hobson in the *Sunday Times* thought it a 'near-miracle' that, after all the endless publicity, the musical was 'not merely as good as we had been told, it is better' (though he added that Julie Andrews's performance as Eliza Doolittle had 'no interest whatever', and that Alan Jay Lerner's book and lyrics had 'foisted on to the most piercing and unsentimental intellect of the English theatre [i.e. George Bernard Shaw's] the outlook of a Berta Ruck)'. The following week's *Any Questions?* picked up that theme. Should 'musical comedy writers', asked Mrs Carter at the Memorial Hall in Ludgershall, Wiltshire, be 'prevented from making a musical out of a straight play after the author's death when he has expressly forbidden this during his life?' 'Well,' answered Harold Wilson, 'I belong to one of the large majority in this country that's absolutely sick to death of all this ballyhoo about *My Fair Lady*.' Wilson went on to express himself worried about what would happen when the copyright expired of Gilbert and Sullivan ('of which we in this country are very rightly proud'). 'Heavens,' he continued, 'if those are going to be turned into New York musical comedies, or ice shows, or for that matter rock 'n' roll popular classics, I shall be extremely upset, and I think so will the majority of decent-minded people in this country.' This puritanical, old-fashioned, selectively modernising Yorkshireman ended by pointing out that 'as with anyone of us here who's been in the Boy Scout movement or Girl Guide movement knows very well, quite a large proportion of the new popular songs, jazz hits and so on, are old songs we used to sing round the camp fire a few years ago, that have been pinched by some Tin Pan Alley spiv and turned into a very big money-making racket'.[5]

The evening before Wilson's outburst, 8 May, saw the London opening at the Globe of Terence Rattigan's new play, *Variation on a Theme*, about a rich woman (played by Margaret Leighton) who had taken up with a young ballet dancer. It was the evening when Rattigan, in his biographer's words, 'finally realised the changes that had been taking place in the London theatre'. An unenthusiastic Heap was typical of the audience, while next day the critics let rip, with even W. A. Darlington, usually very pro-Rattigan, regretfully noting in the *Telegraph* that this time he was 'out of form'. Even so, for all this being the unmistakeable start, four years after the triumph of *Separate Tables*, of what would become a long, painful retreat in Rattigan's reputation, the theatrical revolution as a whole was still far from complete. 'Who will put Life into our theatres?' beseeched Alex Atkinson, a 42-year-old playwright and journalist, in the *News Chronicle* on the 10th about what he regarded as a lamentable failure to follow up the Osborne breakthrough almost exactly two years earlier:

> The Royal Court Irregulars are fighting almost unaided against the forces of reaction and twaddle, and unless a few more enthusiasts will rally to the cause, we may go down in the history of the Drama as the country in which a leg show never closed throughout the Second World War, and the longest-running play was a who-dun-it by a lady whose more serious dialogue has been known to make even seasoned actors giggle . . . Have we no longer the courage to blast the commercial Upper Circle out of its moonstruck reverie? Who will follow Shaw? Did we ever have even the ghost of an O'Neill? Where is our Arthur Miller?[6]

Nine days later, on the evening of Monday the 19th, a chronicler of the Drama needed to be in three places at once. Bernard Kops's enjoyable if sentimental *The Hamlet of Stepney Green* was having a generally well-received premiere at the Oxford Playhouse; the Bob Mitchell Repertory Company was starting a week-long run of *Jane Eyre* at Crewe Theatre, with 22-year-old Glenda Jackson in her first major role as the heroine ('does well', noted the *Crewe Chronicle*); and Heap was taking his seat at the Lyric, Hammersmith. He soon discovered he was in for 'just the sort of lunatic stuff they love to inflict on us at the Court':

> All its characters are clearly insane, all its dialogue completely irrational, and what the whole thing is supposed to convey or signify is beyond understanding. I wouldn't go so far as to call it tedious or boring, for its young author, who is probably just trying to cash in on the stupid contemporary cult for avant-garde obscurity, has at least the knack of somehow holding one's attention. But its utter incomprehensibility becomes irritating, its calculated idiocy, embarrassing, and not even the excellent acting of John Slater, Richard Pearson and Beatrix Lehmann as the three craziest crackpots gathered together in the dingy seaside board-ing-house that comprises the setting, can redeem its lack of sense and sensibility.

The 'young author' of *The Birthday Party* was Harold Pinter, who as a jobbing actor called David Baron had written this, his first profession- ally produced play, during a tour of *Doctor in the House*. The next morning, few if any of the critics dissented from Heap's unfavourable verdict. 'The author never got down to earth long enough to explain what his play was about,' complained the *Telegraph*'s Darlington, bemoaning the lot of critics 'condemned to sit through plays like this'. Alan Dent in the *News Chronicle* ('Mr Pinter Misses His Target') declared, after outlining the plot, that 'the moral would seem to be that every man-jack of us is a raving lunatic'. And for the *Mail*'s Cecil Wilson, though not denying Pinter's 'wit that gleams through his mist of a play', it was altogether a 'baffling mixture'. Pinter himself, some forty years on, recollected in tranquillity the emotion of that Tuesday morning. 'I went out at 7.30 a.m. to get the morning papers, went to a café and had a cup of tea and read them. Each one was worse than the last. I thought I might give the whole thing up and go and write a novel. But my wife at the time, Vivien [Merchant], said, "Come on, you've had bad notices as an actor, pull yourself together."' There was still the *Evening Standard* headline to endure – 'Sorry, Mr Pinter, you're just not funny enough' – but by then the decision had already been taken to pull the plug at the end of the week. Audiences for the rest of the six- day run were desultory, and by the time a eulogising review by Harold Hobson appeared in the *Sunday Times* – 'Mr Pinter, on the evidence of this work, possesses the most original, disturbing, and arresting talent in theatrical London' – it was too late.[7]

Just two days afterwards occured another London debut. Shelagh Delaney, a Salford teenager, had gone to Rattigan's *Variation on a Theme* during its pre-London tour and been so infuriated by what she saw as its insipidness that she had rapidly written her own, locally set play, *A Taste of Honey*. Joan Littlewood at the Theatre Workshop responded positively and, with the Lord Chamberlain agreeing to turn a blind eye so long as the gay character was called an 'art student' and things generally were not made too explicit, it had its first night at the Theatre Royal, Stratford East, on Tuesday the 27th. That morning the *Daily Mail*'s gossip column included a friendly item about Delaney. She was 19, lived with her parents in a council house and had worked as a photographer's assistant. 'It's drawn from my observations and some experience,' she told Paul Tanfield as she sipped lemonade and refused a cigarette. However, the *Mail* giveth, the *Mail* taketh away, and next day's review by Edward Goring was a stinker. After observing that the play 'tastes of exercise books and marmalade', he went on: 'Once, authors wrote good plays set in drawing-rooms. Now, under the Welfare State, they write bad plays set in garrets.' And after giving a plot summary, he concluded: 'It hardly amounts to a play, and for all the shouting it says little. It has a few touching moments, but those stem from the touching quality sometimes found in immaturity . . . If there is anything worse than an Angry Young Man, it's an Angry Young Woman.'

For the most part, however, critical opinion was positive. *The Times* praised it as 'tough, humorous, and close to the ground'; J. W. Lambert in the *Sunday Times* enjoyed the 'curt, quick, funny' dialogue and Delaney's 'wonderfully non-committal attitude' towards 'the grubbier aspects of life'; and Tynan in the *Observer*, while conceding there were 'plenty of crudities' in the play, acclaimed its 'smell of living' and called her 'a portent'. That was also the take of the *Spectator*'s Alan Brien, who reckoned that 'even five years ago, before a senile society began to fawn upon the youth which is about to devour it, such a play would have remained written in green longhand in a school exercise book on the top of a bedroom wardrobe'. A vigilant Wesker went during the second week of the run. 'They shout at each other, interrupt each other, talk to the audience,' he observed of the characters in his appraisal for *Dusty*. 'This seems to be on the way to the real theatre, not quite there but an eye-opener.'[8] *A Taste of Honey* was an important play not only in theatrical history, and not only in relation to social issues (illegitimacy, race, homosexuality), but also in terms of the north of England. So long off the metropolitan cultural radar, it was now just starting to move on to it – a process that had been begun the previous year by John Braine's best-selling novel *Room at the Top*.

For the unknown Wesker, the hour was almost at hand. 'I suppose I'll be branded an angry young man for it,' the 26-year-old told the *Coventry Standard*'s 'Thespis' over coffee at the start of July, ahead of *Chicken Soup with Barley*'s one-week run at the Belgrade Theatre before going straight to the Royal Court for another week, as part of its Repertory Festival. 'My limitation is that I can only write about things that happen to me – but it is also a strength.' Calling his play 'one of a trilogy', he also elaborated on his politics. 'An ardent Socialist,' duly noted his interviewer, 'Arnold Wesker sees Socialism as an attitude to life rather than a political quality. He considers present-day values topsy turvy, producing people in a kind of "rat race". He has strong views on education, and sees much of his art in terms of education.' The week beginning the 7th presented Coventry's theatregoers with strongly contrasting attractions: on the one hand, at the brand new civic theatre, the Belgrade Theatre Company (including Frank Finlay) performing Wesker's semi-autobiographical episodic chronicle of a Jewish – and Communist – family in London's East End between 1936 and 1956, culminating in the anguish of Hungary; on the other, at the long-established, commercial Coventry Theatre, a comedy called *The Bride and the Bachelor* by the future Tory speechwriter Ronald Millar, star-ring three old warhorses in Cicely Courtneidge, Robertson Hare and Naunton Wayne. Conceivably, some may have stayed at home to watch *Ask Me Another* and the *Phil Silvers Show* on BBC, or *Wagon Train* followed by *Free and Easy* (starring Dickie Valentine) on ITV.

Wesker won on points in the local reviews. According to the *Standard*, the Millar farce 'failed to evoke more than a titter for the whole of the first act' and was 'a misfire', while *Chicken Soup* was 'full of life and colour and detail', and was 'quite moving', but ultimately left 'deeply etched outlines that form an unsatisfactory whole'. The *Evening Telegraph* was equally scathing about the 'feeble farce', whereas the Wesker was 'the stuff of life' and 'never fake, never touched up with sentimentality'. On that first night there were cheers and applause at the end, and even the shout of 'Author!', though Wesker preferred to stay in the wings. He was less satisfied on the second evening. 'The audience laughed in all the wrong places, and displayed such stupidity it was unbelievable,' he told Dusty. 'They are so used to seeing corny films and drawing-room comedies that when they come up against a little real-life drama it embarrasses them and they have to treat it as a joke.'

Then came the Royal Court. Not everyone went overboard – a play 'built for pygmies' thought Alan Brien; 'a documentary rather than a play' reckoned Eric Keown; while Harold Hobson found it 'often impressive' but was more interested in *Five Finger Exercise* at the

Comedy by Peter Shaffer ('may easily become a master of the theatre')
– but the general tone was positive. 'John [Dexter, the play's director]
and I stayed up all night walking from Sloane Street in order to get the
papers as they came out,' Wesker reported to Dusty. 'The *Daily Mail*
calls me a playwright of "rare ability and even rarer promise". The
*Standard* says I have "rare understanding . . . passion and urgency".
Even *The Times* and *Telegraph* are favourable.' The longer wait was for
the increasingly influential Tynan, who on Sunday heralded *Chicken
Soup* as an 'intensely exciting play' and asserted that if Wesker could
'survive the autobiographical stage', he was 'potentially a very important playwright'.[9] Tynan called it right: if there was one dramatist over
the next few years who would command the most intense attention,
and simultaneously capture and chase the moment, it was undoubtedly
Wesker.

———

*Tonight* continued this summer to consolidate its hold as television's
most popular current affairs programme. Henry Turton in *Punch*
rounded up some of the 'splendid' team under its unflappable MC:
'high-pitched, querulous' Fyfe Robertson; 'neat and impish' Derek
Hart; 'smooth' Geoffrey Johnson Smith; 'crisp and alert' Polly Elwes.
The leading soap remained *Emergency—Ward 10* – 'the interminably
incident-packed saga of that nice hospital full of photogenic nurses and
terribly British doctors', noted Turton, but 'well done according to the
soap-opera conventions' – while *Take Your Pick* and *Double Your
Money* were the two dominant quiz shows. 'Last week's star,' recorded
John Braine in May about the latter, 'was Plantagenet Somerset Fry,
who decided to keep the £500 he'd already won but just out of curiosity
asked what the £1,000 question would have been. He could have
answered it.' That same week, *Take Your Pick* (hosted by Michael Miles,
with Alec Dane on the gong) was the second-most-watched programme
on either channel, but the most popular (viewed in 4.17 million homes)
was *The Army Game*. 'These slapdash proceedings arouse feelings in
me which verge on the sadistic,' recorded Turton, who saw it as a
particular waste of the talents of Alfie Bass, 'that subtle and delicate
droll'. Such was the show's popularity, however – reflecting in part the
widely shared experience of National Service – that in June its signature

tune went to number 5 in the charts, as, a few months later, did Bernard Bresslaw, aka Private 'Popeye' Popplewell, with an in-character rendition of 'Mad Passionate Love'.

At this stage the BBC's main weapon against *The Army Game* in the comedy stakes was Benny Hill at least as much as Tony Hancock. 'Benny Hill is the king of comedians,' acclaimed one viewer after his show on 26 April; 'he never fails to amuse, is never monotonous and abounds with natural fun and humour.' A rare telerecording of that show survives, revealing a still traditional Variety format – fillers include a glee group, Alma Cogan and a circus double-act – while Hill himself sings two suggestive faux-medieval songs and is the central figure in a series of quick-fire, inventive sketches, with one in drag. The show ends, in his biographer's words, 'with Benny stepping out of character and, for just fifteen seconds, appearing as "himself", accepting the applause of the studio audience, waving, winking at the camera and – for the only time in the entire hour – looking a little uncomfortable'. For straight-up-and-down, middle-of-the-road music, few programmes beat *The Billy Cotton Band Show*, with the good-looking Russ Conway by this time as resident pianist and the host himself one evening remarking to applause that 'skiffle' rhymed with 'piffle'. Cotton would not have enjoyed *Oh Boy!*, ITV's new pop show (masterminded by Jack Good), which made its bow late at night on Sunday, 14 June and, noted an appreciative Tom Driberg, 'crowds more bands and girls and vocal groups on to the stage than you'd think possible and is faster and more frantic than *Six-Five Special*'. The determinedly *au courant* Labour politician went on to express himself especially partial to 'the wonderfully Dadaist Marty Wilde'. Most adults preferred to look elsewhere. 'One of the few singers who sings modern songs pleasantly and quietly, and doesn't fling himself about while performing – such a relief,' declared one such viewer later in the summer after *The Perry Como Show* had ended its series, adding that 'his quiet natural charm and delightfully unassuming manner are most endearing'. Such was the residual dislike among many BBC viewers of almost anything American that another conferred still higher praise on Como: 'Perhaps the least offensive of the all too many imported American show business personalities.'[10]

Was it all too much? 'I have been reading your long article on Television in our lives, sitting out in the warm sun overlooking the sea,' Enid Blyton wrote in April from the Grand Hotel, Swanage to the anthropologist Geoffrey Gorer. 'It was time that someone gave us a clear view of TV and all its implications!' 'I myself,' she added, 'do not watch TV very much but love the things I *do* watch – Peter Scott's programmes, some plays – Dr Bronowski's programmes – good talk – & really *funny* programmes.' Gorer himself was a man of broad human sympathies, but in his *Sunday Times* series he came down hard on working-class viewers. Not only did they eschew 'topical programmes, discussions and brains trusts, serious music and ballet', instead obstinately preferring 'films and serials, variety, and quizzes', but almost half of them were 'addicts' (defined as watching for at least four hours a night), with as a result 'all sense of proportion lost in their gross indulgence, and their family life, if not wrecked, at least emptied of nearly all its richness and warmth, their children's education often imperilled by the absence of any quiet place to do homework'. Even worse, whereas five years previously the owner of a TV set had been likelier to be middle class than working class, now 'there are approximately three owners of a set from the working classes for every two from the middle classes', with every prospect of that trend intensifying. One reader cautioned against exaggerated alarm. 'The article is rather terrifying,' William Empson wrote to Gorer from Hampstead. 'All the same, the race of man is not destroyed so easily; it seems clear that, in the end, if they have time, they will manage to acquire a "tolerance" for their new poison.'[11]

Children naturally were a particular concern. 'I once asked a child,' Blyton related to Gorer, 'why he preferred watching TV to going to the cinema, and he said he liked its "nowness."' As it happened, the most extensive, authoritative survey would appear later in 1958 – namely, *Television and the Child* by the academic Hilde Himmelweit and colleagues, the fruit of several years of research and analysis. 'Television is not as black as it is painted,' she found, 'but neither is it the great harbinger of culture and enlightenment which its enthusiasts tend to claim for it,' adding that 'its capacity for broadening a child's horizons is not spectacularly different from that of any other of the mass media', not least because 'television stimulates interests, but only fleetingly'.

Four of Himmelweit's findings had a particular piquancy: that as many as 60 per cent of the children in the survey said that the TV was left on all evening in their homes; that three out of four 10–11-year-olds viewed until nine o'clock; that middle-class children were glued to the box just as much as their working-class peers; and that almost all children seemed wholly blasé about onscreen violence. Gorer, reviewing Himmelweit's book in the *Listener*, disputed the worth of her overtly paternalistic recommendations about programme content, but was otherwise of a similar mind. 'In so far as television has any influence,' he argued, 'it is as a leveller; it makes the dull brighter, and the brighter duller.'

Himmelweit's was a rather bloodless survey, but fortunately the writer and secondary modern teacher Edward Blishen took charge of a study conducted earlier in the year on behalf of the Council for Children's Welfare. Some 700 parents (weighted a little towards the middle class) spent at least a fortnight watching children's programmes with their offspring, and parental positives were more than counterbalanced by negatives:

- It has quietened him down, as he will now sit and watch.
- It helps to keep them indoors in the evenings.
- Lost his fear of dogs, thanks to Lassie.
- Too much violence. It was a sorry day when ITV began.
- It is difficult to get him to bed.
- They don't want to go to the Scouts or any other movement because there is always something they want to watch.
- Had four books for Christmas, and hasn't read them yet.

As for the opinions of the children themselves, Blishen provided a helpful summary of their favourite programmes generally. 'The boys all plumped for *Zoo Time*, *Zoo Quest*, *Look*, *Lone Ranger*, *The Silver Sword* and *Little Rascals*,' he found, 'with, not far behind, *Circus Boy*, *Crackerjack*, *Sports View*, *Criss Cross Quiz*, *Studio E*, *Onion Boys*, *Sir Lancelot*, *Billy Bunter*, *Popeye*, *Robin Hood*, *Rin-Tin-Tin* and *Lassie*. Invited to let themselves go on their dislikes, the boys proved to be very highly satisfied with everything.' For their part, the girls 'liked most of all *Sooty*, *Emergency—Ward 10*, *Zoo Quest*, *Zoo Time*, *Look*, the quiz programmes and *Little Rascals*'. And they were, he added 'far more disgruntled than the boys, most of them expressing a round feminine displeasure at the many films full of shooting'.[12]

There was at this time no set in the Haines home in Chingford, where instead Judy, after the family's return in early June from half-term week at a Brixham holiday camp (The Dolphin), concentrated on matters at hand. 'Have decided to work to a routine as from tomorrow,' she noted on Sunday the 1st. 'Hope that will get the housework done.' All went satisfactorily to plan over the next few days, and on Friday the 6th she invited Win, from across the road, 'to afternoon tea as my routine doesn't allow of an hour's coffee time', but something more exciting was on her mind: 'I have bought John a summer jacket for our Anniversary. He has bought me a Morphy-Richards steam iron! It is beautifully light and effective.'

By now the World Cup was about to start in Sweden, but even though all four home nations were represented it was far from an all-consuming event, with few mentions in diaries. Quite apart from the sad legacy of Munich, England's campaign under Walter Winterbottom was blighted from the start. Fulham's Johnny Haynes was under attack from the northern press as an overrated 'glamour boy'; the gifted Bobby Charlton was replaced, amidst widespread criticism, by the dogged but lumbering Derek Kevan; and the *Daily Express* published, with censorious commentary, a love letter from captain Billy Wright to the divorced singer Joy Beverley (his future wife). England were knocked out on the 17th, beaten 1–0 by Russia. 'They fought until there was nothing left but heavy hearts and legs wearied to the point of torture,' proudly reported the *Express*'s Desmond Hackett. But the match, he went on, 'unhappily emphasised how wrong England were, from the first kick of this world campaign, to insist that fighting hearts can replace football'. At the end, 'there was something intensely sad about the shirts stained with sweat from their courageous, but unskilled, labours'. Or, as an *Observer* headline bluntly put it: 'Industry Without Skill'. England's early exit provoked a storm of discontent, prompting Haynes to remark that 'everyone in England thinks we have a God-given right to win the World Cup'. Nevertheless, one Englishman did get to the final. George Raynor, a miner's son from Barnsley who coached the Swedish team that lost to Brazil, had previously been in charge at

Juventus and Lazio in Italy, and was renowned for his meticulous, 'scientific' methods. After the tournament he sought a coaching post in England, but the only work he could secure was with Skegness Town, part-timers in the Midland League. British teams, he asserted mildly but unequivocally two years later in his memoir *Football Ambassador at Large*, were 'not yet equipped to win world competitions'.[13]

This was also the summer of the great London bus strike, with Frank Cousins, left-wing leader of the Transport and General Workers' Union, as central protagonist.[14] 'People hearing Cousins in action for the first time are usually struck by the remarkable way he combines a donnish clarity of analysis with the fervour of a demagogue,' noted an *Observer* profile earlier in the year of this 53-year-old miner's son who had become General Secretary of the giant T&G in 1956 and rapidly emerged as 'a national figure' through television and radio appearances. 'His speed of thought and dialectical gifts are familiar to every viewer, so are his watchful eye, his swift changes from evident suspicion to candour and confidence, and the way his relaxed good-natured bearing suddenly stiffens into cold hostility.' As a union leader, continued the profile, his approach could be summed up as 'militancy to be kept high at all times, action to be taken only through the established machinery'. As for his broader politics, 'He is a Socialist consciously, if at times slowly, working to shape a society from which one day the private profit motive will have been eliminated.' About the same time, Julian Symons for the *Daily Mail* interviewed Cousins at his spacious office in Transport House, to which he had driven from Epsom in his Ford Zephyr. Symons observed to him that, sitting behind his large desk, he looked like a big business executive. To which, with a 'pleasant, faintly smiling expression', Cousins replied: 'Yes, you might say that. Of course, I get here earlier [8.30] than most business men seem to do, and I leave a good deal later, and while I'm here I don't do the same sort of thing. There are differences, don't you think?' By 1958 he was undoubtedly the best-known trade unionist, and equally undoubtedly he was in the sights of a Tory government still smarting from its defeat by the engineers and shipbuilders the previous year and now increasingly committed to a policy of wage restraint.

'A London bus strike', noted Macmillan in his diary on 29 April, 'now seems inevitable'. This followed the failure of protracted negotiations over wages between the busmen and the London Transport Executive, and he added that 'it may be salutary'. At a rally of 6,000 London busmen at the Empress Hall in Earl's Court on Friday 2 May, Cousins in effect said that, left to himself, he would not have been pushing for a strike that might well prove very hard to win, but that he honoured the busmen's determination to pursue their just cause and was proud to be leading them. The busmen themselves were virtually solid. 'A strike's deadly action, really, but we want what's right,' one of them told the journalist John Gale. 'Take my own case. The rent's just gone up 15s; National Health's gone up; coal's gone up about a shilling a quarter ton; my wife says she wants more money. Well, what can you do?' Another agreed: 'The job's not what it was. We were the second best paid on the industrial list; now we're fifty-seventh.'[15]

The strike duly began on the 5th, with most of the national press (including the *Manchester Guardian*) hostile, the *Mirror* neutral and the *Express* soon unashamedly demonising Cousins. From the start it failed to be more than an inconvenience. 'John doesn't mind,' recorded Judy Haines in Chingford on the 11th. 'He can park at Turnpike Lane and then by underground to Piccadilly. It has also proved that Central London is far better off without great buses blocking the traffic. I feel sorry for busmen's wives having to feed their families just the same.' Then within days came the major blow of the government settling with the strike-threatening railwaymen, leaving the busmen isolated. Cousins himself, moreover, was equally isolated within the trade union leadership as a whole. 'They wanted Cousins taken down a peg,' recalled Iain Macleod, the tactically brilliant Minister of Labour. 'They didn't like him. They wanted to ensure that the Government didn't cave in to him, because it would have made their job that much more difficult.' 'TUC,' noted Macmillan by the end of the month, 'are obviously pressing Cousins to settle the bus strike somehow. I fear, however, that he is in a sort of Wagnerian–Hitlerian mood. "Fight to the last penny, & bring the whole nation crashing down."'

'Very depressed,' lamented Gladys Langford on 1 June. 'Continued 'bus strike imprisons me in this one room.' Indeed, the public mood now began to harden against the busmen, not least as it turned out to be the wettest June for half a century. 'To blazes with Cousins and his followers,' declared Mrs C. Cheesman of Salisbury Road, Manor Park to the *Evening News* on the 3rd. 'I blame union members for not standing on their own feet. I know who has the biggest worry – the housewife.' Cousins by this time knew that he had either to end the strike or to extend it, with the latter option involving bringing out the oil-tanker drivers, but it was an option that the TUC General Council, told by Macmillan that he would not hesitate to use troops if need be, flatly refused to countenance. The end eventually came after seven weeks. 'The buses start running again tomorrow,' noted an unsympathetic Anthony Heap on the 20th. 'And precious little the fools have gained by it.' Indeed, with Londoners having got accustomed during the strike to using alternative forms of transport, the dispute marked the moment – in London anyway – when gradually declining bus use (with the rise of the private car) turned into headlong fall. 'What is clear to anyone roaming around London is that the buses look strangely empty,' observed Mollie Panter-Downes in early July, and she anticipated the 'sad' day 'when the only note of scarlet on the London streets will turn out to be a fire engine'.

'One of the good things that came out of that dispute,' Cousins would remark many years later about the bus strike to his biographer Geoffrey Goodman, 'was an awareness of the importance of trade unionism: an awareness that had not been there for some time previously.' Arguably, that awareness already existed. 'At the present time the power of the Trade Unions is such that you have a dictator state within a democratic state,' the farmer-writer A. G. Street had declared in February on *Any Questions?*, in the context of a controversial – three men alleged to be in the wrong union – National Union of Toolmakers stoppage; he added (to applause) that 'every time the law of the country is flouted by anybody, even Trade Unions, this nation is going one step nearer to Fascism with all its horrors'. During the bus strike itself, *Punch* (then serialising Alan Hackney's satirical *I'm All Right, Jack*, featuring a Communist shop steward, Mr Kite) ran a full-page cartoon by Illingworth depicting the unions as anti-democratic. Florence Turtle in Wimbledon Park probably spoke for most of the diarists when she reflected, 'What a lot of silly sheep members of trade unions are

– haven't got the guts to say they don't want to strike, do so at the behest of extremists.'[16]

Among Tories generally, a significant element wanted a wholly uncompromising response to almost all wage claims by the unions. 'Of course,' somewhat wearily recorded Macmillan on 11 May shortly before his decisive offer to the railwaymen, 'some ministers & a lot of the Party want a "showdown".' Determined though both men were to see off the London busmen, a relatively soft target, that was instinctively not his or Macleod's approach. 'I am very anxious that the Govt, while firm, sh$^d$ not seem to be obstinate,' Macmillan had noted a month earlier in relation to the railwaymen. 'Above all, we must not "challenge" the T. Unions (as people like Lord Hinchingbrooke w$^d$ like). We must appeal to the Unions, & try to take ourselves some constructive initiative.' Next day, returning to the subject, he observed that 'the middle class' were 'so angry' that needless confrontation with the unions would lead to 'bitterness' and 'class war'. Unsurprisingly, neither man was enthused when in June the Inns of Court Conservative Association published a report, co-authored by Geoffrey Howe and called A Giant's Strength, which asserted that the unions had become 'over-mighty subjects' and argued for ending their long-established legal privileges. Macleod sent a senior Ministry of Labour official to warn off the authors from publicising their pamphlet, while Macmillan, with an election in the not too distant offing, saw no reason to revise his conclusion the previous year that the Tories would not have won in 1951 or 1955 without a sizeable trade unionist vote, and that therefore it 'would be inexpedient to adopt any policy involving legislation which would alienate this support'.[17]

Macmillan's principal domestic concern during 1958 was to get the political and economic cycles roughly aligned, which in practice meant keeping as tight a lid as possible on unemployment through starting to reflate the economy – a process helped by having a largely amenable Chancellor in Heathcoat Amory. His Budget in April was broadly neutral, still targeting inflation and keeping in place the restrictive measures of the previous September. But during the summer, the Bank Rate started steadily to come down, and crucially, in early July, credit controls (particularly in relation to bank lending) were lifted. 'It is now generally agreed that measures to expand the economy are desirable,' purred the *FT*, 'and that a moderate increase in demand for goods and services would not add to the dangers of rising prices; nor would it endanger the position of sterling.' For Macmillan, the Treasury storm of six months earlier seemed a blessedly distant memory. 'The Chancellor of Ex is really handling the economy with great skill,' he reflected at the end of July. 'Cautious where necessary, but not afraid of bolder action. He is worth 20 Thorneycrofts!'[18]

The political mood music did much to inform his buoyant assessment. Back in mid-June, five by-elections 'turned out very well indeed for us'; soon afterwards, the bus strike collapsed, amidst much praise for the government's firmness; by late June the Tories were only 3½ points behind Labour in the latest opinion poll; and on 9 July, Gallup revealed the two parties level pegging at 47½ per cent each, with the brief Liberal bubble having seemingly burst. Altogether it had been, commented the *New Statesman*, a 'breathtaking' swing to the Tories. Five days after that most recent Gallup poll, at a selection meeting for the Finchley constituency, an unaccompanied Margaret Thatcher (with Denis in South Africa) narrowly saw off three men, all of whom had been to public school and all of whom had their wives with them. 'Tories Choose Beauty' was the *Evening Standard*'s headline, but she still had a final hurdle to jump: the acceptance of the whole local Association, meeting on 31 July. This she did with élan. 'Speaking without notes, stabbing home points with expressive hands,' reported the *Finchley Press*,

> Mrs Thatcher launched fluently into a clear-cut appraisal of the Middle East situation, weighed up Russia's propagandist moves with the skill of a housewife measuring the ingredients in a familiar recipe, pinpointed Nasser as the fly in the mixing bowl, switched swiftly to Britain's domestic problems (showing a keen grasp of wage and Trade Union issues), then swept her breathless audience into a confident preview of Conservatism's dazzling future.

As he watched his once-commanding lead being wiped out, these were difficult days for Hugh Gaitskell. On 27 June the *Daily Herald* gave a small private lunch for him in St Ermin's Hotel. The Labour leader, remembered the paper's Geoffrey Goodman, was in 'a passionate mood' as he analysed his party's slippage:

Why, he enquired, aren't the public reacting against the Conservatives? He believed it was because the Labour Party had not departed sufficiently from its old 'working-class attitudes'. People in Britain, he reflected, were in the main 'radical' but not socialist; they wanted a 'left of centre radical party' which would make social changes without being revolutionary or authoritarian. More and more, he believed, the 'Keir Hardie image was becoming a dim and distant feature of the past'. The Labour Party had to find some more modern image if it was to be a successful force. There was now a feeling of prosperity among the working class, he observed, and this was turning the British electorate into a largely middle-class vote.

A fortnight later, lunching at the Athenaeum with Richard Crossman, Gaitskell pursued the theme again. 'Working-class people,' he insisted, 'are week by week becoming less working class, less class-conscious and more allergic to such old appeals as trade union solidarity or class loyalty. Anything we say which can be used as being merely class interest loses us votes.' Did this mean that Labour was inevitably doomed to lose? 'We've got to win the next Election,' Gaitskell kept repeating to Crossman, but a few days later the diarist noted that 'even' Roy Jenkins, 'who was one of the great addicts of the theory that we were bound to win, now admits that we are faced with a possibility of defeat'.[19]

As if on cue, two very different working-class archetypes were on display this month. 'The year was 1957, the morning bright and gay/ On the ninth of February John Axon drove away,' began *The Ballad of John Axon* on the Home Service at 10 p.m. on 2 July – the story of an engine driver who the previous year in a railway accident near Buxton had died heroically to save many others, and the first of the celebrated *Radio Ballads*. Created by the folk singers Ewan MacColl and Peggy Seeger, and produced by Charles Parker, these were pioneering programmes: not only did they celebrate working-class lives, but in a potent blend of music and recorded speech they told their stories through the voices of ordinary people, not professional actors. 'This really was some of the characteristic poetry of the idiom of the people,' declared W. L. Webb next day in the *Manchester Guardian*, being especially struck by the 'gentle reminiscing Northern voices', while Tom Driberg in the *New Statesman* called it 'this superb piece of radio'.

Even so, the programme's Appreciation Index of 61 was five below the Home Service average, and the reaction of individual listeners was at best mixed. 'Unconventional, untraditional, but all completely *right*, nothing jarred,' noted one, another that 'it was refreshing to hear songs which have some relationship with everyday working-class existence, rather than the moon/June noises of tin-pan alley'; but a third listener reckoned that the treatment 'smothered and almost buried the story of a gallant man hurtling to his death', and a fourth that 'John Axon deserved something better than this pseudo-American Annie-get-your-gun-Calypso nonsense'.

'Pop' Larkin's life was not the sort that MacColl et al were ever likely to celebrate. H. E. Bates's new novel *The Darling Buds of May* was, noted Penelope Mortimer in her *Sunday Times* review on the 13th, about 'the family of Larkins – six children, Pop and Ma – who make a fortune out of market-gardening and rather dubious deals, and live in a state of blissful Rabelaisian squalor'. Whereupon: 'A weedy young tax inspector arrives with the absurd intention of trying to get Pop to make an income-tax return. He is persuaded to stay and, transformed by Pop's eccentric taste in drink and by the lovely Mariette, remains to become Pop's son-in-law and partner in future piratical schemes to outwit the Welfare State.' Mortimer, although not much enjoying the book on her own account, had little doubt about its likely popularity, claiming that Bates had 'reached the zenith of his talent for creating life as millions of readers wish it could be'. It was a perceptive assessment of the author's intentions. 'The Larkin philosophy,' Bates himself would recall,

> is all *carpe diem* and the very antithesis of the Welfare State. The Larkins' secret is in fact that they live as many of us would like to live if only we had the guts and nerve to flout the conventions. Pop and Ma demonstrate that they have the capacity by indulging deeply in love and champagne before breakfast, passion in the bluebell wood and encouraging their enchanting daughter to a life of wilful seduction.

Modesty, however, forbade him to quote the novel's most arresting piece of dialogue: 'Pass me the tomato ketchup. I've got a bit of iced bun to finish up.'[20]

Of course, most people (including working-class people) were neither selfless Axons nor look-after-number-one Larkins; and most people naturally enjoyed the rising, if unevenly rising, sense of prosperity and widening range of material goods. Anthony Crosland was on the right side of the historical curve when in May he produced a highly critical report on the Co-operative movement, including its many shops. 'In many areas the word "co-operative" is associated with a drab, colourless, old-fashioned mediocrity,' with 'too many societies' being run 'complacently and unimaginatively'. This, he insisted, was 'not good enough for the consumer in 1958'; indeed it betrayed 'a somewhat patronising and insulting attitude to the wants and expectations of the ordinary co-operative member', whose tastes were 'changing and rising rapidly'. The reaction from Labour's left was predictably negative ('Why,' wondered *Tribune*, 'should Co-ops ape the capitalists?'), as it was from the Co-operative movement itself, and to Crosland's intense frustration his report – recommending fundamental change, including a drastically slimmed-down structure to the whole unwieldy organisation – largely gathered dust. Instead, the consumer future lay elsewhere. 'Our many outlets make it possible for us to take advantage of bulk buying to the full and we are constantly on the look-out for new lines and new ideas,' declared an unblinking champion of private enterprise, Jack Cohen, at Tesco's AGM in July, as he announced trading profits up by more than 50 per cent. 'Our policy is to give the best possible value.' Looking ahead, he promised a 'programme of constant modernisation of branches'.[21]

By this time some 4,250 self-service grocery shops were doing around 17 per cent of the UK's grocery trade, with those shops including 175 supermarkets (i.e. self-service with a sales area of at least 2,000 square feet) – of which 83 were owned by the Co-op and 75 were in London and the south-east, though Ken Morrison was getting going in Bradford (with all of three checkouts). Even so, a Gallup survey this summer of housewives' shopping preferences revealed that small independent shops were still much preferred, often involving considerable residual loyalty and/or conservatism, with 65 per cent buying their groceries from the same shop, and 75 per cent from the same butcher. 'Their main criticism against large multiple stores [preferred by only about 17 per cent of housewives] is that they are unfriendly,' reported the *News Chronicle*. 'They complain that the self-service stores encourage them to buy too much; then that lack of over-the-counter warmth pops up again.' Increasingly, though, supermarkets (led by Tesco and, from July, followed by Sainsbury's) were significantly reducing their prices on branded goods, especially foods. 'I am not cutting prices,' an independent grocer in a well-to-do London suburb so far reasonably free of supermarkets defiantly told the *Mail*. 'My customers want delivery and monthly bills. I need big margins to give this service.'

The problems for that business model would become increasingly apparent, while in 1958 other signs of change were the start of Green Shield Stamps (begun by Richard Tompkins, who had seen trading stamps in action in a flourishing petrol station near Chicago) and of another phenomenon, cash-and-carry (pioneered by a Huddersfield wholesaler, Lawrence Batley). The multiples, meanwhile, were offering an increasingly attractive shopping experience. Florence Turtle, a stationery buyer for British Home Stores, visited in Birmingham 'our Super Duper new Store which really is a store to be proud of', while a full-page advertisement in the *Kentish Mercury* for Lewisham's 'beautiful new C&A' set out its wonders:

- Great modern arcades of superbly lit windows – you can window-shop to your heart's content!
- Big, modern showrooms, beautifully decorated and arranged so that you can reach out anywhere and touch a bargain
- Twice as many self-contained fitting rooms, where you can try things on in comfort and privacy

Importantly, there also seems to have been a greater willingness on the part of shoppers to buy on credit. A survey in August found that 58 per cent of people (and 65 per cent of those under the age of 45) approved in principle of the practice, and that 23 per cent of all adults were at that time making payments. It was an area of life that could cause domestic tensions. 'Your father and me were talking about TV Friday night,' Tom Courtenay's mother Annie wrote to him earlier in the summer from working-class Hull. 'He seems to think he can get one that gradually reduces to 1/- a week. So we nearly ended up arguing.'[22]

Advertising roared on, in 1958 for the first time since the war regaining its pre-war proportion of 2½ per cent of all consumer expenditure, as naturally also did commercial television. 'Three in every four viewers affirm that the advertisements on television interest them,' noted a survey in June. 'Cartoons with jingles continue to lead the popularity stakes. The most popular advertiser in 1958 to date: Sunblest. The least popular advertiser in 1958 to date: Omo.' New brands on the market this year included Blue Daz and Tango (heavily promoted through the 'Tango Wobbly Ball' offer), while successful rebranding campaigns included Kattomeat (hitherto struggling, in a pre-Whiskas world, behind the market leader Kit-E-Kat) and the continuing Bronco story, with first a 'gay' wrapper pushing up sales and then the testing in Tunbridge Wells of the toilet paper itself in pastel shades of pink, blue and green demonstrating a clear public preference for colour. Two new television advertisements, meanwhile, had particular resonance, becoming in their way classics: 'Go to work on an egg' (contrary to myth *not* devised by the copywriter and future novelist Fay Weldon but by a colleague of hers at Mather & Crowther) and the creation of the impeccably middle-class, long-running Oxo family, with the young, attractive housewife Katie (played by Mary Holland) happy to 'give a meal man appeal' – virtue that husband Philip would occasionally reward with a patronising 'good girl'.[23]

So much was new in 1958, such as stereo 'hi-fi' equipment and discs, throwaway Biros, and eye-level grills on gas cookers. For teenage girls there was now, in shocking pink and peacock blue, the 'Pink Witch' bicycle, produced by Triumph and recommended by Jackie Collins: 'My, if you'd gone round asking girls what they wanted it couldn't have been nicer. It's so *vivid* – and so *gay* – and so marvellously *sensible* too.' The Continental influence was becoming ever more apparent. Italian Lambrettas and, to a lesser extent, Vespas dominated the motor-scooter market; for the young Howard Jacobson and friends, the moment when 'the first Italians opened up a coffee bar on Oxford Road in the centre of Manchester' around this time 'changed our lives'; and even in a 'poorish suburb' of Bournemouth with 'nothing in the least imaginative in the shopping line', related an amused Frances Woodsford in April to her American correspondent, there was a new shop which was 'all frills and flounces, and they have called it "Mes Petits"'.[24]

Yet as always there were limits to the appetite for the new. 'Confident and distinctly modernist' is how Terence Conran's biographer describes his 1958 furniture catalogue, but the range flopped commercially. Nor, owing presumably to lack of consumer demand, was the sandwich revolution even remotely in the offing, with the travel writer Arthur Eperon lamenting in July how he had 'recently been charged 3s in pubs for a sandwich consisting of dry scrapings from an old chicken carcase between hunks of cardboard bread'. Instead, 1958 saw in Reading the first of a chain that would become the reliable home of the unreconstructed breakfast fry-up: an 11-seater Little Chef, modelled on an American roadside diner.[25]

---

On 26 July, at the close of the Empire and Commonwealth Games in Cardiff, the Queen's recorded voice announced that Prince Charles, future hammer of the modernists, was to be known as the Prince of Wales – surprise news that, noted Mollie Panter-Downes, 'seems to have caused emotion among the middle-aged and over, for whom it revives memories'. Over the next few days three other stars were born or at least sighted. From nearly 3,000 talking budgerigars from across Europe, the winner of the BBC's Cage Word Contest was revealed as Sparkie, a budgie not only possessing a wide vocabulary and capable of singing in Geordie but also soon to become a household name and, almost half a century later, to inspire a Michael Nyman opera. 'Look, an original comic!' was the *Mirror*'s 'Telepage' headline above praise for Bruce Forsyth's appearance on the *The Frankie Vaughan Show* as that of 'an original performer who takes trouble with his material, has a deft delivery, and tops it with a personality which, though assured, is not in the least cocky or big-headed'. And also in the *Mirror*, Patrick Doncaster's weekly column on new records looked ahead to the release on 29 August of the first single by 'a 17-year-old dark-haired dark-eyed singer and guitar twanger from Cheshunt Herts', reckoning that Cliff Richard had 'a personality that shines through the grooves' and 'could succeed in discland'.[26]

Kenton and Shula Archer were born on 8 August, and the Australian novelist Patrick White, staying in London, might have preferred to be in Ambridge. 'It is so terribly dirty, ugly, the people so drab – also ugly

and dirty – the women like uncooked dough, the men so often suggestive of raw veal,' he informed a friend on the 12th, adding that during a
recent lunch with his English publisher he had been struck by Douglas
Jerrold's 'habit of chewing his words in the best English manner – as if
they were a difficult and unpleasant meat'. On the 23rd the BBC finally
consented to give starting prices with its racing news; two days later
Midland announced it would be the first high-street bank to offer
personal loans; and on Wednesday the 27th Madge Martin went to a
matinee of *My Fair Lady* ('well-nigh perfect'), Gladys Langford treated
herself to a long ride on the 179 bus to Grove Park (where, with female
toilets 'conspicuously missing', she 'had to take a 2d platform ticket,
find someone who would unlock lavatory & found it smelly, cistern
chain not working'), Ted Hughes had a selection of his work read on
the Third Programme ('It is not often that one is so excited by the work
of a new poet,' said the *Listener*), and Philip Larkin boldly predicted to
Monica Jones that the England cricket team ('swollen with pride') that
had been selected to tour Australia would 'come a cropper'.[27]

These were not the all-time-best summer holidays. 'Wakes week'
may have been the episode that on 14 July finished the first series proper
of radio's *The Clitheroe Kid*, but such was the seriousness of the down-
turn in the Lancashire cotton trade that, as the *Rochdale Observer*
gloomily reflected about this time, some would have no alternative but
to 'regard the annual holiday as a luxury which will have to be sacri-
ficed this year'. Nor did the weather help, with Macmillan himself
noting on 20 August that 'it has now rained, practically without ceas-
ing, for 6 weeks in every part of the country'. Still, there was always
plenty to see and do in 'The Most Magnificent Gardens In The British
Isles'. An advertisement itemised the attractions of Staffordshire's
Alton Towers:

> Fully Licensed Bars and Catering – Boating – Children's Paddling Pool
> – Miniature Railway, and many other amusements for all ages – Unrivalled
> Woodland Walks – Flag Tower – Chinese Temples, etc., etc.
>     Also the world's largest 'oo' Gauge Model Electric Railway.
>     Celebrated Bands Sundays and Bank Holidays. (The Jaguar Car Works
> Band will play in the Gardens on Sunday, August 17th.)

Judy Haines spent a Sunday morning in early August in Littlehampton. 'Butlin's have a place there right on the front,' she noted. 'But for that it's very pleasant.' The Butlin's in question was only an amusement park; for the real Butlin's experience she should have gone to the holiday camp at Clacton-on-Sea, where soon afterwards Cliff Richard and the Drifters began a residency at the Pig and Whistle Bar. 'Campers used to go for a knees-up and a sing-song,' recalled a Redcoat, Stan Edwards. 'They thought Cliff's music was a racket and nobody went in there when he was playing. Cliff only knew about eight numbers at the time, and they were all Elvis Presley songs. He used to look like Elvis, and wiggle in the same way. You can imagine the campers who wanted a sing-song liking that sort of music!' It transpired that Cliff had been put in the wrong bar; on transferring to the recently opened South Seas Coffee Bar, 'he went down well' and also did afternoon sessions in the Rock 'n' Roll Ballroom. One night towards the end of the season a terrific thunderstorm left the top end of the camp completely flooded, including the South Seas. 'It had glass tables with live goldfish, and was really sprauncey,' remembered another Redcoat, Roy Hudd. 'The place was three feet deep in water, and the drains couldn't take any more. We were all woken up at three in the morning, and told to get up there.' A less than gruntled Hudd reluctantly did so. 'About 2,000 campers were there, baling out the water, cleaning the tables, checking everything was OK as if they were employed by Butlin's. One of them wading in the water turned to me and said, "Marvellous, isn't it? Just like the Blitz."'[28]

On Saturday, 30 August, while a teenage Jimmy Greaves scored five at Stamford Bridge against the usually formidable Wolves defence, the Empire Theatre in Portsmouth prepared for its last performance. Variety theatres around the country were by this time closing down at a rapid rate, and a supermarket was to be built on the site. That evening, for the second house, there was standing room only to watch Terry (Toby Jug) Cantor's 'Folies à la Parisienne', with others on show including the Hungarian acrobats the Great Alexis troupe and the double-jointed comedian Dale Robertson. After it was all over, and the audience had departed, some stagehands took to the stage and started to sing. Whereupon, according to the local *Evening News*:

Someone opened a side door, just as 63-year-old Mrs Lilian Salmon was going by on her way home. She paused as the noise flooded out into the almost deserted Edinburgh Road, and went inside. Through the maze of passages and stairways she found her way to the stage – and took command.

This was no longer Mrs Salmon, of 21 Sommerville Road, Southsea. This was Lilian Ravenscroft, 'Lancashire's Singing Mill Girl' of World War I, when the theatre was in its heyday.

On that same stage she made her professional debut in 1914 as one of The Six Red-heads. Another member of the group was Gracie Fields . . . A pianist joined in, and soon the theatre was ringing with The Singing Mill Girl's rich contralto voice.

Song after song she sang, and before long there was a small gathering at the open side door, including a police sergeant and two constables. Their interest was not surprising, since it was long past midnight.

Eventually, a stagehand announced that everybody had to go home. The Singing Mill Girl led 'Auld Lang Syne', and the Empire Theatre was dead.[29]

# 8

# Get the Nigger

Just after closing time on the evening of Saturday, 23 August, exactly a week before the curtain came down on the Portsmouth Empire, a 21-year-old blonde, Mrs Mary Lowndes, and her miner husband were leaving a pub in the rundown St Ann's district of Nottingham, to go back to their two small children, when she was apparently punched in the back by a black man. 'The next thing I knew,' she related afterwards, 'my husband was being punched from one side of the road to the other by a group of coloured men. I heard bottles being smashed and everyone started screaming and shouting.' Things rapidly escalated. There were knife attacks on several white men; a crowd of some 1,500, mainly white, rapidly gathered; counter-attacks began against blacks; and it took the police an hour and a half to restore order. Over the next day or two it emerged that the initial events had been a reaction against the previous fortnight's series of assaults by white Teddy boys on the area's heavy concentration of black residents – assaults mainly fuelled by an atavistic dislike of black men having white girlfriends and eventually leading to some West Indians taking the law into their own hands. The following Saturday, the 30th, Teds and others turned up in St Ann's en masse, a milling mob of up to 4,000, with revenge on the agenda amidst cries of 'Let's lynch them', 'Let's get at them' and 'Find some niggers', but with their targets almost all staying prudently at home, they fought instead with the police, resulting in 24 arrests. 'This was not a racial riot,' insisted the Chief Constable, Captain Athelstan Popkess. 'The coloured people behaved in a most exemplary way by keeping out of the way. Indeed, they were an example to some of our rougher elements.'

Between the two Saturdays, the *Manchester Guardian* had on Wednesday the 27th an optimistic headline: 'Other cities not perturbed about Nottingham: It-couldn't-happen-here feeling'. Even so, the accompanying report did note that in the Notting Hill Gate–Shepherd's Bush area, where 'between three and five thousand West Indians are living, mostly in poor housing conditions, among a white population largely composed of people who are themselves not Londoners and have little community life', the previous three weeks had been 'unsettled', including 'fights and attempts to run down pedestrians with cars on Saturday nights'. Meanwhile the Hammersmith area had witnessed 'a recent outburst by gangs of Teddy boys said to be cruising the streets on week-end evenings, looking for Africans or West Indians', with those gangs 'said to choose streets where only the occasional coloured person is to be seen, and then attack in the ratio of half a dozen to one'. In fact, there had been a particularly vicious episode the previous Saturday night – just an hour or two after the first Nottingham battle – when a gang of nine white youths, mainly from Shepherd's Bush, had gone out 'nigger-hunting' (their term) and, armed with iron bars and other weapons, had wantonly indulged in unprovoked attacks, injuring five black men, including three seriously. On Friday the 29th the *Kensington News and West London Times* noted more broadly that 'Nottingham must be a warning to North Kensington' (aka Notting Hill), where almost 7,000 'coloured' people lived, approaching a tenth of the population.[1]

Taking place in increasingly warm weather at the fag-end of what had been a dismal summer, the 'Notting Hill Riots' – by some distance the most serious civil unrest of the decade – began shortly before midnight on Saturday the 30th. 'A bottle bomb was thrown through a basement window of a house in which coloured people rent rooms,' reported the *Daily Express*, and over the next few hours other 'coloured' houses were attacked, as were random black men as well as white women known to be going with blacks, often by roaming white gangs with, according to another report, 'iron railings, choppers and in some cases bicycle chains'. It was worse on Sunday night, with threatening, violent crowds of some 500 or 600 on the streets, and 17 arrests made after, noted the *Kensington News*, 'West Indians had been savagely assaulted and petrol bombs had been thrown by the mobs into the homes of coloured people'. For four hours, stated the ensuing police evidence, 'there were running fights continuously between coloured and white people and, at times, the two opponents were ganging up against the police'.[2]

Monday, 1 September was the climax. 'I have seen nothing uglier, or nastier, than this,' declared one reporter, Merrick Winn, about an incident that became emblematic:

> A young man, coloured, a student, walks alone in the middle of a shabby road, Bramley Road, Notting Hill, London. It is three in the afternoon. He carries a brown bag, for he has just come to the area. He looks about him, jumpily, wondering about the silent people, white people, crowding the pavements. He has not heard about the race riots.
>
> The people watching, violently. Suddenly a voice yells: 'Get him.' Other voices yell: 'Get the nigger.' The people sweep after him. Middle-aged people, but most of them young people. And many are children.
>
> They hit the student. A youth flings his cycle at him. He pleads and cries out, then breaks away, into a greengrocer's shop. The greengrocer locks the door. The student stands trembling and says: 'They'll kill me.'
>
> Then police cars come and a police van with a dozen policemen. They take the student to safety and the greengrocer says to me: 'They'd have murdered him.'

The man running for his life was Seymour Manning, a 26-year-old African student living in Derby, who had come down to London for the day to see friends; the greengrocer's wife who bravely let him in and kept the pursuers at bay was Mrs Pat Howcroft. 'I was one of the three that first got 'im,' an angry white boy in a red shirt told another reporter. 'I half-twisted his leg off anyway. We'd have tore 'im apart if it hadn't been for the police.'

That evening, as darkness fell, huge, rampant mobs of white youth – shouting 'Kill the niggers!' and estimated as up to 2,000 strong – smashed their way through a large swathe of Notting Hill. By this time the local blacks, supplemented by Jamaicans from Brixton (itself in a highly volatile state), were fighting back, including an all-out pitched battle in Powis Terrace, with the philosophy being, recalled one, 'In for a penny, in for a pound'. A *Daily Express* reporter caught something of the flavour of a chaotic, violent night:

> Youths surged from the Bramley Road area, through Oxford Gardens into Blenheim Crescent. They shattered windows of a Jamaican woman's home with palings torn from the garden fence of her English neighbour.
>
> A Fascist meeting in Barandon Street nearby lost its audience as youths marched away to Blenheim Crescent. A bottle containing lighted petrol was hurled among them from the roof of a four-floor tenement. A rain of milk bottles followed. The road was littered with broken glass. An old lamp-lighter going his rounds on a bicycle was felled by a brick. Two more petrol bombs followed, sending sheets of flame up from the road.

Early next morning a politician, living in nearby Holland Park, toured the battle zone. 'I saw the debris and the corrugated iron up behind the windows of the prefabs where the coloured families live,' recorded Anthony Wedgwood Benn. 'The use of petrol bombs and iron bars and razors is appalling. There is a large area where it is not safe for people to be out.' That Tuesday afternoon he toured again – 'even at 5 o'clock there was an ugly atmosphere and people hurried along the streets' – and indeed another night of trouble lay ahead, with 55 people (mainly white) arrested, often for possession of offensive weapons such as broken milk bottles and loaded leather belts. 'In one street where some of the ugliest fighting has taken place your Correspondent found a group of men in a public house singing "Old Man River" and "Bye Bye Blackbird", and punctuating the songs with vicious anti-Negro slogans,' noted *The Times*. 'The men said that their motto was "Keep Britain White", and they made all sorts of wild charges against their coloured neighbours.' Rain at last arrived on Wednesday to damp things down, and though Thursday was another hot, tense day with some disturbances, a degree of normality began to return from Friday onwards.[3]

It was hardly news, of course, that not all whites in Britain viewed the 165,000 or so non-white immigrants with unalloyed enthusiasm. 'I have been living in Hartington Street for over 30 years and I have seen the deterioration which has been caused by the coloured people,' Mrs F. L. Greenwood, a widow from Moss Side, Manchester, told a local paper the previous autumn. 'We are all made by the same Creator, but I think the coloured folk should live together in one district, as they do in Birmingham.' Or from Paddington, take the views (as elicited in April 1958) of some of the white residents of Oakington Road:

- I've got nothing against them, but they should have a place of their own like Maida Vale. I was brought up prejudiced against them.
- There's 10 people sleeping in a room over there.
- They should not be allowed to flood here. They must be stopped. They give white girls babies.
- They blow their nose as they pass you.
- Their windows and curtains are filthy. They are noisy.
- God made black as well as white, but if you see all the black prostitutes in Piccadilly, it's awful.
- They don't interfere with me. I don't like them around. I don't know why.

Two months later it became a national story when local magistrates renewed the licence of the Scala ballroom in Wolverhampton even though it was operating a colour bar. 'The fact is people don't want them,' the manager, Michael Wade, explained. 'They have said to me: "We have to work with them; some of us even have to live next to them. We want to get away from them sometimes."' So too elsewhere in the West Midlands. 'Are there too Many Coloured Folk in Coventry?' was the title at the start of August of an editorial in the *Coventry Standard* – noting how 'each day a stream of them wends its way down Grey Friars Lane to the Employment Exchange, and most of them have savings accounts at the banks' – while later in the month the *Birmingham Mail*'s industrial correspondent, Clem Lewis, argued that, in the context of 'no longer enough jobs to go round', the time had come for action: 'The problem is one of people coming from impoverished countries to a country with standards and a way of life that they cannot immediately understand or accept. For their sake and our own it has to be faced honestly, fairly, and imaginatively – NOW.'[4]

For their part, non-white immigrants undoubtedly continued to encounter significant prejudice and discrimination – but the question is to gauge how much. A glance at the small ads for furnished apartments in the *Kensington News* on 22 August, just before the troubles began, is suggestive, being full of phrases like 'English only', 'Europeans only', 'White business people only', 'No coloured people' and, regretfully, 'Sorry, no coloured'. Moreover, as the sociologist Ruth Glass found not long afterwards, the omission of such a phrase was no guarantee of an open door. Only one in six of 'neutral' private advertisers in the *Kensington Post* were in practice, on being rung up, willing to countenance West Indian tenants. With council housing almost out of the question in the context of the ongoing housing shortage – 'It would be quite unrealistic,' frankly stated a housing minister, Reginald Bevins, in November 1957, 'to expect local authorities to give priority to immigrants over other local families who have often been on the waiting-list for several years' – the most common recourse was to dilapidated housing owned by fellow immigrants, too often far from scrupulous about issues of sanitation and overcrowding. As for employment, where non-whites by now were often doing the menial or ill-paid jobs that whites no longer wished to do, it was a more mixed picture: the colour bar virtually gone in sectors like the NHS and public transport, but explicitly or implicitly often present elsewhere, not least through local branches of trade unions operating colour quotas with the tacit consent of employers. 'We do not get past the factory door because we are told "No coloured workers wanted" as soon as they see us,' a Jamaican in Birmingham told a journalist in March 1957. 'Even when we know there are jobs vacant we are told, "Sorry, there is nothing." Sometimes they are very polite, but politeness and rudeness mean just the same thing.'[5]

One should not exaggerate the general severity of the prejudice. 'Wherever there are tensions, these tend to be subdued,' reckoned Ruth Glass about the customary workplace situation. 'West Indians sometimes complain that they have been slighted or insulted by their workmates. More often they tell stories of incomplete "integration": they say that all goes well at work, but once it is done, the white workers do not mix with them in the canteen or on their way home, nor do they ask them to come along to the local pub.' That is probably right: incomplete integration as typical rather than, say, the more dramatic experience in 1958 of the future actor Delroy Lindo, living in Eltham as the six-year-old son of Jamaican parents, and one day terrified out of his skin when a Teddy boy got his attention in the street and then drew a finger across his throat. Either way, it was piquant timing for the singalong smiliness of the BBC's *The Black and White Minstrel Show*, which, complete with The Television Toppers and Kenneth Connor as MC, had its first outing on 14 June and was an instant hit. 'Very much to my taste,' applauded *Punch*'s Henry Turton in pregnant late August. 'I am glad that most of the creaking conventions of the old-time minstrel-show have been dispensed with. George Mitchell's merry men black up, certainly . . . otherwise little pretence is made at reproducing the rather flat-footed routine of the genuine burnt-cork-and-tambourine troupes.'[6]

Inevitably, whatever the prior rumblings, the lurid events of Nottingham and Notting Hill came as a considerable shock to activators. Ten years after *Windrush*, and with non-white Commonwealth immigration during 1955–7 running each year at well over 40,000 (compared to 2,000 in 1953 and 11,000 in 1954), the question naturally arose of whether 'the emigration of coloured people to this country should be limited' – as the opening questioner put it at the Leisure Hall in Mere, Wiltshire, on the return of *Any Questions?* on 12 September from the programme's summer break. The panel's response was unanimously negative. The Tory MP Ted Leather said there could be 'no possible excuse for intolerance and mob violence of any kind'; the Labour MP Anthony Greenwood insisted it would be 'morally wrong' to impose such a limitation; the would-be Liberal MP Jeremy Thorpe declared that 'if the brotherhood of man means anything, well then let's share what we have got'; and the farmer-writer A. G. Street was likewise against restrictions ('to stop immigration would wreck the Commonwealth'), though he observed that 'this coloured thing is very difficult, it is based on physical repulsion, if you like on sex jealousy'. A last word went to the chairman, Freddie Grisewood, who added that 'as a corollary to what has been said it wouldn't be a bad moment just to pay a tribute to the police in the way they have handled these shocking riots'.[7]

That all sounded more or less fine, dandy and liberal, but for both the main political parties the reality this autumn was more complex. In the immediate wake of the troubles, only *The Times* of the Tory-supporting national dailies came out unequivocally against immigration controls, declaring in a leader on 'A Family of Nations' that such a policy would 'almost certainly have unforeseen and harmful effects', was 'a counsel of despair' and 'should not be countenanced'. With an election probably only a year away, however, the last thing Macmillan wanted was a major, divisive furore, and on 8 September – two days after Butler as Home Secretary had asserted in a speech at Maldon that it would need 'considerable force of argument' to alter the 'right of British citizenship to come in and out of the mother country at will' – the Cabinet was entirely in agreement that it was 'important to avoid, if possible, any major pronouncement on Commonwealth immigration'.

Over the next few weeks most Tories adopted a measured tone – 'faults on both sides' was the overriding theme of the analysis in the *Smethwick Telephone* by that constituency's prospective Tory candidate Peter Griffiths, before he dropped in the assertion that 'it would seem reasonable to restrict immigration into this country to healthy people who have jobs to go to' – but it became increasingly clear that there was a divide between on the one hand the party leadership, on the other hand some backbench MPs and the bulk of the party membership. In October the party conference was at Blackpool, where (despite Butler's insistence that 'we should maintain the long and respected tradition of allowing citizens of the Commonwealth to come here'), delegates endorsed by a large majority a motion calling for immigration controls. No backbencher was keener on those restrictions than Cyril Osborne, who later that month in the Commons declared that 'it is time someone spoke for this country and for the white man who lives here', and expanded upon what he claimed to be the idleness, sickness and crime that coloured people brought to the country. Few other Tory backbenchers openly supported him, however, and at a meeting of the 1922 Committee he was humiliated and indeed reduced to tears. One backbencher watching it all, and keeping his counsel, was the MP for Wolverhampton South West, Enoch Powell, who 35 years later would tell his biographer Simon Heffer that he had felt ashamed ever since of staying silent during the attacks on Osborne.[8]

It was not wholly different in the Labour and Labour-supporting ranks, from where in early September there were four significant interventions. 'The Government must introduce legislation quickly to end the tremendous influx of coloured people from the Commonwealth,'

North Kensington's MP George Rogers told the right-wing *Daily Sketch*. 'Overcrowding has fostered vice, drugs, prostitution and the use of knives. For years the white people have been tolerant. Now their tempers are up.' Another Labour MP, the usually liberal-minded Maurice Edelman, wrote a fairly balanced but ultimately pro-control piece for the *Daily Mail* that was given the exaggerated headline, 'Should we let them keep pouring in?' – a piece that earned him praise for his 'courage' from the *Daily Mirror*, which itself did not just declare that Commonwealth citizens should only be allowed to come to Britain if they already had a job and home lined up but also called for greater powers of deportation: 'Some of the coloured people who have settled here are no-goods. As Commonwealth citizens, they cannot be deported. That is ludicrous.' The fourth intervention came from the TUC, meeting at Bournemouth, where its General Secretary, Sir Vincent Tewson, spoke in favour of immigration control, asserting that 'there should be gates in their land of origin and here through which people must pass'.

Nevertheless, the majority opinion among Labour MPs was almost certainly the other way, with Benn on the 7th expressing it in a *Reynolds News* article which claimed that the introduction of immigration controls would in effect be 'the start of apartheid', given that the object of such controls could only be 'to keep out coloured people'. For many on the Labour side, including the leader Hugh Gaitskell, haunted by memories of the 1930s, the much-publicised presence of Sir Oswald Mosley's fascist followers during the Notting Hill troubles was probably a decisive consideration in their determination to brook no compromise. Later in the month, just before its conference, the party issued a statement unambiguously rejecting immigration controls and promising that the next Labour government would 'introduce legislation making illegal the public practice of discrimination'.[9]

What of public opinion? It is easy enough to locate individual viewpoints – 'It's high time the growing resentment felt in the country against the black invasion of Britain was thus made violently and forcibly manifest,' noted an approbatory Anthony Heap on 1 September about the 'racial riots', while letters received by Edelman after his *Daily Mail* article were largely supportive – but the only reliable representative guide is the Gallup poll conducted nationwide on the 3rd and 4th.

The key findings included: 55 per cent wanting restrictions on non-white immigration from the Commonwealth; 71 per cent disapproving of 'marriages between white and coloured people'; 54 per cent not wanting 'coloured people from the Commonwealth' to be 'admitted to council housing lists on the same conditions as people born in Britain'; and 61 per cent definitely or possibly moving 'if coloured people came to live in great numbers' in their district. These were striking enough figures – with the first especially at variance with the broad party political consensus – but need to be set against others: only 9 per cent definitely moving, and 21 per cent possibly, 'if coloured people came to live next door'; and only 7 per cent objecting 'if there were coloured children in the same classes as your children at school'.

Altogether, as Ruth Glass dryly put it, the poll showed that 'the veneer of racial tolerance is a rather thin one'. But at the same time, at least that thin veneer existed, and arguably owed at least something to a widespread underlying decency on the part of a socially still very conservative population. 'Discussed the Colour problem, Jewish problem, & agreed that the 4 years sentence on the Teddy Boys who beat up the Colour chap was just,' noted Florence Turtle after lunch with a friend on the 17th, in the context of the recent deliberately punitive sentences given to the nine white thugs who had presaged the Notting Hill troubles. Not dissimilarly, speaking in some sense for Middle England, there was the Giles cartoon of the 7th, showing three Teds walking out of a surgery where the battle wounds they had brought on themselves had been treated by a black nurse and doctor. Even on the part of averagely decent whites, though, a strict limit applied to their appetite for the whole issue. As BBC Television's autumn schedule unfolded, members of the viewers' panel found it 'a pleasure to watch such an artist' when Harry Belafonte was on, but not so with *The Untouchable*, a worthy-sounding Sunday-night drama about an impoverished widow taking an Indian law student into her home as one of her lodgers. 'To a good number,' noted the report, 'this play about the colour bar seemed "ill timed" – there was "too much talk and controversy" already and they were "sated with the subject".'

Probably for many anyway, it was still a rather academic question, given that only 49 per cent of those polled by Gallup had actually ever known a non-white person.[10] But for those living in the areas of non-white settlement it was far from academic, and in three of them there were some particularly strong reactions during these charged days and weeks.

Starting in Notting Hill itself, so much in the national spotlight that on 5 September the nine o'clock news on the radio had five minutes shaved off in order to include a special report on the area that featured the views of white people living there. 'Some of those interviewed, after disavowing any racial prejudice, agreed,' noted the *Listener*,

> that 'This here trouble with the blacks' as one of them called it, all started by coloured men forcing white girls into prostitution and living hand-somely on their earnings and often drawing national assistance as well. Others alleged that coloured immigrants bought up houses in the area, evicted the original tenants and then filled them up with their friends, five and six to a room, when they further outraged the feelings of the local inhabitants by rowdy parties lasting all night.

Three days later, nearly fifty teenagers (almost certainly all white) attended the newly opened Dale Youth Club to take part in a subse-quently reported discussion:

> They felt that it has been a small minority of the coloured population that has provoked the white people in the area. The general consensus of opinion was that mixed marriages were wrong and that there was a certain amount of feeling against white girls who married coloured men. During the discussion many of the teenagers quoted actual cases of their own experience, of the appalling low standards of living, among the coloured people. As regards the housing problem, they were annoyed that 'West Indians could come here and get houses when white people are overcrowded and have not got houses'. They agreed that some sort of immigration restriction should be imposed particularly in their area.

Finally, these four dozen white youths were asked whether the riots had been justified. 'They would give no definite answer,' the club leader, Mr Hale, told the local paper, 'but they would rather say yes than no.'

Up in the West Midlands (which had the second-biggest concentra-tion after London of non-white immigrants) there had been no serious disturbances, with the partial exception of Dudley, but that did not prevent some uninhibited correspondence in Wolverhampton's *Express and Star*:

> I do not advocate an inhospitable attitude towards foreign elements within our midst, but surely we have the undeniable right to choose our guests and 'weed out' the sick, the lame and the lazy? Our outraged intellectuals would do well to visit their local pubs where more common sense is aired than in many a Parliamentary gathering. *('Geordie')*
>
> Jobs are scarcer, rent and rates higher, yet people are entering this land and going straight on to public assistance. It is completely wrong. Friction in such circumstances is inevitable, regardless of colour or creed. If common sense and less sentiment were employed, everyone would stand to gain. *(Florence Beamand, 49 Butts Road, Penn, Wolverhampton)*
>
> We dread the summer or any nice weather, as a crowd of Jamaicans gather in the next-door gardens to play cards, and make the neighbourhood hideous with their noise ... It is useless for Cabinet ministers or anyone else to attempt to whitewash. They should live amongst these coloured immigrants and suffer as we have done. *('Long-Sufferer')*

Colin Quayle of Himley Road, Dudley also had West Indian neighbours. 'The lines of clean washing which hang above their well-tended gardens testify to their cleanliness and industry,' he insisted. 'They are good neighbours, who wish to interfere with my way of life as little as I wish to interfere with theirs.'

The third place was Kentish Town in north London, where a local by-election was due to be held on 25 September. The Conservative, Labour and Communist candidates all agreed to keep race issues out of it, but a fourth candidate stood as an independent specifically on a 'Keep Kentish Town White' platform. He was William Webster, a 51-year-old publican and former boxer at whose pub, the Black Horse in Royal College Street, only whites were admitted. 'My platform is primarily a moral one,' he explained. 'The so-called Teddy boy era is the most healthy reaction we have had to date. Even if the coloured people were acceptable biologically there is neither work nor accommodation for them in this area.' And to another journalist about his opposition to a multiracial society: 'It is a matter of racial survival and

I can see in this a lowering of standards. The Negro is on a lower evolutionary plane so far as I can see.' As for his policy at his pub, Webster maintained that 'if I did not keep coloured people out of my house I should have no customers at all'. Shortly before polling day, the brewers Watney, Combe and Reid gave him a year's notice to quit, and the chairman of the Central Panel of the Brewing Trade wrote to *The Times* making it 'abundantly clear' that 'this trade dissociates itself entirely from all forms of racial discrimination', prompting in turn a letter from Webster's wife Emmeline, who claimed that all her husband was trying to do was 'to keep the area in which his wife and children reside, and the house wherein he earns his living, morally and socially respectable'. The voters (predominantly white) duly gave their verdict: 479 votes for Webster, out of a total of almost 6,500 cast.

In other words, the non-white immigrants – of which there were by now a critical mass – were here to stay. Including Sylvester Hughes, who in his early thirties had sailed from Antigua on Christmas Eve 1957, started in London as a kitchen porter in Lyons Corner House, and over the next 15 years would work as a carpenter (rising to foreman) before turning himself into a self-employed stallholder, eventually becoming in the early 1980s the first-ever West Indian stallholder in the Portobello Road fruit-and-veg market. Year-round, on stall 109, he wore the same outfit, recalled his obituarist Emily Green in 1991:

> Tweed hat, pressed cotton shirt, knotted tie, wool jumper. He never hawked. There was no easy familiarity. He addressed others as 'Miss', 'Missus' or 'Mister' – never 'Love', 'Lovey' or 'Darling'. And he was known locally, even by those who knew him well, as 'Mr Hughes'.
>
> His produce, too, was an exercise in contrast . . . Jamaican peppermint, white and yellow yams, plantains, ackee, limes, several types of root ginger, a good variety of chillies, coconuts, smooth Jamaican avocadoes and the exotic squash *chayote*.

On the day of Hughes's funeral, at All Saints' Church, Notting Hill, 'stall 109 was heaped with bouquets from shoppers and neighbouring stallholders, who had grown quite fond of the quiet man with the queer fruit'.[11]

'Today the Do-It-Yourself Exhibition opens at Olympia,' noted the *Evening Standard* on 4 September, adding that 'in no section has there been such a boom as in sailing craft'. Marinas and suchlike, however, were not on the minds of those gathered at Bournemouth that week for the Trades Union Congress, with Frank Cousins an increasingly vexed participant. 'The general atmosphere of apathy & display of unreadiness to enter into a real examination of major problems was increasingly apparent,' he privately reflected after it ended, and went on:

> It seems we have too many men in the Council of the T.U.C. who either do not believe fully in the principles of public ownership or do not understand it in relationship to the control of the country's economy . . . Even subjects such as security in employment, mobility of Labour, social services, full employment, productivity & the like appear to be matters of no concern . . . Many of the leaders seem to have no forward purpose except to maintain their individual status. Not a solitary lesson was learned from the Bus Strike of May 1958 & every one seemed satisfied to have reached a position where no one was wrong & no one was right on the issues involved.

Even more disenchanted, though, was Les Cannon, the ex-Communist trade unionist who was by now in bitter dispute with his union, the Communist-dominated Electrical Trades Union, over its shameless ballot-rigging practices. On the eve of the TUC he gave a high-profile press conference. But in the event he received precious little support (Vic Feather an honourable exception), with the sympathy of the capitalist press, together with the ETU's vehement line that an attack on one union was an attack on the movement as a whole, probably having the effect of turning many trade unionists against his cause, or at least just wishing it would go away.

In terms of employer–employee relations it was in many ways still a paternalistic world. Take the giant ICI, whose Billingham sports club, the Synthonia (a portmanteau of Synthetic Ammonia), had a new ground, superbly appointed for both football and athletics, officially opened by the Earl of Derby on Saturday the 6th. 'I must express on behalf of the members our sincere and grateful thanks to the Company for yet one more act of supreme generosity towards us,' declared the club's president at the ceremony. Paternalism was also usually the order of the day in the many small or medium-sized family-run firms that largely comprised the City of London. The merchant bank Antony Gibbs & Sons was one such, holding this autumn for family, partners, staff and pensioners a cocktail party at the Grocers' Hall to celebrate its 150th anniversary. 'Mac', the recently retired Stanley McCombie, naturally received an invitation after 44 years' service, but, stricken with dermatitis, he warned 'Mr Antony' he might be unable to attend. 'So far I don't consider my retiring to be an unqualified success,' he wrote on the 20th from his home in Leytonstone, 'and my wife is threatening to send me back to the office as a washout so far as home is concerned . . . I miss you very much, but I'm sure all goes on as usual without me.'[12]

By this time *Sunday Night at the London Palladium* had a new host, following Lew Grade's abrupt sacking of Tommy Trinder, possibly for telling a racist or anti-Jewish joke. This was the 30-year-old Bruce Forsyth, who a year before had talked of giving up comedy to run a tobacconist's. Clifford Davis on the *Mirror*'s 'Telepage' charted Forsyth's early progress. In his first show, 14 September, 'a likeable personality – without being too forceful'; a fortnight later, 'packed in some topical material' but 'will have to stop overworking the word "wonderful" every time he interviews contestants for "Beat the Clock"'; and a week later, 'managed to hold this rather indifferent show together . . . versatile . . . tailor-made for the job . . . gets better each week'. The *Mirror* in September also gave its appraisal of a new British film. 'Unabashedly relies on beating customers over the head with a bladder of lard,' reckoned Dick Richards, adding 'the jokes come thick and fast' and that, although 'sometimes the comedy sags', this was 'only while the cast is getting its second breath'. *Carry On Sergeant* owed a fair bit to television's *The Army Game*, not only being similarly set amongst a bunch of National Service squaddies but also featuring three of its stars in William Hartnell, Charles Hawtrey and Norman Rossington, who helped out Bob Monkhouse, Dora Bryan, Kenneth Connor and Kenneth Williams. In any case, it was such an instant hit that at the Last Night of the Proms a huge banner proclaiming 'Carry On Sargent' was waved behind the unwitting conductor, Sir Malcolm.

At the outset the film had been conceived by producer Peter Rogers
and director Gerald Thomas as a one-off, but within weeks *Carry On
Nurse* was in production.[13]

On a damp Thursday four days after Forsyth's debut, an American
professor of genetics, George W. Beadle, arrived in Oxford with his
wife Muriel and son Red to take up a visiting professorship. Their brisk,
matter-of-fact landlady showed them round their rented house – small
and cluttered – in Headington and, as recalled by Muriel in her nicely
humorous memoir of an often baffling year, offered some local guidance: '"Thursday is early closing," she said, "and if you wish to lay on
supplies you must get to the shops before one." The butcher shops shut
their doors on Monday and Saturday afternoons, in addition, she told
us; and the wine merchant was open (for the purchase of spirits) only
during "hours", which I later found out meant during the same hours
the pubs were open.' Umbrellas in hand, they set out for some immediate groceries:

> At Berry's, the bakery, I bought a small round loaf of bread, receiving it
> with a piece of thin paper loosely wrapped around part of it. At
> Murchison's the Headington greengrocer, I added newspaper-wrapped
> potatoes, carrots, and a limp head of lettuce to the bundles in Red's arms.
> Our final stop was H. E. Weaver's Quality Meats, and there I made a
> mistake. Walking along, I had made a quick calculation as to what might
> be the simplest menu to prepare, and I had answered myself: a good Irish
> stew. So I asked Mr Weaver for 'a pound of beef for stew', expecting the
> succulent squares of chuck that the same request would have produced at
> home. I don't know what he gave me, because I never ordered it again.

That evening at 8.30, with a fork still unable to penetrate the meat
despite four hours of cooking on top of the Rayburn, Muriel's patience
snapped:

> I said, 'Let's eat it. If we cut it into small enough pieces, we won't even
> have to chew it.' I *did* chew one piece of mine to see what it tasted like,
> and it didn't have any taste.
>
> Red, sensing my distress and doing his best to relieve it, said, 'The
> potatoes are awfully good, Mom.'

'I'm glad you like them,' I said with savage politeness, and burst into tears.

Later, she lay awake for hours, listening to the rain. 'I let my thoughts drift back to the electric range in my California kitchen, and to the furnace we lit by pressing a button, and to the big living-room in our Spanish-style house.'

One of John Bloom's washing machines would probably not have made the difference. 'Britain's Greatest-Ever Washing Machine Value!' boasted an advertisement on the back page of the *Mirror* six days later for the 'Electromatic Washing Machine and Spin Drier'. 'From 49 [in huge type] Gns. A Brand New Combination ... A Complete home laundry for 1/3rd deposit and only 7/3 a week for 2 years!' A remarkable story was under way. The 26-year-old Bloom was the son of a Polish-born tailor and had grown up in the East End before leaving school at 16. By 1958 he had tried his hand at various things (salesman at Selfridge's, running a road-haulage business, selling paraffin door-to-door), but not got very far in any of them. But that year, in quick succession, he started selling cut-price washing machines imported from Holland, grew a beard to make himself look older, and now, in September, took a punt by advertising in Britain's best-selling daily paper – so successfully that more than 8,000 readers sent off the coupon requesting details about the Electromatic. It was a propitious moment. Hire-purchase controls were about to be abolished, washing machine sales for 1958 would be 44 per cent up on the previous year, the market leader (Hotpoint) largely eschewed price reductions, and at this point Bloom was one of only two entrepreneurs who saw the gap in the market for (to quote the historian of domestic electrical appliances) 'really cheap and less indestructibly durable appliances, using high-pressure salesmanship to sell them', mainly to 'working-class homes, still so understocked with many appliances'. Bloom's rival was the Manchester-based A. J. Flatley, who in the course of the year began to make clothes dryers and gave his name to the advertising jingle 'Mum deserves a Flatley'.[14] History, however, would remember Bloom.

These were still early days after Nottingham and Notting Hill, and, quite apart from issues of immigration and race relations, there were the implications to be considered of the Teddy boys' violent behaviour.

The industrialist Sir Halford Reddish, appearing on a *Brains Trust* television panel just before Forsyth's Palladium debut, had no doubts: 'I would like to see corporal punishment brought in and these young thugs given a good thrashing.' A few weeks later, at the Tory conference, Butler managed to fend off vociferous demands to restore flogging, though at the price of promising harsher youth detention centres to 'de-Teddify the Teddy Boy', while also in October the government set up a committee under Lady Albemarle to consider the youth problem, including the question of facilities. Phyllis Willmott, meanwhile, offered a beady perspective. 'The Committee members absolutely appalled me at first sight,' she wrote after attending in late September her first meeting as a member of the Managing Committee of Westlea Hostel for the aftercare of teenage girls. 'They seemed very middle-aged, rather frumpish, and overpoweringly middle class.' Next day she and other committee members visited Dixcot Hostel, a large Edwardian house near Tooting Common that catered for 'difficult' girls of 11–15:

> The hostel is ridiculously spic & span for a *children's* home. Poor little dears, no wonder they spend all their free time out on the Common. The Warden seemed a very stiff person. I should think most children would feel immediately uneasy with him . . . It was like a hotel not a home . . . 'Not a single scribble on the wall' as one handsome well-dressed Tory woman said. One can't help wondering in such a place whether the hostel is run for the children or the adults supposed to be caring for the children . . .[15]

'The publisher who accepted the manuscript told me that it was the sort of book he liked to have on his list, a very reputable work, but of course very few people would want to read it,' recalled Raymond Williams. 'He said: "I've got another book called *The Uses of Literacy*, of which I would say the same."' The publisher was Ian Parsons of Chatto & Windus, and Williams's *Culture and Society, 1780–1950* eventually appeared in September 1958, a year and a half after Hoggart's book and four months after Crossman's disconcerting evening listening to him speak at a New Left meeting. *Culture and Society*, like *Uses*, hugely exceeded expectations: some 200,000 copies sold by 2005, and over the years it has often been identified as the start of 'cultural studies'. Williams was 37, the son of a Welsh railway signalman; via Abergavenny Grammar School, he had gone to Cambridge – for a time falling, like so many, under the influence of the powerfully moralising F. R. Leavis – before (in 1946) becoming an adult education tutor in East Sussex. *Culture and Society* was not his first book, but it was his breakthrough into a much wider readership, and over the next three decades he emerged as arguably the leading British public intellectual.

At the heart of *Culture and Society* was its sympathetic recapitulation of the views of those English writers (including Coleridge, Carlyle, the 'Condition of England' novelists, Mill, Morris, Lawrence and Orwell) who, according to Williams's reading, had reacted, whether from a conservative or a more socialist standpoint, *against* the utilitarian assumptions of laissez-faire industrialism – the phenomenon that in his eyes, looking back over the previous two centuries, was the worm in the Enlightenment bud. Williams wrote with particular warmth, and clear personal empathy, about D. H. Lawrence:

> He had the rich experience of childhood in a working-class family, in which most of his positives lay. What such a childhood gave was certainly not tranquillity or security; it did not even, in the ordinary sense, give happiness. But it gave what to Lawrence was more important than these things: the sense of close quick relationship, which came to matter more than anything else. This was the positive result of the life of the family in a small house, where there were no such devices of separation of children and parents as the sending-away to school, or the handing-over to servants, or the relegation to nursery or playroom ... in such a life, the suffering and the giving of comfort, the common want and the common remedy, the open row and the open making-up, are all part of a continuous life which, in good and bad, makes for a whole attachment.

'A whole attachment': that was the ideal. Raphael Samuel would write illuminatingly after Williams's death of how 'the socialism which he advocated was not a utopian blueprint, but rather the recovery of a lost wholeness ... a matter of age-old solidarities reasserting themselves, in conditions of difficulty, and complexity'.

Where lay that wholeness in the third quarter of the twentieth century? In an ambitious, more explicitly personal concluding chapter, Williams seemed to pin his hopes on 'working-class culture', a culture which he (like Hoggart) contrasted with the inexorably rising, commercialised mass culture, but which he (unlike the pessimistic Hoggart) saw as having an intrinsic, deep-rooted strength that would carry the day. This culture, he insisted,

> is not proletarian art, or council houses, or a particular use of language; it is, rather, the basic collective idea, and the institutions, manners, habits of thought and intentions which proceed from this ... [it] is primarily social (in that it has created institutions) rather than individual (in particular intellectual or imaginative work). When it is considered in context, it can be seen as a very remarkable creative achievement.

Citing Edmund Burke's fear of the 'swinish multitude' trampling down learning, Williams ended this passage by comparing the historical record of collective working-class culture favourably to that of individualistic bourgeois culture: 'This, indeed, is the curious incident of the swine in the night. As the light came, and we could look around, it appeared that the trampling, which we had all heard, did not after all come from them.'

*Culture and Society* was reviewed widely if not always favourably. John Jones in the *New Statesman* noted 'a generosity of temperament which gives moral stature to his work', but Denys Harding, an out-and-out Leavisite, charged Williams in the *Spectator* with failing to 'squarely face the fact that vast numbers of people want, and pay for, rather low-quality work, and only a small public wants work of the quality discriminatingly appraised in this book', while the *TLS* called his approach 'at times suffocatingly abstract'. A typically shrewd, balanced verdict came in *Encounter* from the rising literary critic Frank Kermode. While admiring the book's intelligence, candour and seriousness, he was sceptical about the exaltation of working-class culture – 'I do not feel that it retains the value that Mr Williams allows it. Specially, I think the harm being done by television advertising is catastrophic.' In due course two of the strongest critiques came from a pair of historians much more deeply embedded in the Marxist tradition than Williams himself was at this stage. 'The prime requisite for any study of cultural history is a firm framework of historical fact – economic, social, political ... The one great deficiency of the book is the lack of just this,' declared Victor Kiernan the following summer in the *New Reasoner*. Then later, in its successor journal, E. P. Thompson wrote disparagingly (if fairly) of the book's 'procession of disembodied voices' whose 'meanings' had been 'wrested out of their whole social context'; he particularly mourned the apparent absence of 'struggle', especially class struggle, in Williams's cultural tradition. For most readers, though, in the book's early life, any reservations were far outweighed by a sense of excitement. Williams's first biographer, Fred Inglis, put it best: 'It was a life-changer for young-ish readers in 1960 or so (including me). Its large, never-quite-grasped purpose was to find and recharge the lost veins of English romantic socialism, to make them glow again in the body politic.'[16]

Within a week or two of *Culture and Society*'s publication, an essay by Williams appeared in *Conviction*, a collection edited by Norman MacKenzie. Entitled 'Culture is Ordinary', the piece argued forcibly that, for 'the Socialist intellectual', there were 'no masses to save, to capture, or to direct, but rather this crowded people in the course of an extraordinarily rapid and confusing expansion of their lives'. A year after the Angry Young Men had made their *Declaration*, this was generally a more sober gathering, with the contributors – again, all under 40 – generally on the left of the Labour Party but for the most part at some distance from the New Left. They included the Labour politician Peter Shore, the journalists Paul Johnson and Mervyn Jones, the historian Hugh Thomas and Richard Hoggart, the last with a piece characteristically called 'Speaking to each other', a plea for what he called 'a decent classlessness'. Two essays that attracted particular attention were on welfare issues: Brian Abel-Smith sought to demonstrate that the middle class was benefiting disproportionately from the welfare state, and Peter Townsend, shaping up for what would become almost a lifetime's work, attacked the myth that poverty had been abolished. But arguably the most striking essay was the last, and the only one by a female contributor: 'A house of theory' by Iris Murdoch. Starting with a comprehensive demolition job on the inadequacies of current and recent British philosophy, she then demanded not only a more rigorous, systematic theory of socialism but a return to the ideals of William

Morris – without which, in the alienating conditions of modern industrial life, the 'proletariat' would remain 'a deracinate, disinherited and
excluded mass of people'.

It was stirring if *de haut en bas* stuff, but in the event Murdoch's
subsequent, mainly understated political journey would be to the right,
as ultimately was the trajectory of the collection's already sceptical
reviewer in *Socialist Commentary*. 'I detect in this book a condescen-
sion to the goodness of ordinary people, as opposed to the radicals
whom they philosophically admire, or the careless submerged, whom
they envy but dare not emulate,' wrote John Vaizey. 'I detect a reluctance to live their own ideals.' And he asked:

> What is the socialist vision today? I strongly suspect – much as I detest it
> – that it has more to do with the kind of hunger for achievement that we
> see in the New China than with any Scandinavian arcadia. Either that, or
> the socialist vision is now a private vision; a turning-away from public
> causes; a decision to live one's own life concerned with one's relationship
> with other human beings and with oneself, in which socialism is the
> political equivalent of turning down the neighbour's noisy wireless
> because it interferes with our children's sleep.

Vaizey in 1958 was a young, leftish economist specialising in education,
but in the end he would be the intellectual par excellence who, in Noel
Annan's words about this 'mercurial, erratic, ingenious' man, 'declared
that he [i.e. Vaizey] and his generation had got it wrong and they should
shake out a reef and sail on a new tack'.[17]

Sadly, neither *Declaration* nor *Conviction* took a line on the rapidly
changing built environment, but towards the end of September the
*Architects' Journal*'s 'Astragal' (probably J. M. Richards) described his
recent visit to the almost completed, already part-occupied showpiece
of public housing. 'If you drive across Richmond Park towards the
towering slabs and point blocks of the LCC's Roehampton estate,' he
began, 'you will feel that this is what the approach to a city ought to be
like – open country leading to rolling parkland punctuated by buildings.' Admittedly there were faults – 'the access balconies are sordid
bleak places, and there isn't any relief from the spartan *matières brutes*
once you get inside the maisonettes' – but overall these were 'faults that

are easy to forget when you look at the scheme as a whole and compare it with any other local authority work in this country'. Around this time, one Sunday afternoon, Florence Turtle also had a look:

> We toured Richmond Park & the Roehampton LCC Estate – this latter a terrible eyesore from Richmond Park, it resembles seven or eight tall piles of matchboxes surmounted by a drum, and at some angles it looks like a giant industrial plant. Letters in the 'Telegraph' praising it & others the contrary. I suggest the 'pros' don't have to live in sight of it. The occupants of the flats complain about travel, shopping, & entertainment facilities, during the bus strike they were cut off. They have some justification, many of them rehoused from the East End. To us who appreciate the amenities of the district it is 'The Murder of a Neighbourhood', it used to be one of the loveliest districts in London.

There had indeed been a vigorous correspondence in the *Daily Telegraph*, and a few days later the last word went to W. R. Atherton, who had moved in February into one of the estate's new high-rise flats. 'I found myself at home,' he said, despite not being a natural modernist. 'I hate rock 'n' roll, toneless music, abstract painting, and all sculpture after Jacob Epstein. I am a Cockney in exile. And yet I am content.'

So too in Bristol this autumn, where one sky-blue Saturday morning a local MP inspected Barton House, a new 14-storey block. 'We went right to the roof and visited various flats,' recorded Anthony Wedgwood Benn. 'To see the bright airy rooms with the superb views and to contrast them with the poky slum dwellings of Barton Hill below was to get all the reward one wants from politics. For this grand conception of planning is what it is all about. The people were happy, despite the grumbles about detail.' Up in Sheffield, it was a less grand outlook for Mrs Mary Slinn, who since 1899 had lived at 50 Woodside Lane, Pitsmoor, in a small but comfortable house due to be demolished as part of the Corporation's Burngreave redevelopment scheme. 'Nobody is going to shift me away to some estate outside the town,' she told the *Sheffield Telegraph* a few days before her 90th birthday. 'I am too old to put roots down somewhere else now . . . It doesn't look much, but it is a friendly street. You couldn't ask for nicer neighbours and that means a lot at my age.' In Hertfordshire a whole town, Ware, was seemingly being demolished. 'A holocaust of antiquity', with 'medieval timbers and kingpost roofs, Elizabethan wall-paintings, a Regency assembly room, all gathered round a handsome red-brick Georgian Inn, swept away', was a local description in October of what had been taking place in recent years, with this letter-writer to an architectural magazine adding despairingly of how 'the homeliness of brick and tile is replaced by carpets of concrete dotted with municipal bedding plants'.

In the City of London a wonderful Victorian building by now under threat was the Coal Exchange, recommended for demolition as part of a road-widening proposal. On 25 October *The Times* published a plea from Betjeman, repudiated a few days later by David Young of Sloane Avenue, Chelsea: 'The Coal Exchange may be "a pioneer building in cast iron", to quote Mr Betjeman, but it is in bad repair, cold, dirty, and no longer of any use to the coal industry. We must not be sentimental about buildings of this type.' Would J. B. Priestley have agreed? The day after Betjeman's letter, the BBC broadcast *Lost City*, showing the crusty Yorkshireman making a rare return trip to Bradford, his boyhood city, still strikingly Victorian in character and appearance despite the redevelopment recently under way. For the most part nostalgia ruled, but at the end, as the London train prepared to pull out, he offered his considered verdict on present-day Bradford and how it needed fully to embrace the second half of the twentieth century: 'It's not as good as it promised to be once. It's not bad, but it's not good enough for the real Bradfordians.'

T. Dan Smith had no doubts that the Newcastle of 1958 was not good enough for Geordies. 'I talked a different language,' he recalled about his failure (only 14 votes out of 60) to be elected leader of the city's Labour Party after it had won power in the local elections in May. 'My arguments were about inner cabinets in local government, efficiency as a complement to caring, and planning as the handmaiden of a civilised life. Their talk was of drains and majorities and rates. These were important things, but not priorities in a city which was being strangled by traffic, humiliated by lack of opportunity and murdered by mediocrity.' Instead, he had to make do with the chairmanship of the Housing Committee, where he put new drive into the existing slum-clearance programme and, faced with nearly 10,000 families on the waiting list and no spare building land within the city boundaries, saw no alternative but to build high.

Smith's immediate focus was on Newcastle's rundown West End, including the Scotswood Road area, and that autumn he wrote a long poem
about his hopes and ambitions for it that began by emphasising the determination to clear the 'horrid slums'. Smith was an intelligent, rounded
man, whatever his flaws, and the poem's most interesting passage conveys
a certain ambiguity – even regret – about the process, often a brutal one,
that was now starting to unfold:

> Here and there a gable wall
> Exposing papers to us all –
> Flowered, plain, in stripe or check
> Silent parchments watch men wreck
> As building after building falls
> Leaving exposed those few odd walls;
> Wherein once sheltered windows clean,
> Now only broken glass is seen.

Ultimately, though, he believed there was no alternative, and the final
lines looked ahead to that glorious day almost four years thence, the
centenary of the Blaydon Races:

> Old Scotswood Road must live again
> To carry further still its fame.
> We're soon to have a celebration –
> Let Tynesiders rise in jubilation
> A century has marched along
> Since first we heard that Tyneside song.
> On June the 9th in '62
> We will tell the world anew –
> Together with the sculptors' art,
> A Festival to play its part.
> We'll make Tyneside thus loud proclaim
> How just and right its shout of fame –
> Tomorrow, then, we all will see
> That Scotswood's making history.[18]

In the early days of October, 18-year-old Ronnie Wycherley was auditioned in Birkenhead by the impresario Larry Parnes and would soon be known as Billy Fury; *Saturday Skiffle Club* on the Light Programme transmuted into *Saturday Club* (introduced by Brian Matthew in a non-BBC, cross-class voice); and the first single by Harry Webb (aka Cliff Richard) entered the Top Twenty. 'So rock 'n' roll is dead, is it?' the jazz critic Steve Race had asked in *Melody Maker* in June. 'My funeral oration consists of just two words: good riddance.' An incensed young songwriter, Ian Samwell, had seen Cliff perform at the 2i's coffee bar in Soho and then penned for him an authentic rock 'n' roll number, 'Move It', inspired musically by Chuck Berry. Released in late August, the song was taken up by Jack Good, the strong-minded TV producer who had become disenchanted with the BBC's antiseptic *Six-Five Special*, started *Oh Boy!* on late-night commercial television during the summer, and in September was able to get his fast-paced, cutting-edge show directly competing on Saturday evenings against Pete Murray et al. Good's trump card was Cliff, and vice versa. 'It was Jack who created the beginnings of Cliff Richard,' recalled the singer half a century later. 'He didn't want an Elvis lookalike, so off came the sideburns, away went the guitar, and in came the sneer, the curled lip, and that sultry look up at the camera. I was 100% directed by him but, oh boy, did he know what he was doing.' Not that, even on the pop scene, the pouting young Cliff was everyone's cup of tea. 'Violent hip-swinging and crude exhibitionism', the *New Musical Express* would call his performing style, adding tartly that 'Tommy Steele became Britain's teenage idol without resorting to this form of indecent, short-sighted vulgarity.'[19]

The start of *Saturday Club* on 4 October coincided with the return of a national champion. Back in 1952 the De Havilland Comet had inaugurated the jet age, but three crashes in less than a year meant that all Comets had been grounded from 1954. Four years on, two wholly redesigned Comet IVs now flew the BOAC flag from London to New York – the world's first transatlantic passenger jet service, beating (amidst considerable national satisfaction) Pan Am's Boeing 707 by a little over three weeks. A momentous occasion in the wider transport sense, with 1958 the last year in which more passengers crossed the North Atlantic by sea than by air, it did not in the event signal a lasting British triumph. The process of getting Comet IV into service had been too slow to secure decisive first-mover advantage, the plane's seating capacity was only half that of the 707 or the Douglas DC-8, and it was only a few years before BOAC was looking to Boeing for its long-haul needs. Symbolically, within days of the initial moment of glory, BOAC found itself beset by an unofficial strike of 4,000 maintenance men – a strike overseen by a rising trade unionist, the supremely self-confident and articulate Clive Jenkins. 'While the Comet IV is a delightful aircraft in which to fly,' he observed soon afterwards in his analysis of the dispute, 'it represents a marginal commercial operation. This is easy to see when it stands alongside the large Boeing 707 on the apron at London Airport.' And as for 'the Tories and their plans for hobbling the unions in civil aviation and further traffic-diversions to the under-cutting private operators', he quoted a Spanish proverb: 'Have patience and you will see your enemy's funeral procession.'[20]

Two days after the Comet soared was 'Decontrol Day' – the coming into operation, after a 15-month standstill, of the government's contro-versial Rent Act. Around six million dwellings were owned by private landlords, with some 40 per cent of London's population living in the private rented sector. The purpose of the legislation was to give those landlords an adequate return after many years of rent control and generally to try to restore the forces of supply and demand to the hous-ing market, which ultimately – ministers believed – would help to reduce the dire housing shortage. Many middle-class tenants, enjoying the genteel advantages of protected tenancies and rents, were appalled by the prospect. 'Why should a wicked act be passed?' Mrs Philips Guise in January 1958 asked the Housing Minister, Henry Brooke – an act that allowed 'unscrupulous landlords' to 'put up rents more than double, causing misery and distress to thousands of people who have fought for their country & have always strived to live within their means'. The novelist Ivy Compton-Burnett was especially wrathful. 'The Rent Act is looming over everything here, and it has fallen on me with thunderous force,' she wrote from South Kensington to a friend abroad in September 1957. And again, some nine months later: 'It would be of little good to move as the same thing is happening every-where and there is nothing to be done but suffer it, though in my case not in silence.' To a cousin indeed, she was positively apocalyptic, declaring that 'these are hard days and we are the doomed class'.

Unforeseen by its creators, and presumably not affecting Dame Ivy, the Rent Act would through reducing security of tenure also give birth to 'Rachmanism': in essence, the systematic, often brutal use of intimidating methods by landlords – usually slum landlords – to induce or coerce sitting tenants to leave, so that with vacant possession they could either sell the property at a handsome profit or pack it with new tenants (often West Indian immigrants) paying inflated rents. Perec (Peter) Rachman himself was an immigrant from Poland in his late thirties who by this time had already built up a slum empire of some 70 or 80 houses, mainly in Paddington and North Kensington, by unsavoury means; the new legislation played into the hands of this 'short, chubby-faced, plump and balding' man, who, adds a biographer, 'dressed in silk shirts, cashmere suits and crocodile shoes', as well as always wearing 'dark glasses and a gold bracelet which was locked to his wrist and inscribed with serial numbers of his Swiss bank accounts and safe-combinations'.[21]

Tenants rather than owner-occupiers gathered at White Hart Lane on Saturday the 11th to see Tottenham, with Bill Nicholson as new manager, run out 10–4 winners against Everton (Albert Dunlop in goal). It was not a final score that BBC television's new rolling sports programme, making its debut that afternoon, could immediately bring. *Grandstand*, introduced by Peter Dimmock (who had wanted to call it 'Out and About'), started at two o'clock and featured golf, horse racing and show jumping, but at 4.45 had to give way to *The Lone Ranger* followed by *Jennings at School* before, at 5.40, *Today's Sport*, introduced by Kenneth Wolstenholme, at last gave the football results, read by Len Martin. Elsewhere this Saturday, Philip Larkin in Hull bought a new tie – 'black, with gold horizontal stripes: *nearly* Teddy Boy but not quite, at least I hope not quite', as he informed Monica Jones – and in London Paul Robeson gave a half-hour recital, singing spirituals, during Evensong at St Paul's, with a crowded congregation of 4,000, including many non-whites, watching a significant, reconciling moment some six weeks after Notting Hill.[22]

Culturally, though, the defining event of the weekend was the reviews in the two upmarket Sundays of Alan Sillitoe's first novel, *Saturday Night and Sunday Morning*. 'The rowdy gang of singers who sat at the scattered tables saw Arthur walk unsteadily to the head of the stairs, and though they must all have known that he was dead drunk, and seen the danger he would soon be in, no one attempted to talk to him and lead him back to his seat,' began this story by a working-class Nottingham man of a working-class Nottingham anti-hero, the cynical, hedonistic, newly affluent young Arthur Seaton. 'With eleven pints of beer and seven small gins playing hide-and-seek inside his stomach, he fell from the topmost stair to the bottom.' It struck an immediate chord, with Richard Mayne in the *Sunday Times* praising its 'authenticity, bolshie anarchism' and John Wain in the *Observer* welcoming the realistic characterisation of Seaton, 'not ... a displaced intellectual but a genuine working man, who doesn't hanker for a dimly glimpsed world of books and ideas, but differs from his mates only by being more rebellious'. A few days later, Peter Green in the *Telegraph* was even more complimentary, calling it 'that rarest of all finds: a genuine, no-punches pulled, unromanticised working-class novel'. An alternative type of literary exotica was available this month, though, in the form of Lawrence Durrell's *Mountolive*, the third of his *Alexandria Quartet*, now starting to be provisionally judged as an entity. 'Not much more than an Arabian Nights Entertainment,' was the sceptical view of fellow novelist Pamela Hansford Johnson, who deemed it 'an entrancing, odorous maze without a centre'.[13]

'Looked in at Television, such a lot of it is drivel,' Florence Turtle noted on Thursday 16 October. 'Hughie Green's double your money is quite a good programme, but what a lot of illiterate people they get on it.' In retrospect, though, the main TV event that day had already happened, at five o'clock on the BBC. 'Toys, model railways, games, stories, cartoons' was the subtitle given in the listings for *Blue Peter*, 'a new weekly programme for Younger Viewers, with Christopher Trace and Leila Williams'. He was a handsome 25-year-old actor, she was Miss Great Britain 1957 (and also an active Young Conservative). The under-11 target audience soon gave their verdict:

> Almost without exception they found this programme very enjoyable to watch. For the small boys, of course, Christopher Trace's demonstration of toy trains and model railways was an especial attraction ... The demonstration of mind reading passed almost without comment, but a

number of young viewers (boys and girls alike) seem to have found the cartoon – 'Sparky and the Talking Train' – very appealing.

Children over 11 mainly dismissed the programme as 'babyish', though a few girls 'reacted favourably to the doll collection item' as presented by Williams, who also talked about their trousseaux.

Three days later a daredevil, good-time motor racer from Farnham, 29-year-old Mike Hawthorn, became world champion, courtesy of an act of the utmost sportsmanship by Stirling Moss, who, following a controversial incident at the Portuguese Grand Prix earlier in the season, had given testimony that allowed his rival to keep second place. Hawthorn on becoming champion immediately retired, but for Tommy Steele the next career move was a change of direction, with his manager announcing next day, 'He wants to get away from rock 'n' roll,' in the context of Steele signing a film contract to play a British seaman who gets involved in a Spanish bullfight. By this time, Monday the 20th, the president of the German Federal Republic, Dr Theodor Heuss, had begun a state visit. 'The sight of Germany's black, red, and gold flying alongside the Union Jack on government buildings has given many Londoners a mighty queer feeling,' commented Mollie Panter-Downes, adding that along the Mall 'most of the crowds watched silently when he drove past them in the open royal carriage'. No doubt some had been reading the *Mirror*'s 'Cassandra', who that day categorically called Germany 'the cause of the greatest bloodshed and misery the world has ever known' and insisted that 'Papa' Heuss, for all his 'good manners', would be unable to 'wash away the nature of the nation that he represents'. Two days later the unforgiving columnist reprised, arguing that 'the ageing professor has successfully been sold to an amiable but significantly silent British public, as a benign and scholarly man', though in reality 'a skilful apologist for the German people'; he signed off with a reference to 'the stench of the gas ovens still in the air'.[24]

That same day, Wednesday the 22nd – three weeks after being 'tremendously heartened' by how on his tour of the West Midlands 'everyone seemed very cheerful & very friendly', and four days after noting that 'the Socialists are working up a "slump" scare', with unemployment having tipped over the then politically invidious half a million mark – Macmillan recorded a cardinal moment in the pre-election cycle:

I had a good talk today with the Chancellor of the Ex$^r$ on the 64,000 dollar question – is it a boom? is it a slump? is it slack water? If the last, will the tide go in or out? The people have now a pathological fear of even a little unemployment. Yet 1% means *over*-employment and a financial crisis. 3% means almost a political crisis . . .

It is a great pleasure to talk with Heathcoat Amory, after having dealt with Thorneycroft. The former is *very* intelligent, flexible, & courteous. The latter was fundamentally stupid, rigid, & 'cassant'. We agreed on the things we *might* do to 'reflate' the economy.

Five days later, on the 27th, the government announced the end of the remaining restrictions on hire purchase and the renting of goods: no longer would it be compulsory to make a minimum deposit of one-third or to pay in advance for the first four months' rental. 'We can give this extra bit of freedom because the credit squeeze and the other stern measures we took a year ago have worked,' declared the president of the Board of Trade, Sir David Eccles, though the *Manchester Guardian* observed cautiously that 'no Chancellor can lose sight of the balance of payments' and that the government was bound to be criticised for having 'favoured consumption before investment'. The public, however, was willing to take the risk: a Gallup poll soon afterwards revealed 58 per cent approval for this green light and only 26 per cent disapproval.[25]

Tuesday the 28th saw the state opening of Parliament being televised for the first time, with two commentators in direct competition. As 'Her Majesty returns to the Robing Room and thence to Buckingham Palace,' solemnly intoned the BBC's Richard Dimbleby near the end, 'she leaves behind in all of us, a memory of a state occasion at its most magnificent.' Over on ITV, Robin Day was altogether crisper and more informal: 'The crown will go back to the Tower of London. All the scarlet and ermine robes will go back to wherever they came from. And Parliament will go back to work.' In the afternoon, Gladys Langford again 'went 'bussing': 'Finsbury Park – Golders Green – Victoria – Green Park – Highbury Barn. But my world is gone. Cliff-like flats, girl children in colourful pants, old women raddled & "permed".' That evening Anthony Heap dutifully attended the Royal Court for the first night of Samuel Beckett's *Krapp's Last Tape* and *Endgame* ('these dreary sleep-inducers'), and Dr Bronowski's guests on ITV's *New Horizon* programme, discussing the good and bad effects of science, were Aldous and Julian Huxley. 'Move It' was meanwhile moving up the charts – number 3 by the end of the week, tucked behind Connie Francis's 'Stupid Cupid' and Elvis's 'King Creole' – while on Saturday 1 November *Grandstand*-watchers noted a changing of the guards, with Dimmock now co-presenting with an unknown face, 32-year-old David Coleman. Then from the 8th it was Coleman on his own.

The new man was, in Frank Keating's apt words, 'smart, street-wise and regional', having previously been the first non-international athlete to win the Manchester Mile and played for Stockport County reserves as well as working on the *Stockport Express* and in the BBC newsroom in Birmingham. The time was ripe for a new, non-public-school approach to covering sport. 'Out,' as Jim White puts it, 'went the clipped, detached, patronising dinner-jacket style inherited from radio presentation, and in came a much more engaged manner.' It was an elevation that undoubtedly owed much to *Grandstand*'s producer, the fiercely driven 31-year-old Bryan Cowgill, who had been to grammar school in Clitheroe and was at this stage convinced that his lack of a university education would block his progress at the BBC.[26] Coleman and Cowgill: part of a fresh breed – call them meritocrats – whose hour was seemingly at hand.

The Bradford Empire just before demolition, 1957

Birmingham, May 1957: Aston Villa players and mascot parade the
FA Cup at Villa Park

Unrationed sweets: London, 1957

Clarendon Crescent, Paddington, 1957

Notting Hill at night, 1958

Fishermen carry coracles to the River Teifi in Cardiganshire, March 1958

Cherry-picking: West Malling, Kent, July 1958

Redevelopment in Everton Heights, Liverpool, 1959

Youth club float, New Malden, Surrey, July 1959

St George's Day parade, St Helier Estate, South London, 1959

Harold Macmillan (*right*) in the north-east, January 1959

Hugh Gaitskell (*left*) at the Midland Area Miners' Gala, June 1959

Election night, October 1959

# 9

# Parity of Esteem

Just as Coleman was preparing to take the hot seat (and a peasant's son was being elected Pope John XXIII), the first reviews started to appear of Michael Young's *The Rise of the Meritocracy* – the book for which he would be remembered even more than *Family and Kinship*. Contrary to subsequent assumptions, Young did not in fact coin the term *meritocracy*: two years earlier, writing in *Socialist Commentary* (a magazine to which Young contributed), the sociologist Alan Fox had put the word in quotation marks and defined it as 'the society in which the gifted, the smart, the energetic, the ambitious and the ruthless are carefully sifted out and helped towards their destined positions of dominance, where they proceed not only to enjoy the fulfilment of exercising their natural endowments but also to receive a fat bonus thrown in for good measure'. But it was certainly Young who popularised it.

The book itself – in which 'Intelligence and effort together make up merit (I + E = M)' – is set in 2034 and comprises two parts. The first traces the rise, well under way by 1958, of a meritocratic elite chosen largely through intelligence-testing and educational selection; the second relates the disturbing consequences, as those deemed unmeritorious become an increasingly alienated underclass, with the threat looming by the 2030s of a 'Populist' revolution. Although the first part reveals Young as far from unsympathetic to the meritocratic case, ultimately the book is a dystopian warning against a rampant, self-serving, IQ-driven, intolerant meritocracy. 'Were we to evaluate people, not only according to their intelligence and their education, their occupation, and their power, but according to their kindliness and their courage, their imagination and sensitivity, their sympathy and generosity, there could be no classes,' asserts the 'Chelsea Manifesto', issued by a local group of the Technicians Party (as the Labour Party has been rebranded) in 2009. 'Who would be able to say that the scientist was superior to the porter with admirable qualities as a father, the civil servant with unusual skill at gaining prizes superior to the lorry driver with unusual skill at growing roses?'[1]

The notices were respectful rather than wholly enthusiastic. The *Financial Times* waited 'in vain for the sound of a human voice or a glimpse of earthy people'; the *TLS* reckoned the final revolt 'too sketchily contrived to be convincing'; and in the *Spectator* the literary critic Boris Ford regretted that Young's satire 'operates at a comparatively simple debating level', with 'little command of the undertones of irony, let alone of the verbal compression, that one associates with Swift'. On the substance of the satire, Young was attacked from both directions. 'He seems to think that if we now chose comprehensive schools, with a common curriculum for all children, the cleavage in society would never take place,' observed *The Times*. 'But in a country whose economic survival depends on discovering and promoting the best brains, even such schools would still be selective instruments. There is no getting away from the rise of the meritocracy in a scientific world.' By contrast, reviewing in the *Manchester Guardian*, Raymond Williams was unconvinced by the reach of the new meritocracy: 'I see no evidence, in contemporary England, of *power* being more closely connected with merit, in any definition. The administrators, professional men and technicians are increasingly being selected on educational merit, but the power is still largely elsewhere, "and no damned merit about it".'

Perhaps the most searching critique, looking ahead and similarly sceptical, came from Charles Curran in *Encounter*, arguing that Young was 'guilty of a gross over-simplification' in assuming that 'the road to Meritocracy' lay wide open without obstacles. Instead, he contended, 'the British masses', far from seeking a meritocracy, 'want a society that protects and cares for the untalented many', and he identified 'three great barriers to the attainment of Meritocracy in Britain', which collectively were 'impregnable': first, an increasingly elderly electorate, who had 'outlived their competitive years' and were now 'social pacifists, against change and struggle'; second, the power of the family unit,

involving parents 'caring fiercely, irrationally, instinctively, combat-
ively' for their offspring, so that the family was 'the historic fortress of
favouritism, the nest of nepotism, the protective shell that guards the
dull, the timid, the slow, the non-competitive weakling'; and third, the
deep roots in British history of status being 'fixed by inheritance and
tradition, rather than achieved as a prize in competitive struggle'. In
short, Young had constructed a meritocratic straw man. And, he added,
'the lower classes need not start advertising for a Spartacus just yet'.[2]

But undoubtedly, even if their numbers and potency were exaggerated, the meritocrats – advancing largely by dint of their own endeavours, as opposed to socio-economic background and connection – were
on the march in the course of the 1950s, and Young's analysis was
tapping into a real trend.

'Lucky Jim Dixon is the first hapless hero to climb from the crib of
the Welfare State,' Philip Oakes wrote in the *Evening Standard* in
September 1957, almost four years after Kingsley Amis had given birth
to a literary-cum-social phenomenon. 'His bones are reinforced by
Government dried milk. His view of the world is through National
Health spectacles. And he looks back – not in anger – but with surprise,
that he has been allowed to barge through the privileged ranks of bores
and phonies, towards some kind of success.' In short, 'he is the man
most likely to move into the room at the top'. The last four words had
a particular resonance, just six months after the publication of John
Braine's instantly best-selling novel *Room at the Top*, the story of the
aspirational, socially climbing, lower-middle-class (like Braine himself)
Joe Lampton, newly arrived in a prosperous northern provincial town.
'A callous, ambitious, sexy L-cky J-m,' declared John Davenport in his
*Observer* review. 'He is a ruthless rather than an angry young man.'
Over the summer, Richard Crossman read this 'nauseating new vulgar-
ized Lucky Jim book' and pondered its success. 'It is lower middle-
class, anti-working-class, describing the working classes as dirty, smelly
people, eating fish and chips and favouring the upper class as people
who have tiled bathrooms and beautiful voices.' Only a Wykehamist,
of course, could fail to appreciate the allure of tiled bathrooms, and
over the next few years Joe Lampton increasingly replaced Jim Dixon
as the symbol of new, meritocratic social forces dynamically and
hungrily on the move.

'GRAMMAR SCHOOL BOYS DID IT' was the *Daily Sketch*'s exultant headline in January 1958 after the Atomic Energy Authority announced that a team of young British scientists at Harwell had produced the world's first controlled fusion reaction. This was ZETA, the Zero-Energy Thermonuclear Assembly, 'a 120-ton yellow and black painted reactor' that was a man-made sun on earth and held out the promise of limitless fuel. Sadly, that promise flattered to deceive, but the emphasis on 'a team of grammar school and scholarship boys' was a reminder of how the scientific and technological thrust of grammar schools and red-brick universities was an increasingly frequent element in the advance of the new men. Two of engineering's notable new men by the late 1950s were James Drake and Denis Rooke. Drake, Accrington-born and spiky, was Britain's first great motorway creator, with a vision of roads like 'sculpture on an exciting, grand scale', carving and moulding 'earth, rock and minerals into a finished product'; the lantern-jawed, no-nonsense Rooke, in his mid-thirties and the son of a south London commercial traveller, had recently joined the North Thames Gas Board to explore the crucial possibility of importing natural gas. In 1959 he was in charge of the technical team aboard the *Methane Pioneer*, as it transported liquefied gas from the Gulf of Mexico to Canvey Island on a storm-tossed, 23-day voyage.[3]

The meritocratic businessman was also afoot, with a trio poised around the end of the 1950s for great things. For the implacably rational Arnold Weinstock, son of Jewish refugees from Poland, the start of a remarkable career in electronic manufacturing was the 30-year-old's arrival in 1954 at the firm of his father-in-law Michael Sobell, who made radio and television sets. 'With colossal self-confidence he immediately took charge, largely ignoring his 63-year-old father-in-law, who was suffering from prostate problems,' records a biographer. 'Weinstock concentrated on producing – efficiently and profitably – basic products that worked, in contrast to his competitors, dominated by engineers who did not believe as did Weinstock that "the customer is king".' By 1958, when the firm was floated under the name of Radio and Allied, Weinstock was 'established as among the most formidable operators in the whole electrical sector'. At the textile manufacturers Courtaulds, the rising star was Frank Kearton, whose way to the top was blocked

by the ageing, indeed failing, Sir John Hanbury-Williams. The thrust-
ing Kearton had been educated at Hanley High School, the gentlemanly
Hanbury-Williams at Wellington College, and the former's 'barely
concealed contempt' was reciprocated by the latter's 'active dislike'.
There were no tantrums at the merchant bank Schroders, where Gordon
Richardson was on a rapid upward curve. The son of a Nottingham
provision merchant, he had become a successful barrister before in 1955
trying his luck in the financial world, going to the Industrial and
Commercial Finance Corporation (the future 3i). There he was
unhappy, according to a mole, because 'it is not the kind of business nor
does he in general meet the sort of people which he hoped for when he
left the Bar'. But by 1957 this handsome, imposing, intelligent man,
vanity his only Achilles heel, was ensconced among the City's crème de
la crème, just as the post-war revival of the Square Mile was at last
getting under way.[4]

Inevitably, the meritocrats – almost all of them male – would flourish especially in the media and the arts. Robert Robinson, a product of
Raynes Park County Grammar School under the famed headmaster-
ship of John Garrett, wrote sardonic radio criticism for the *Sunday
Times* and from 1959 was the astringent presenter of television's *Picture
Parade* about current films. The *Manchester Guardian*'s features editor
Brian Redhead, son of a Newcastle printer, would also make the transition to the small screen, though in his inveterately loquacious case
radio ultimately loomed. Another northern journalist, Harold Evans,
son of a railwayman, was a wiry, energetic assistant editor of the
*Manchester Evening News*; meanwhile Jean Rook, Hull-born daughter of an engineer and an usherette, was gearing up on the *Sheffield
Telegraph* to take on the world. Keith Waterhouse, whose father
walked about Leeds selling produce from a barrow, was on the *Daily
Mirror* and by 1958 writing his second novel, about an undertaker's
assistant (as he himself had been) who was a habitual fantasist; another
young novelist, Malcolm Bradbury, first-generation grammar school
let alone university, debuted in 1959 with *Eating People is Wrong*,
about the dilemmas of a red-brick university professor. The as yet
unpublished B. S. Johnson, undergraduate at King's College London
and son of a stock-keeper, threw a party at his parents' home in Barnes,
but not before taking down from the wall of the lounge the three

horribly tell-tale flying ducks, unfortunately leaving marks that
provoked amused comments. John Carey, accountant's son and from a
grammar school in East Sheen, had his first teaching job at Christ
Church, Oxford, full of window-smashing public schoolboys, and
spent his time 'totting up how much more their clothes had cost than I
earned'; a more attractively self-possessed Oxford undergraduate, Ian
Hamilton, launched the literary magazine *Tomorrow*, having already
at grammar school in Darlington started *The Scorpion* and got Kingsley
Amis, Angus Wilson and Cecil Day Lewis among others to contribute.
Two young, already well-established theatre directors, Tony
Richardson (son of a pharmacist) and Peter Hall (son of a stationmaster), were facing the future with high artistic ambition and seemingly
inexhaustible drive, while John Thaw, son of a Mancunian lorry driver,
arrived as a 16-year-old at RADA in 1958 'dressed like a typical teddy
boy', whereas 'the other kids all looked so bloody superior, I've never
felt so alone in all my life'. Stanley Baker, from the Rhondda Valley
and close to rivalling Dirk Bogarde as Britain's leading male film star,
brought working-class machismo and sexual arrogance to Joseph
Losey's 1959 *Blind Date*; that same year Terence Donovan, from the
Mile End Road, set up his own studio, just before Leytonstone's David
Bailey, while the third of what Cecil Beaton would ruefully call 'The
Terrible Three' of fashion photographers, East Ham's Brian Duffy,
was already shooting for *Vogue*, 'an easy way to make money'. A defiantly non-fashion photographer, Don McCullin, whose Finsbury Park
childhood had been dominated by weekly trips to the pawn shop, had
his picture of a gang posing on an old bombed-out building published
by the *Observer* in 1959 and suddenly was in demand ('that little thing
inside me knew this was the only hope of having a life'). The artist
Peter Blake, son of a Dartford electrician, was starting to embrace, in a
contemporary yet nostalgic way, the popular culture of postcards and
pin-ups. The self-educated, self-made Bryan Robertson, who had had
a hard childhood in Battersea, was several years into the directorship
of the Whitechapel Art Gallery and becoming the witty, generous
presiding spirit of the British art world. Zandra Rhodes, her mother a
fitter at a fashion house, was at Medway College of Art; Lionel Bart,
son of an East End tailor, wrote his first songs for Tommy Steele and
enjoyed claiming he could not tell the difference between A flat and a

council flat; and Joe Meek, whose father had run a fish-and-chip shop on the edge of the Forest of Dean, was the engineer on 'Last Train to San Fernando' and, by 1958, was writing home that 'I'm sure your Son is going to be famous one day Mum, as things are going I am very well known in the whole record world and have a very good name too.'[5]

Few if any of that gallery, though, were classic meritocrats – 'classic' in the sense of passing the triple historical test of (a) being born in 1933 or later, (b) being working-class and (c) going to grammar school as a direct beneficiary of the 1944 Education Act and using that education as a ladder for further advancement. It was those meritocrats who were, par excellence, 'Britain's New Class', as sharply described in *Encounter* in February 1958 by Frank Hilton, himself from a grammar school (though born in 1929) and now a teacher:

> Our underdogs are on the move today . . . In some ways everything and anything is possible. But they don't know where to start. They have no background that could have nursed their talents and trained them how to use them. They have only their intelligence, their energy, and too much choice. So they have no confidence and approach everything with suspicion. They loathe the scullery, the kitchen, and the front room they've left behind, and most of them – whatever they may care to say to the contrary – look upon their mums and dads as semi-prehistoric creatures, evolutionary missing links between the gin-and-work-sodden 19th-century working-class ape-man and the modern Grammar School-Redbrick university-Sergeants'/Officers' Mess working-class 'cream'.

This arguably overheated depiction prompted Joe Lampton's creator to respond from Bingley. 'As for the New Men,' predicted Braine, 'they will be quite content with a little house, car, wife, TV, and a bottle of gin in the sideboard. And if they work hard enough they will get them. And what on earth is wrong with that? Only a tiny minority, thank God, ever wants power.'

Dennis Potter was undeniably a classic meritocrat. The son of a coal miner in the Forest of Dean, he went to Bell's Grammar School in Coleford and then, in 1956, to New College, Oxford, richly populated with Wykehamists and Etonians. 'The few other grammar-school boys were creeps, adopting as many mannerisms of Oxford as they could and distancing themselves from their past,' he recalled. 'I took to being aggressive and making an issue of it.' Part of that aggression was keeping his accent intact, and he rapidly began to make a university name for himself as both a debater and an actor, as well as writing for *Isis*, with a first article unashamedly describing his personal background. 'There's nothing more terrifying than a young man on the make,' he conceded many years later. 'And of course I was feeling these things, but at the same time I was manipulating the very feelings that I was in a sense enduring. Therefore I went out of my way [to say] "My father is a miner." Which of course is a slightly more complicated sort of betrayal.' Potter's second year featured an acrimonious spat with fellow undergraduate Brian Walden, an article in the *New Statesman* on being torn between two worlds and a book contract for a state-of-the-nation tract, culminating in August 1958 in a lengthy interview on a BBC television documentary about class. 'Do you want to become classless, Mr Potter?' asked Christopher Mayhew. 'No,' he replied. 'Well, I did at one stage, I think, like most people from the working classes want to get away from the working class, but I certainly want to keep a sense of identity, as it were, with that background.' Yet, as Potter went on to explain, that sense of identity was far from untroubled:

> By now my father is forced to communicate with me almost, as it were, with a kind of contempt, now and again. It is inevitable. I mean, he does everything he can possibly do to get through to me, and I to him, but it is just that our circumstances make this communication rather difficult. I mean, he is likely to ask me a question through my mother, for example. And a little thing like the allocation of radio time – it might seem small, petty. If I want something on which is likely to be – in fact very often is – very different from what the rest of the family want, then, well, this is likely to spotlight the tensions. The little petty things like that. I mean, I have a row with my sister, inevitably, over whether we should have something like *Life with the Lyons* on, or not. And, well, I – it's at times like this that I think, oh darn, why does one have one way of life, and you just can't come to terms with it ever again?

Potter by his last year was an established star at the Oxford Union – 'in a slashing peroration he denounced the Tory chrome-plated coffee-bar civilization,' reported Peter Jay in November 1958 – and, after taking an undistinguished Second (having barely worked) he slipped into a BBC traineeship in July 1959.

Two other 'classics' began at Oxford in 1957, a year after Potter. 'My room in Somerville was on the ground floor of the library block, a large, square, high-ceilinged room with a mullioned window overlooking a lawn shadowed by a huge cedar tree,' remembered Margaret Forster, daughter of a fitter at the Metal Box factory in Carlisle. 'It was easily four times the size of any room at home and the sheer space thrilled me.' Writing essays about medieval history proved less thrilling – 'it was such an unreal task, so removed from my mother's life' – but Forster loved being pulled into a different social and political world. 'I'd thought political allegiances were according to class and money but now I saw they could not be – it was as odd that my working-class mother voted Tory as that my Somerville friends voted Labour. They were all upper middle class, all from wealthy (to me) homes, and yet they all passionately wanted to align themselves with the working class.' In the more traditional (and right-wing) culture of a men's college, her contemporary Melvyn Bragg, son of an RAF sergeant and (later) publican, was making a largely cautious transition from Wigton in Cumberland to Wadham College. 'I took it all on "their" terms,' he reflected many years later. 'I was trying to learn the secrets of those in the educational and social citadel.' Significantly, this did not lead to chippiness:

> I knew an awful lot they didn't, but I sort of thought it didn't count. I mean, at breakfast in college they'd have really detailed conversations about Africa or Malaysia. Some of these men had led people into battle. But I'd been to places like Manchester and Blackburn about which they knew nothing. I knew about a whole range of life that simply didn't appear on their agenda. It was as if your past was locked away at the age of 18, as if they were saying 'put that away, you won't need that for the journey, dump that over the side of the stagecoach'. I didn't resent it, frankly, I just thought 'that's the way it is.'[6]

*Crossing the Lines* would be the title of Bragg's subsequent novel about his Oxford experience. Probably for most meritocrats, certainly including him, they were at this point not enemy lines.

---

For Potter, Forster and Bragg, as also for Ian McKellen, Trevor Nunn, Tom Courtenay, Alan Plater, Alan Bennett, Alan Bates, Glenda Jackson, Hunter Davies, Joan Bakewell, Neil Kinnock, Tim Bell, David Hockney, Roy Strong, Dudley Moore and many other meritocrats starting (or about to start) to come through by the late 1950s, the grammar school had been the formative, indispensable education. 'What is the most important factor in getting to the top?' a *Sunday Times* survey into teenage aspirations asked in 1959. Specifically, was it hard work or personality? Among public school boys, 48 per cent plumped for hard work and 45 per cent for personality. Among grammar school boys, the respective figures were 80 per cent and 16 per cent. Going to a grammar was of course a variable experience, both within the school and between schools. But a trio of retrospective accounts for these years is particularly suggestive about an educational world where for the most part charm was not the name of the game.

Anton Rippon's recollections of Bemrose School, Derby (1956–61) are largely benign. He enjoyed the daily morning assembly (Victorian hymns accompanied by the magnificent school organ) and was appreciative of the general lack of bullying; his only real complaints were over the 'silly rules', especially the regulation school cap to and from school, and the house system, 'particularly because of its obsession with cross country running', an obsession that once caused him to be 'spectacularly sick' at the top of Rykneld Rec hill 'not long after I'd enjoyed two helpings of treacle pudding and custard on the second sitting for school dinner'.

Mary Evans's take on her unnamed girls' grammar (1957–64) in her trenchant memoir-cum-essay *A Good School*, is markedly more critical – though with a similar exasperation about the petty rules, such as 'never going upstairs on buses (since they were apparently dens of iniquity, or more precisely men smoking cigarettes), always wearing our school hats in the streets, never walking along a pavement more than two abreast, never, ever, eating in the street, never going outside in our indoor shoes and never bringing into the school either sweets or books or magazines that were not part of our school work'. During these years, she notes, 'pupils were still sufficiently intimidated by the authority of their teachers to believe that school rules had the force of absolute law'.

It was the first year, though, that set the tone, a year in which Evans not only had her posture continuously assessed (with the reward of a posture stripe, to be sewn into her navy-blue tunic, if she proved herself not to be a sloucher), but spent all the domestic-science lessons on smocking a pinafore – seemingly futile and pointless, but 'we were quite explicitly told that our performance at this task would be taken as a measure of our "patience" and our ability to do something called "work steadily".' Indeed, the emphasis throughout was on diligence and steadiness, with Aesop's fable of the hare and the tortoise 'much favoured as an illustration of the virtues of plodding away'. With the academic work, teachers imparted the inflexible virtues of what she calls 'the conventional sandwich essay' (defined as 'beginning with a proposition to examine, examine it and then reach a conclusion'), and where 'to have an essay returned as "badly organised" was the greatest shame'. Was it an ultra-competitive environment? Evans's answer is interestingly nuanced: yes, in the sense that there was rigorous stream-ing from the start, and at one level the dominant ethos was all about individual achievement, yet at the same time, by sixth form anyway, 'our civics classes were weekly exercises in being taught that individuals were not allowed to act merely for themselves'. Altogether, she reck-ons, 'a reliable product, the grammar school child, emerged at the end of a seven-year education, and the product was reliably well schooled in writing legibly, writing grammatically, being punctual and having at least the appearance of respect for authority'. *A Good School*, written in the early 1990s, ends with a thought as double-edged as its title: 'We emerged into the adult world with extensive and authoritative evidence of our ability to carry out given tasks and to live a disciplined and sober life. Little wonder that many people still dream fondly of the institu-tions that apparently created us.'

Roy Greenslade is the most negative of the three. Looking back on his time (from 1958) at Dagenham County High School (very far from one of the country's top-rated grammars), he highlights 'the communication barrier' between the middle-class staff and mainly working-class pupils; the widespread disaffection and divisiveness, caused in his analysis by a mixture of the streaming system, the pressure of exams and differences in home status; the general absence of class-room discussion, with teachers 'preferring instead the these-are-the-facts-now-go-away-and-learn-them approach'; and the prevailing conformity, with 'dissent the school's dirtiest word'. Caustically, Greenslade describes the education that he received as 'simply a five-year course in how to succeed without understanding why':

> At school the propaganda was subtle, but it combined well with the thrust from home. 'Pupils, you are in a privileged position; take your chances while you can; don't fall behind; don't end up like the secondary modern layabouts; there really is room at the top.' Classroom competition was fostered with the front-runners constantly exhorted to do better; and those at the bottom put under pressure to do much, much better. I hardly need add that the sports field was another element in the same indoctrination.

Accordingly, 'the boys of County High emerged into the adult world bursting with enthusiasm for little more than money', a long way removed from 'the once-favoured ideal that grammar schools would carry on the public school tradition of training for community service'. And when Greenslade interviewed many of his contemporaries in the mid-1970s, he was dismayed by their apathy and complacency towards the wider world – characteristics that he largely attributed to the narrow, reductive efficiency of their grammar-school training.

Ashby-de-la-Zouch Boys' Grammar School was almost certainly of a higher standing than Dagenham County High, perhaps somewhere in the middle range. The report in the school magazine for 1957–8 about the activities of the Literary and Debating Society, written by a sixth-former, nicely conveys the grammar culture – not least its ineradicable whiff of priggishness – in this its final classic phase:

> *3rd October, 1957*
> In two embryo debates, we considered the relative merits of BBC and Commercial Television *and* the advisability of continuing experiments

with nuclear weapons. The eloquence and humour elicited by the former discussion was soon surpassed by the zest with which the scientists defended their colleagues' activities, to the great joy of the members.

*17th October, 1957*
The House debated the motion 'That gambling is socially and morally indefensible'. Impassioned appeals to our conscience earned little but scorn and eventually the suffrage of precisely half our number: the Chairman's casting vote alone preserved the Society's reputation for moral rectitude, while the need for it left room for grave doubts.

*20th February, 1958*
Candidates ranging from *Machiavelli* to *Gilbert Harding* were proposed to fill the last place in Heaven; every speaker had cogent arguments for his protégé, and it is doubtful whether the final choice of *Babyface Nelson*, the notorious American gangster, reflects genuine anarchical sympathies, or merely the eloquence of his advocate.[7]

Of course, these debaters were only there because they had passed the 11-plus. The exam itself was usually taken in January and often at the actual grammar school, with masters invigilating. 'Even I feel nervous,' wrote one in 1957 about the experience of superintending a classroom of excited hopefuls:

The starting bell makes one sallow child visibly start, but only for a second. Immediately all are at work: their fingers nervously nicked to their pens, their lips pursed or tacitly murmuring as they do their sums. Somehow they looked years older than when they came in; already on their foreheads frowns are beginning to appear which time will etch more deeply. Ten minutes have passed; according to my instructions, I remind them that there are more questions on the other pages of their answer books. Some have already started on them. Some have finished five minutes before the end of the fifty-minute paper.

After a ten-minute interval they get down to English ('Do not forget to put your number on the top of the paper'). Now I begin to see them more clearly. There is little difference in their size although the two largest boys are already in long trousers. Only two of the thirty wear glasses.

Some are in their Sunday suits, others wear cardigans and sweaters, sometimes with a watch (Dad's or Uncle's?) fastened over the sleeve. Somehow it seems that the most poorly dressed have the grandest fountain pens.

One boy upsets his ink-well; I help him to mop up the ink which has divided his answer book into blue and white sections. I notice that his hand shakes. Another boy absorbed in work sits on his own leg and rather dirty shoe. Yet another picks his nose and then puts his finger in his mouth. I feel embarrassed that he has noticed that I have noticed; he probably thinks that I will take a mark off!

I wonder if it is possible to estimate their intelligence from their physiognomy. Surely that intense boy with the tousled hair is intelligent? I walk up the aisle only to discover that he not written down anything. His vacant-looking neighbour who has at least half a dozen badges on the lapels of his green blazer has half-finished the paper.

At the end of English they go out to break, and I warn them to use the toilets before returning to the classroom. In the Common Room where I go for coffee they are discussing the illiteracy of some of the candidates and the foolhardiness of some of the examiners. Somebody says that even the Parliamentary Secretary to the Ministry of Education has not been able to do some of the questions that have been set. No wonder that two candidates have been sick and one has had a fit.

Back to the classroom for the General Paper ('Put your examination number . . .') and then English Composition ('. . . at the top of the paper'). Some children have their own personal spelling ('cushion' for 'cousin'; 'duck' for 'Dutch'; 'arrisen' for 'horizon'), others write very creditable conversation passages in idiomatic prose. Only two write in italic hand; their penmanship creates a very favourable impression when contrasted with the others. One boy in describing 'An Enjoyable Outing' describes a trip to France; in another row a boy describes 'the flicks and fish an chips and sweets.'

At last, at 12.30, the final bell shatters the silence. I collect in the papers and tell them to be careful crossing the road. They become young again, and some even say 'Ta-ta, sir!' as they leave the room. It is over. Some parents are already at the school gates to take their offspring home after what for most will be their one and only visit to a grammar school.

So much, in every sense, depended. Jacky Aitken (later Jacqueline Wilson), from Kingston in Surrey, sat the exam that year and had 'one of those head-filled-with-fog colds, when you can't breathe, you can't hear, you can't taste, you certainly can't *think*'. The result was a nightmare ('I'd never felt so frightened in my life'), especially the arithmetic test ('I couldn't calculate in my bunged-up head, I had to use my ten fingers, like an infant') and the number sequences in the intelligence test. A year later, on a Friday morning in January 1958, it was the turn of Ione Haines at Chingford. 'I feel sick,' noted an apprehensive Judy, but Ione herself 'awoke happily and tucked in to a three-course breakfast'. They set off for the High School, Ione taking with her the '"success" cards' she had received and 'many lucky charms, including 3*d* bit from Daddy'; nearing their destination, 'the children poured off buses and along to the school in the snow'. An anxious few hours followed, before Ione returned at lunchtime, 'eyes shining, and saying she had had a lovely time', with 'questions not too bad', and that 'she enjoyed using my fountain pen'.

Then came the waiting. Eventually, Jacky was informed by her primary teacher, in front of the class, that she had failed and ought to be ashamed of herself, leaving the poor girl to tell her parents. As for Ione, her mother's diary recorded the outcome:

> *24 April.* Gwen had told me 11+ results would be out today and I waited and waited for post. Suddenly I wondered if a tearful Ione would come home from school. Relieved this was not so and nobody appears to have heard anything.

> *25 April.* No post.
> Ione came rushing home from school with the good news that she *has passed General Admission Examination*. What a thrill! We 'phoned Daddy, me in tears . . .
> By the way, the official card came at mid-day.

A year or so later, in the Cheshire village of Bunbury, there was elation too at the Blakemore home after a little brown envelope popped through the door:

I'd come downstairs to get some breakfast and found Mum waiting for me in the hall, smiling. And then something totally unexpected happened. With a whoop of joy she held me round the middle and danced around the hall with me.

It was one of those moments that stay with you forever. The fresh green summer morning, sunlight dappling through the windows, the threadbare carpet on the stairs, the press of my mother's apron against my face, the giddy feeling as she swept me off my feet. And all this from a mother who'd rarely put her arm around me. For those few seconds I'd been grabbed and returned to early childhood.

When she stopped I smiled, embarrassed. It felt good, though the evident relief and joy in her face led me to wonder whether my parents had really expected me to fail. From Dad I just got a cheery smile and a 'well done' as he sat at the breakfast table neatly polishing off his bacon and tomato.

Ken Blakemore then went to school, where he found that though two of his friends had passed, the one who had really wanted to, Clive Bevan, had failed: 'He was sullen, red-faced with anger and disappointment, and couldn't bring himself to talk to us.' Several months later, in September after Ken had started at the grammar, he decided to go round to see Clive at his home, a little bungalow. 'It was an attempt to ask whether we could still be friends. We couldn't. He couldn't wait for me to leave.'

Passing the exam did not necessarily clinch the deal. A quite common impediment was financial, despite the 1944 Act, and revolved round the purchase of a uniform and other expensive, compulsory accoutrements. 'They felt exploited by having to go to the school's selected outfitters and paying prices they, rightly or wrongly, felt were higher than elsewhere,' recalled Roy Greenslade about Dagenham's working-class parents. 'For some it was undoubtedly a financial burden and a real sacrifice. For a few, it was an impossibility and their children were never equipped in County High's sombre black, blue and white.' Another possibility was that the child might demur. In May 1958, for instance, Kent Education Committee notified John Jones that his son David (the future Ziggy Stardust) had, having passed his 11-plus, a choice between Bromley Grammar and the new Bromley Technical School, due to open in the autumn. Mr Jones initially preferred the former but David strongly the latter, and so it was – though not before the council's education officer had interviewed the 11-year-old about his career plans.[8]

---

The Britain of the late 1950s was not conspicuously characterised by equality of either outcome or – rising meritocrats notwithstanding – opportunity. In terms of the former, despite some redistribution during the 1940s, not only did the richest 5 per cent own some 75 per cent of total wealth, but also the share of incomes (both before and after tax) enjoyed by the different occupational strata was not yet fundamentally different from what it had been shortly before the First World War. In terms of the latter, some eloquent detail peppered Tom Bairstow's analysis of 'The Establishment' in the *News Chronicle* in April 1958. All but two of Macmillan's Cabinet had been educated at public school, including almost one-third at Eton; all but four had gone to Oxbridge; the two Opposition leaders, Gaitskell and Grimond, had backgrounds of (respectively) Winchester and New College, Eton and Balliol. The top three ambassadors had all gone to Eton or Winchester, while in the City, the governor of the Bank of England was an Etonian, and the chairmen of the Big Five banks included two Etonians, one Harrovian and one Wykehamist.

Bairstow did think, though, that the power of the old school tie was perhaps waning in industry at large, and he cited Sir Alexander Fleck, head of ICI, 'who came up the hard way from an elementary school'. Or as one industrialist, A. D. Bonham-Carter, had recently put it in a radio talk on 'The Way to the Top in Industry': 'Social and educational backgrounds are now immaterial. What matters is the way in which a man uses his qualities and knowledge, not how he acquired them.' Yet almost certainly this was a gross exaggeration, to judge by the statistical evidence of a trio of surveys conducted between 1955 and 1958 into the backgrounds of Britain's business leaders. 'These three studies agree that, while some men have managed to get to the top without special advantages, the odds were heavily against them,' concluded Roy Lewis and Rosemary Stewart in their 1958 book *The Boss*. 'The men who were most likely to succeed were those with family connections in business, although this was less important in the larger firms, and those who had been to public school. Most likely of all were the Old Etonians.'[9]

Of course, by the late 1950s the effects of the 1944 Act had not yet started to work through into these sort of surveys. What is striking, though, is the extent to which – even in the new dispensation – the working class as a whole was still seemingly being shut out of the mer-itocratic race. Take the key question of social composition of the gram-mar schools, systematically investigated by Jean Floud and colleagues in their much-quoted *Social Class and Educational Opportunity* (1956), based on grammar admissions in 1953 in two contrasting parts of the country. The following were the percentage chances, from the parents' occupational groups, of their sons being selected for admission:

|  | *South-West Hertfordshire* | *Middlesbrough* |
| --- | --- | --- |
| Professional workers, business owners and managers | 59 | 68 |
| Clerical workers | 44 | 37 |
| Foremen, small shopkeepers, etc. | 30 | 24 |
| Skilled manual workers | 18 | 14 |
| Unskilled manual workers | 9 | 9 |
| All social classes | 22 | 17 |

It is unlikely that these figures changed markedly during the second half of the decade, and in late 1959 the Crowther Report, *15 to 18*, was unequivocal that in secondary moderns – overwhelmingly the most common destination for those who had failed to pass the 11-plus and thereby get into a selective school (usually a grammar) – 'the children of non-manual workers are much under-represented, and the children of semi-skilled workers over-represented'.

In theory, there was 'parity of esteem' between the roughly 1,200 grammar schools and 3,800 secondary moderns. In practice, not only did most people view the secondary moderns as vastly inferior but there was a shocking relative shortfall in their resourcing. 'It is likely,' noted John Vaizey in his 1958 treatise *The Costs of Education*, 'that the average Grammar school child receives 170 per cent more per year, in terms of resources, than the average Modern school child.' Teachers at secondary moderns were paid less, only about a fifth were graduates, and even by the end of the 1950s barely 10 per cent of the buildings they worked in were new and purpose-built.

The gulf in expectations was even greater. Surveying in 1961 that year's school-leavers from a semi-skilled and unskilled background at five Leicestershire schools (two grammars and three secondary moderns), William Liversidge found that 93 per cent of the grammar boys anticipated moving into a higher class of employment than their parents – whereas only 18 per cent of the secondary modern boys did. 'The general conclusion that emerges from this study,' he reflected, 'is one of startlingly accurate appraisal of life chances by the children, and a shrewd appreciation of the social and economic implications of their placing within the educational system.' Not long before, in 1959–60, another sociologist, Michael Carter, had sampled 200 boys and girls (overwhelmingly from working-class homes) who were about to leave, or had just left, secondary moderns in the Sheffield area. Among those still at school, three-quarters 'expressed their satisfaction that they would soon be workers – independent, recognised as grown-up, no longer "school kids"', while half the overall sample, including those who had left, 'objected strongly' to the very idea of raising the school-leaving age to 16. 'I don't think I could have lasted,' said one girl, and a boy was equally adamant: 'It is not fair; we left at 15, so the others should be able to.'[10]

Social class was not just relevant to grammars vis-à-vis secondary moderns; it also did much to determine outcomes *within* grammars. In 1954 an official report on *Early Leaving* found that whereas children from the semi-skilled and unskilled working class represented over 20 per cent of grammar school intakes, by the sixth form that proportion was down to barely 7 per cent. Given which figures, it was unsurprising that by the mid-1950s a middle-class child who had been to a grammar was five times as likely to go on to a university as was a child from an unskilled working-class background who had also been to a grammar. Why was this? Towards the end of the decade, Eva Bene sought part of the answer by surveying 361 boys from the Greater London area who were in the third year at their grammars; she revealed by social class the percentages of replies to various suggestive statements such as 'If he had a chance he would like to go to university'. There was a telling

20-per-cent gap between that working-class minority wanting to stay on after the age of 16 (45 per cent) and that working-class majority wanting to go to university (65 per cent).[11]

The university system itself was gradually expanding – 50,000 university places just before the Second World War doubling to some 107,000 by 1960–61 – and plans were afoot by the end of the 1950s for a clutch of new universities, including what would become Sussex, York, East Anglia, Essex, Kent and Warwick. 'The elite of tomorrow' was the *Observer*'s headline in 1960 for an article by Mark Abrams on the 1.6 per cent of the adult population – some 570,000 people – who were university graduates or who had comparable professional qualifications. 'Since the war the graduates have not looked back,' he declared. 'Today they are still far from having completely supplanted the pre-war elite, but by the end of the 1960s they will be well on the way towards doing so.' And, according to Abrams, 'the rise of the graduates has been resisted only in trade union leadership, industrial management, popular journalism and the entertainment industry'. It was heady, Whiggish stuff, but Abrams did not pretend it would be a wholly open elite. 'Where yesterday's elite was based on birth and wealth, tomorrow's will rest largely on education and wealth. And because of this difference the gap between the elite and the rest of society will surely be just as great as it was in the past.' Indeed, in 1960 itself, only 2.6 per cent of 18-year-olds from working-class homes went to university – compared to 16.8 per cent from middle-class homes. At the pinnacle of the university system, Oxbridge, the public schools continued to dominate: 56 per cent of the 1955 intake at Cambridge came from there; two years later, 70 per cent of scholarships and exhibitions awarded at Oxbridge men's colleges went to public schoolboys; and Abrams in his 1960 article cited a recent survey of the latest Cambridge graduates, showing that a majority still came from public school and only 9 per cent from the working class.[12]

There were many reasons – including institutional bias, going back to primary school – why most working-class children failed to thrive in a largely middle-class educational system, but arguably the most important revolved round parental attitudes and expectations. Floud et al found in their study of grammars in South-West Hertfordshire and Middlesbrough in the early-to-mid-1950s that over half the working-class parents 'either desired no further education for their children or were uncertain in the matter', while when Abrams in 1956–7 interviewed some 200 married couples in London, mainly from the skilled working class, he seldom encountered 'that degree of personal ambition which is likely to carry them socially upward'. This also applied to their aspirations for their children, even though a majority hoped they would go to either a grammar or a technical school (the latter thin on the ground, but viewed as good for learning skills and job security), and only 15 per cent positively wanted a secondary modern – where, of course, most of their children would in the event go. As Abrams reflected:

> For most people in the sample, 'education' is something provided by the authorities for which parents do not have to pay but over which, correspondingly, they can exercise no control . . .
>
> It is difficult to persuade oneself, from the general tone of the results of this enquiry, that the majority of working-class parents or children yet regard education as being so important that the frustration of their hopes is a major disaster. The system is still new, still imperfectly understood, and its possibilities are still rather vaguely glimpsed. The parents themselves, almost without exception, left school at 14 or 15, and most of them see no reason why they should be unduly disturbed if their children have to do the same, provided that after they leave school they can get decent jobs which they are unlikely to be thrown out of.

So too with other studies. Interviewing working-class couples in Dagenham (mainly in 1958–9, on the LCC's huge inter-war Becontree estate), Peter Willmott 'found some support for the view that most parents on the estate are not educationally ambitious for their children, and do not take a keen interest in their schooling', typified by a trio of vox pops:

> I've never really thought about it. I've always taken it for granted he'll leave school at 15 unless he turns out brilliant and goes to College.
>
> I don't care a lot myself. The main thing is for the children to be happy.
>
> It's immaterial to us. If he wants to go in for the 11-plus, we wouldn't stand in his way.

The classic, most nuanced account of this whole charged area is by Brian Jackson and Dennis Marsden, whose *Education and the Working Class* (1962) was a groundbreaking survey, conducted in about 1959–60, of 88 young working-class people who had been to grammar school in Huddersfield during the 1950s. Coming out of the Institute of Community Studies (run by Young and Willmott), and combining sociology with anthropology, it gave a detailed, moving picture of the social, cultural and psychological pressures faced by working-class pupils – especially over such matters as sport, uniform and friendship groups – and their often baffled, frustrated parents. Jackson and Marsden identified on the part of those parents a familiar pattern. Initial pleasure at their child's 11-plus success and, during that child's early terms at grammar school, flickers of intellectual excitement for themselves, were followed, by the third year, by 'a growing sense that the child was out on its own, moving into worlds to which the parents had no access'. At this point many of those parents, usually the fathers, 'sought to reassert control over their children's education by demanding some clear statement about the kind of job this was leading to'. They quoted one: 'I always wanted education for myself, and then I thought our lad would have it. But what I thought was the technical side, something that I could understand. That was what I thought education would be. I never thought about that Arts side, literature and language and all that stuff. That was new to me; that didn't come into my reckoning about education at all.' There was also, explained another parent, the problem of the neighbours:

> Many a time you'd be out and the neighbours would say, 'Eeh, is your lad still at school? What's he going to be then?' And I'd have to say, 'I don't know what he's going to be yet.' And they'd say, 'Doesn't *he* know yet?' . . . I hadn't got an answer and I felt soft. They'd look at you as much as to say, 'Staying on at school all that time and don't know what he's going to be, well!'

The obvious solution was for the parents to talk to teachers about courses and choices, but, suffused by a sense of 'them' and 'us', they seldom did, even if their children were in the A stream and there was no shame involved. Altogether, noted the authors, 'by the time the leaving age was reached and the General Certificate taken, many wondered whether there was much to be gained by leaving their child at school'. Or, as one father put it about the whole unsettling experience: 'Tha can't *afford* to send t'lasses to t'grammar schools. Tha sends 'em and when they come back they're no good to y'. They don't want a mucky job even if that's where t'brass is. They won't look at it!'

Still, it was sometimes the teacher who thwarted a parent's aspirations. From Sheffield in about 1960 is this emblematic account of a leaving pupil's interview with the headmistress of a secondary modern and the Youth Employment Officer:

The YEO enquires – with a smile designed to put mother and child at ease, but standing no chance of overcoming the suspicion which mother feels for officials – what job the girl would like to do. Before the girl has a chance to speak, mother jumps in, saying with a determination made more formidable by the certain knowledge that she will shortly be contradicted, 'she ain't going to work in a warehouse.' The head teacher disregards mother and turning to the girl says 'What do you want to do?' The girl blurts out that she wants to be 'one of them shorthand-typewriters'. The YEO now has something to work on, and enquires of the girl whether she is good at spelling. There is a dull silence, broken by the head teacher, who says in a significant tone, 'One out of ten'. An enquiry about English Composition leads to the comment 'Four out of twenty'. The head teacher is becoming impatient, and tells the girl that this is a waste of time: that there is no likelihood of her getting an office job: that she would not be happy doing office work: and that she *would* be happy doing packing work in a warehouse. Mother has by this time reached 'the sniffing stage'. The head teacher turns her attention to her and says, 'Look here, Mrs So-and-so, things have changed since you and I were children. Lots of valuable things are packed nowadays. It is an important job. Factories have good conditions, girls can earn good wages, wear nice clothes and be happy doing the work.'[13]

---

On 31 July 1958 the Yorkshire professional cricketer Johnny Wardle was, reported the *Daily Mail*, 'cheered all the way to the wicket by the Sheffield crowd' – the day after the club had announced it would be dispensing with his services from the end of the season. He had fallen out badly with Yorkshire's new amateur captain – 39-year-old Ronnie Burnet, who had never played first-class cricket before this season – and though in the rest of the match he performed brilliantly, taking eight wickets at fewer than ten runs each, he never played for Yorkshire again. The following week he was back in the pages of the *Mail* with two prominently displayed articles, 'Why I Was Sacked' and 'We're Carrying the Captain', claiming that Burnet's 'lack of experience' had made it 'desperately hard for the key men of the side'. Later in August, offended by Wardle's trenchant criticism of the Yorkshire committee, the MCC (which still ran English cricket) withdrew his invitation to tour Australia.

The amateur-professional divide continued to run deep: an amateur, Surrey's Peter May, would be captaining the English tourists, and, earlier in the year, an MCC committee chaired by the club's president, the Duke of Norfolk, had concluded that 'the distinctive status of the amateur cricketer was not obsolete, was of great value to the game and should be preserved' (though at the same time, in terms of the financial recompense of those nominally unpaid performers, the committee admitting to being 'disturbed by the apparent over-liberal interpretation of the word "expenses" in certain cases that had come to their notice'). The hypocrisy was rank, with a range of different methods being found to pay the socially more prestigious, so-called amateurs. Ahead of the tour, England's other spinner, also a Yorkshireman, gave George ('Gubby') Allen, chairman of the selectors, stockbroker and a pillar of the Lord's Establishment, a bad quarter of an hour. 'I told Gubby that I was considering becoming an amateur and I wondered how he would feel about this,' recalled Jim Laker. 'He asked me if I'd given it serious consideration and said that, if I had, he thought it was absolutely splendid but wondered why I wanted to do this. He didn't look best pleased when I told him that I thought I would be better off in financial terms playing as an amateur in the England team in Australia with expenses rather than drawing professional pay.'[14]

The Wardle Affair, the introduction of life peerages (Sir Eric James, High Master of Manchester Grammar School and arch-meritocrat, on an early list), satire about the complacent incompetence of the traditional ruling class (the Boulting brothers' film *Carlton-Browne of the*

*FO*, with Terry-Thomas as the bumbling diplomat), Basil Bernstein's pioneering study ('Some sociological determinants of perception') of the different affective and cognitive equipment of working-class children compared to middle-class, even some daring cross-dressing (the fashion photographer Antony Armstrong-Jones taking a riverside room in Rotherhithe, the metropolitan intelligentsia starting to form Sunday morning soccer teams) – one way and another, quite apart from the celebrated new wave of plays and novels, class and related issues were bubbling away strongly in the late 1950s.[15]

'Despite (and sometimes because of) the Welfare State,' declared the *Radio Times* in August 1958 in its preview of Christopher Mayhew's television series 'Does Class Matter?' (including the Dennis Potter interview), 'we British are still one of the most class-ridden peoples in the world.' Produced by Jack Ashley, this was a notable examination of a ubiquitous but seldom overtly discussed subject, and, noted BBC's audience research, 'many viewers found it an enjoyable and interesting experience to be looking at themselves "from outside", though some questioned the wisdom of stressing class distinctions'. Not long afterwards, in January 1959, Tom Lupton and C. Shirley Wilson published their pathbreaking analysis 'The Social Background and Connections of "Top Decision Makers"', taking as their starting point the recent evidence given to the Bank Rate Tribunal. This detailed with unambiguous clarity the narrow social and educational background of the City elite, as well as its multiple interconnections, and, though appearing in an obscure academic journal, it received considerable publicity. So much so that four months later, at the City of London Society's annual luncheon at the Mansion House, that body's chairman (the self-made Harley Drayton) was compelled to declare, boldly if unconvincingly, that 'if a young man has talent, integrity and courage, not only is there nothing to stop him going to the top, he will almost be kicked there'.[16]

Among those watching 'Does Class Matter?' were Florence Turtle and Tom Driberg. 'He is a Socialist & somewhat prejudiced against Public Schools,' Turtle noted unenthusiastically of Mayhew, but the Labour politician (and regular TV reviewer for the *New Statesman*) was struck by how '95 per cent of those questioned put education as the first determinant of class', reflecting further that it was 'hard to believe that most people will acquiesce for much longer in an educational system which artificially reserves so many of the best jobs for those with a particular kind of education, identified by a particular accent'. Two years earlier Anthony Crosland in *The Future of Socialism* had had strong words about the existing 'system of superior private schools' – 'open to the wealthier classes, but out of reach of poorer children however talented and deserving ... much the most flagrant inequality of opportunity, as it is cause of class inequality generally, in our educational system' – while there was a degree of unease even among some Tories. After referring in 1957 to 'the almost comically overwhelming predominance of Old Etonians in the Conservative Party', the writer and former MP Christopher Hollis went on in the *Spectator*: 'I think that the time has come when it would be for the advantage of the nation that the Conservative Party should be somewhat less "U" in its higher personnel and when a party which pays lip-service to equality of opportunity should in practice treat at least (shall we say?) a Rugbeian as the equal of an Etonian.' The next year, more seriously, the Education Minister Geoffrey Lloyd (Harrow and Trinity College, Cambridge) privately expressed some sympathy with 'elements on our side, e.g. The Bow Group, which thinks that basis for entry should be widened, and not restricted, as for all intents it is, to those who can meet the heavy cost of a preparatory, as well as of a public school education'. But, anxious about charges from elsewhere in his party that direct government subvention to enable 'deserving' children to take up places would threaten the independence of the schools, he opted for a policy of masterly inaction. And those institutions themselves? 'You Can't Write Off the Public Schools' was a *Daily Mail* headline in May 1958, with the article revealing that numbers had increased since the war from 50,000 to 80,000 and that many had no vacancies until 1966 or 1967.[17]

Although their academic superiority over the better grammars was now questionable, they were continuing to deliver the goods where it mattered, and when the *New Statesman* later in 1958 published statistics definitively revealing their dominance of Oxbridge entrance, a flurry of letters ensued. It was all 'simple enough', insisted the constitutional expert Ivor Jennings, Master of Trinity Hall, Cambridge: 'It is that the number of applicants from public schools is more numerous

– in this college much more numerous – than the number of applicants from other schools: and all are meritorious because they are supported by the schools, which are familiar with Cambridge standards and help us enormously in our selection.' Other correspondents were unconvinced, with some (including John Vaizey) calling for the integration of the public schools into the state system, while a youngish Oxford historian, Lawrence Stone, conceded there were 'too many' public-school men at Oxbridge 'who in a world of equal opportunity would not be there at all'. About the same time, another Oxford fellow, J. R. Sargent of Worcester College, elucidated in *Socialist Commentary* the three 'ineluctable factors' at work:

> First, there is the classical tradition of the public schools, combined with the large number of classical scholarships offered at Oxford or Cambridge. Secondly, there is the fact that public school masters are old hands at the complex procedure for getting admission. They make less mistakes than grammar school masters with less experience, and this does not simply mean that they are better at 'nobbling'. Thirdly (let's face it), there is the fact that many public schools provide very good teaching and can do so because many people are willing to pay large sums in order to get it.

There was an Oxbridge coda the following spring, when scientists at both universities led campaigns to get the Latin exam dropped from admission requirements. Cambridge agreed to relent, but Oxford narrowly not, before eventually permitting those with a maths or science A level to be exempted.

'I have never been able to understand,' declared Crosland in *The Future of Socialism*, 'why socialists have been so obsessed with the question of the grammar schools, and so indifferent to the much more glaring injustice of the independent schools.' Yet it was clear which issue had the greater traction in the popular mind. Certainly, the BBC television documentary in February 1957 on the 11-plus, featuring a secondary modern in north London, engendered no shortage of viewer response:

> The answer is, Eleven Plus is bad, comprehensive schools not the remedy. The remedy is better teachers and less crowding of classes. Look at that

nondescript lot of stuff you showed us tonight. No wonder you chose a powerful commentator, otherwise we may have dozed off. *(Technician)*

There is a good standard of education in these schools [i.e. secondary moderns]. It would be a poor sort of world peopled with academic types only. We must have practical men and women. *(Engineer's Wife)*

I feel too much pressure is brought to bear on the children at this age and they are far better left alone, with a natural interest in their work being shown by the parents. *(Correspondence Clerk)*

The 'do-or-die' attitude of many parents towards their children – pass and so win a place to a grammar school or else . . . – has as its basis near snobbishness. *(Cashier)*

Despite all that has been written and spoken about those children who do not gain Grammar School status, in attempting to alleviate their feelings at having *failed*, failure is in fact the cold clear truth, and nothing can now change this. *(Architect)*

Hard words, and a teacher (unstated at which sort of school) could offer only another cold, clear truth: 'The Grammar Schools can only take a certain number of pupils, and in most parts of the country there are not enough Grammar Schools.'[18]

---

In fact, by the late 1950s the dynamics of this whole inter-related cluster of issues – 11-plus, grammar schools, secondary moderns, comprehensives – were changing quite rapidly. Above all, it was becoming increasingly apparent that the future of the widely admired grammars was being threatened by deep dissatisfaction with two things beyond their control: the 11-plus and the secondary moderns.

A significant part of the 11-plus problem was that a child's chances of passing the exam hinged to an alarming extent on where he or she lived, depending on the availability of grammar-school places. Those chances were as high as 35 per cent in the south-west, 33.5 per cent in Wales, and 31.6 per cent in London and the south-east, but as low as 24.1 per cent in the Midlands, 22.4 per cent in the north-east, 18.9 per cent in the south and, in one particularly ill-favoured city, Nottingham, a mere 10.1 per cent. More generally, beyond that, there was the key question of misallocation. In practice, 11-plus failures had relatively few opportunities to transfer across at a later stage to a grammar, yet even in 1954 the *Early Leaving* report was revealing, on the basis of 1951 O-level results, that whereas 45 per cent of those who had been at state grammars since the age of 11 got five or more passes, the comparable figure for those who *had* subsequently been transferred from secondary moderns was 45.7 per cent.

But the first real heavy lifting in the debate on intelligence testing and selection came from a committee of leading psychologists led by the Institute of Education's Professor Philip Vernon. In their 1957 report, *Secondary School Selection*, they declared, in contradiction to the theories of genetic determination popularised by Cyril Burt, that

> psychologists should frankly acknowledge that completely accurate classification of children, either by level or type of ability, is not possible at 11 years, still less on entry to the junior school at 7 [a reference to the prevalent streaming at primaries], and should therefore encourage any more flexible form of organisation and grouping which gives scope for the gradual unfolding and the variability of children's abilities and interests.

Moreover, they added, 'only among the top 5% or so and the bottom 50% do we consider that allocation to grammar, technical and modern schools can be made automatically from test scores and scaled estimates', with 'all intermediate pupils' to be 'regarded as border-zone'. Later that year, a detailed report on how selection worked in practice (*Admission to Grammar Schools*, commissioned by the National Foundation of Educational Research and written by Alfred Yates and D. A. Pidgeon) found that, even if all possible improvements were made in the selection process, there would still be an ineradicable misallocation of at least 10 per cent. 'Whether a 10% error for all the country at large, involving 60,000 children per annum,' reflected Professor Ben Morris in his preface to the report, 'is to be regarded as reasonable or intolerable of course depends upon what particular educational values are regarded as most important.'

Nevertheless, what in most people's eyes ultimately did for the 11-plus was its inherent cruelty and divisiveness – prompting even a Tory minister, the liberal-minded Sir Edward Boyle (the Parliamentary

Secretary at the Ministry of Education who had apparently struggled with some of the questions), to refer publicly in 1957 to its 'evil effect' and to how it 'casts a shadow over the classroom'. Understandably, many parents voted with their feet, it being estimated at the time that nearly half that year's eligible children were not in the event sitting the test. And when, soon afterwards, a *Daily Express* poll asked whether the 11-plus should be left as it was or replaced by an assessment based on the child's general school record, only 25 per cent opted for the status quo, with little difference between Tory and Labour voters.[19]

As for the other Achilles heel of the existing system, a bald statement in the *Manchester Evening News* in April 1956 said it all: 'With shock and disbelief many parents have learned this week that their own son or daughter will be going to a Secondary Modern school next September.' A year later, Manchester's recently retired, strongly pro-selection chief education officer, Norman Fisher, accepted that 'even where there are secondary modern schools in first-rate buildings, it has seldom been possible to persuade parents or children that they offer a reasonable alternative to the grammar school'. And in June 1957 the *Spectator* published a stark piece by Colm Brogan based on the experience of a female teacher he knew who had recently worked in a co-ed secondary modern on a housing estate near London. 'Nearly all the teachers devote time, labour and anxious care,' he concluded, but in the end it was 'the apathy and the negative attitude of the pupils', from a work-ing-class East End background, that prevailed, including a total lack of discipline and corporate spirit:

> The school had nothing to offer them that they believed to be of any value whatever. Educationists may talk of deepening the aesthetic experi-ence, rounding the personality and enriching the lives of secondary modern pupils, but these words are as thorns crackling under the pot for the pupils themselves. With the exception of the minority who have agreed to stay on, the sole aim and object of the children is to get out the instant the law releases them. The world outside is Eldorado, to which their eyes and thoughts are ever straining.

The negative depictions continued. 'Run away to sea rather than go to a secondary modern,' was the sage advice of A.J.P. Taylor later in 1957;

in 1960, in his manual *Secondary Modern Discipline*, Richard Farley called secondary moderns 'the focal point of the duller, less responsible, maladjusted and potentially criminal young people', so that as a result 'ninety per cent of the work in a Secondary Modern School is control and discipline'.

Inevitably, among those teaching in the secondary moderns, a deep defensiveness prevailed. 'Why is it that when I go into your secondary modern schools the teachers are so apologetic?' a visiting educationalist from abroad was quoted as asking in 1956. '"You must remember," they tell me, "that these are not the brightest children. You must realise that we do not have the best." And so they warn me not to be disappointed. They make excuses for the work I shall see.' But it could hardly have been otherwise, as the *Times Educational Supplement* (still strongly pro-selection) went on in its report: 'The visitor was surprised that the teachers expected him to judge the secondary modern school by the grammar school. The teachers, of course, could have told him that the public as yet had seldom done anything else. This was not an apology the teachers were offering the visitor. It was seasoned self-defence.'[20]

Yet for all this – including (not least) press treatment of secondary moderns in which, as one observer wearily put it, 'the stress is upon physical violence and the threat of the adolescent' – the larger reality was perhaps not quite so bleak. In implicit riposte to Brogan, the *New Statesman* in September 1957 ran a five-page survey by Judith Hubback in which she did not deny that the 59,000 secondary modern teachers, almost half of them taking classes of over 30, were often mediocre, so that 'most of the dull classrooms will go on witnessing dull, over-crowded, incompetent and undisciplined lessons for the next few years'. But, she stressed, 'the majority of classes do not get out of control, the majority of children are moderately well taught and most of the regular teachers do not have discipline problems'. A more whole-hearted defence came the following year from Harold Dent (educationalist and former editor of the *TES*) in his *Secondary Modern School: An Interim Report*. By his calculations, over half the secondary moderns were doing good work, almost half sound work and only 5 per cent bad work; vocational courses, tailored to a wide range of aptitudes and interests, were giving 'a lively sense of purpose and reality'; and altogether, the 'incontestable fact' was that 'hundreds of thousands of girls and boys in secondary modern schools' were now 'being given a much better, much more genuinely secondary education than were even their elder sisters or brothers who attended the self-same schools only a few years previously'. The picture was positive too in 1959 in E. R. Braithwaite's *To Sir, With Love*, his justly celebrated account of a black teacher at a secondary modern in the East End – drawn from his real-life experience at St George's-in-the-East Secondary Modern, located amidst the grimness and periodic violence of Cable Street, Stepney, but where a remarkable, inspiring head, Alex Bloom, made every child feel counted and created a real sense of school community.

Even so, this was undoubtedly the exception rather than the rule. More representative – but still positive in its own terms – was the experience of Julia Gunnigan, teaching in 1959 in the secondary modern at Pimlico and encountering an atmosphere that was rough but friendly. 'The boys queuing to hand over their lunch money would sometimes pause at the head of the line and demand: "Fulham or Chelsea, Mam?",' relates her son John Lanchester. 'The wrong answer would get a scowl and sneer; the right answer would be met with "Buy ya dinner."' And, relevant not just to the typical working-class secondary modern, he also describes what his mother found during her London sojourn:

> No one would ever admit it, but people were happy where they were. They were especially happy with the level of complaint and grumbling, which often seemed one of life's most important pleasures. A few of her brightest pupils had passed the eleven-plus and been offered a place at grammar school, but their parents had not allowed them to take it up. She raised the question with one of the parents and they shuffled and looked shifty and embarrassed and eventually admitted to her – as they perhaps wouldn't have if she hadn't been Irish – 'We didn't want him to think he was better than us.'[21]

Middle-class parents, alarmed by the possibility (however statistically slight) of their children failing the 11-plus, felt very differently. 'In some of the Home Counties and other areas where there is a large middle-class dormitory population, the abolition of entry to the County Grammar schools by payment of fees has caused a great deal of bewilderment and intense public pressure upon the authorities to provide some outlet of comparable value,' noted F. S. Marston in the *Journal of Education* as early as 1954. 'Indeed, it may be that parents with this social background will, despite their preference for the Grammar school, join with others having very different ideas to replace it by the comprehensive [i.e. non-selective] school unless some other acceptable solution is forthcoming. It is only too probable that the unilateral Modern school is engaged in a race against time.' In practice, this race against time meant not an 'education for life', the vocational model upon which the secondary moderns had originally been conceived in the 1940s, but instead something more akin to grammar school lite, through the provision of exam-tested extended courses. 'The knowledge that others in such a [secondary] modern school are succeeding and going to college or a student apprenticeship is the greatest educational tranquilliser for parents and is worth 1,000 pamphlets describing the methods of selection!' declared Rhodes Boyson, head of a secondary modern in Lancashire's Rossendale Valley and a Labour councillor, in a letter to the *Sunday Times* in February 1958. 'What parents fear in the 11+ is not technical error, but an alternative choice which will cut their children off from later educational opportunities.' Progress along these lines, however, was relatively slow, and by 1960 there were still only 21,680 secondary modern pupils staying on after 15 to take GCE exams.

From Tory politicians, for the most part viscerally committed to the grammars, mere boosterism of the ill-favoured but indispensable secondary moderns was no longer enough. In late 1958, Geoffrey Lloyd unveiled the government's White Paper *Secondary Education for All: A New Drive*, promising among other things a five-year £300 million programme of new school building, mainly for the secondary moderns, as well as a greater emphasis at the secondary moderns on supplying examination courses for academically abler pupils. Altogether, reckoned *The Economist*, 'it embodies the Conservative tactic for grasping the political thistle of the eleven-plus: to level up educationally without seeking to stamp flat socially; to overbid the comprehensive school with the new-style secondary modern (renamed high school); to put the really big money behind a practical "parity of esteem" which will alone take the sting out of selection'.[22]

From this perspective, there was no doubt about the identity of the elephant – or potential elephant – in the room. 'Have you heard about what are called comprehensive schools?' asked Gallup earlier in 1958, a reasonable question given that there were still fewer than a hundred – one of which, Holland Park, started in September that year under reassuringly traditional lines (uniforms with school crest, house system, streaming). By a narrow majority, most people *had* heard of comprehensives; by a much larger majority, 58 to 19 per cent, those who had heard of them thought they were 'a good idea'. Accordingly, it was an urgent political context in which Lloyd's White Paper served, in *The Economist*'s sympathetic words, 'blunt warning' that the Conservative government 'will not approve attempts by local authorities to "comprehensivise" schools if they would damage existing grammar schools'– a warning designed to ensure that 'the grammar schools can be left to get on with their essential job of training the country's upper quartile of intelligence for the major academic and scientific skills'.[23] Grammars and selection on the one hand, comprehensives on the other: by the late 1950s a national debate was gathering steam.

There were already some predictable anti-compers. 'Greater equality of opportunity is not to be attained easily by some administrative reorganisation of our schools,' but rather by 'the civilising effects of extended education on the homes and on the whole community', warned Eric James of Manchester Grammar School, reviewing Floud et al; 'a veneer of confidence is being spread about the comprehensive school which has no substance to support it', claimed the *TES* soon afterwards, in February 1957, in a fierce attack on the LCC's determination to push ahead with more comprehensives; and later that year *The Economist* visited one (probably Kidbrooke in south-east London) and worried not only about 'too ready a flight in the new schools from academic subjects into pottery and cookery and dressmaking' but also whether the staff was 'so "comprehensive-minded" that duty to the majority is all and a special effort with the bright ones thought rather unfair'. In his sceptical response to Lloyd's White Paper, which he interpreted as the government trying 'to catch votes by buttering up the secondary modern schools rather than by thinking out what is their purpose', Christopher Hollis in the *Spectator* declared that selection went with the grain of the fundamental human reality that there were many children who were 'simply of the type that learns by doing rather than by reading', whereas at a comprehensive, 'if the non-academic boy is to leave school at fifteen and the academic boy to stay on till eighteen, then the non-academic can never in the nature of things attain to a position of prominence and responsibility and is likely to feel more frustrated than if he stayed in a school [i.e. a secondary modern] of his own kind'.

Another seemingly entrenched anti-comper was Harry Rée, liberal-minded head of Watford Grammar School, who in his 1956 book *The Essential Grammar School* rejected the comprehensive alternative as requiring huge, unwieldy schools and strongly defended the grammars as ladders of social mobility and as the democratic alternative to what he saw as the dying public schools. So too a promising playwright, who had taught at a grammar, in his letter to the *New Statesman* soon after Hubback's survey of the secondary modern. 'The fact is that if a child has failed his 11-plus he is probably stupider, or lazier, or both, than the child who has passed,' wrote Robert Bolt. 'Socialists don't quite like to say this because it seems to imply second-class citizenship, but a human being has his citizenship, not in virtue of his attainments, but in virtue of his mere humanity.' And, Bolt continued, it was the 'special style and *panache*' of a grammar sixth form 'which enables children of ability from moneyless homes to compete on a footing of absolute equality with the sprigs of the upper class', thereby making 'a Grammar school sixth the only wholly successful intrusion of democracy into the special reserve of the rulers'. A starker warning still, also from a leftish perspective, came in the same magazine a year later (October 1958) from B. Laslett:

> Unhappily, these schools [comprehensives] are too new to have the confidence of many parents who care about education, and many, given a choice, will feel unable to take a risk, and will struggle to find money for fees in a misguided effort 'to buy the best' for their own children. Among grammar school teachers there is at present strong prejudice against comprehensive schools, and many will get out, if they can, into fee-paying schools.

The comprehensive threat to grammars would, in short, 'make it more certain than ever that fee-paying schools will flourish'.

Two heads of new comprehensive schools naturally on the other side of the argument were Miss Margaret Miles of Mayfield in Putney and Mrs Harriet Chetwynd of Woodberry Down in Stoke Newington. The comprehensive principle, claimed Miles in a Third Programme talk in 1957, recognised through its heterogeneity that pupils had 'widely varying interests and abilities and long- or short-term objectives', whereas in the avowedly homogeneous grammar 'the average girl' was 'often regarded as a dud'. As for the assumption that, in order to provide courses for all abilities, comprehensives by definition would be too big, she asserted that 'size can give dignity to an institution and it can give stimulus and a sense of adventure'. Chetwynd, writing in the *New Statesman* in February 1959 to counter an 'Against the Comprehensive' article by Rée, impatiently summarised the familiar anti-comp negatives ('size, chaos, teachers will not mix, children will not mix, parents will not mix, the most able will be neglected, the least able will suffer, schools will be sausage machines, there will be no room for the individual, leadership will go only to the academic seniors') before setting out her credo:

> The Comprehensive school exists to develop a new conception of secondary education based on a positive moral philosophy – that it is right for all children (or at any rate a full cross-section) who will be the next generation's adult society to spend their adolescent years together; that it is right for their education to be concerned not only with the brain, important though that is, but with the mind and character, the body, the spirit, the standards of judgment – both personal and to the community; that it is right for the individual to have the means to grow to his full stature and yet to discipline himself as a member of the society in which he will live, with its obligations, its rights and limitations.

Others onside included two tireless educationalists, Brian Simon and Robin Pedley, the latter writing the influential *Comprehensive Education: A New Approach* (1956) and declaring soon afterwards that the abolition of the 11-plus would be 'a giant stride towards the achievement of national prosperity and individual happiness'; Professor Vernon and his fellow psychologists, arguing that 'on psychological grounds there would seem to be more to be said in favour of comprehensive schools than against' while not denying that 'it would be unwise to ignore the strength of tradition and parental prejudice'; and of course Michael Young, so alert to the dangers of a meritocratic elite.

But what about the ladder for the working class? Raymond Williams did not specifically refer to grammar schools, yet – even though he had been to one himself – they were surely in his sights in a passage towards the end of *Culture and Society*. Arguing that the ladder was essentially a 'bourgeois model' that had 'produced a real conflict of values within the working class itself', he claimed that it was especially 'objectionable' because 'it weakens the principle of common betterment, which ought to be an absolute value' and 'sweetens the poison of hierarchy'. Williams concluded with unshakable moral certainty: 'In the end, on any reckoning, the ladder will never do; it is the product of a divided society, and will fall with it.'[24]

Increasingly the debate would be played out also at local level, nowhere more pertinently than in Leicestershire. There, a *Conservative*-controlled authority sanctioned in 1957 the ingenious, attention-attracting 'Leicestershire experiment', initially applied to two areas of the county and inspired at least in part by the Leicester-based Pedley. 'It is the county's boast,' explained the educational journalist Dinah Brook, 'that it is not only the first education authority to abolish eleven-plus but also the only one to give parents the freedom to choose a grammar school for their children if they want it.' Essentially, it was a two-tier approach: 'All children go from primary school at the age of eleven to a new version of the secondary modern school, called the high school. At fourteen, children whose parents undertake to keep them at school until they are sixteen can transfer to grammar school.' The *TES*'s response to the announcement of the scheme was scathing – 'a wholly needless abdication of leadership' – but on the ground the early signs were positive, to judge by the reports of the headmaster (Rev. E.S.C. Coggins) of Oadby Gartree High School, one of the county's new-style secondary moderns. 'I have not received a single parental objection to the Scheme,' he reported to his governors in September 1957. As for the open meetings held that term for parents, some of whose children might have been admitted directly to grammar school under the previous system, 'I did not encounter any feelings of injustice or snobbery. The parents of children in the less academic streams were equally enthusiastic.'

Ironically, in Labour-controlled Leicester itself, selection and the traditional ladder-climbing 11-to-18 grammar remained the order of the day, though from 1959 the external 11-plus examination did give way to what the city's director of education reassuringly called 'a standardised junior school assessment of each child's ability'.[25]

Passions ran higher in Bristol, and along somewhat more orthodox party lines. 'If the babblement of confused voices demanding the destruction of grammar schools – and the latest one is that grammar schools breed Tory voters – showed less envy and prejudice and more hard thought about what is to replace them if they are destroyed, they might convince us that they care something about education and less about playing politics,' declared the headmaster John Garrett at Bristol Grammar School's prize-giving in October 1957. 'At a time when trained minds are more than ever necessary to enable the nation to skirt the edge of the abyss of bankruptcy; at a time when men unafraid of doing a hard day's work are desperately needed, is it wise to jerrymander with schools which have shown they can produce both?' This was too much for Alderman St John Reade, before the war a teacher at the local public school (Clifton College) but now Labour chairman of Bristol Education Committee and pushing hard for comprehensivisation, including of Garrett's 425-year-old grammar school: 'We must, I suppose, expect that our future leaders, now being trained at Bristol Grammar School, will be stout supporters of the "separate but equal" principle advocated by Mr Garrett and Governor Faubus and Little Rock.' Readers of the *Western Daily Press* would have picked up the allusion to American bigotry; even so, another letter-writer chose to distance himself from Reade's structural ambitions. 'Generalisations about a whole class of school are rash,' reflected an anonymous Labour Party member who was also a teacher. 'A really first-rate school of its kind, be it Grammar, Technical, Secondary or Comprehensive, is as different from most of its kind as from quite another kind of school. Where such a school exists, it should be cherished and preserved for the sake of the whole community.'

Up in the north-east in autumn 1958, educational ferment seized Darlington after the town council narrowly voted, despite a split in the ruling Labour group, to establish a comprehensive school at Branksome. 'We believe every child in this town has the right to a proper education and proper standard,' declared Councillor Whelan, while Councillor O'Brien was more emollient: 'We want to absorb the Grammar Schools, not supplant them. We hope the best traditions of these schools will be carried over into the new.' There ensued a flurry of mainly hostile letters to the *Northern Despatch*, typified by L. Davis writing sarcastically that 'when Coun. Whelan has demolished our Queen Elizabeth Grammar School and our sons are receiving their diplomas for rock 'n' roll at the comprehensive schools, he may turn his attention to other ways in which he can promote our community's welfare'; that grammar's Old Boys' Association took out a half-page ad on 'YOUR CHILD'S FUTURE' ('If Comprehensive Schools are set up in Darlington, no child will have the opportunity of the best education now available ... Grammar School education requires special gifts and great application ... It would be harmful to force it on children who are not really fitted for it'); early in 1959 both Macmillan and Gaitskell paid visits to Darlington, touring respectively the grammar and a secondary modern; and finally, in April, the minister, Lloyd, refused permission for the new school to go ahead as proposed, a decision confirmed in June largely on the basis of 2,500 local objections, mainly parental.[26]

Or take Bradford, whose City Council was bitterly divided during 1957–8 about a seemingly innocuous proposal from the controlling Labour group to build a new secondary school in Flockton Road in the south of the city, next to Bolling Girls' Grammar School. 'It must have a disturbing effect on the teachers of that school, knowing that they were going to be integrated into a comprehensive school,' claimed Councillor J.E.B. Singleton for the Tories in December 1957. 'What effect would it have on the pupils? They were going to lose the grammar school environment ... It was all very well saying: "Put them under one roof" but it did not work out in education practice. They had to have a certain amount of environment and they could not bring the clever ones down to the level of the dull ones.' This provoked, later in the meeting, a telling Tory–Labour exchange:

*Coun. Audrey Firth* said she did not want a comprehensive school in Bradford. There would be some sort of remote control and it would be a great barrack-like place where the child was not going to be an individual. It could not be with 2,000 children in the same building. Someone mentioned environment, and someone called 'snobbery'. Surely there was nothing wrong in giving a child environment and background. They should be proud to provide it.

*Coun. J. T. Tiernan* said the mention of snobbery brought back memories to him. He went to an ordinary elementary school and had to pass a grammar school. The children there told them: 'My mother has told me we haven't to play with you.'

Almost a year later the issue was still unresolved, with Labour's Alderman R. C. Ruth, leader of the anti-selection, pro-comprehensive lobby within the Labour group, giving the larger picture:

*Ald. Ruth* said it was proved over and over again that children with brains were being denied an opportunity to go to University because of the test made at the age of 11-plus. Was it suggested because they were building a Secondary School near a Grammar School that it was going to reduce the social status of the Grammar School because of the adjacency of boys and girls who fail to pass the 11-plus examination?

Singleton refused to yield ground. 'Alderman Ruth appeared to have forgotten that in Bradford they had a transfer system between Secondary and Grammar Schools, and no pupil was denied the possibility of going forward to Grammar School and then to University,' insisted the councillor. 'It was known in educational circles that schools of a smaller population had a better opportunity of encouraging pupils than had the larger schools. Alderman Ruth had accepted the fact that all children had the same educational attainment. That was not so . . . They could not all be put in one school and attain the same standard at the end.'

Muriel Beadle, wife of the visiting professor of genetics at Oxford in 1958–9, despaired. This keen-eyed American came – after immersing herself in educational debates, visiting several schools of each type and following the 'hot controversy' in the spring of 1959 over whether north Oxford should get a comprehensive – to 'the inescapable conclusion' that 'England's educational problems are not likely to be solved as long as schooling and social status remain so inextricably entwined'. And, like the Bristol letter-writer, she drew a parallel between racial segregation in the USA and educational segregation (whether private/state or grammar/secondary modern) in England:

> The sad thing is that secondary education, as education, is so much better overall than it was before 1944. A pity it had to get mixed up with social class, and the business of having a proper accent. That hopeful phrase, 'parity of esteem', is as hollow as our 'separate but equal'. The main difference is that we discriminate against a minority and the English against a majority.[27]

Amidst the swirling controversies, Labour's challenge by 1957 was to forge a coherent education policy ahead of the next general election. The Study Group on Education that met for the first time in March comprised mainly MPs, including two Wykehamists in Gaitskell and Crossman, Anthony Greenwood (Merchant Taylors) and Michael Stewart (Marlborough). Soon afterwards, Stewart was in public conversation with Edna Healey, who chaired the managers of a group of schools in London, and they touched on the issue of whether and how comprehensives needed to build a 'tradition' of good reputation in order to compete with established schools:

> *EH* – It is true that we don't want to create a mystique of tradition, but neither do we want to throw the baby out with the bath water. The grammar schools understandably take the view that since they are doing a good job already, why interfere with them . . .
>
> *MS* – The question that matters is: what is the whole education system turning out? Is it doing the best for the average as well as the clever pupil? History gives no instance of a civilization collapsing because it neglected its élite; but it tells of many which perished because they paid insufficient attention to the mass and allowed a gap to yawn between the élite and the ordinary citizen. Is there not a lesson here for modern England?

Throwing the baby out with the bath water: Healey's understandable fear reflected a party still deeply conflicted about the grammars, though ultimately it would be Stewart's take-no-prisoners line that spoke the loudest.

Over the rest of the year the Study Group considered a series of memos and submissions. 'Our real enemy is, surely, not the examination of children but the *separation* of them at 11,' argued Stewart in tandem with Margaret Cole, while on the other key front, it was 'an illusion' that 'if the Labour Party leaves the public schools alone and concentrates on creating comprehensive schools, these latter will become "Everyman's Eton", and the special advantages enjoyed by those parents who can pay public school fees will disappear'. For his part, Crossman did not deny the socially pernicious consequences of the old boy network, but warned against policy 'actuated by motives of envy' and was adamant about the need to recognise 'one basic human right – the right of the parent to pay twice for the child's education'. The great historian and radical R. H. Tawney advocated 'establishing not a small percentage of free places at a large number of schools, as the Fleming Committee recommended [in 1944], but a large percentage of free places at a smaller number of schools', claiming that 'nothing would do more to knock on the head the boarding school social snobbery of today than the existence, side by side with the one-clan Eton, Harrow and the rest, of equally successful boarding schools recruited from all sections of the nation'. And, in another memo, Eric James solemnly stated that grammars had been 'the strongest solvents of class divisions', given that 'Manchester Grammar School, and a few others like it, represent probably a wider social cross-section than almost any other schools, not in England alone, but in the whole Western world (this is literally true), and an academic standard which challenges the very best independent schools.'

The Study Group also heard evidence in December from Mark Abrams, commissioned to survey parental attitudes to education. In terms of working-class parents and the maintained sector, a predictable enough set of findings emerged: that most were 'quite happy to leave things as they are'; that 'while emphatic that children with good brains should be given every chance to develop, most parents seemed convinced that their own children were unlikely to obtain this opportunity because of lack of ability'; that 'they did not feel that their own children were likely to benefit particularly from any improvements in education'; and that 'the idea of the comprehensive school had made practically no impact upon them'. As for private education, Abrams noted that his survey had revealed 'an overwhelming majority of parents', including working-class ones, 'in favour of private spending on education', with 'the general feeling' being that 'if parents wanted to send children to private schools there was no reason why they should not do so'. Accordingly, concluded Abrams, 'any attempt' to abolish private education 'or even to stir up hostility against private education would probably only seem curious to the electorate'.

In February 1958 the Study Group decamped to Clacton-on-Sea for a weekend conference, listening to the views of some 18 outside experts. 'There was no criticism of Labour's proposals for reorganisation of secondary education on comprehensive lines,' recorded the official summary of the proceedings, 'provided that these were submitted in terms of a 15/20-year plan and full provision was made for flexibility in implementing the new system.' Crossman, however, privately recorded that 'everybody emphasised how impossible it was to go too fast towards a comprehensive system'.

Gaitskell looked in on the Sunday session and expressed his preference for 'Flemingism', in effect the extension of free places, chosen by intellectual ability, in about 30 public schools, but this was dismissed by Crossman as 'totally impractical', an opinion that most of the Study Group apparently shared. Altogether, noted the official summary of the session, 'the discussions were largely inconclusive but seemed to indicate the view that under present circumstances the public schools were best left alone'. Next day, writing up his diary, Crossman reflected wryly how 'at the conference there was almost universal bewilderment and amazement at the idea, and all for the right reasons – that to attack Manchester Grammar School, while leaving Eton, is the act of a zanie'.[28] The syntax was confusing, but the sense was dismayingly clear.

*Learning to Live*, Labour's policy document on education (largely drafted by Stewart), was published in mid-June. Under a future Labour government, all local authorities would be required to produce plans ending selection at 11; but at the same time, there was an acceptance that, in terms of the precise mechanics, local circumstances would demand a degree of flexibility. What about the public schools? The document yielded nothing in its ferocious denunciation of the current system – 'damages national efficiency and offends the sense of justice . . . all who desire equality of opportunity and social justice will agree that the existence of this privileged sector of education is undesirable' – but the nub, it insisted, was the question of priorities:

> There is a risk that argument over this question may give it an importance which, in proportion to the whole field of education, it does not possess. Compare, today, the free national system of education and the private fee-paying system. It is the national system which provides the greater variety and attempts the most difficult tasks. Despite all its present inadequacies, it is vigorous and capable of great advances. To make the nation's schools fully worthy of the nation will be an immense achievement. Smaller classes, better-qualified teachers, better equipment and a higher proportion of sixth formers in our own schools will open the door of opportunity and steadily reduce the influence of the privileged fee-paying schools in public life. We believe that the next Labour Government should concentrate its educational endeavours on this work.

And 'therefore', as Mollie Panter-Downes not long afterwards informed her *New Yorker* readers, 'Eton, Harrow, and the others will be left as they are'.

The document inevitably provoked some strong criticism. 'We are afraid to tackle the public schools to which the wealthy people send their sons,' lamented the working-class 'Manny' Shinwell (a former Labour minister) in *The Times*, 'but at the same time are ready to throw overboard the grammar schools, which are for many working-class boys the stepping stones to the universities and a useful career – I would rather abandon Eton, Winchester, Harrow and all the rest of them than sacrifice the advantage of the grammar school.' The journalist Geoffrey Goodman, in a letter to the *New Statesman*, was equally appalled: 'It is almost inconceivable that a party dedicated to the concept of greater equality (to say nothing of Socialism) can argue that privilege of any kind will wither away in an acquisitive society, provided you offer "suitable" alternatives.' And in the same magazine, the Cambridge literary critic Graham Hough offered a caustic prediction: 'There will remain to the Labour Party the glory of messing up the grammar schools, the oldest and best of English educational institutions; and of continuing the nineteenth-century public school system for the very few who can afford to pay for it.'[29]

The party conference was at Scarborough at the end of September. In the same debate that endorsed the anti-11-plus aspect of *Learning to Live*, Fred Peart, a dissenting member of the Study Group, moved a resolution calling for the integration of public schools into the state system. In support, Gillingham's delegate, the young Gerald Kaufman, declared that 'a progressive measure of this sort would be advancing Socialism and gaining middle-class support', while for Frank Cousins the issue was that something needed to be done about the fact that 'this country's economic, international, political and industrial affairs are in the hands of a privileged group who hand the privileges on from place to place, whether it is in the Tory Party or in our Party'. On the other side, Alice Bacon (also of the Study Group) argued that the practical problems of integration were too great and its immediate relative importance too limited, but promised that the 'scandal' of public schools getting 'priority of entry into Oxford and Cambridge' was 'something we can stop', while Stewart dismissed Peart's resolution as irrelevant: 'Ask yourselves how many members of your own constituency party want to send their children to public schools.' The outcome, on a card vote, was a defeat for Peart by 3.54 million votes to 3.07 million. 'Some day,' reflected the *New Statesman* soon afterwards, 'Labour must clearly make away with the fee-paying public schools; but it had better choose its own time, which will not be until the comprehensive schools have been firmly established in sufficient numbers and have had time to show their merits.'

A range of reasons had contributed to Labour's unwillingness to take on the public schools – not least an honourable dislike of interfering with people's liberty, a dislike felt as much by Bevan as by Gaitskell and Crossman. But perhaps the last word should go to Sir Richard Acland, reviewing Michael Young's *The Rise of the Meritocracy* in 1959. According to this singular man – Rugby and Balliol, from 1935 a Liberal MP, then founding member during the war of the socialist Common Wealth Party, later a Labour MP until in 1955 resigning from the party over its support for nuclear weapons – Young's optimistic forecast that by the end of the 1970s the public-school question would be (in Acland's paraphrasing words) 'quietly and effortlessly eliminated' as a result of vastly increased educational expenditure on the state system was 'almost wholly divorced from reality':

> The privilege of public school education has little to do with better teach-ers – man for man I doubt if they are very much superior to grammar school staff. Still less has it anything to do with some subtle atmosphere distilled from the spirit of Matthew Arnold hovering in the quads. It is based on something far more material which I very seldom see mentioned. Having them under their hands all day long *the public schools can give their pupils many more hours of education per week.*
>
> At a typical public school known to me the boys have 38 hours of organised instruction per week, including all games, and 1½ hours prep. per night in quiet study or under discipline in hall. The corresponding figure for Wandsworth School (comprehensive) where I taught last year is 28 hours, including 1 hour's prep. in a home where there may be no escape from the tele. The other material factor is size of class – averaging about 22 compared with 32 at Wandsworth.
>
> Speaking to a sixth form at a public school recently I had to say to them: 'Of those at Wandsworth who will seriously try to reach univer-sity this year and will fail, two-thirds would succeed if they could work under your conditions; of you who will succeed in entering university, two-thirds would fail if you worked under Wandsworth conditions.'
>
> *This* is the measure of the educational privilege which the rich can buy. *This* is the reason why no wealthy socialist can do other than send his son to public school – he cannot face the vision of his own son, aged 21 and perhaps by then a keen Conservative or Liberal, saying to him: 'You had the means of giving me the best chance, and for your blasted political humbug you didn't do it.'
>
> And *this* is the reason why the Labour Party, in the present temper of the nation, does not and dare not propose to end public schools. Putting it quite brutally, they know that against such an appalling invasion of privilege and inequality, the rich would 'go on strike' in one way or another and bring the economic life of the community to chaos in which (once again in the present temper of the nation) the government would

not receive such zestful backing from workers and middle-classes as would win from the chaos a government victory over the rich.

Therefore, let it be perfectly clear, we are not going to have Michael Young's Meritocracy or anything like it merely by accentuating our present tendencies.[30]

# PART THREE

# 10

# Unnatural Practices

Pinky and Perky, not yet sundered by musical differences, starring on *Sunday Night at the London Palladium*; a television critic laying into the fake bonhomie of ITV's 'Show Biz Corps' ('Mr Michael Miles's awful relish . . . Mr Hughie Green's twangy transatlantic archness . . . Mr Bruce Forsyth's twinkle-toes and strident congratulations'); *Grandstand* starting to show rugby league (commentator, Eddie Waring); Cliff Richard's 'Move It' peaking at number 3, 'Hoots Mon' by the novelty act Lord Rockingham's XI climbing to number 1; Walter Allen praising Stanley Middleton's first novel *A Short Answer* as 'a sharp and fruitful picture of middle-class provincial life'; reading Angus Wilson's *The Middle Age of Mrs Eliot* feeling for Pamela Hansford Johnson like being 'hobbled with the author in a sort of three-legged race'; Arnold Wesker issuing his first major blast ('Let Battle Commence!') on the need to bring art to the masses ('It is the bus driver, the housewife, the miner and the Teddy Boy to whom I should like to address myself'); Philip Larkin admiring a newspaper photo of London Zoo's Guy the Gorilla ('I felt considerable kinship with him'); John Fowles, on his way to the Whitechapel Gallery's Jackson Pollock exhibition, walking through the 'eighteenth-century streets' of Spitalfields, 'full of Indians, Jews, poverty, beautiful door-ways painted in tatty varnish, dirty, ragged children'; a Gallup poll finding 81 per cent had a favourable view of the Royal Family, 71 per cent of the House of Commons, 52 per cent of the House of Lords and 51 per cent of the trade unions; Marian Raynham in Surbiton rebelling one Saturday ('Why should I spend all morning making cakes & scones? Seem to be spending all my life doing these foolish things. I just won't . . .'); Judy Haines's younger daughter Pamela doing an old 11-plus paper at home one evening ('Nearly screamed when I found she had gone wrong in two of the simplest sums . . . Must get her a tonic. This swotting for 11+ is getting on her nerves'); and Anthony Heap citing 'the latest craze' among girls and young women – 'rotating an old fashioned child's wooden hoop (now called a "hula-hoop") around one's waist as long as possible without letting it drop' – as further evidence it was 'a mad world' . . .[1] Yet nothing mattered more in November 1958 than the fact that on the 26th the House of Commons at last openly debated the issue of homosexuality – almost fifteen months after the Wolfenden Report, six months after the founding of the Homosexual Law Reform Society and by chance just a few days after a high-profile episode had thrown the whole issue into uncomfortably stark relief.

On the night of Wednesday the 19th Ian Harvey – rising Tory MP, junior minister at the Foreign Office, married with two daughters – was walking along the Mall shortly after 11 o'clock. 'A young guardsman in uniform passed me at a slow pace and I knew what that meant,' he recalled in his memoir *To fall like Lucifer*. 'I turned and caught up with him and we went together into the Park.' There they were 'caught by a park official accompanied by a policeman', taken (not without a struggle on Harvey's part) to a police station, and, next morning, stood side by side in the dock at Bow Street Court, each charged with 'committing an act of gross indecency with another male person' and 'behaving in a manner reasonably likely to offend against public decency', with both men being remanded until 10 December. It was the end of Harvey's political career. 'If (as I fear) he is guilty, it means that he must resign his post in the Govt *and* his seat in Parl[t],' recorded Macmillan on the Friday. 'I saw him this morning, & did my best to comfort him. But it [is] a terrible thing & has distressed me greatly.' In the event, Harvey resigned both post and seat on Monday the 24th, well aware that in his constituency association at Harrow East there were 'many people who, whilst they were my supporters, regarded what I had done as unspeakable'. On 10 December each man was found guilty and fined £5 – with Harvey paying not only for the guardsman but also, as his counsel accurately predicted, for the rest of his life. He found himself rapidly being cut off by former colleagues in politics and advertising, with one remarking that 'the only thing for Ian Harvey to do is to change his name and go to Canada'; the Carlton Club accepted his resignation without comment; the Junior Carlton Club hoped he would retain his membership, but asked him to promise not to enter the premises for two years; and the War Office had to be persuaded not to have this former lieutenant colonel in the Territorial Army cashiered. 'I remember him,' wrote Matthew Parris in 2002 (15 years after Harvey's death), 'a sad old man, living alone and forgotten in a small flat.'[2]

The proposed decriminalisation of homosexual relations was of course only one part of Wolfenden; on the other part – the recommendation that prostitutes be outlawed from the streets – Rab Butler as Home Secretary made it clear, opening the thinly attended debate, that he was fully in accordance, leading in due course to legislation to that effect. The story goes that an uncertain Butler had sought the opinion of the stationmaster in his Saffron Walden constituency, who had told him that people did not mind prostitutes, but had no wish to see them in public places. As for the more contentious question, Butler's unyielding line, on behalf of the government as a whole, was that 'there was at present a very large section of the population who strongly repudiated homosexual conduct and whose moral sense would be offended by an alteration of the law' – a no-change policy backed by a narrow majority of the speakers, among them Labour's Fred Bellenger. 'I can well understand the pleas of those who say that those who practise this cult in private are inoffensive citizens,' he conceded. 'Perhaps they are, if it is meant that they do not break windows or behave riotously. Nevertheless, they are, in my opinion, a malignant canker in the community and if this were allowed to grow, it would eventually kill off what is known as normal life.' A Tory backbencher, William Shepherd, agreed: 'I think there is far too much sympathy with the homosexual and far too little regard for society . . . I believe that it is our duty as far as we can to stop this society within a society. I believe that to a great extent, perhaps 90 per cent of the cases, these men could be deviated from their path . . .' Perhaps the most emphatic speaker was his colleague Cyril Black, an inveterate campaigner for traditional morality. 'These unnatural practices, if persisted in, spell death to the souls of those who indulge in them,' he declared. 'Great nations have fallen and empires been destroyed because corruption became widespread and socially accept-able.' On the morning of the debate *The Times* had contended that though it was 'a foregone conclusion that the homosexual laws will not be reformed yet', it was 'equally a foregone conclusion that reform must come eventually', given that 'the majority of well-informed people are now clearly convinced that these laws are unjust and obsolete'. But for the moment, as Butler accurately indicated, public opinion as a whole continued to run the other way, and a few weeks later a Gallup poll revealed only 25 per cent wanting decriminalisation, as opposed to 48 per cent favouring the laws staying as they were. Ironically, it was in Shepherd's own constituency – at Bilston in Staffordshire – that a fort-night after the debate two men (aged 66 and 41) gassed themselves to death, having been questioned by police in connection with (consent-ing) 'indecent actions between men'.

More bleak years lay ahead. *A Minority: A Report on the Life of the Male Homosexual in Great Britain* was produced in 1960 by Gordon Westwood (pseudonym for Michael Schofield), based on a survey of 127 'self-confessed' homosexuals. 'It is impossible to work on a research of this kind,' noted the book's first sentence, 'without becoming imme-diately aware of the repugnance with which homosexuality is regarded by many people.' And Schofield itemised how 'all sorts of difficulties were put in the way of the research', not least by 'the Medical Committees of some hospitals', which 'refused to allow doctors on their staff to help'. Inevitably, the interviewees themselves spoke eloquently of the attitude of heterosexuals:

> They think it's disgusting. The kind of remarks I get are, 'Be a man,' or 'You're not a proper man.'
>
> It's very difficult for a normal to understand. There are no expressions they would not use to show their disgust. It's horrifying how men or women who in every other way are decent and sensible can lose their sense of proportion on this subject.
>
> The normal men I work with simply don't understand. They say, 'Why do they have to do such things when there are plenty of women about?'
>
> Many people – like my brother, for example – think it's all a huge joke and just don't take it seriously.

Inevitably it affects your social life. I always seem to go on holidays alone and sometimes I get a pitiful feeling, knowing that I'll live the rest of my life in solitude.

A homosexual cannot relax in ordinary company.

The effect of acting a part can be exhausting. I envy people in jobs where they haven't got to act a part. In the business world one spends a lot of time taking care – making sure one doesn't give oneself away.

But of course, it all depended. 'If you are a failure in the world, they look down on you if they know you are queer. But if you are successful and queer, you become rather quaint.'[3]

Even so, to an extent sometimes under-appreciated, there were clear signs by the late 1950s of the hold of 'respectable' morality starting to break up. Specifically, three pieces of essentially liberal legislation had been enacted – not without difficulty – by the end of the decade. The Mental Health Act, by abolishing the categories of moral defectiveness and feeblemindedness, made it impossible to lock up in Victorian mental institutions women deemed promiscuous or otherwise troublesome; the Legitimacy Act significantly extended the legitimisation of children born illegitimate; and the Obscene Publications Act, piloted through by Roy Jenkins, greatly reduced the powers of censorship over the printed word.[4] Significantly, this last piece of legislation was not yet enacted when in spring 1959 Vladimir Nabokov's controversial *Lolita* was at last published in Britain, by Weidenfeld and Nicolson – who were not subjected to prosecution. A battle had seemingly been won.

―――

Two key industrial announcements were made in the closing months of 1958. The first, on 18 November, concerned steel strip mills: the expectation had been that the government would back the construction of a huge new continuous one at Llanwern, near Newport in South Wales; but instead, in the general context of worryingly high unemployment in the old 'depressed areas', political pressure from Scotland was such that Macmillan decided – exercising what he called 'the judgement of Solomon' – to back *two* smaller, semi-continuous new mills, namely one at Llanwern and another at Ravenscraig in Lanarkshire. This call, justly comments the historian Peter Scott, 'resulted in neither being sufficiently large to obtain the economies of scale achieved in continental plants'. But at least at this point there was not a problem of inadequate demand, quite unlike the ominous, rapidly developing situation in the coal industry. There, total consumption during 1957 had abruptly fallen by over 6 million tons, followed in 1958 by a drop of a further 13 million tons, as coal found itself being brutally undercut by oil. 'Coal is still our main source of power – and a vital part of our natural inheritance,' proclaimed a full-page National Coal Board advertisement in November 1958, exhorting 'young men' to become 'the next generation of managers, engineers and scientists' in the coal industry. Soon afterwards, on 3 December, the NCB announced that 36 pits would have to close (including 20 in Scotland and 6 in South Wales), most of them in the next few months, with some 4,000 mineworkers to be made redundant. Still, from a Tory point of view, this would hardly lose votes, whereas another sector in deep trouble, the Lancashire cotton industry, was a different, more troubling matter. The upshot was not only detailed negotiations to reduce Commonwealth imports but, in summer 1959, the passing of the Cotton Industry Act, in effect a state-supported scrapping scheme designed to eliminate excess capacity as painlessly as possible. 'A sop to Lancashire,' the historian of the Lancashire cotton industry brusquely calls this politically motivated, taxpayer-funded piece of government interventionism that did little to equip the industry for challenges ahead that might anyway have proved impossible to overcome.[5]

The housing trends by the late 1950s had an even more significant political dimension, as is suggested by the annual breakdown for permanent dwellings built in England and Wales:

|      | Local authorities | Private builders |
|------|------|------|
| 1956 | 149,139 | 119,585 |
| 1957 | 145,711 | 122,942 |
| 1958 | 117,438 | 124,087 |
| 1959 | 102,905 | 146,476 |

Macmillan was fully alert to the potential dividend of stimulating the number of owner-occupiers, and during 1958 (the year that Lawrie Barratt formed a house-building company in Newcastle, initially focusing on first-time buyers) he overrode Treasury objections and pushed his Housing Minister into developing the concept of 100-per-cent, government-supported mortgages, as enshrined in due course in the House Purchase and Housing Act of 1959. 'Whatever the Opposition may say now,' declared the junior Housing Minister Reginald Bevins in the Commons debate on the Bill in December 1958, 'the fact of the matter is that the Labour Party has always been secretly, not publicly, contemptuous of the conception of a property-owning democracy. [HON. MEMBERS: "Nonsense."] Of course, they have. Indeed, from their own point of view, they are probably right, because it is not part of the Socialist mission in this land to manufacture Conservatives.'[6]

Nevertheless, those Hon. Members opposite were by and large in an optimistic frame of mind during the winter of 1958–9, notwithstanding the recent tightening in the polls and an instantly celebrated Vicky cartoon in the *New Statesman* in November dubbing the PM as 'Supermac'. Rising prices, rising unemployment (up by February 1959 to 620,000, the highest level since 1947), a deteriorating balance of payments – no wonder that, in Geoffrey Goodman's words, 'both Left and Right wings of the Labour Movement felt that 1959 would bring a Labour Government to power with Gaitskell as Prime Minister'. Admittedly the temporary accord between Left and Right was paper-thin – 'Gaitskell's piddling all the time for fear of losing the Election,' Nye Bevan scornfully told Dick Crossman in December – but at least it existed. There was even a glossy new policy document in place, *The Future Labour Offers You*, launched during the autumn in tandem with a notably effective party political broadcast. Yet two indicators this winter might have given pause for thought. In November a detailed analysis in the *Financial Times* concluded that 'the long post-war decline in the economic position of the middle class has now been halted'; and in January the publication of weekly averages of shop sales for 1958 revealed that a sharp drop in the early months had given way, following the end of the credit squeeze, to a steep rise between August and the end of the year. Bevan, though, was adamant. 'We shall win the Election,' he informed Crossman, 'and the trouble will come very soon afterwards.'[7]

One direction in which Labour did not look for lessons was from the New Left. On the same evening as Bevan's predictions, Brian

Abel-Smith read a paper to the Fabian Society, with Anthony Wedgwood Benn among those present. In it he advocated that the Fabians become more like the *Universities and Left Review*, which (in Benn's words, reporting Abel-Smith) 'got five or six hundred to their meetings', whereas 'we were completely missing young people'. Abel-Smith further urged the Fabians to 'meet in a coffee house instead of in large bare halls'. Whereupon: 'Tony Crosland opened the attack. He said that he could see nothing of interest in the *ULR* except that "there's a man who seems to be able to run a coffee house". He thought that political activity under the age of thirty-five was not of great interest to the Fabians ... All this was said in a most bored and offensive way.' The others who spoke 'agreed with Tony to a greater or lesser extent', except for Benn himself, who argued that 'the question we had to face was whether we had anything relevant to say in the modern world'.

The coffee house that Crosland so disdainfully referred to was the Partisan at the *ULR*'s premises at 7 Carlisle Street in Soho – a place not only for food and drink ('Bill of fare includes Farmhouse Soup ... Borscht ... Irish Peasant Stew ... Liver dumplings ... Boiled Breconshire Mutton with caper sauce ... Apple dumplings with hot lemon sauce ... Whitechapel cheese-cake and pastries ... Vienna coffee ... café filtre ... Russian tea') but also chess, music and debate. The venture was run by the ebullient, charismatic, hopelessly disorganised young historian Ralph (later Raphael) Samuel, by this time based at the Institute of Community Studies. 'He obviously has tremendous faith in people and in his beliefs,' reflected Phyllis Willmott after talking to him at a Christmas party. 'I find his earnest idealism most wonderfully touching.' In January, intrigued, she visited the Partisan and found 'mostly odd cranks and broken-down "artists"', often 'sporting beards or berets', as well as serious-looking young students. 'Girls in duffle coats and black stockings, young boys in old jackets. A coloured man began to play the guitar more or less spontaneously as I could judge. I felt very sophisticated and elegant by comparison, although I wasn't.'[8]

Benn's 'modern world' was coming on apace. On the morning of 5 December, two days after the pit-closures announcement, Macmillan inaugurated the 8.5-mile Preston Bypass, Britain's first stretch of motorway and, subsequently, part of the M6. 'In the years to come,' the

PM declared, 'the county and country alike may look at the Preston Bypass – a fine thing in itself but a finer thing as a symbol – as a token of what is to follow'; pressing a button, he cut the traditional tape by remote control; and then, watched by 200 cheering schoolchildren from what *The Times* called 'one of the futuristic-looking bridges that straddle the motorway', he was driven along in a Rolls-Royce Landau. On another front, though in public call boxes it was still a case of insert four pennies and press button A, there was major progress too, for later that day the Queen visited Bristol telephone exchange and directly dialled an Edinburgh number (031 CAL 3636), thereby inaugurating the new subscriber trunk dialling (STD) system. 'Those present then heard an amplified voice reply: "The Lord Provost of Edinburgh speaking," to which the Queen replied: "This is the Queen speaking, from Bristol. Good afternoon, Lord Provost."' Back in Preston, the AA in the evening reported traffic flowing at 400 vehicles an hour at an average speed of 70 mph, with excellent lane discipline and 'exemplary' signalling, though it did regretfully add that 'the speed and density of the traffic' would probably make a traditional salute from their patrols 'impracticable'.

Literary tastes – like many other tastes – remained for the most part defiantly unmodern. 'Mr and Mrs Brown first met Paddington on a railway platform,' began Michael Bond's *A Bear Called Paddington*, inspired by a stocking-filler bear he had bought for his wife at Selfridges the previous Christmas Eve. The *TLS* was only cautiously enthusiastic about Bond's creation ('it must be said that a 6-year-old to whom the book was read laughed himself sick over some of the slapstick'), but the entire first print run rapidly sold out. So too did John Betjeman's *Collected Poems*, though not without the odd dissenting note amidst the general enthusiasm. 'I wish he wouldn't appear to be writing off some millions of his fellow humans because they say "Pardon",' reflected Janet Adam Smith in the *New Statesman*, while K. W. Gransden in the *Listener*, after acknowledging the poet was 'in the rare position of being both chic and popular', teased out the implications of how Betjeman's 'own emotions enter into everything he writes':

He really feels it and means it. Does class matter? By jove, yes. Down with vulgar new rich City men; down with suburban pseudo-gentility;

down with supercinemas, neon, fish and chips, chromium; down with the phoney picture-postcard England of the brewers' advertisements. Up with romantic Baker-street buffet; up with churches; up with the Home Counties and horses. Down, in short, with the century of the common man, and up with the past from about 1880 to 1914.

And of course one sometimes agrees. Mr Betjeman is an extraordinarily accurate observer and recorder of middle-class manners and prejudices, some of which are endearing and even good. But at times the exclusiveness and triviality of this point of view seems ignoble and, like all rearguard actions, rather pathetic. It is all very funny; but how seldom one laughs without a pharisaic snigger; and how unscrupulously Mr Betjeman beguiles and flatters us into accepting his values along with his verbal felicities. We may feel cleverer, 'nicer', or even more U after reading him; we rarely feel better.

Shortly before Christmas, at the Hyde Park Gate home of Enid Bagnold, Betjeman was presented with the Duff Cooper Prize by Princess Margaret. 'A really thrilling moment of triumph,' Betjeman wrote afterwards to his publisher Jock Murray, while another publisher present at the ceremony, Rupert Hart-Davis, told his old schoolmaster, 'My dear George, she is exquisitely beautiful, very small and neat and shapely, with a lovely skin and staggering blue eyes.'[9]

Tom Driberg's swoon of choice was Cliff Richard. 'Though he is said to be in private life a modest and likeable Hertfordshire lad,' the politician noted about this time following his latest performance on *Oh Boy!*, 'he has been taught to assume just the right look of delinquent fretfulness: his eyes have the smouldering but fixed glare of a sulky basilisk; his coiffure is mountainously upswept. A menacingly one-sided Ozymandias curl of the lip reveals strong incisors.' A few days later, the *New Musical Express* reported that Cliff now had a new manager (the tough-minded impresario Tito Burns, keen from the start to turn him into 'an all-round entertainer'); that his parents, with whom he still lived in Cheshunt, had been promised for Christmas 'a 17 in. console television set'; and that his plan for Christmas Eve was to go for 'a bumper Chinese spread' at Edgware Road's Lotus House (London's first upmarket Chinese restaurant, run by John Koon). Elsewhere in pop-land, Tommy Steele was now

already taking his first step on the primrose path to all-round entertainer, starring at the Coliseum as Buttons in *Cinderella*, alongside
the 'handle-bar moustached comedian' Jimmy Edwards (of current
*Whack-O!* fame) and 'Television glamour girl Yana', an altogether
'odd, not to say outlandish conglomeration of talents'. The descriptions were by Anthony Heap, present of course at the first night (18
December) and his usual implacable self: the 'rock 'n' roll idol'
brought 'to his first stage acting part little but an atrocious cockney
accent', while Edwards 'seldom contrives to be funny, least of all in
his long-winded trumpet-playing solo act'. Alan Brien in the
*Spectator* agreed about Steele's deficiencies ('his timing is embarrass-
ingly erratic and he moves as stiffly as a stilt-dancer'), with the
panto's only redeeming feature being Kenneth Williams as a 'campy
sister'.

In the days after Christmas, two faces of the future were sighted on
the small screen. On ITV's *Small Time* for younger viewers, Muriel
Young read 'Little Rocky: The rocket who was afraid of heights', and
on the BBC, the quiz game *Ask Me Another* (produced by Ned Sherrin)
included Ted 'Farmer' Moult, praised by viewers for his 'wonderful
good humour' and treating the programme 'certainly seriously, but as a
game, and not as a grim contest'. There were plaudits too for the chairman Franklin Engelmann – 'firm, fair, friendly, quick-witted and always
very natural', noted an insurance agent – while a marine fitter called the
whole thing 'not only instructive, but also very interesting and entertaining'. Even so, the show captured only 16 per cent of the working-
class audience, with 36 per cent opting instead for *Emergency—Ward 10*
on the other channel.[10]

---

The trade unions may have trailed far behind the Royal Family in terms
of the public having a 'favourable' attitude, but with 51 per cent they
did better in Gallup's November poll than the City and Stock Exchange,
which managed only 44 per cent, though with a high 'neutral' (in practice indifferent?) rating of 40 per cent. 'The City must often to foreign
eyes seem deceptively sleepy; it does not take fleets of lawyers to reach
an agreement; it often likes to pretend that it is more old-fashioned than
it is,' the *Financial Times* complacently reflected a few weeks later. 'At

Christmas we can allow ourselves the favourite English pastime of congratulating ourselves on being a lot shrewder than we are taken for. Let other people be "too clever by half" so long as we can be "not such fools as we look."' But as it happened, two stories at the end of the year and going into 1959 suddenly put the City unusually and at times uncomfortably in the national spotlight.

Shortly after Christmas the government announced the full convertibility of sterling held by non-residents. 'Pound Flies High' (*Sunday Express*), 'This Proud, Free £' (*Daily Express*) and 'The £ Stands Firm on Freedom Day' (*Evening Standard*) was the patriotic chorus of the Beaverbrook press, while the *FT* declared that sterling's convertibility, following on from the end of credit controls, meant that 'now, for the first time, it is possible to claim that the post-war period, with all its artificial pressures and constraints, is over and done with'. *The Economist*'s line on 'An Act of Bravery?' was altogether more cautious: 'The main meaning of the move is that Britain, as the world's leading short-term banker, will now be more formally (and therefore possibly more forcefully) committed to take the strain upon its gold reserves whenever any other currency in the world is regarded as temporarily more desirable to hold than sterling.' And, accepting that 'to voice these misgivings is just another way of saying that Britain is, for better or worse, in the international banking business', it concluded: 'Sterling sets sail on a long voyage in a fair weather ship at a moment when the weather forecast is favourable. Let us hope, indeed everybody must hope, that it will remain favourable. But it is rash to bet that it will do so for ever.'

What were the domestic implications of what one economic historian calls 'Britain's new cosmopolitanism'? Although the announcement itself provoked no great controversy, Anthony Crosland would state the potential downside forcibly in a Third Programme talk in early February. Claiming (probably correctly) that the 'strongest pressure' behind the decision had come from the Bank of England and the City, wanting convertibility 'in order to enhance the position of London as a world banker and financial centre', he called it 'a disastrous approach' – given not only that 'the financial earnings of the City from overseas business are trivial in relation to our balance of payments' but that 'every step in the direction [i.e. of financial liberalisation, ultimately leading to the end of exchange controls] increases our vulnerability to speculation'. And:

> The really serious thing about all this is that our *domestic* policies are increasingly dictated by the holders of sterling – by bankers in Zurich and London, by speculators all over the world, and by traders using sterling as an international trading currency. These people are not, unfortunately, as the City likes to think they are, highly rational and sophisticated judges of the true state of the British economy. On the contrary, they are often naive, volatile, and ill-informed – as they were, for example, when they caused the sterling crisis of 1957; or else they are plain incompetent, as the City syndicate was in the recent British Aluminium dispute. Yet the fear of what they may do to sterling increasingly influences our Bank rate policy, our rate of economic expansion, our wages policy, and now – to judge from a recent leading article in *The Economist* – even what taxation policy we are allowed to pursue. Heaven alone knows – or rather I can easily guess – what their attitude would be to the policies of a Labour Government.

In short, in characteristic Crosland tones (and, no doubt, drawl): 'All this seems to me an intolerable derogation of British sovereignty; the more tiresome since bankers and speculators are all natural deflationists and their influence is invariably against a rapid rate of growth.'[11]

The 'British Aluminium dispute' to which Crosland referred was the other story.[12] In essence it was a disputatious, high-profile City setpiece arising out of the contested takeover of British Aluminium (BA), an ailing company whose chairman was Viscount Portal of Hungerford, Chief of Air Staff during the war and now president of the MCC. The rival bidders were on the one hand the Aluminium Company of America, favoured by BA, and on the other hand an alliance of an American company, Reynolds Metals, and a British one, Tube Investments (TI). The prestigious, ultra-respectable merchant banks Hambros and Lazards were advising BA, while for the other side the principal adviser was Warburgs, a recently created Jewish merchant bank headed by Siegmund Warburg that was still regarded with considerable suspicion by the City Establishment. 'Rather a "Gentleman v.

Players" affair', was how Macmillan privately characterised the Aluminium War (as it became known), and the whole episode would prove richly symbolic.

Amidst considerable acrimony between the two camps, the dramatic denouement began in the last few days of 1958 when Hambros and Lazards formed a City consortium of the great and the good (including Morgan Grenfell, Brown Shipley and Robert Fleming) to protect BA from the attentions of Reynolds/TI, a grand alliance prompted less by a dispassionate analysis of what was best for BA than a visceral dislike of hostile takeover bids, still a relative rarity. Kim Cobbold, governor of the Bank of the England, tried to arrange a truce between the two parties, which in practice meant persuading them not to engage in further buying of BA shares. But during the early days of 1959, while the City consortium heeded Cobbold's wishes, Warburgs did not, deploying the black arts of what Cobbold himself crisply called 'monkey business'. Put simply, one side played cricket, the other did not. By 6 January, Reynolds/TI had achieved majority control; the following week, *The Times* published an extraordinary letter by Olaf Hambro, claiming that the wishes of the City had been violated.[13]

The Aluminium War was the making of Warburgs, ushered in an era of contested takeover battles and generally struck a blow – though not a fatal one – at the City's traditional ethos of gentlemanly capitalism. For Portal, it was part of a distressing winter, with his MCC tourists taking a pounding down under against a notably uncompromising Australian side. 'Cowdrey,' noted Philip Larkin on 27 December shortly before the Second Test, with England already one down, 'is clasped in some cloudy private inhibition: Bailey is like the old horse in *Animal Farm* – "I will bat slower"; Dexter, well, don't know much about Dexter: *pas sérieux*, I'd say. Fenner's playboy.' All three were amateurs, the team's captain (Peter May) was an amateur, and of course the dissenting professional, Johnny Wardle, had been left behind. Things failed to improve at Melbourne, with the visitors being rolled over in their second innings for a miserable 87. 'Never can I remember such a dismal batting display,' declared one old salt, Alec Bedser, while Frank Rostron in the *Sunday Express* blamed May and the manager Freddie Brown (yet another amateur) for 'their staggeringly slack attitude and complacence from the beginning of the tour'. It got still worse. England eventually went down 4–0, and in one match the supremely professional off-spinner Jim Laker, pausing as was his habit to check his field before coming in to bowl, noticed that down at deep square leg the young Cantab Ted Dexter was ... practising his golf swing.[14]

# Morbid Sentimentality

A suburban vignette, and an ill-natured turn against a sporting hero, helped mark the start of 1959. At Finchley Central on the evening of the 2nd, a Friday, passengers travelling on the Northern Line – for so long 'the misery line' – refused to leave their carriages when 'all change' was called. Holding the doors open to prevent the train from moving, they wanted, according to eyewitness Ernest Lindgren of 57 Ventnor Drive, N20, 'to know what the reason was'. Eventually most got out, after the police had been summoned, but Lindgren in his letter to *The Times* was adamant that 'this sudden, spontaneous demonstration was not provoked by one incident or one official, but by the accumulated resentment of rational people at being treated habitually and consistently as unreasoning cattle'. The mood was also dark the next afternoon at Old Trafford, where, after winning a penalty for his visiting Blackpool team, Stanley Matthews found himself being booed for the first time in his 28-year career.

Three days later, on 6 January, Anthony Heap took his nine-year-old son to the King's Cross Gaumont to see Norman Wisdom's latest, *The Square Peg*, with the star taking a 'gratifying – and well seized – opportunity to get away from his customary cloth capped "little man" character'; on the 8th the *Daily Express* exposed in 48-point type the double life of Edwin Brock ('PC 258 CONFESSES I'M A POET . . . THE THINGS HE THINKS UP AS HE POUNDS THE PECKHAM BEAT'), after he had had some poems published by the *Times Literary Supplement*; and at Earl's Court on the 12th, Bellingham's Henry Cooper became British and British Empire heavyweight champion by outpointing Blackpool's Brian London over 15 gruelling rounds – 'an extraordinary fight!' declared Philip Larkin, as he listened on the radio to what one reporter called Cooper's 'superbly judged' perform-ance against the 'bull-like rushes' of his opponent, left at the end looking like 'an over-grown schoolboy receiving a caning'. Macmillan meanwhile was heading for the north-east, for a three-day tour that included a series of factory visits, largely convincing him that, with order books still thin, it would be sensible to postpone the general election until the autumn. In Sunderland on his final morning, the 15th, he toured the North Sands shipyard of Joseph L. Thompson and Sons. 'There was Mr Macmillan, in a nest of girders, watching the workmen watching him,' recalled an accompanying journalist, Alan Brien. 'Then the noon-day hooter gave its bronchial blast. The motionless men sprang to life and poured past him in a hurrying, preoccupied flood. His eyebrows twitched in surprise and he muttered something to his wife. Lady Dorothy was quicker on the uptake. "When the whistle blows," she explained, "they all go off for their luncheon."' That evening in Newcastle was the first night of Tyne Tees Television, and Macmillan gave an interview. 'They are rather like fish, the further north you go the better they get,' he said of the people of the north-east. And, after noting how impressed he had been by the sight of workers and employers pulling together, unlike in the old days, he added: 'It has given me a tremendous inspiration – even a few days like this. In London you really don't see what is going on.'[1]

The weather during much of January and February was miserable – peasoupers, a flu epidemic carrying chesty complications, and, as Mollie Panter-Downes put it, 'every theatre, train, and bus crowded with customers barking like a vaudeville dog act'. Frost damage caused the famed Preston Bypass to be closed for over a month, but the weather was probably not responsible for the death on 22 January of the recently retired motor-racing champion Mike Hawthorn, racing his customised Jaguar against a friend's Mercedes on the Guildford by-pass. 'About ten minutes of the fifteen minutes was wholly concerned with it,' grumbled Kenneth Preston after the six o'clock news on the radio. 'It is a comment on the time that so much should be made of a young man for travelling fast in a car. What sort of values have we got nowadays?' A week later in Chingford was the eve of Pamela Haines's 11-plus exam. 'I set her hair and got clean blouse, cardigan, etc, ready for tomorrow,' recorded Judy. 'Cleaned shoes, too, as I intend going to school with her, even though she's taking the exam at her own school.' Next day: 'I went down with her. She looked lovely and at this eleventh hour – relaxed. I am so grateful . . .' And even better: 'Pamela came home radiant (as did Ione last year) saying she had had a lovely time.' By now it was almost exactly five months since the Notting Hill riots, and late on Friday the 30th the BBC showed live from St Pancras Town Hall half an hour of the first Caribbean Carnival. Its stars included Cleo Laine, The Southlanders and The Mighty Terror; a Carnival Queen beauty contest was won by the very black Faye Craig; and decorative palms from Kew Gardens gave a suitably tropical feel. The presiding spirit of the event (direct forerunner of the Notting Hill Carnival) was Claudia Jones, a Trinidadian Communist who had been deported in 1955 from the United States and who in March 1958 had founded the *West Indian Gazette*. 'West Indians newly transplanted to British soil,' she wrote in the souvenir brochure, 'strain to feel and hear and reflect their idiom even as they strain to feel the warmth of their sun-drenched islands and its immemorable beauty of landscape and terrain,' while the events of the previous summer had been 'the matrix binding West Indians in the United Kingdom together as never before', so that 'those who have filled St Pancras Hall' were 'determined that such happenings should not recur'.[2]

Most politicians spent the first week of February reading with horrified fascination Labour MP Wilfred Fienburgh's posthumous novel *No Love for Johnnie*, accurately acclaimed by Bernard Levin as 'a modern *Fame is the Spur* . . . a dagger-sharp observation and a deep understanding of the itch that bites at a politician'. Among public condemnations, Richard Crossman in the *Daily Mirror* called it a 'nauseating caricature of Labour politics', and J.P.W. Mallalieu in the *New Statesman* complained that Fienburgh had 'almost totally excluded' from his hero's character (apparently based in part on James Callaghan) 'any trace of integrity or any real feeling for the movement of which he is a member'. Privately, George Wigg thought the book an epitaph not only for social democracy but for the parliamentary system itself, and Macmillan reflected that if Fienburgh 'hadn't died, the other Labour MPs would have killed him'.

The latest death in the news, though for the most part far from banner headline, was Buddy Holly's. Four days after the plane crash, early in the morning on Saturday the 7th, the eight-year-old Brian McHugh heard 'a loud scratching' from the particularly squalid Glasgow tenement next to his rather better one and looked across:

> A window was open, and the ragged remnants of a curtain were pulled to one side. A young man was standing gazing out of the window. Suddenly, the loudest noise I thought possible exploded from the window. It was Buddy Holly singing 'That'll Be the Day'.
>
> I can still remember [in 2011] the look of sad but bewildered ecstasy on the man's face. The music was blaring from a brand new portable Dansette record player. As the music finished there was commotion in the further recesses of the room; I could make out a young woman and two small, semi-clad children scurrying about.
>
> The window was closed and there was more noise – wailing, arguing, someone crying . . .

The noise was more decorous that evening, as the married couple Pearl Carr and Teddy Johnson zestfully performed 'Sing, Little Birdie' to become the British entrants for the Eurovision Song Contest. How would they fare the next month in Cannes? 'Although it has a catchy tune,' reckoned one viewer, 'I can't imagine it having much chance on the continent.'³

Undeniably there was a whiff of the Continental about Jack Clayton's film of the bestselling John Braine novel *Room at the Top*, and not only because of Simone Signoret's starring role. 'Its camera-work has an unheightened truth so foreign to our feature films that one often drifts into looking for the subtitles,' noted an admiring Penelope Gilliatt in the February issue of *Vogue*. 'Casually and baldly, as Fellini would, it states what a Northern town is like: cobbled streets, smudged views of chimneys, women cooking at ranges, wet slaps of washing to be dodged by children playing in the street.' The film also involved – despite the British Board of Film Censors insisting that words like *lust* and *bitch* be removed – a serious examination of sex and social class, and altogether marked the start of the British New Wave in the cinema. 'So moving, so raucous, so pertinent', wrote the *Spectator*'s Isabel Quigly; 'a British film that shatters the pattern', agreed the *New Statesman*'s William

Whitebait; and even in the *Sunday Express*, Derek Monsey praised its 'sheer, blatant honesty', claiming that 'in this case at least, and at last, the X certificate [introduced in 1951 for adult-only films] looks like a badge of honour'. Inevitably, there was the odd facetious snicker. 'Now Britain joins the BEDROOM BRIGADE ... and adds a slice of Yorkshire pudding,' was the *Daily Herald*'s headline; 'By gum,' declared *Picturegoer*, 'this scorching analysis of bed and brass in a Yorkshire town rates its X certificate.' *Room at the Top* deservedly proved a considerable commercial success. 'Only once before in the history of the Plaza cinema [in London] has more money been taken by a film,' noted the *Birmingham Mail* at the end of February, shortly before its local opening, 'and that was *The Ten Commandments*, which ran at increased prices.' For any Brummie doubters, the paper applauded the movie for being 'up-to-the-minute in its audacious frankness'.[4]

A more British type of frankness characterised the year's most popular film, hitting the nation's screens during March. 'Mr Bell?' asks the nurse, a glamorous Shirley Eaton. 'Ding dong, you're not wrong,' replies the patient, an urbane Leslie Phillips. *Carry On Nurse* begins with an ambulance hurtling to hospital, the crew urgently wanting to hear the latest racing results; Matron is criticised for her pettifogging rules; and throughout there is a mildly subversive streak. The critics were divided. 'Script and director rely for laughs on nurses' endeavours to undress men and supervise their baths,' complained the *Manchester Guardian*, but for Dilys Powell in the *Sunday Times* this hospital farce brought 'a welcome breath of good, vulgar music-hall fun'. In due course Anthony Heap took his son to the Century. 'Something of a sequel to that surprising box office hit of 1958, "Carry On, Sergeant",' he noted, finding that 'the humour – mainly, as one might expect, anatomical – is on much the same broad, unsophisticated level'. Even so, *Carry On Nurse* is now generally viewed as the first authentic Carry On film, and in Charles Hawtrey, Kenneth Williams, Joan Sims, Hattie Jacques and Kenneth Connor the nucleus was in place for what would become a rolling – and in its early years still fresh – national institution.[5]

Following that astonishing burst between the previous April and July, the theatrical revolution continued in early 1959 to cause ripples and occasionally waves. *The Long and the Short and the Tall*, opening at the Royal Court on 7 January, was the title that the director Lindsay Anderson gave to Willis Hall's claustrophobic anti-war play about young working-class British soldiers in the Malayan jungle. Hall himself was from Hunslet, as was the 26-year-old Peter O'Toole, praised by Alan Brien for 'the arrogant casualness of his performance', having 'exactly the right blend of sardonic irreverence and aggressive satire for the unspoiled Jimmy Porter from the Lower Depths'. Perhaps 'not a great play', conceded Brien, but it was still 'a great portent . . . another one of the trail-blazers towards a live British theatre'. The following Monday, at the Birmingham Theatre Centre, saw the first performance of Harold Pinter's *The Birthday Party* since its Hammersmith debacle. It was performed by Stephen Joseph's pioneer-ing theatre-in-the-round Studio Theatre – based in Scarborough and aimed, as Joseph told the *Birmingham Mail*, at getting audiences 'to take part in the actual excitement of creation, of imagination at work' – and the playwright had travelled to the resort for pre-tour rehearsals. 'He was in a very defensive, not to say depressed state,' recalled Alan Ayckbourn, then a 20-year-old actor charged with playing the part of Stanley. 'I remember asking Pinter about my character. Where does he come from? Where is he going to? What can you tell me about him that will give me more understanding? And Harold just said, "Mind your own fucking business. Concentrate on what's there."' In the event, the *Mail*'s critic found it 'a profitless form of playmaking' for all Pinter's technical adroitness, whereas the *Post* reckoned it 'not a pleas-ant play' but 'impossible to dismiss lightly'; among those providing 'its tautly theatrical effect' was Ayckbourn's 'tormented pianist'. A month later, Joan Littlewood's Theatre Workshop had another new play, in fact a quasi-musical, to present at the Theatre Royal, Stratford East. This was *Fings Ain't Wot They Used T'Be*: music and lyrics by Lionel Bart, book by five-time former convict Frank Norman and the whole, heavily cockneyfied performance set in a gambling den. 'Matter-of-fact, jocular, argumentative, and optimistic', noted Brien about what became an instant hit; in addition to Littlewood's 'slap-up, street-party production', he had especially warm words for Yootha Joyce, 'surely genuine star material', as one of the three whores: 'She looks like a leopardess – beautiful, intelligent and terrifying, all in one feline glance.'[6]

*Fings* appeared the week after Littlewood's most acclaimed production of 1958, *A Taste of Honey* by Shelagh Delaney, began a much-publicised run in the West End. 'Just because we have some big money now, we have no plans to leave our council house,' her 43-year-old widowed mother, down from Lancashire with the rest of the family, told the press shortly before the curtain went up at Wyndham's on 10 February. 'What has happened has made no difference between us and the neighbours.' The play got eight curtain calls (though Delaney herself declined to take a bow), Michael Foot called it 'absolutely first class', and among those in the audience were Margot Fonteyn, David Niven and Vivien Leigh. A local government official from St Pancras presumably did not join in the applause. 'How the censor came to pass this first crude play-writing effort of Shelagh Delaney, a 19-year-old Salford ex factory worker, is as much of a mystery as why any reputable management should have brought it to the West End from the East End where it first got presented under the odious auspices of the communist Theatre Workshop,' wrote Anthony Heap that night. 'A squalid and thoroughly obnoxious story of a gormless teen age slut who, neglected by her whoring mother, has a baby by a nigger seaman and is befriended and nursed through her pregnancy by an equally half-baked young homosexual, it is about as savoury as a sewer and as edifying as a dung-hill.' Next morning, Alan Dent in the *News Chronicle* tended to agree. Condemning the play's 'all-pervading murkiness', and deploring the West End succumbing to 'the kitchen-sink', his review declared it 'an odd sort of evening altogether when the one likeable character is the young coloured sailor' who 'at least knows what he wants, gets it, and gets out'.

It was the start of a short but intense storm, further fuelled by a front-page letter in the same paper on the 13th. Attacking Dent's 'air of patronage and insensitivity', John Osborne declared that the critic had 'an image of Britain which seems to be derived principally from the pages of the daily newspapers, Jane Austen, and glossy magazines devoted to gun dogs and girls at point-to-point meetings' – whereas, he went on, 'Miss Delaney has written an acutely sensitive play about a group of warm, immediately recognisable people.' Dent the next day flatly dismissed her play as 'squalor, impure and simple . . . the latest example of the Lavatory School of drama', adding that 'Miss Delaney has a gift for pungent natural low dialogue, and no other discernible talent as yet.' On the 15th the Sunday heavies came to her defence – 'a dramatist born, not one manufactured by study', insisted Harold Hobson in the *Sunday Times*; 'a very intelligent, moving and original play', asserted Angus Wilson in the *Observer* – but Derek Monsey in the *Sunday Express* took no prisoners: 'It has its few moments of truth, but it also has acres of hooey, whole slices of sheer incompetence, and long stretches of boredom.' Next day the *News Chronicle* published an avalanche of letters – including one from Correlli Barnett, author of *The Hump Organisation*, calling Osborne 'a Welfare State Byron without a Missolonghi' – and by Thursday, when the editor called stumps, opinion was running three to one in Dent's favour.

T. C. Worsley in the *New Statesman*, meanwhile, frankly expressed the hope that, now the English play had shown it could 'break through the class barrier at will', its 'period of intoxication' with working-class plays would be 'short'. Worsley's hope led to an equally frank riposte from 15 Clapton Common, E5:

> So, we 'prole' playwrights must make the most of it, must we? We've been given our little say and now the hierarchy is a bit tired and we must finish amusing them, is it? . . .
>
> Now, listen to me, Mr T.C.W., I've been waiting for twelve years and it's only in the last year that I've been given my chance. I didn't write *Chicken Soup with Barley* simply because I wanted to amuse you with 'working-class types' but because I saw my characters within the compass of a personal vision. I *have* a personal vision you know, and I will not be tolerated as a passing phase. You are going to see my next play soon, and I am going to write many more and you are going to see them as well, *not* because I'm a young '*primitive*' writer out on a leash for a bit of airing but because I'm a *good* writer with a voice of my own!

A fellow playwright not quite yet in Arnold Wesker's camp was in London a couple of months later. 'I went to *A Taste of Honey*,' recorded Noël Coward, 'a squalid little piece about squalid and unattractive people.'[7]

Television was doing its bit for the revolution. There would be 'no costume dramas, no classical plays, nothing of a contemplative nature', Sydney Newman, a forceful Canadian producer who looked like a Mexican, had promised after taking over *Armchair Theatre* the previous autumn on Sunday nights on ITV, with a new emphasis on plays by British writers. By March he was declaring his ambition 'to marry the intellectual idea to the requirements of a mass audience'. Some two-thirds of Britons now had a set, with no programme still more consistently popular in early 1959 than the farcical comedy *The Army Game*. Tony Hancock continued to ride high. 'What *can* one say further than my small son's remark: "He's so funny even when he's not"?' rhetorically asked a viewer in January after the latest episode (including Rolf Harris as a sailor) of Hancock's fourth series. But for another gifted comedian, Tyneside's 'Little Waster', the small screen proved a disaster. *The Bobby Thompson Show* began on Tyne Tees in March, with a sketches format quite unsuited to his stand-up talents, and, after a reasonably promising start, the series bombed, almost wrecking Thompson's life and career.[8]

The highbrow critics could be harsh. *The Black and White Minstrel Show* may have been a viewers' favourite ('a grand show, wonderful songs, wonderful singing, great comedy and bags of talent all round'), but the *Listener*'s Ivor Brown saw 'no point in white singers (and fine ones) putting on a grotesque make-up, which has nothing to do with the natural good looks of an African, in order to sing popular songs which have nothing to do with the coloured world'. Tom Driberg found Huw Wheldon's presentation of *Monitor* – for which 'Kenneth' Russell directed on 1 March a filmed portrait of Betjeman – 'too arch for my taste and too mannered in his emphases and pauses: the upper-middle-brow's Pete Murray'. And Henry Turton compared Richard Dimbleby's fronting of *Panorama* ('almost uncomfortably polite . . . a holy attitude to the rich and glittering things of life . . . pronounces most words elaborately . . .') unfavourably to Ludovic Kennedy's of *This Week* ('achieves his atmosphere of urgency by crisp reading or a stern expression'). Turton also had it in for the anchorman of *Sunday Night at the London Palladium*. 'I understand that he has won a great following (much of his own act was devoted to telling us so), and I am glad for him,' he wrote in March. 'At the same time I cannot believe that a compère should fluff quite so often when announcing the names of performers.' Even more unkindly, Turton referred to Forsyth's 'vague resemblance to Tommy Trinder, a trickle of lame gags, a strange London accent and a matey grin'. Hughie Green, star of *Double Your Money* (in which the footballer Bobby Charlton appeared in January and won £1,000, promising to buy a car for his father, a miner), put it all in perspective. 'Highbrow – low rating,' he crisply told an interviewer.

> I'm not interested in the people who live in Mayfair and Westminster, but those in Wigan and Bermondsey . . . We like people at home to feel that they might be able to answer some of the questions. That's why some of the first questions are not too hard. It's a matter of audience participation nowadays. People like to see someone like themselves on the screen. They like to feel that it might be themselves up there.[9]

It was 'The Miner-Author', a regular columnist on the *Neath Times*, who bitterly anticipated St David's Day. 'Where are our harps in these days?' asked B. L. Coombes.

> Where are the small orchestras which used to be in every village? Where are our first-class instrumentalists, or our really top-class singers? Yes, and dramatists also who can truly depict the life of our folk? How many of our choral singers can read music? No! The land of song is a comforting piece of ballyhoo to make our folk feel they can do one thing at least better than other nations.

On 1 March itself, television had two more victims, as Universal and Gaumont closed down their cinema newsreel operations; next day in Leeds, Holbeck Working Men's Club voted that members' wives should be permitted to become lady members; and on the 4th, Bertrand Russell was John Freeman's second interviewee on *Face to Face* (following on from the celebrated lawyer Norman Birkett), while in the *Romford Times* a 'quick-witted, fast-talking' would-be magnate had his first newspaper profile ('money rolls in faster than John Bloom ever dreamed it would a year ago as he tramped streets, persuading housewives to buy washing machines'). On Monday the 10th, the notoriously divisive Cutteslowe Walls in north Oxford at last came down, having according to a local journalist become not only pernicious but also illogical, given that 'the size of a wage packet may now be higher in a council home than in an owner-occupied home'. Next day, Florence Turtle visited the recently much-extended Woolworths in Dundee ('a really fine store'); Ernest Marples announced that telephone operators were to have greater freedom to be themselves and sound like human beings; and Britain's Pearl and Teddy came second at Cannes to Teddy Scholten's *'Een Beetje'*.[10]

The following day was the last *Take It From Here* written by Frank Muir and Denis Norden (though the programme limped on for a final series); Muriel Young in *Small Time* on Friday the 13th was inviting young viewers 'to meet Joan, Angelica and Jeremy the Cat'; and by the end of Saturday the last three left in the FA Cup comprised an improbable trio. 'I don't mind about Norwich particularly,' Philip Larkin conceded graciously enough about a Third Division club that had overcome Manchester United, Cardiff, Tottenham and Sheffield United. 'I can't say I want any of them to win the cup – in *my* day Luton were 3rd Div$^n$, Nottingham Forest, oh, 2nd I'd say, & Norwich didn't exist. None of them seems quite serious to me.' In the event the Canaries went out 1–0 in a replay against Luton the following Wednesday, the same day that 19 students from Hatfield Technical College secured a world record by piling into a telephone kiosk and two days before Madge Martin had 'a horrible shock' lunching in the Grill Room at the Regents Palace Hotel: 'Gone the old-fashioned, comfortable ordinary surroundings, gone the attentive familiar waiters, gone the large extensive menu. Now given place to harsh modern décor, colouring, lighting. Small, uncomfortable plastic tables, "floozies" as waitresses, fresh from school, paper "serviettes", food served all on one plate, wines in ugly jugs.' Still, it was better than being a horse at Aintree, where at next day's Grand National only four finished out of 34 starters, and among the 14 fallers at Becher's Brook one had to be destroyed after breaking its back. A 'disgusting, bloody circus', complained the League Against Cruel Sports, but the course's managing director, the formidable Mirabel Topham, yielded no ground: 'They don't know what they are talking about. How dare they talk of banning the race!'[11]

On the 18th, the political terms of trade changed significantly. 'Mr Iain Macleod, the immensely able Minister of Labour, unexpectedly rose in the House to announce – with obvious enjoyment, and minus notes to help him with the complicated statistics that he reeled off to the silent benches opposite and to the cheering ranks behind him – the first significant drop in unemployment figures,' reported Mollie Panter-Downes. 'He got a relieved ovation from his party, which now feels that its major election worry has been removed.' This was hardly cheering news for Gaitskell, who had something else weighing on his mind. 'Hugh made one observation to me which he had got from Mark Abrams,' recorded Crossman next day.

> One of our long-term problems, he said, is that the kind of emotions and behaviours which held the Party together in the past were all based on class. Yet, since the war, progress has all been such as to weaken these senses of class loyalty upon which the Labour Party is based. More and more the younger people don't feel class-conscious in that sense of the word, and they are actually repelled by what they feel to be the fusty, old-fashioned, working-class attitudes of the people who run the Labour Party.

The perception was probably not inaccurate: 'tired, grizzled men and grey-haired careworn women', was how a *Times* journalist had described Labour workers at the recent Southend West by-election.

Ultimately, of course, the question for the left as a whole was whether it would be able to grasp – let alone empathise with – the larger social and economic forces now at work. John Vaizey for one was sceptical. 'Surely the problem for socialists is to understand the life of the suburbs, the problems of the semi-detached society – attached in part to the working class in its origins, but to the middle class by aspiration,' he argued in that month's *Socialist Commentary* in a swingeing attack on the backward-looking romanticism of the Bethnal Green school of sociology (i.e. Young and Willmott's *Family and Kinship*, supplemented by Peter Townsend's *The Family Life of Old People*).

> These are the people who are becoming articulate, who provide the new social problems – lonely life, ambitious life, but a secure life, and a life with often surprisingly broad horizons and directed by a serious

intelligence that has enabled its people to rise into the ranks of the skilled and the white-collar people. These people call beer beer [a dig at George Orwell's preference for calling it 'wallop'], and prefer babycham. To do otherwise voluntarily is dangerously near sentimentality.

Women's magazines pointed in the same direction. Old-fashioned, un-glossy, non-aspirational ones like *Home Chat* and *Everybodys* had recently folded, but to glance at an issue (14 March) that spring of the hugely successful *Woman* is to be struck by a world of colour, of burgeoning consumerist modernity, of apparent classlessness – and of a seemingly total disconnect with current affairs of any sort, let alone politics as such. Instead, jostling with 'My Strange Life' by the Duke of Bedford and 'Learning to Wait' by Anna Neagle (a regular columnist), 'The Wooden Spoon Club' assembled this week at the Brighton home of reader Eileen Timms, who with six other 'keen cooks' chatted to the magazine's cookery editor about 'everyday eating':

> *Pat Taylor*: Half our trouble is that families are so conservative about food. I'm so tired of all this cooking a Sunday joint, but my husband and children don't like anything else.
>
> *Eileen Timms*: They will if you make it sound exciting. Every now and then I promise my family a continental dish as a special Sunday treat. We call it 'going travelling'. The favourite, up to date, is Hungarian Goulash.
>
> *Mary Carter*: That sounds most exciting, but isn't it terribly difficult to make?
>
> *Eileen Timms*: Not really, it's only another name for veal stew . . .
>
> *Elizabeth Taylor*: High tea is my problem. My children are tired of eggs.
>
> *Jane Fraser*: It's mine, too. My husband likes something savoury to eat in the evening.
>
> *Pat Taylor*: I find the new condensed soups and packet soups used half-strength like sauce are good for quick snacky dishes. You can make all sorts of egg, fish and meat dishes with them. I often use two kinds of soup mixed together.

The last, robustly sensible word went to Mary Carter: 'My standby for all occasions is Irish stew. It cooks itself and there's only one saucepan to wash up.'[12]

And the young, those objects of Gaitskell's special concern? They were not yet voters, but about the same time some 2,000 'candid' teenagers were surveyed for the *Woman's Mirror*. Four in five said they would bring up their own children in an organised religion; 35 per cent intended when they were 21 to vote Conservative, 35 per cent Labour, and 20 per cent were 'don't knows' or would refuse to vote; and half the girls thought it wise to marry before they were 21, their favourite dream was to be a model (no longer an air hostess), and 68 per cent said that parents were right to disapprove of premarital sex (compared to 40 per cent of the boys in the sample). The girls' favourite TV stars were Robert Horton of *Wagon Train* and Clint Walker of *Cheyenne*, while the boys plumped for Tony Hancock and Popeye; on the big screen, the respective favourites were Dirk Bogarde and Brigitte Bardot; and the majority had no favourite politician, though among those who did, Churchill was 'easily' the front-runner. What about work? Two-thirds of Britain's youth were in employment by the time they were 16. Soon afterwards, the Industrial Welfare Society published recently written, unedited essays on 'What I expect from work' by a cross-section of school-leavers:

> I have chosen to be a scientist because I have always felt a sense of vocation for this type of work. I know that society should, and will, provide me with a job suited to my capabilities. *(Norman, 18)*
>
> One thing I hope to gain is really a combination, poise, self-confidence and good taste. *(Patricia, 14¾)*
>
> I dont suppose I will have much choice of work, but I will just have to be satisfied with the Job I get and hang on to it. I will not expect high wages at first, and will learn to respect the manager. I know most of my libities will be cut out a little when I am earning my living, but theres always the feeling you get that you'r no longer a child and wish to be treated as a grown up. *(Frank, 14¼)*
>
> The Civil Service offers security which forms the basis of any man's life especially if he intends to marry. *(Raymond, 17½)*
>
> Every one wants a well decorated house with all the modern

conveniences fridge, washing and so on. I am sure a dustman could not afford this. *(Peter, 14)*

I would like to work in a shipping office, where you have a full Navel dress, shoes, shirts, tie and be well respected with all the office workers. *(Maurice, 15)*

At the moment, I have doubts about being a shipping magnate or head of an atomic power station. *(Leonard, 14)*[13]

———

'Seems to be leaving realism further and further behind and developing only in the direction of an atomic, sophisticated Sapper,' was Maurice Richardson's verdict in the *Observer* on 22 March on Ian Fleming's *Goldfinger*, with Bond himself becoming 'from a literary point of view ... more and more synthetic and zombie-ish'. The villain was almost called 'Goldprick', after the hot-tempered, left-wing architect Ernö Goldfinger had threatened to sue; indeed, back in the 1930s, Fleming had been among those protesting against the demolition of cottages in Willow Road, Hampstead to enable the building of Goldfinger's modernist house. Neatly enough, the book's publication almost coincided with the outcome of another Hampstead run-in, this time over Goldfinger's plans for an ultra-modern four-storey block of flats, resting on pillars over a car port, to be built in the Vale of Health. One nearby resident, Anthony Greenwood, Labour MP and chairman of the Hampstead Labour Party, claimed that it would 'help to make us a Mecca for students of architecture from other parts', but 53 other local residents disagreed, signing a petition that described the proposed development as 'out of keeping'. At the two-day public inquiry in November 1958, Goldfinger's expert witness, the recently knighted John Summerson, described 'the greater part' of the Vale of Health's architecture, full of 'dreadful little Victorian villas', as 'rubbish chaotically arranged', while Goldfinger himself not only was equally adamant that the surrounding buildings had 'neither architectural nor aesthetic merit, nor any charm in their own right' but insisted that working-class people in the Vale were fully behind him. In the event, the Housing Minister (and Hampstead MP) Henry Brooke deliberately sat on the decision so long that by the time consent was given, in early March 1959, the architect's client had gone elsewhere. 'It was Goldfinger's misfortune in the

1950s,' his biographer would reflect in 2004, 'to have come up against a succession of proto-Prince Charles figures with their ill-thought-out conservative mantras of "local character" and "fitting in".'[14]

It had been a triumph for 'the Hampstead preservationist lobby', as the *Architects' Journal* noted crossly, but of course Hampstead was not London. 'Whichever party won the next election there would be an enormous amount of work for them to do,' Lord Stonham, who until recently had been Shoreditch's MP as Victor Collins, reassured the London Master Builders' Association at a luncheon in December 1958. 'Some people said that it was a shame to pull down some of the old buildings,' replied the Association's president, 'but each generation must build for its own needs and many of the new buildings were very fine indeed.' By this time work was under way on what would become the Stifford Estate – three 17-storey towers dominating the Stepney Green skyline, replacing (in Paul Barker's words) 'low terraces, built by the Mercers' Company in the early 19th century, which had lasted satis-factorily for about 130 years' – while a few months later *The Times* surveyed Bethnal Green, where 'from Spitalfields to Victoria Park the whole face of the borough is being changed'. No fewer than 15 blocks of 10 storeys or more had been built or were being built in the square mile of Bethnal Green alone; by the end of the process, a third of the borough's 50,000 inhabitants would have moved into new flats built since the war. Walking round the borough's eastern end, between Roman Road and Old Ford Road, the special correspondent observed that 'whole streets have already been demolished in the Cranbrook Street scheme', adding how 'again and again someone has chalked on the shattered walls "I lived here", with the dates'.

Not so far away, but a world apart, the City of London's redevelop-ment was moving up a gear by early 1959. The City Corporation was poised to give approval to the Paternoster scheme, with that precinct (just to the north of St Paul's) envisaged as London's premier modern shopping centre; the impending construction of large new office blocks was necessitating the widening of historic Cheapside; and between Aldersgate and Moorgate, the construction of the urban motorway that was Route 11 was pushing ahead, notwithstanding the contractors having to build a covered pit to store the 200 or so skulls and other bones they had accidentally disturbed beneath the old Barber-Surgeons'

Hall – a pit that children managed to get into at weekends, using the skulls for games of Cowboys and Indians. So too in the capital at large, but for almost the first time with a whiff of controversy that went beyond merely nimby-ism. 'All of a sudden,' noted Mollie Panter-Downes in March, 'Londoners seem to be looking around at the new London that is rising out of the bombed or demolished areas and to be asking critical questions.'[15]

What sort of questions? The LCC had just given the go-ahead to a 31-storey building on Millbank, it was negotiating with the property developer Harry Hyams a deal by which it would consent to the Seifert-designed 35-storey office tower (the future Centrepoint) at St Giles Circus in return for Hyams 'giving' it £1.5 million of adjacent land on which to build a roundabout (which never happened), and the unlovely 17-storey Bowater House had just gone up in Knightsbridge. But for the briefly much-publicised Anti-Uglies – students mainly from the Royal College of Art but also from the Architectural Association – the villain of the piece was dreary neo-Georgianism, above all in the City. Two particular targets were Sir Albert Richardson's defiantly non-modernist Bracken House (the new home of the *Financial Times*), on which the Anti-Uglies marched, and the elephantine new Barclays head office in Lombard Street, with the RCA's duffle-coated but glamorous Pauline Boty photographed outside scattering rose petals on the coffin of British Architecture. Far from a modernist in most things, Panter-Downes tended to sympathise, while like 'most Londoners' she found the LCC's housing projects 'something to be proud of' – not least 'the enormous Roehampton Estate of small skyscrapers, which you can see glittering in the sun these spring mornings as you motor in from Kingston, and which are brilliantly sited among the cedars of the Victorian suburban mansions they have replaced'.[16]

Outside London, it was Birmingham that now set the pace. On 25 February a Corporation spokesman reiterated to the local press that the Market Hall (1828), in the way of the Inner Ring Road and the redevelopment of the whole Bull Ring area (which already included 'The Big Top', the giant, 160-foot City Centre House shop-and-office block erected by the rising local and increasingly national property developer Jack Cotton), was to be demolished 'as soon as possible'. Next day, opening the British Road Federation's exhibition ('Town Roads for

Today – and Tomorrow') at the Civic Centre, Alderman Frank Price, about to step down after five years chairing the Public Works Committee, declared that people who advocated banning cars from city centres were like 'ostriches' and expressed the hope that the city's Inner Ring Road, due for completion in 1969, would give a lead to the rest of the country. And on the 27th the *Birmingham Mail* issued a 'Progress Report on the New Birmingham', accompanied by a photograph of the broad sweep of the showcase first section of the Inner Ring Road, starting to take shape in Smallbrook:

> In and around the city centre, building work totalling some £65,000,000 is now in progress. Enormous changes have been made in the past five years. But this is only the beginning.
>
> Ugly old buildings are being wiped away. The city centre changes almost daily. The visitor returns to find white new buildings mushrooming amid the architectural debris of the past. The city's list of post-war new buildings, either completed or proposed, covers no fewer than 45 substantial projects.

Price himself – Labour, mid-30s, from Birmingham's slums, previously a toolmaker, now a public relations officer – was quoted: 'In 20 years from now the future citizens of Birmingham will look back on this period of their city's history and will say: "This was Birmingham's finest and most courageous period."' But soon afterwards the *Mail* asked this 'tough, ambitious realist with more than a touch of the visionary' whether any mistakes had been made in the city's redevelopment plans. 'Obviously we have made some,' he replied. 'At times I think we should stand still and try to get into perspective what we are attempting to do. I think certain buildings in the city could have been improved upon. But, by and large, I think a magnificent effort has been made.' At this stage almost the only detectable opposition to all this came from small traders. 'Ask any local retailer [in Smallbrook] for his views on this wonderful city of the future,' wrote F. D. Walkley to the *Mail*. 'He will reply in words not usually found in the dictionary.' J. F. Munro agreed: 'Moderate redevelopment in any city is welcome, but wholesale bulldozing is another matter. Small traders, after years of service to city and citizens, are being indiscriminately turned out

– many to face ruin and the end of all their efforts.' Still, a city's pride was at stake, and in April the pedestrian subway under Smallbrook Ringway opened – the first in the country.

Alderman Price featured prominently in *Who Cares? A New Way Home*, a BBC documentary about slum clearance in Birmingham broadcast on 24 February. Calling the slums 'caves' and 'holes in the wall', he argued that young families moving to new blocks of flats would benefit from the open space around, opposed mews-type development, conceded that the lack of the extended family on the new estates was a problem – and claimed that Birmingham was on the way to becoming 'one of the most beautiful cities in Europe'. The TV programme as a whole was relentlessly upbeat. 'One must admire the drive and enthusiasm of the Housing Department,' declared the presenter, Douglas Jones, who at one point asked the city engineer, Sir Herbert Manzoni, about the 'comprehensive manner' of the slum-clearance programme and, specifically, whether people were enthusiastic. 'Of course it's difficult for those who are being disturbed,' Manzoni replied, adding that he usually found them 'getting enthusiastic' once they were in their new homes.[17]

The documentary was transmitted barely a fortnight after BBC television's *Second Enquiry*, in which (after an interval of over six years) Robert Reid paid a return visit to Glasgow and its housing issues, including the redevelopment of the Gorbals. 'This programme didn't mince matters,' noted one impressed critic. 'Years of neglect have created a colossal problem; it may be twenty years before Glasgow clears the last of its tenements. But one felt it would be done; and that this time the citizens of this "no mean city" will not have to leave Britain as their fathers did to find a decent life, but will receive their birthright in their own country.' Reid's programme won from the Viewers' Panel a notably high Reaction Index of 78. 'Without seeing, who would believe that people had to live in such awful surroundings in Britain today?' asked a housewife, while a chemical worker's wife declared, 'Surely slum clearance which is needed as obviously as this demands tip-top priority above everything else.' Even so, the odd comment did query whether Glaswegian slum-dwellers possessed a high-enough quota of the self-help ethos. From a research engineer's wife: 'These people seemed quite content to put their names on a list for council houses and then sit back and wait. My husband and I have struggled to buy our house.' Perhaps inevitably, several viewers took exception to the 'mournful and monotonous mouth organ music'.

By this time the Sub-Convener of Glasgow's Housing Committee was David Gibson, an idealistic, high-energy left-winger (and former Independent Labour Party stalwart) described by Miles Glendinning and Stefan Muthesius, historians of the tower block, as 'arguably the most remarkable of Western Europe's postwar municipal housing leaders'. Gibson's passion was to rehouse Glasgow slum-dwellers in the city itself, not to banish them to overspill estates on the periphery; his means was the high-rise flat. 'Gibson,' they note,

> intuitively grasped that, if the multi-storey blocks proposed by the planners for mixed development use in the CDAs [Comprehensive Development Areas] were instead built by the Committee *outside* those areas on gap-sites, much higher blocks would be possible, unfettered by planning restrictions and acquisition delays. This would allow a cycle of decanting within the city, without resorting to overspill.

There ensued during 1958–9 'much agonised discussion' on the Housing Committee, but for the moment its natural conservatism prevailed.

One approach, though, that lamentably failed to produce any worthwhile discussion was Tom Brennan's in his book *Reshaping a City*, published in early 1959. Focusing especially on Govan (rundown centre of the shipbuilding industry and home to Glasgow Rangers) and Pollok (site of a huge peripheral estate), his 'arresting conclusion', as the *TLS* reviewer fairly summarised it, was that 'the process of decanting people to the outskirts and radically rebuilding the centre may have gone far enough and is not the true answer to the situation as it now exists', especially given that 'overcrowding in the central districts is no longer serious and the dispersal of industry and services has not kept pace with the dispersal of population'. What was the true answer? For 'the majority' of Govan's population, Brennan himself argued, 'the obvious solution, if it could be managed, would be to make available to them the components for a better life – not in a new town in ten or twenty years' time, but in Govan now. The idea should be one of repairing, reviving, and thereby renewing Govan rather than waiting until it has deteriorated sufficiently to be replaced altogether.' It was an analysis backed up by detailed evidence of how in Govan's older properties the occupants (who revealed little wish to move to new towns or overspill estates) were already using their new prosperity to upgrade their living conditions, and backed up also by a call for 'a judicious combination of commercial, public and private enterprise' to stimulate renovation – a very different route to Glasgow becoming, through local-authority demolition and local-authority redevelopment, 'Corporation-owned and Corporation-managed'.[18]

If a similar diagnosis had appeared at this time about any other large British city, it would almost certainly have received an equally nugatory response from the activator class. 'It will be of particular interest to the residents of 375 of Liverpool's darkest acres, those 39,000 people living in the forest of 90 to 130-years-old terraces of the municipal wards of Netherfield, Vauxhall, St Domingo and Westminster,' promised the *Liverpool Echo* in November 1958 about a new exhibition, *Liverpool of the Future*, on the Everton Heights Redevelopment Scheme, in which some 6,500 houses were to be replaced by mixed development, including 21-storey blocks of flats. 'They will see what the future holds for the dreary, narrow streets and blackened houses which have been their familiars for so long.' The paper went bullishly on about this 'attempt at creating a closely-knit community':

> Already the new North Liverpool skyline is taking shape, with the majesty of Creswell Mount crowning the slope on which are huddled the mean and narrow streets of the old Liverpool.
> The two new blocks, The Braddocks, already have nestling near them a number of modern buildings, colourful and fresh in contrast to the black dreariness surrounding them. They are the forerunners of what is to come.
> It is a brave project, charged with imagination, but well capable of realisation.

The old Everton Heights had one shop for every 65 people, and when 'a brains trust composed of four leading council officials, with a senior lecturer in social science at Liverpool University as chairman, answered questions on the scheme, the audience's main concern, after the question of the housing, was what would be the fate of the little shops'.

Little shops were not on Anthony Wedgwood Benn's mind when, the following February, he took Boris Krylov, a Russian academic, on a tour of Bristol. This featured 'the worst slums' plus 'an old smoky school with overcrowded classes and no proper playground' plus 'the prefabs' and 'the horrible, dull red brick pre-war council houses', before 'finally the new housing':

> I took him to Barton House, the 16-storey block of flats in the centre of the Barton Hill redevelopment. We went to the roof and then knocked on a flat door and were shown round by a railwayman and his wife. It was lovely and they were very happy.
>
> Then we went out to Hartcliffe estate – a 50,000-people new suburb. It really is a lovely place, well laid out and planned with different types of houses and the finest school I have ever seen anywhere in the world. I spotted it in the distance, not knowing what it was. But we walked in the front door bravely and asked if we could look round. It was Withywood Comprehensive School and the headmaster insisted on taking us on a tour. We started by going up in the lift to the top and walked down and through the beautifully equipped laboratories and classrooms. The school has enormous playing fields, two gymnasia and lovely design in aluminium and glass.

'It really knocked Boris sideways,' concluded Benn.[19]

So too in Newcastle, where in March – not long after reports about the local authority's intention to demolish Dobson's Royal Arcade and replace it with a roundabout – the City Council decided to proceed with T. Dan Smith's recommendation, as chairman of the Housing Committee, to build high-rise blocks of flats (12 to 15 storeys) in the slum-cleared or to-be-cleared areas of Heaton Park Road, Shieldfield and Cruddas Park. This last was just off the Scotswood Road in Newcastle's West End and near to Rye Hill, a particularly rough area where in the mid-1950s the Tory-run council had been responsible for erecting the much-criticised Noble Street flats: five storeys, no lifts, badly designed, done on the cheap, a slum before the first tenants moved in. The new breed of flats, insisted Smith, would be wholly different. 'The Council need have no fear at all about this scheme,' he declared after listing in great detail all the mod cons and suchlike (including gas water-heater, gas-heated clothes-drying cabinet, full-size bath and centralised aerial system) that would be available. 'The external is as attractive as any block of flats I have seen built anywhere else, and more attractive than most. The flats will make a tremendous contribution not only to the housing problem but to the brightening up of areas which hitherto have been depressing.' The female perspective came from a fellow councillor, Mrs Wynne-Jones. 'It has always surprised me that flats have not been popular in this part of the world, and we hear people say "I would rather have a proper house,"' she observed. 'Here, quite obviously, the architect and the people responsible have not forgotten that it is the ordinary, practical running of a house that is going to matter so tremendously to the women who are to live there.'

Manchester since the war had been rather slow to embrace the modern high-rise, but no longer. 'Albert Bridge House shows signs of blowing some of the cobwebs away, but they have been there a long, long time and it looks as if a howling gale will be required finally to dislodge them,' was the somewhat grudging appraisal by the *Architects' Journal* in April of a newly completed 18-storey block to house Manchester's tax officials. Elsewhere in the city centre, work had just started or was about to start on not only the Co-operative Wholesale Society and Co-operative Insurance Society cluster of buildings (including the 25-storey CIS tower modelled on Chicago's Inland Steel Building) but also Piccadilly Plaza, described by a latter-day Pevsner as 'a huge commercial superblock' that 'completely fails to take any account of its surroundings', though 'the sheer confidence and scale impress'. The residential nettle was also being grasped. News that an 11-storey block was to be built in Chorlton-on-Medlock once 54 acres had been cleared was welcomed in November 1958 by the *Manchester Evening News*, which 'has campaigned for years for multi-storey flats blocks, well designed and equipped, to be built near the city centre for people who wish to stay in Manchester'.

In nearby Salford, such good progress was being made in major multi-storey building programmes that by April 1959 the slum-clearance schedule there was expected to speed up – with most of Walter

Greenwood's 'Hanky Park' (now in the Ellor Street Clearance Areas) likely to be cleared by the end of the year. 'It is a district of people whose roots are firmly embedded in the hard ground, and there is every sign that they are not going to take kindly to the sudden upheaval,' observed a visiting reporter. 'There was a sense of uneasiness around, which is in many cases hidden by a joke or a resolution to face the new life – the sort of resolution one reaches when facing a visit to the dentist to have that worrying tooth removed. The jokes take the form of suggestions that the Royal Oak Hotel [i.e. a pub] should be removed en bloc as it is and put down in the new area of habitation, a joke obviously based on a feeling of lack of security.' Some were happy to move – 'mostly women who see in the new life a chance to throw the kids into a bath at night-time with the steaming hot water coming out of a tap instead of a kettle' – but tellingly, 'everybody in the area' wanted 'to go to Southgarth [likely to be Salford's last new council estate built of houses] and don't want to be on the eighth floor of any flats'. 'They all know they are going,' concluded the reporter, 'but to where, and to what, they do not know.' Later in the month, the Housing Committee announced plans for 15-storey blocks in the St Matthias Clearance Area – Salford's highest yet.[20]

Modernity did not try to spare the town of the crooked spire. 'Chesterfield's old, cobbled Market Place, which for centuries has been the hub of the town's shopping area, seems doomed to disappear,' began the *Derbyshire Times*'s story in early 1959, with the Labour-run Town Council expected on 3 February to agree to move the market area some 400 yards, demolish the old Market Hall, and instead develop a modern shopping centre in the Market Place. At the meeting, discussion was predictably 'stormy', as was the 23–11 vote in favour of the plan. 'A lot of this is sentimentality,' was the (ultimately unsuccessful) opposition-quashing line of Councillor H. C. Martin, chairman of the Town Planning Committee. 'I have had the same feeling. I was reared in Chesterfield. It is my town. I don't like to see the Market Place developed, but am I to allow morbid sentimentality to prejudice the future development of the town?'

A few weeks later, in the city of the dreaming spires, a local paper endorsed John Summerson's charge that Oxford was too timid in its attitude to new buildings, but chose not to blame the Planning Committee. 'The fact is that there is still a large body of public opinion which is a great deal more timid than the Committee seems to be,' argued the *Oxford Mail*. 'These people, to whom high buildings and modern design are the Devil's works, make the noise that frightens Committees – be they City, college or University – and ensure that new buildings in public places must be either archaic or tame.' Even so, the *Mail* was pleased that Arne Jacobsen, 'the greatest Danish architect', had been invited to design the new St Catherine's College, while Sir William Holford had been asked to scrutinise the plan for the redevelopment of St Ebbe's: 'They, and more like them, must be encouraged to do their finest and boldest work here. Only in this way can a modern Oxford be created worthy to stand beside historic Oxford.'

Soon afterwards, in Lancashire, the fourth estate was even more trenchant. 'I shudder to think what posterity will say about us when they see the buildings we are handing down to them,' claimed Councillor S. Preston about 'Picasso-like buildings' at the monthly meeting of Orrell Council, in the context of a new school being built in the district. 'I do not see anything picturesque in them, but there is apparently little we can do about it.' Other councillors seemingly agreed, but not the *Wigan Examiner*: 'The architects who design these schools are professional men who have spent a lifetime learning their business. Their designs are fundamentally good and reflect the mood and character of the age we live in. That laymen don't like them, is a point in their favour, for laymen have never liked advances in the arts.' After a pop at local authorities' penchant for 'neo this and neo that' in the tradition of the 'revolting imitation Gothic which our Victorian grandfathers have inflicted on us in such vast and nauseating quantities', the paper went on:

> From our new schools, our children will derive considerable benefit of an unobtrusive kind. They will subconsciously learn to appreciate the beauty of unfussy, functional design. They will benefit from the light and space which modern methods and modern materials allow the designer to incorporate in his conceptions and, since they will not be surrounded by clutter, let us hope their minds will be uncluttered too.

In short: 'More power to the modern architects say we.'[21]

So also, unsurprisingly, said the architects themselves. 'A battle has to be fought against public ignorance and apathy, and sometimes aggressive retrogression,' declared Basil Spence in November 1958 in his inaugural presidential address at the Royal Institute of British Architects. He made clear his particular target:

If ever an objective of the lowest common denominator of ignorance and bad architecture had to be achieved, the planning committee precisely fits the bill. That is my own personal conviction . . .

We are in an adventurous new period of architectural development, and architects must be helped, not hindered, by this form of bureaucracy if we are to allow our native genius to flourish in the future.

It had of course to be native genius of a particular type: around this time Quinlan Terry, a student at the Architectural Association, was submitting classical designs, only to be informed he would fail if he continued to do so. Yet though the supremely arrogant example of Le Corbusier still bewitched, at least some rising architectural stars were showing a degree of critical detachment. 'Graeme Shankland felt that Le Corbusier's tendency to make man in his own image, to project this image on society and often to impose a formal pattern regardless of circumstances, in some degree vitiated his contribution,' noted in February a listener to a Third Programme appraisal of the exhibition *Le Corbusier and the Future of Architecture* at the Building Centre. 'James Stirling expressed the opinion that the spatial luxury which was necessary to all his achievement was now beginning to detract from the viability of his forms, and proposed that in the post-Corbusier world a more down-to-earth empiricism was to be desired.' Soon afterwards Peter ('Joe') Chamberlin – of Chamberlin, Powell & Bon, which had recently won the commission for a massive reconstruction of Leeds University and would soon be tackling the Barbican – gave a lecture at the Housing Centre on 'High Density Housing' that seems to have been modernism at its best:

His general approach was to analyze the qualities that could make life in a closely-packed urban environment enjoyable, and then to suggest how these qualities could be achieved in new developments.

People had fled to the suburbs, not because they disliked high density as such, but because of the negative qualities of the central areas as they knew them – noise, smoke, smell, dirt, dangerous traffic and a general restrictiveness as to the detail of daily life: there was nowhere to potter around and 'do it yourself,' pets were often prohibited and so on. These negative qualities were not essential to high density living, it was our job as architects to get round them, and offer many 'plus' qualities to set against them. A dazzling slide of a Van Gogh pavement café night scene – intensely evocative of the excitement of eating out together – suggested the sort of quality he had in mind.

Other specific, attainable, with-the-grain recommendations followed, prompting a revealing reflection at the end of the admiring report in the *Architects' Journal*: 'The approach to high density housing from the humanist angle of "how can we make city life as enjoyable as possible" ought not to be unusual – but it certainly is, and how.'

Ian Nairn was surely in sympathy. 'The Antiseptic City' was the title of a typically trenchant recent *Encounter* piece, in which he argued that the missing dimension in too many projects, however good they looked as architectural models, was 'ordinary people in all their idiosyncrasy and variety of temperament'. As a result, the new urban pattern taking shape in London (including much-vaunted Roehampton) was 'chopped-up, monotonous, inhuman yet overcrowded – and this in a city whose outstanding virtue is in its contrasts and sudden incongruities and irrepressible vitality'. Nairn went on to explain his credo – one that 'so few' modern architects were 'prepared to accept in practice' – namely, that 'buildings ought to fit the people who will use them':

There should be no building for a mean, but simultaneous building for every kind of extreme; and everybody is extreme in one way or other. On a larger scale the city should be a place for everyone – tarts as well as good girls, spivs as well as model husbands and honest men . . . You can no more separate good and evil to create a clean, rational, social-minded city than you can separate the poles of a magnet.

Condemning 'use-zoning' (i.e. zoning by function) as 'a disaster for the vitality of a city, which makes its impact from the multiplicity of things all thrown together', and emphasising the need for 'some continuous change for the eye to hook on to', as opposed to 'separate staccato impressions, however grand', Nairn summed up his advice to architects 'in nine words: look at people, look at places, think for yourselves'. The alternative, he signed off, was that 'we will rapidly build ourselves an inhumane, cliché-ridden, and antiseptic nut-house'.[22]

The search for the right kind of urbanism was fuelled in part by a degree of deepening disenchantment – arguably much exaggerated by commentators and observers – with the post-war trend of dispersal to new, outlying estates. Take Coventry, where early in 1959 not only did a survey of Tile Hill reveal a huge gap between planned and actual amenities (no community centre, youth centre, branch library, day nursery, swimming baths or cinema) but a report by the local Labour Party found generally that 'the tenant feels that the centre of authority is too remote from him', with the council being 'too big and imper-sonal, despite the best efforts of the elected representatives and officers concerned'. In Birmingham the *Mail* soon afterwards focused on Kingshurst, an overspill estate (out past Castle Bromwich) with almost 9,000 residents. Eyes and ears told different stories: the reporter 'saw pleasant homes, with bright paint and neat curtains, wide roads, rural street names, grass and the wide, wide vista of winter sky that no central area can offer', but he 'heard, as I talked to people who live there, a tale of bewilderment, disinterest, loneliness and dislike'. Lonely, bored young wives, almost nothing for young people to do ('they hang around together, talking and daring each other,' said a mother, adding that 'wickedness is sure to happen'), old people cut off from their Birmingham roots left 'to wilt and pine in their new homes', poor and expensive public transport – the litany was becoming increasingly familiar. 'In solving the problem of homes and city overcrowding by "spilling" into the country, have we raised a host of subtler problems which will be much harder to solve?' wondered the reporter. 'Can we form a commu-nity from people who still persist in feeling that they are exiles from somewhere else?'

By this time, moreover, relatively few – certainly relatively few acti-vators – believed that the New Towns were necessarily the answer. *Socialist Commentary* in April featured a coruscating analysis by Nottingham University's Geoffrey Gibson of 'New Town Ghettos', in which he argued that the planners had got it fundamentally wrong – above all through their misguided concept of the self-contained neighbourhood unit, which had almost completely failed to foster community spirit. A *cri de coeur* came soon afterwards from Nicholas Hill, who had lived for the past 15 months in the new town at Hemel Hempstead. 'There is no imagination or planning behind the lay-out of the community,' he wrote to the *Spectator*.

> The houses are jerry-built ... The few shops are built and look like matchboxes. They are situated at the edge of the community rather than in the middle, and sell a meagre selection of second-rate goods ... The community resembles a modern chicken farm, every chicken alone in its identical box ... Let someone who loves people, and not uniformity – beauty, and not drabness – build the next town.[23]

'I proceeded to Turnham Green (10.30 a.m.) and watched some of the marchers move off, split into contingents by the police, presumably to inconvenience the traffic less,' recorded a non-committal Henry St John on 30 March. 'There were several hundred of them, average age about 20, of the intellectual type, hardly a hat among them.' It was Easter Monday, and whereas the pioneer 1958 march for nuclear disarmament had gone from London to Aldermaston, this time (under CND's auspices) it was the other way round, an implicit recognition that direct action was not going to close down the Atomic Weapons Research Establishment. Later that day, the march – with architecture the only profession to be represented by its own banner – was some four miles long as it approached Trafalgar Square, and, according to another, more sympathetic observer, 'the vast majority were quite ordinary young men and women, serious, politically minded and indistinguishably working and middle class'. Up on the Ayrshire coast (Glasgow's 'lung'), the first sunny weather of the holiday weekend attracted thousands of 'flu-wearied, smog-ridden' city-dwellers. 'At Ayr railway station where 14 special trains brought around 3,000 visitors, it was the good behaviour of the crowd that caught the attention of the staff,' noted a local paper. '"The best-behaved holiday crowd we've had in years," said one official. "Not a rowdy among them."'[24]

Further down the west coast, Nella Last in Barrow had at last succumbed to the urgings of her children and neighbours by acquiring a television set. 'Knowing my husband's love of an old time Variety show I tuned in to the Bob Monkhouse Show on ITV – a really good show & to see & hear my poor dear chuckle and laugh was a real pleasure,' she wrote on the first Saturday of April. Even so, caution still prevailed:

> An hour, or one & a half hours at most, is quite enough, & I will have to vet programmes on TV as closely – no, more so, than on wireless. Last week in Emergency Ward 10, a man died under a serious operation & it did upset my husband – lingered the next day – while any violence or 'savage' grimaces make him dream he says. A Quiz programme is his delight – we both grieved for that 'Double or Quits' contestant, who so gallantly tried to turn £500 into £1,000 – & lost the lot. I've *no* courage like that!

Nella was never a likely candidate for *Drumbeat* – debuting that evening as BBC's latest hopeful riposte to *Oh Boy!*, with Adam Faith and the John Barry Seven among the regulars – while on the radio she missed 'Faces in the Crowd', a Third Programme talk in which Asa Briggs regretted how social history lacked the 'academic prestige' of political history. Next evening, also on the Third, *New Poetry* included a reading of Philip Larkin's as yet unpublished 'The Whitsun Weddings' ('any supercilious note should be rigorously excluded', insisted the poet in advance) – presumably not listened to by Jean Bird, receiving several doses of pethidine that day at a maternity hospital before on the Monday, under general anaesthetic, giving birth to her son James through a complicated high-forceps delivery:

> When I came round, the baby had already been taken away. It seems quite shocking now [1996], but it was par for the course in those days. He'd had a difficult start, and the drill in those days was 'cot nursing', which meant the baby wouldn't be touched any more than was absolutely necessary for 48 hours. He was kept in the nursery, so I didn't even see him until he was nearly two days old. I remember they brought him along in his cot and left him by my bed just before the 48 hours was up.

Of course I was desperate to look at him and hold him, so I picked him
up and put him to the breast. He was ravenous – he'd only had a bottle
of half-strength milk – and latched on straightaway.

'But then,' she added, 'the curtains were pulled back and I got a real
ticking off for getting him out of his cot too soon.'[25]

During the interim, on Tuesday the 7th, the year's seminal economic
event had taken place, one with powerful political resonance. 'Budget
statement was very effective,' recorded a satisfied Macmillan, who for
many months had been pushing Heathcoat Amory hard to do exactly
what at last he now delivered. 'The C of Ex' got rather tired at the end
of his 2 hour speech & we thought he was going to faint. But he got
through.' Amory himself was sufficiently recovered to give a television interview in the evening, reassuringly calling it a 'Steady Ahead'
Budget, but in reality it was far more expansionary than that: ninepence
off the standard rate of income tax, cuts in purchase tax, twopence off
a pint of beer, and altogether, as the *FT* approvingly noted, 'a Budget
of large concessions', designed to 'restore economic confidence' and
'combat recession'. Even *The Times* – temporarily forgetful of its
earlier, anti-Keynesian sternness at the time of Thorneycroft's resignation, but instead mindful that this was almost certainly an election
year – was similarly positive, after managing with a certain amount of
legerdemain to satisfy itself that consumers were 'not getting more
than their share' of Amory's largesse. Among the politicians, Reginald
Maudling in the Budget debate robustly insisted that disapproving
talk by the Shadow Chancellor, Harold Wilson, of 'a consumers'
spree' was a 'particularly silly' way of describing what was in practice
'leaving more money in the pockets of the public to spend as they
wish', but it was Wilson's colleague Richard Crossman who really –
albeit privately – let the cat out of the bag. 'My first reaction, I am
afraid, was that I had saved about £100 on my new Humber Hawk by
postponing delivery until after the Budget,' he wrote. 'In fact, as far as
I can calculate, I shall also get nearly £200 in reduced income tax.' On
more mature reflection, the following week, he would call it 'a selfish,
egotistical Budget', but his rival diarist had already had the right of it
on the 9th: 'Budget has been *very* well received in the country & by
the Press,' noted Macmillan. And he added: 'The 64,000 dollar

question remains – When? I am feeling more & more *against* a "snap" election.'[26]

There were few complaints about the Budget in middle-class Woodford, which was not only Churchill's constituency but also the subject this spring, two years after *Family and Kinship*, of intensive study by Peter Willmott and Michael Young. They found, further out on the Central Line but not as far as Debden, an utterly different world from Bethnal Green – from where (or thereabouts) many upwardly mobile Woodfordians had come over the years. 'How few people there seemed to be in Woodford, and how many dogs!' they wrote in their subsequent *Family and Class in a London Suburb* (1960). 'In Bethnal Green people are vigorously at home in the streets, their public face much the same as their private. In Woodford people seem to be quieter and more reserved in public, somehow endorsing [Lewis] Mumford's description of suburbs as the apotheosis of "a collective attempt to lead a private life."' Almost two-thirds of their general sample were middle class, roughly reflecting Woodford's composition: a typical middle-class house had 'thick pile carpets, rooms fashionably decorated with oatmeal paper on three walls and a contrasting blue on the fourth, bookcases full of Charles Dickens, Agatha Christie and *Reader's Digest* condensed books, above the mantelpiece a water-colour of Winchelsea, VAT 69 bottles converted into table-lamps, french windows looking out on to a terra-cotta Pan in the middle of a goldfish pond, the whole bathed in a permanent smell of Mansion polish'. And Willmott and Young were struck by the district's 'general adoption of middle-class standards', with electricians and bank clerks (and their respective wives) wearing 'the same sort of clothes', driving 'the same sort of cars' and inside their homes watching 'the same television set from the same mass-produced sofa'.

Yet for all this, much of the middle-class vox pop – gathered while the authors held glasses of sherry 'gingerly in the left hand while unchivalrously scribbling notes with the right' – revealed keen status anxieties and resentments:

There's all this emphasis on material possessions. People seem to think that if they've got something you haven't got they're better than you are. And they're not really what I would call well-educated people. They're people who've got the money but not the educational background to go with it.

As soon as next door knew we'd got a washing machine, they got one too. Then a few months later we got a fridge, so they got a fridge as well. I thought all this stuff about keeping up with the Joneses was just talk until I saw it happening right next door.

The working class is better off, which is a good thing *if* they know how to use their money. Which they don't, I'm sorry to say.

I think the richest class today is the working class, and they don't know how to spend their money. They waste money on fridges, washing machines, TVs and cars. It's the old tale – the person born to money knows how to use it, the person new to getting it doesn't.

Those people from the East End are good-hearted folk, but you couldn't make friends of them. Sounds a bit snobbish, I know, but we've got nothing in common with them.

Unsurprisingly, the working-class interviewees were far from oblivious to this censorious disapproval:

In Woodford they haven't got much, but they're what I class as jumped-up snobs. They think they're better than what you are.

The middle-class people here are snobs. They put on airs and graces. They are all out for show – nothing in their stomachs but nice suits on.

Some people here are more classy – or they try to be. They're just the same as we are, but they try to be something different.

'Inside people's minds,' concluded Willmott and Young about this Essex suburb, 'the boundaries of class are still closely drawn. Classlessness is not emerging there. On the contrary, the nearer the classes are drawn by the objective facts of income, style of life and housing, the more are middle-class people liable to pull them apart by exaggerating the differences subjectively regarded.' In short, there were 'still two Woodfords in 1959, and few meeting-points between them'.

Such sociological concerns, though, were not the stuff of parliamentary debates – unlike the question of the moral state of the nation, on its way to becoming a hardy perennial. 'The disease is in the body politic itself,' declared Lord Denning in the House of Lords the day after the

Budget. 'It is a loosening of moral standards, a decay of religion. It is up to us, each of us, to do our part in leading our country to a strong and healthy opinion, condemning wrongdoing and upholding the right.' Perhaps he should have visited Gardenstown in Banff, a male-dominated fishing village (population 1,200) that was a stronghold of the Plymouth Brethren. From there, earlier in April, the national press reported not only the disapproval directed towards 'fair-haired' Mona Tennant (manager's wife in the solitary pub) for wearing slacks, but also the case of Diana Norman, the only girl to wear make-up. 'I find the Lord is sufficient,' replied a Plymouth Brethren girl, her long hair tied in a bun, when asked her views. Elsewhere in Scotland, at almost the same time, the *Weekly News* (from the hugely successful D. C. Thomson stable in Dundee) published a letter by Miss A. F. of Maryhill, Glasgow in which the 17-year-old complained how she found it 'very humiliating' to be spanked with a slipper by her mother after she had returned from a dance after midnight, and asking what other readers thought. 'Miss A.F. should be thankful her mother uses only a slipper on her,' reckoned 18-year-old Miss J. S. of Dundee. 'My aunt keeps a tawse, and regularly warms my fingers and posterior with it.' And among 'dozens' of other letters, 19-year-old Miss A. Davidson of Drongan spoke for the majority: 'I'm always home by 10.30. As long as she is under her parents' roof, they have a right to spank her, whether she is 17 or 37.'[27]

It all depended. Few had a bad word to say about Russ Conway – twinkle-eyed pianist, regular on *The Billy Cotton Band Show*, favourite of the Queen Mother, his honky-tonk 'Side Saddle' topping the charts in early April – but the troubled rock 'n' roll singer Terry Dene (former bicycle messenger, timber-yard labourer, plumber's mate and odd-job boy in a clock factory) was another matter. 'DENE DRINKS CHAMPAGNE – to the Army that found he was unfit,' announced the *Daily Mirror* on Easter Saturday, two days after his discharge from National Service after only eight weeks, most of them spent in psychiatric wards. 'The Army has made a new man of me,' he told the press from his 'luxury flat' in Gloucester Place, Marylebone. 'I was a crazy, mixed-up kid. Now I have been straightened out. I hope my public will stay loyal to me. It will be several months before I can even think of going back to the stage.' In fact, less than three weeks later, the manager of a cinema in Burnley went on stage to test audience reaction to the news that Dene had been booked as part of a forthcoming Dickie Valentine bill touring mainly northern cinemas. 'The response was shocking,' a Star circuit executive revealed. 'They booed. But during the interval we talked to teenagers individually and discovered they were anxious to welcome Terry.' On 20 April the *Derby Evening Telegraph* broke the news to locals that the following Sunday, the 26th, would be the start of Dene's comeback, at the Majestic on the outskirts of Derby. 'He is able to make the Chaddesden stage appearance at short notice because he recovered from his breakdown earlier than expected.'

Coming hard on the heels of Marty Wilde's exemption from National Service on account of flat feet, a week of controversy ensued. 'In view of the fact that he is a "rock and roll" expert, has the War Office consulted the Admiralty as to whether he would be suitable for sea service?' asked Herbert Morrison in the Commons, while Gerald Nabarro promised, 'I would have smartened-up Terry Dene's parade for him.' And in Derby itself, not only were there hostile letters in the local paper – 'I wonder what the veterans of two wars are thinking of it' and 'In my opinion the only emotional strain Terry Dene suffered was the fact that his wages dropped from hundreds of pounds per week to a mere 17s 6d and he wasn't man enough to take it' – but anti-Dene slogans (such as 'GET ON PARADE!' and 'GET YER 'AIR CUT') were daubed overnight in yellow on the Chaddesden Majestic. On Saturday, despite protest letters to the BBC, Dene appeared on *Drumbeat*, and then on Sunday evening came the big test:

> As soon as he appeared cheers were mingled with a storm of booing. Some of his songs were completely drowned by the din as the barrackers jeered, booed and chanted: 'LEFT RIGHT LEFT RIGHT.' As the boos reached a crescendo so his fans cheered even louder . . . right through his 16-minute act.
>
> And while the uproar raged, Terry Dene sang and quivered, oblivious to the noise. His show went on.

'That was good,' he told a journalist afterwards. 'I think they still like me.' Sadly, they did not. Dene's next single, 'There's No Fool Like a Young Fool', failed to trouble the charts, and by the end of the year he was a forgotten man.[28]

'M still looking pretty grim with no top teeth and it seems likely to remain so since they won't make her an upper denture unless she has all her lower teeth out as well,' related Anthony Heap on Sunday the 26th after a second visit to his mentally unwell wife Marjorie (who during the winter had gone missing) at Horton Hospital, Epsom. 'To which, of course, she won't agree and I don't blame her ... Why *must* these dentists be so damned awkward?' Three days later, 11-year-old Gyles Brandreth, at a prep school near Deal, bought Rolos at the tuck shop ('They don't have Aeros or Spangles, but can order them if enough people want them') and Accrington Stanley had their last match of the season, going down 5–0 at Reading, barely a week after a 9–0 drubbing at Tranmere. 'It is now very strongly rumoured that 11+ results come out next Tues,' noted Judy Haines on Thursday. 'I fluctuate between quiet confidence in a satisfactory result to agonies in case it isn't.' Friday, 1 May was a suitable date for the consecration service of the leftish Mervyn Stockwood at Southwark Cathedral (Princess Margaret present 'in a grey two-piece velvet suit and a pink hat'), while elsewhere the local comedian Arthur English crowned the Fleet Carnival Queen ('Gor blimey, there are some real smashers up there'), Nella Last watched 'that moronic Army Game', Richard Crossman addressed Labour's annual rally at Grantham ('just over 100 people, stolid and totally apathetic, all of them waiting for the dance to begin'), and, in the small hours, the plucky but limited Brian London was knocked out by world heavyweight champion Floyd Patterson in Indianapolis, despite the support of 'a party from the north of England, who had flown over, complete with bowlers and umbrellas'.[29]

Next afternoon, Marian Raynham in Surbiton took a walk along the Ewell Road ('How everywhere is changing, flats going up everywhere'); Crossman joined Betty Boothroyd to speak to 38 people at Stamford Labour Club, before 'we went across the passage to the bar, where some 50 people had been sitting throughout the meeting!'; Ted Dexter got married at Bray to the model Susan Longfield, with the Bishop of Gibraltar officiating; in South Wales, Briton Ferry Town's first home match of the cricket season was 'an uninspiring display' drawing 'only a handful of people', with the visitors from Clydach recovering to win after losing three early wickets (G. Davis c. Mainwaring b. E. Jones 2, Will Jones b. D. Jones 0, Eifion Jones c. N. Jones b. E. Jones 0); and

Arthur English was in Ash (near Aldershot) to crown the May Queen at the Red Cross May Fair. 'I was going to Wembley for the Cup Final, but I wouldn't let the Red Cross down. They do such a lot of wonderful work. I'll see the last few minutes of the game on the TV at home.'[30]

He was in time to watch Luton Town doggedly but uninspiringly trying to equalise against Nottingham Forest, down to ten men after Roy Dwight (uncle of Reg Dwight, later Elton John) had been carried off with a broken leg. 'Syd Owen ran up towards the end,' wrote Alan Hoby in his *Sunday Express* match report about Luton's veteran defender playing his last game, 'and even vaulted the rails when the ball went loose.' But Hoby, like almost every other neutral observer, agreed that Forest deserved their 2–1 triumph. Both TV channels covered the match, though neither lingered: by 5.05 on BBC it was children's TV, by 5.10 on ITV it was (appropriately enough) *The Adventures of Robin Hood*, with Richard Greene as Robin and Richard O'Sullivan as Prince Arthur, Duke of Brittany. One more football issue still needed resolving, and that evening the visitors at Dulwich Hamlet won 3–1 and thereby clinched the Isthmian League title. 'Although they take some stopping,' noted *The Times*, 'Wimbledon are not a graceful side.'

Crossman's dispiriting jaunt ended on Sunday afternoon in rain-swept Nottingham. 'The May Day procession was about half a mile long, with 15 big floats and 4 bands,' he recorded of a downbeat occasion, 'but I should guess that not more than 1,200 people were marching.' At the ensuing rally he referred in his speech to 'the shameful Budget', but the bigger cheer came when John Silkin, prospective Labour candidate for Nottingham South, declared, 'Look what we brought you – we brought you the Cup!' In fact, everyone had to wait until the next evening to see the trophy itself, when the homecoming heroes made a memorable tour along seven miles of the city's roads. As the *Nottingham Evening News* reported:

> At every point were gathered crowds to see the coach carrying the players with skipper Jack Burkitt waving aloft the FA Cup, and in the old Market Square there gathered the biggest crowd (some 50,000) ever seen in that arena. The thousands who had come to see Forest bring back the Cup, cheered and screamed themselves hoarse and sang 'Robin Hood' as vociferously as it had ever been sung. Bells were played and rattles were

plied as the seething sea of red and white demonstrated its appreciation of the team's achievement.

No royal visit has ever brought out the tumultuous turn-out on this occasion.[31]

# 12

# A Merry Song of Spring

'There's gold in them there stock markets – and how it shines this bright May morning!' proclaimed the brazenly pro-Tory tabloid the *Daily Sketch* on the 5th, the day after Nottingham's loving cup:

> These are great days for anyone who has a stake in Britain's drive for prosperity. Share values are UP yet again. From TV to textiles . . . radio to rubber . . . banks to breweries – the markets sing a merry song of spring.
>
> Car sales – always the best index of a boom – are hitting new heights. And the peak season is still to come.
>
> *Can we keep it up? Yes – and yes again.*

Indeed, only one thing was missing from the feel-good prospectus: '*All we want now is for the summer to follow the market's example – and get in the golden groove, too!*'

Two families this Tuesday had unashamedly local preoccupations. 'I'm afraid Essex is a very competitive county,' a Woodfordian had recently admitted to Willmott and Young about parental anxieties concerning the 11-plus, and Judy Haines in Chingford would probably not have pretended to be any different. Happily, a year after Ione's success, it turned out fine again: 'At 9.30 (as I was trying to concentrate on ironing) a loud rat-a-tat-tat came on the front door, and there was Pamela with Cynthia Gayton. "I've passed," she cried. What joy. I pinched myself to make sure I was awake and then kissed them both.' Up on Humberside, the preoccupation was with Hull's imminent appearance in the Rugby League Cup Final. 'I shall be pleased when it's all over,' Tom Courtenay's mother frankly wrote to him in London. 'There seems to be an atmosphere all the time.' Tom's father wrote also, making plans for his 10.15 arrival at King's Cross on Saturday morning: 'I am looking forward to a real good day. Our programme will be a drink to give us an appetite then a good feed so I'm hoping you know where a good pint and a meal can be had. We shall have plenty of time. I think if we get to Wembley Stadium by 2.30 we should be in clover.' But for John Osborne, it was thorns all the way on Tuesday evening. The first night at the Palace Theatre of his satirical, anti-Establishment musical, *The World of Paul Slickey*, featured booing during the show, more booing at the end, and afterwards Osborne being chased up the Charing Cross Road. Heap reckoned it 'crude, tawdry, puerile and putrid'; in Noël Coward's eyes, it was a case of 'bad lyrics, dull music, idiotic, would-be daring dialogue', the whole thing the work of 'a conceited, calculating young man blowing a little trumpet'. Reviews were almost unanimously hostile, Larkin noting with bipartisan pleasure that 'it got a bashing in *both* the *D. Telegraph* & the *M. Gardener*', and when Mollie Panter-Downes a few weeks later attended a matinee performance, 'the seat holders in the stalls huddled together like shipwrecked mariners in a sea of red plush'. Of course, the conceited Osborne had had it coming, and *Slickey* was clearly a second-rate (or worse) piece. But Michael Billington also has a point when he argues that the way in which it was 'elevated from a resounding flop into an instrument of generational revenge' – John Gielgud among those booing at the curtain calls – revealed the 'cultural chasm' across which 'mutually hostile groups' were now glaring.[1]

This was not the only chasm. On Thursday the 7th, two days after Osborne's debacle, C. P. Snow gave the Rede lecture at Cambridge, taking as his theme 'The Two Cultures and the Scientific Revolution'. It did not come out of the blue – Snow himself almost three years earlier had written in the *New Statesman* about 'The Two Cultures', i.e. literary and scientific, while Richard Crossman more recently had lamented how 'the preservation of an anachronistic elite educational system', in the form of public-school-dominated Oxbridge, had created 'an Establishment with a set of cultural values hostile to technology and applied science, and with an arrogant belief that a mind trained in

mathematics, classics or pure science can solve any problem to which it
gives attention'. But it was this celebrated lecture, almost instantly
printed as a book, that crystallised public attention around the subject.
Ostensibly, Snow was the meritocratic (son of a Leicester clerk),
Olympian, dispassionate observer – on the one hand an accomplished
novelist who would coin the phrase 'the corridors of power', on the
other hand Scientific Adviser to the Civil Service Commission – but in
reality, although of course he called for a better mutual understanding
between the two cultures, his principal target was men of letters.

'If the scientists have the future in their bones,' Snow declared, 'then
the traditional culture responds by wishing the future did not exist. It is
the traditional culture, to an extent remarkably little diminished by the
emergence of the scientific one, which manages the western world.' He
continued with an attack on what he saw as the elitist guardians of that
Luddite, anti-scientific culture:

> They still like to pretend that the traditional culture is the whole of
> 'culture', as though the natural order didn't exist. As though the explo-
> ration of the natural order was of no interest either in its own value or
> its consequences. As though the scientific edifice of the physical world
> was not, in its intellectual depth, complexity and articulation, the most
> beautiful and wonderful collective work of the mind of man. Yet most
> non-scientists have no conception of that edifice at all. Even if they
> want to have it, they can't. It is rather as though, over an immense range
> of intellectual experience, a whole group was tone-deaf. Except that
> this tone-deafness doesn't come by nature, but by training, or rather
> the absence of training.

Almost inevitably, a year and a half after Sputnik had apparently
revealed the Soviet lead in the global power game, he looked east for the
solution. 'I believe the Russians have judged the situation sensibly,'
boomed Snow.

> They have a deeper insight into the scientific revolution than we have, or
> than the Americans have. The gap between the cultures doesn't seem to
> be anything like so wide as with us. If one reads contemporary Soviet
> novels, for example, one finds that their novelists can assume in their

audience – as we cannot – at least a rudimentary acquaintance with what industry is all about.

At the end, he issued a ringing call for education to become more scientific, more technological, more progressive, more *modern*:

> All the arrows point the same way. Closing the gap between our cultures is a necessity in the most abstract intellectual sense, as well as in the most practical. When those two senses have grown apart, then no society is going to be able to think with wisdom. For the sake of the intellectual life, for the sake of this country's special danger, for the sake of the western society living precariously rich among the poor, for the sake of the poor who needn't be poor if there is intelligence in the world, it is obligatory for us and the Americans and the whole West to look at our education with fresh eyes.[2]

This sunny Thursday was also the day of local elections. Labour overall sustained some 200 losses – 'the Tories have got in!' exalted Kenneth Williams in St Pancras, adding 'so that's got rid of all those Red Flag merchants who have queened it so arrogantly & for so long' – but soon afterwards a cautious Macmillan definitively confirmed that there would be no general election before the autumn. 'On a hot summer night,' wondered a Labour agent about the poor turnout, 'was Diana Dors or Bob Monkhouse more important than exercising the long-fought-for right to vote?' Results were still coming in when on Friday morning, at Pentonville Prison, a 25-year-old scaffolder, Ronald Marwood, was hanged for stabbing to death a policeman outside a dance hall in Seven Sisters Road, Holloway. 'Cassandra is out of touch with public opinion when he suggests that the case against Marwood was prejudiced because the victim was a policeman on duty,' a letter to the *Daily Mirror* asserted earlier in the week after the paper's star columnist had vainly called for a reprieve (as had 150 MPs, almost all of them Labour). 'The reverse is the case, for the public, in the main, do not like policemen.' A few weeks later, an opinion poll showed over half of British adults believing that '*all* murderers should be liable to the death penalty', with barely a tenth wanting outright abolition. On the evening of Marwood's execution, *Frankly Howerd*, the new TV sitcom starring Frankie Howerd, had its second outing, and it was already clear it was shaping up to be a humiliating flop. Whereas 'we never quite know how Hancock will respond,' observed *Punch*'s Henry Turton, the Howerd character was 'entirely predictable'; soon afterwards an unforgiving BBC executive privately called him a 'neurotic performer unable to make up his mind whether he wants to be a slapstick comedian or a comic actor'. For Howerd himself, as with Bobby Thompson up on Tyne Tees, it seemed a career-destroying moment. Next morning, Saturday the 9th, Tom Courtenay's father duly caught the 5.45 from Hull and the duo made it to Wembley, but the RADA student was distracted by the prospect of performing in Chekhov that evening at Senate House and had to leave shortly before half-time. Hull crashed 30–13 to a Wigan outfit spearheaded by Billy Boston – powerful, Welsh and black.[3]

Dealing 'tactfully' with 'all shades of opinion in a controversial issue', was how *The Times*'s film critic the day before had praised Basil Dearden's London-set whodunit, *Sapphire*. The issue in question was race, and Oswald Mosley – veteran fascist and now the Union Movement's prospective parliamentary candidate for North Kensington – spoke on the Sunday for an hour in Trafalgar Square, undaunted by continuous chanting of 'Down with Hitler', '*Sieg Heil*' and 'Gestapo', as well as being struck on the shoulder by an orange. 'Mosley is back, here in London, and anyone who thought Fascism was dead in 1945 is a fool,' Alan Sillitoe wrote soon afterwards to his brother. 'He and his thugs are on the streets, organising meetings, stoking hatred.' Then, in the early hours of the following Sunday, the 17th, a young black carpenter from Antigua, Kelso Cochrane, was attacked and murdered in Notting Hill by white youths, as he walked back – bespectacled, with hand in bandages – from Paddington General Hospital after going there for tablets to ease the pain of his broken thumb. That Sunday evening, with the news of the murder having rapidly spread, the local reporter Colin Eades toured North Kensington. 'Young white boys walked the streets in twos and threes giving an occasional whistle and jeer at known coloured men,' while in West Indian clubs 'the general attitude was one of patience and determination – a determination not to be pushed around'. Two days later, with the police insisting to general disbelief that the murder had no racial significance, Mosley issued a statement, describing as 'nonsense' the suggestion that he had contributed to racial tension and thus Cochrane's death. Would the murderers be found? 'Notting Hill has closed its eyes and its ears to this crime,' conceded the *Kensington News and West London Times* on Friday the 22nd. Indeed they never were tracked down – at least in part a reflection of how deeply and impermeably there ran in the police culture at this time what one can only call institutional racism.

That Friday evening, the journalist John Gale stood outside a youth club in Notting Hill and found out what a handful of white youths thought about the blacks:

> With the white women and that. The birds. Whores, like. Buying up all the houses. Riding around in big cars. Layabouts.
>
> Well, they do jobs you don't like. You wouldn't like to work in the gasworks or the sewers, would you?
>
> They don't like to work. They're lazy. I've worked with them. Metal polishing. Do they work? Do they nothing!
>
> Between you and me, as long as there are coloured blokes in this district there'll be trouble. Giving the area a bad name. If you're on holiday, and you say you're from Notting Hill no one wants to know you. We was in Southend and a copper picks us up and we was in the nick all night.

Altogether, Gale discerned in the youths 'a reflection of the environment: of the peeling stucco, littered newspapers, festering basements'.[4]

Next day, Colin Jordan – a 35-year-old Coventry schoolteacher, visiting North Kensington at weekends in his capacity as national organiser of the recently founded, pro-repatriation White Defence League – spoke to the press. 'We are reflecting an opinion,' he insisted. 'It may be that it goes unspoken most of the time, but it is held by the overwhelming majority of people in this country.' Parading the banner 'Keep Britain White', the League held a meeting in Trafalgar Square on the Sunday, as students chanted in riposte, 'No Colour Bar in Britain' and 'Who Killed Kelso Cochrane?' In the event, contrary to some expectations, Notting Hill did not blow up as a result of the Cochrane murder – on the 26th, Eades walked at dusk around 'a troubled area' and found 'emptied streets' and a 'deathly hush', with 'people watching the streets below from open windows, or, more cautiously, from behind curtains' – but after Cochrane's packed Ladbroke Grove funeral on 6 June, some 1,200 mourners formed a procession a quarter of a mile long from there to Kensal Green cemetery. 'I was pregnant with my second child and I stood in line feeling the shame of my colour,' remembered (many years later) Maureen, an Irishwoman who earlier in the decade had married a black musician called Ozzie. 'Those near me were all white, all feeling that it was our fault for not stopping the poison. Ozzie changed from that day. He was so carefree when we met. I was a singer. He became dark, afraid, and sometimes he took it out on me. He saw me as white, not the woman he had fallen in love with. When he died [in 1970], I was the only white woman at his funeral.'

Racial harmony, let alone racial integration, seemed a distant prospect in the summer of 1959. 'The immigrants are living in tight pockets turning inwards to themselves and it would seem intent on creating a "little Jamaica" or the like within the City,' reported Mr A. Gibbs, Birmingham's Liaison Officer for Coloured People, to the City Council at around the time of Cochrane's killing. After spelling out some salient facts – 35,200 non-white immigrants in Birmingham occupying only 3,200 houses; those immigrants including 24,000 West Indians, 7,000 Pakistanis and 2,000 Indians – most of the well-meaning, deeply paternalistic report was a plea for a properly resourced home-visiting service, on the grounds that by the time immigrants reluctantly visited his office it was usually too late to help: 'They talk things over with each other, follow suggested courses of action which are ill-conceived and doomed to failure, and they finish up talking "colour bar" when they finally come to the office.' Situations where a home-visiting service would be able to help, went on Gibbs, included child welfare when mothers went out to work, complaints by tenants, domestic troubles, health issues, employment problems and voluntary repatriation. Such situations were epitomised by (in a local paper's summary of the report) 'the prostrate mother of a murdered girl; the father in Jamaica asking for news of his son – last address Birmingham; the West Indians who lost their house deposits "through criminal activities of certain estate agents"; the West Indian who wrote to the Queen asking for help'. And Gibbs himself solemnly (though in the event to little avail) made his case:

The normal outside influences which are brought to bear within the homes of white people are absent because there is no way open at the moment to introduce them. Unless the apparent mistakes of the present are rectified, neither integration nor a stable community will be achieved. There will exist a coloured quarter made up of people who wish to have the best of both worlds yet are not prepared to accept the moral obligations of either. Very few people will have access and very little information will leak to the outside.

He might have wished, though, for a rather different headline in the *Birmingham Mail*: 'White Women Who Live With Coloured Men'.[5]

During the second half of May, intense scorn was directed at the England football team for losing successive friendlies in such minor outposts as Peru and Mexico; the days of the Aldershot Show seemed numbered after disappointing attendances despite Princess Margaret's presence; the first Commonwealth Day (replacing Empire Day) was marked in a low-key way; Dame Margot Fonteyn appeared on *Sunday Night at the London Palladium*; Gladys Langford lamented how 'boys & girls, tiny or adolescent, wear gaudy trousers, long or short, plastic hair slides, multi-coloured, plastic rings for horse-tail hair styles'; and the property developer Charles Clore provoked virulent opposition by bidding for Watneys. 'I disapprove of take-overs,' declared A. P. Herbert soon afterwards. 'It's simply not right for someone to reap the benefits of other people's work just by offering a ridiculous amount of money. What does this Mr Clore know about pubs, anyway?' The two great emerging Marxist historians were in contrasting modes. E. P. Thompson declared in the *New Reasoner* that the New Left of the future would 'break with the administrative fetishes of the Fabian tradition, and insist that socialism can only be built from below, by calling to the full upon the initiatives of the people', just as Eric Hobsbawm (no friend of the New Left) was publishing, as 'Francis Newton', his survey *The Jazz Scene*. Larkin's *Observer* review was respectful enough – though 'there are times when, reading Mr Newton's account of this essentially working-class art, the course of jazz seems almost a little social or economic parable'. He added that 'Mr Newton has little charm as a writer'.[6]

Class could not be avoided. Ian Rodger's radio column in the *Listener* besought the writers of *Mrs Dale's Diary* to create 'something more than permanently ignorant "proles" and continually omniscient middle-class managing women', while the release of the film version of Osborne's *Look Back in Anger* (by now 'easily digestible and mildly dated', according to Leonard Mosley in the *Daily Express*) prompted discussion about whether Richard Burton had become too grand to play an authentic working-class anti-hero. On Saturday the 30th, *Oh Boy!* – live from the Hackney Empire, as usual – bowed out with a Cliff Richard/Marty Wilde duet, and two days later pop music on television took a decisive 'family' turn with the first *Juke Box Jury*. The impeccably smooth David Jacobs was in the chair, and – in addition to 'Britain's number one Dee-Jay', Pete Murray – the pioneering panel comprised 'the popular songstress' Alma Cogan, 'popular recording star' Gary Miller and, almost *ex officio*, 'a typical teenager' in Susan Stranks. The programme was immediately followed by the first British showing of *Bronco*, with the BBC trusting to Ty Hardin as the roving cowboy to challenge the dominance of a hugely popular genre that ITV had established through *Cheyenne*, *Gun Law* and above all *Wagon Train*.

These TV developments coincided with the piquant case of Eftihia Christos. 'SCANDAL OF THE HARD WORKING MOTHER' was the *Sketch*'s indignant front-page headline on Friday the 29th after Mrs Christos, from the council estate at Dog Kennel Hill, East Dulwich, had been sentenced by the Lambeth magistrate to two months' imprisonment, waking up this morning (her 39th birthday) in Holloway Prison. She was a widow, her husband having died six years earlier of TB; three of her four children had TB; and her crime was concealing the fact that on various occasions in the past four years she had supplemented a National Assistance allowance by earning two or three pounds a week at home – mainly by sewing hooks and eyes on clothes, with the two shillings per dozen garments set aside for the benefit of her children. The *Mirror* was similarly indignant, fiercely attacking the magistrate, 69-year-old Geoffrey Rose, for his lack of compassion; next day it was able to report that over a thousand London dockers had not only signed a petition calling for Christos's release but were collecting money for the children. The double denouement came on Monday, 1 June, as

Christos was released on bail and Rose was taken ill at his Oxfordshire farmhouse, dying hours later. Even-handedly, the London dockers sent a telegram of condolence to the magistrate's widow.[7]

The rest of June was the time of part of Southport Pier burning down (machines crashing apart on the beach, people instantly gathering to pocket still-warm pennies); of the Minister of Supply, Aubrey Jones, going to Paris to propose the joint building of a supersonic civil aircraft; of Vanessa Redgrave appearing in Peter Hall's production of *A Midsummer Night's Dream* ('played Helena in the tradition of that fine old English schoolgirl, Joyce Grenfell', observed Al Alvarez); and, in Madge Martin's words, of 'such a spell of lovely weather', though on another day 'hotter and more trying than ever'. On the 8th, Nigel Pargetter was born and George Lyttelton in Suffolk hosted his old pupil John Bayley and his wife Iris Murdoch ('I liked the tousled, heelless, ladder-stockinged little lady'); on the 9th, Heap took his son to Littlehampton, where 'in a dingy café alongside the Funfair' tea was served in 'small cardboard cartons at 5*d* a cup!'; on the 15th, Macmillan recorded with satisfaction ('the crowds were enormous, & very enthusiastic') the first time the Trooping of the Colour had been on a Saturday; on the 17th, Liberace won £8,000 damages plus costs after the *Mirror*'s Cassandra had strongly implied that the pianist, a 'slag-heap of lilac-covered hokum', was homosexual; and on the 19th, Charles Clore bowed to the hostile mood music by reluctantly withdrawing his bid for Watneys. The following week, some five dozen miners at the Devon Colliery near Alloa in Clackmannanshire spent 52½ very cold hours underground – 'singing, playing card games and draughts', with local people sending down food at regular intervals – in protest at the colliery's announced closure (along with 15 others). Eventually, recalled one of them, 'the pit committee called us up. The Coal Board had agreed to meet a delegation of miners in Edinburgh to discuss the closures. But the net effect was that the pit still closed.'[8]

The collapse in the demand for coal, the sunshine blazing, a national printers' strike under way that affected magazines, local papers and book publishers (including delaying the last volume of Lawrence Durrell's *Alexandria Quartet*), the Tories ahead in the polls – June would have been a difficult time for Labour even without the start of a major defence row, particularly unhelpful just as Gallup was about to show only 15 per cent in favour of unilateralism. 'I have led more controversies and rebellions than anyone else here,' Nye Bevan as shadow Foreign Secretary admonished the unilateralist Frank Cousins at a heated meeting on the 23rd between Labour Party leaders and the TUC, 'but whenever Elections approach I call for unity against the common foe.' Eventually a form of wording was temporarily agreed, causing Macmillan to worry that Labour's '"compromise" policy on the H Bomb' might 'have a rather spurious success'. But a lengthy private letter to Gaitskell on the 26th made it clear that Cousins would continue to press for a pledge that Britain not only would not use the nuclear bomb first but would suspend production of it – 'in the firm belief', he helpfully explained, 'that ambiguity on any aspect of our defence policy would be the most damaging thing in our approach to the electorate'. Gaitskell's even lengthier reply to Cousins on the 30th gave little ground, insisting that if Labour won the election he did not want to find himself in the position 'in a year or two hence unable to do something which I believed to be right for the country because of some commitment I have made now'. He ended by pointedly expressing confidence that 'you will appreciate the great importance of presenting, as far as we are able, a united front at the moment'.[9]

Also on the 30th, Arnold Wesker's *Roots*, his second play of a projected trilogy that had begun with *Chicken Soup with Barley*, had its London opening. Joan Plowright (about to become Lady Olivier) starred as Beatie Bryant, 'an ample, blonde, healthy-faced young woman' who had returned to impoverished rural Norfolk after living in London, and Heap that first night called it 'an exceeding well written and richly rewarding play, frequently funny, occasionally moving and never in the least dull', all of which made Wesker 'a far more promising playwright than John Osborne'. Reviews were mixed, but most were favourably struck by Wesker's full-frontal, unsentimental treatment of the working class. 'Even in the Welfare State,' reflected Alan Brien,

a large section of the population still lives on a hostile and unmapped planet where the invisible dragons of disease and loneliness and poverty wait outside the light of the camp fire. Conversation is the interchange of ritual, repetitive magic formulas which dull the edge of their fears. *Roots* not only captures the occasional surface eruptions of humour and anger but also exposes the banked fires beneath the surface.

He added that, although a left-wing dramatist, Wesker (unlike most such) 'does not start off with the assumption that the working class are noble victims of a selfish conspiracy'.

Phyllis Willmott was unconvinced. 'I hated the points where he seemed to be saying to the audience "Look at the funny, ludicrous ways of these clods!"' she noted after going to the Royal Court a week or two into the run. 'And even more the amusement of the audience in response.' So too Charles Parker, middle-class producer of the *Radio Ballads*, who in early July complained directly to Wesker that his portrayal of the gracelessly boorish agricultural labourer had all too easily enabled 'an intellectual Royal Court audience' to 'hug to themselves the comfortable feeling that these uncouths did not significantly touch their own humanity at any point'; 'corrupt and moronic though the common people are seemingly becoming,' he added, 'only in the common people can the true work be rooted, the true tradition rediscovered and re-informed.' Wesker's unapologetic reply was suggestive of how much his play had been influenced by the challenging, largely pessimistic implications of Hoggart's *The Uses of Literacy*: 'I come from the working class and I know all their glories but I know their faults also, and this play was written *for* them ... It was aimed at the muck-pushers for pushing the third-rate and at them for receiving it. It must have been obvious that I saw these people as warm and worthwhile.'

It was a more nuanced, complicated perspective than another playwright's. 'Graham [Payn] and I have taken a great shine to the East End,' recorded Noël Coward shortly before *Roots* opened, 'and we drive down and go to different pubs, where we find the exquisite manners of true cockneys, all of whom, men and women, are impeccably dressed and none of whom is in the least "look back in angerish", merely cheerful and friendly and disinclined to grumble about anything.'[10]

———

During a long, memorable summer, the new world continued, especially in London, to come inexorably into being. In the City, central

London's first new highway since the war, Route 11 (now named London Wall), was formally opened, with a car park beneath for 250 cars, while just to the north the City Corporation was preparing to give the go-ahead to Chamberlin, Powell and Bon's hugely ambitious Barbican proposals, hailed by the architect-planner Graeme Shankland as 'Britain's most imaginative scheme for big-scale central area redevelopment'. In the West End, Basil Spence's 14-storey Thorn House was completed ('somehow the human scale of the St Martin's Lane area has been preserved', thought the *Architects' Journal*), designs appeared for the towering New Zealand House at the foot of Haymarket, and Richard Seifert lodged the formal planning application for Centrepoint, crisply informing the City of Westminster that 'we shall be glad to discuss any amendments, but it is most important that the bulk of the building should not be reduced'. South of the river, Ernö Goldfinger won the LCC's competition for office development at Blitz-ravaged Elephant and Castle, for what became the Ministry of Health's Alexander Fleming House – more popular (concedes even Goldfinger's biographer) with architects than with occupants and eventually infamous for 'sick building syndrome'. And in the East End, the LCC announced that Chinatown, in the Pennyfields district of E14, was to be wholly demolished, while officials of the LCC and the British Transport Commission met to discuss a proposed reconstruction of the whole of Euston station, with its famed Doric arch to be moved to Euston Road.[11] Elsewhere, Croydon's first major new office block, Norfolk House, was approaching completion – the start of 'Croydonisation'; Coventry decided to liven up its new shopping centre by building blocks of residential flats above it; the highest block in the Midlands, 16 storeys in the Lyndhurst estate on the outskirts of Birmingham, was almost finished, giving 'an unrivalled vista over green-belt Warwickshire'; and in Hull, the new university library was ready by the end of the summer to receive books. 'Some bits are awful: others are not bad,' the hard-to-please librarian informed Monica Jones. 'It is a clumsy, rather graceless building, lacking intelligence at all levels, but not without a certain needless opulence in parts.'[12]

Understandably, few if any activators denied the need for pressing on with at least a substantial measure of slum clearance. 'At Anderston Cross, built in the middle of the last century, I visited the worst slums I have ever seen,' wrote John Betjeman in June in a *Telegraph* piece about Glasgow.

> Enter one of the archways to the court-yards which they enclose, and you will see the squalor. Small children with no park or green space for miles play in rubbish bins with dead cats and mutilated artificial flowers for toys. Spiral stone stairs, up which prams and bicycles have to be carried, lead to two-storey tenements with one lavatory for four families. One such tenement I saw housed five children and the parents. The coal and the marmalade and bread were in the same cupboard. There was one sink with a single cold tap. There was a hole in the roof and a hole in the wall, and the only heat was from an old-fashioned kitchen range on which was a gas ring for cooking.
>
> Yet these people, though they complained, were not bitter and I was told that there were 150,000 such houses in Glasgow . . .

That city's housing problems were of course unique, but by 1959 in England and Wales only some 18 per cent of the 850,000 dwellings estimated four years earlier as unfit for human habitation had been demolished or closed. The Housing Minister, Henry Brooke, declared later in June during an inspection of slum clearance in Bethnal Green that 'many of these mothers and fathers are putting up a splendid fight in the surroundings they have to put up with. It is libellous to dub them slum dwellers. They may have just a tap and a sink in a black hole under the stairs, and a tumble-down closet shared with their neighbours in an open yard at the back, but they are trying to keep decent standards in their homes all the same.' He added: 'We are going to win this battle. I am determined to get all slums down.'

Among architects by this time, if Basil Spence firmly represented the acceptable face of the modernist push – 'he belongs to the modern school', noted an *Observer* profile, 'yet he and his buildings have a charm well calculated to mollify the feelings of those who are normally affronted by modern architecture' – then Alison and Peter Smithson were still defiantly uncuddly. 'The use of traditional forms in traditional ways is sentimentality,' they bluntly informed students at the Architectural Association. 'It is possible that a future architecture will be expendable, and that an urban discipline of few fixed points and the pattern of change will be developed. In such an architecture the short-ness of life can allow of solutions in which the first process is the last process. There would be no problem of maintenance. At present most buildings are assumed to be permanent.' Many of those students contin-ued to be bewitched by Le Corbusier, and by this time the high-profile, high-rise, Corb-inspired, hard-modernist estate at Roehampton was finished. Among those making the pilgrimage to it were members of Dundee's Housing Committee and the young, uber-modernist architect Rodney Gordon (future partner of Owen Luder), profoundly shocked to witness the unreconstructed taste of the early tenants: 'The windows were covered with dainty net curtains, the walls were covered with pink cut-glass mirrors and "kitsch", and the furniture comprised ugly three-piece suites, not even the clean forms of wartime Utility furniture.' The estate's special eminence was recognised in a lengthy piece by Nikolaus Pevsner in the July issue of *Architectural Review*. Admiring its 'pride in *béton brut*', its 'delight in chunky shapes' and its 'instinctive refusal to compromise with sentimentality', he approvingly asserted that alto-gether the estate was a 'vast, yet not inhuman, composition'.[13]

In many towns and cities, the juggernaut – which some dared criti-cise, or even resist – was still only revving up, but in September the *Shrewsbury Chronicle* printed a heartfelt letter ('Stop knocking Shrewsbury about') from B. Dodd of 9 Combermere Drive:

> The Crown Hotel is to be knocked down and replaced by shops. The Raven Hotel may be demolished and its place taken by more shops. On the old Smithfield site – a splendid setting for a public garden – there is to be more 'development' in the form of a large block of shops. Next April, the market clock is to be knocked down and a characterless modern structure is to be erected in the place of that charmingly ugly piece of Victoriana, so essentially a part of the Shrewsbury skyline.
> Can nothing be done to halt this maniacal 'progress'? . . .
> We can see the kind of proposed 'improvements' in any of a hundred other towns. There is, sir, at present, only one Shrewsbury. Has not the time come to cry halt and keep it that way? Or is it already too late?

Lurking increasingly by this time was the sometimes barely visible hand of the property developer. 'We knew nothing about the matter;

nobody has approached us and the suggestion that someone can come along and pull down our property like that is quite laughable,' declared (in August) the indignant managing director of the Tolmer Cinema in Tolmer Square, just north of Euston Road, after St Pancras Borough Council rejected a planning application to demolish the cinema and redevelop the island site:

> This cinema is regarded with a great deal of affection locally and many of our elderly patrons come along three and four times weekly and they like us because we do not hustle them out; if they want to stop for three or four hours, they are welcome. I am certainly looking further into this matter because I want to know if it is really possible for someone to seek planning consent in respect of property that they do not even own.

The Hippodrome at Golders Green was also under threat, with Hallmark Securities Ltd seeking to have the theatre demolished and turned into a 13-storey block of flats, but during September some 25,000 people signed a protest petition, stars of stage and screen attended crowded 'Save the Hippodrome' meetings ('If I were in charge,' announced Bruce Forsyth, 'this would never have happened'), and eventually Hendon Council unanimously recommended to Middlesex County Council that the application be rejected.[14]

Two situations this summer highlighted the gulf between planners and planned. 'Pit Village Preferred to New Town' was the *Manchester Guardian*'s story in June after over 1,700 of the 2,000 adults in the Durham mining village of South Hetton had signed a petition protesting against the rehousing of 620 of them in the new town of Peterlee. The county's planning department could not understand, observed the special correspondent, why they did not want 'good new houses' in Peterlee in preference to the back-to-backs in South Hetton scheduled for demolition. The answer, he went on, was partly the six miles between new town and pit head, but also 'the community spirit built up through 120 years of living and working together', making South Hetton 'a large, close-knit family'. Accordingly, 'its new and handsome miners' institute is not an experiment in social living, it is an elegantly painted roof over a thriving social life to which the happiest citizens of new towns may sometimes look back in wistfulness'. In another mining area, South Wales, the conflict in Aberdare, running for almost two years, was between the Labour-run council supporting Glamorgan County Council's town plan – one-third of the buildings (including over 3,000 houses) to be demolished, with instead comprehensive development areas releasing the townspeople from an 'outworn environment' – and the many local residents who bitterly opposed it. 'They will have to get the bloody army to get me out,' declared one. 'Whether they want my house for a bus station or a car park, I just don't intend to go.' Ralph Samuel wrote up the case in August in the *New Statesman*. 'The Glamorgan planners did not set out to destroy a community,' the young historian reflected. 'They wanted to attack the slums and give to the people of Aberdare the best of the open space and the amenities which modern lay-out can provide. It did not occur to them that there could be any opposition to a scheme informed by such benevolent intentions; and, when it came, they could only condemn it as "myopic".' In the spirit of the New Left, he concluded: 'When bureaucracy is at work in the institutions of welfare, its intentions are quite frequently benevolent, and its face is always bland. As a result, its sway is generally unresisted and its assumptions rarely challenged. But the people of Aberdare have shown that its advance need not be inexorable.'

Overwhelmingly, the sense in 1959 was of being on the eve of not only a new decade but also of urban change of a fundamental nature with unknowable consequences. 'This is a very ambitious project and one can only wish its sponsors luck,' John Osborn, a prospective Conservative candidate in Sheffield, told the local *Telegraph* in June after touring show flats among what the paper called 'the giant honeycomb of future homes' at Park Hill, just a few months before the first residents were due to arrive. 'It is indeed a social experiment and the architects have given a lot of thought to the problems involved,' he went on. 'This trend for building upwards is new to the city and it is something we have got to accept.' Osborn was asked if high-rise development was the answer to the problem created by the huge Sheffield housing list. 'We shall know that only in the future,' he replied. 'When, in fact, people have the choice of living on estates or in multi-storey blocks. I would like to walk around these flats – which I consider very good – in five years' time. Then we shall know how successful the project has been.'

Or take the thoughts of a clergyman, observing at close quarters the whole fraught process of slum clearance and subsequent development. Norman Power, occupant of about-to-be-demolished Ladywood Vicarage, wrote in the *Birmingham Post* of Ladywood's 'strange appearance', as 'besides the shells of the condemned back-to-back houses, the new flats rise in hygienic, impersonal majesty'. He did not pretend to be regret-free. 'I do think it is very tragic that some fine old roads, with real charm and character, should also be swept away. Surely a civilised city would wish to preserve roads like Calthorpe Road, Hagley Road, and Beaufort Road? Surely its citizens would insist that it should?' He found it impossible too to quell his doubts about 'the great, American-looking blocks of flats' that were making up the new Ladywood. 'Splendid as they look, there is something very cold and impersonal about the new flats. And each block seems curiously separate – here are people without any community where once thrived the intense social life of a city centre.'

Yet overall, Power's glass was at least half full. 'On the whole, it is impossible not to rejoice. I have seen too much of what living in "back-to-back" does to the third or fourth generation to have many regrets.'[15] A perceptive witness with humane concerns, he was still travelling hopefully. And so, to a greater or lesser extent, were most people.

# 13

# We're All Reaching Up

'I turned on BBC Television – so often hopeless, & we were agreeably surprised to find it as clear as ITV,' reported Nella Last about her reception on 3 July, the same day that the three reassuring words *Sing Something Simple*, as performed by the Adams Singers (directed by Cliff Adams), were first heard on the Light Programme. 'Morecambe area, like up on the East Coast, often has a poor "shimmering" screen,' Last continued. 'We hope for better results when the new receiving station is built in this district.' She had always been preoccupied by her listening habits, and now she and her neurasthenic husband had to juggle the viewing too. 'I like Tuesday night – The Flying Doctor & Twenty Questions & little or no Television,' she wrote four days later.

> Far from 'becoming a fan' as friends told me, we seem, now the 'novelty' has worn off, to be as 'choosy' as over sound transmission, & as our watching time can only begin when my husband has heard The Archers & finishes at 9 o'clock – except Sunday night, if he is enjoying a Variety show from 8.30 to 9.30 – & he won't have cowboy, Emergency Ward 10 or 'crime' shows where there is shooting or killing, it's a bit restricting. I'm often wryly amused at his attitude of 'nothing to interest *me*'.

The following Friday, 'doing several little jobs at once' in the 'kitchenette', Last heard on the radio (from the adjoining sitting room?) the Adams Singers, so she 'sat down & listened to the gentle, "sweet" voices, as they sang the years away for me'.

Predictably, Frances Partridge had not yet yielded to the box in the corner, but soon afterwards, visiting Robert Kee in his London flat, she had no choice but to give *Tonight* a try. 'It certainly riveted one's attention in a horrid, compulsive sort of way, yet I was bored and rather disgusted, and longed to be able to unhook my gaze from this little fussy square of confusion and noise on the other side of the room,' she recorded. '"Ah, here's one of the great television personalities – the best-known face in England!" said Robert, and a charmless countenance [presumably Cliff Michelmore's] with the manner of a Hoover-salesman dominated the screen.' Yet among the millions who did watch regularly, there were perhaps signs of changing taste. 'He is vulgar and gives the rest of the country a horrible impression of Northerners,' noted one among several critical viewers later in July in response to the BBC's *Blackpool Show Parade* featuring a well-known, long-established variety comedian. 'Dave Morris is still doing the same act he did twenty years ago . . . His usual "bar" or "club" humour does not work on a stage, or on television.' And perhaps most damningly: 'Probably OK for those on holiday there and out for the evening, but not for a television audience.'

Reporting this month, under the BBC's auspices and chaired by Antony Jay (the future co-writer of *Yes Minister*), was TICTAC, acronym for Television's Influence on Children: Teenage Advisory Committee. 'Teenagers,' it found, 'are bored by politics.'

This is rather a bald statement, but it does seem to be true of an astonishingly large proportion of them. 'It's all talk', 'it's boring', 'I don't know what they're talking about'. Again and again all of us came across these comments and others like them. Western Germany, steel nationalisation, the constitutional future of Rhodesia and Nyasaland, the Singapore elections – nearly all of them seem incapable of the slightest interest in, let alone enthusiasm for, any of these topics. The reason seems to be that they cannot see how 'politics' impinge on them, or what they have to do with their lives . . .

We found a widespread disenchantment with politicians. 'It's sort of corrupt'. 'They're too dogmatic'. 'It's all fixed'. 'They're just keeping to the party line'. At the back of it seemed to be the feeling that their views were conditioned by their party allegiance; they didn't honestly believe what they said, or at least you couldn't be sure they did; and that discussion between, say, Labour and Conservative was pointless since neither was open to persuasion by the other.

Other findings were that teenagers were more interested than adults in 'the large issues of ethics and morality' such as 'the colour bar, crime, punishment, marital fidelity, social justice, religion, the H-Bomb'; that they were highly observant of television techniques, criticising 'bad cueing, unconvincing studio exteriors, fake props and set dressing, bad camerawork, etc'; that they were often 'outraged' by insincerity in a speaker or programme; and that particular dislikes included the quiz games watched by their parents (seeing 'if some bloke was going to go on and win £3 2s'), period drama ('I can't bear all those "'pon my soul's" and overacting') and slow-paced BBC programmes ('Victor Sylvester and all that'). Altogether, concluded TICTAC, 'the more we talked to teenagers about television, the clearer it became that for them it was solely a source of entertainment. They never volunteered this fact, because it had clearly never occurred to them that it might be anything else. Its function in the home was that of Court Jester: to pass the time, to keep boredom at bay, to hold the attention, to interest, to amuse, but always to entertain.' Or, put another way, 'neither they nor their parents looked to the television set to serve as private tutor, chaplain, woodwork instructor, occupational therapist or Youth Leader'.[1]

Nor were Cousins or Gaitskell in the entertainment business. 'I have never believed that the most important thing in our times was to elect a Labour Government,' declared the T&G's leader in early July at his union's conference on the Isle of Man, shortly before it voted unilateralist. 'The most important thing is to elect a Labour Government determined to carry out a socialist policy.' The press gave him a predictable lashing – 'COUSINS LOSES THE ELECTION' (*Daily Sketch*); 'COUSINS GOES WRONG' (*Daily Mirror*); 'IS COUSINS A DANGER TO BRITAIN?' (*Sunday Express*) – and shortly afterwards a poll conducted for Labour found almost half the electorate agreeing with the proposition that the party was 'severely split by disagreement', an impression presumably confirmed when Gaitskell on the 11th, speaking at Workington, repudiated unilateralism and insisted that 'the problems of international relations' would not be 'solved by slogans, however loudly declaimed, or by effervescent emotion, however genuine', but by 'very hard, very clear, very calm and very honest thinking'. By now, everyone was expecting an autumn election, and Labour's anxieties were compounded by industrial troubles, especially in the motor industry, while the printers' strike dragged on until early August.

'I am sure your sensitive adolescent souls will burn with righteous indignation when you read that some poor motor car builders simply had to go out on strike because they were earning only £30 a week,' Dr J. E. Dunlop, rector of Bell Baxter High School at Cupar, Fife sarcastically surmised on 3 July at senior prize-giving. 'Try to rise above this horrible example set by your elders,' he urged the school-leavers, 'and you will gain what they have missed, the greatest prize in the world – a tranquil soul.' Within a fortnight, in a different dispute, a major, almost month-long strike had started at Morris Motors (part of the British Motor Corporation) in Cowley, following the instant dismissal of chief shop steward Frank Horsman – 'because', according to management, 'of a continuous and deliberate policy of obstruction, insubordination and insolence over a period of many years, culminating in the incident of July 14, when he instructed certain men to stop work'. Mrs W. Lawrence, a farmworker's wife and mother of three, was unimpressed. 'What must other countries think of England?' she asked in a letter to the *Oxford Mail*, shortly before Cousins managed to settle an increasingly invidious dispute by arranging for Horsman to be transferred to Pressed Steel. 'Is it *Great* Britain when it seems the unions try their best to stop workers' efforts by these constant strikes?' A few weeks later, in early September, Gallup found that those viewing trade unions as on the whole 'a good thing' had declined from 67 per cent in 1955 to 60 per cent now; given the overwhelming press hostility, arguably the surprise was that the figure was as high as that.

Not only the press was hostile. The Boulting brothers (John and Roy) had been making low-to-medium-strength anti-Establishment comedies for several years, and now, with *I'm All Right, Jack*, they hit the jackpot. Set in a munitions factory, and in theory attacking equally both sides of industry (with Terry-Thomas playing the useless, pompous manager, Major Hargreaves), in reality the film had as its principal target hypocritical, self-serving trade unionism, as embodied by the shop steward Fred Kite (played – indeed created – by Peter Sellers with cruel brilliance, including short-back-and-sides haircut, Hitler moustache, ill-fitting suit, waddling walk). 'All them corn fields and ballet in the evening,' is how he imagined his beloved Soviet Russia. As for concepts of economic efficiency: 'We do not and cannot accept the principle that incompetence justifies dismissal. That is victimisation!' Crucially, most reviewers from the left portion of the political spectrum found little to object to. The *Manchester Guardian* on 15 August reckoned it 'not so far from the reality as told in the daily news of strikes', while the day before, Dick Richards in the *Mirror* gave 'full marks' to the 'witty, irrepressible' Boultings for their 'latest thumb-to-the-nose mickey-taking piece of gaggery', in which they 'shrewdly, and with very little malice, poke fun at every phase of industrial life'. 'Maybe,' conceded Richards at the end, 'it's not an accurate picture of 1959 factory life, but it's splendid comedy.' Splendid enough for the Queen, who watched it while on holiday at Balmoral – apparently in the company of Macmillan. 'If that doesn't win you the election,' said someone to the PM, 'nothing will.'[2]

Macmillan himself had spent the last Thursday of July at his Sussex home, Birch Grove. 'Butler, Heathcoat Amory, Hailsham, Macleod, & a lot of TV experts to luncheon,' he noted. 'We then did about 50 minutes discussion (to be cut to 15 minutes) wh. it is hoped w$^{\text{d}}$ do to open the election campaign ... We did it in the Smoking Room & the whole house was in confusion, with 40–50 electricians, technicians & what-not who made havoc of the place.' The following week he toured three new towns (Basildon, Stevenage and Harlow, with a 'good' or 'very good' reception everywhere), while on the 7th came a feel-good announcement from the Palace. 'The Queen is to have another baby in January or February,' recorded Harold Nicolson. 'What a sentimental hold the monarchy has over the middle classes! All the solicitors, actors and publishers at the Garrick were beaming as if they had acquired some personal benefit.'

Nothing, though, improved the national mood more this summer than the heady cocktail of sun and affluence. 'For week after week, the skies have been deeply blue and cloudless every day, followed by warm, starry nights in which people have sat out in pavement cafés and on their own doorsteps and in every slip of a back garden to enjoy the rare, un-English balminess,' wrote Mollie Panter-Downes.

> Though the old idea of London in August is of empty streets becalmed
> in a dead season, the city has never appeared more lively and booming,

with the hotels, restaurants, and theatres all packed; the chauffeurs waiting beside their Rolls-Royces and Jaguars at West End curbs; the television masts seeming to sprout thicker each day over the suburban hous-
ing-estate roofs; and crowds from the provinces, dressed in their holiday
best and with money to burn obviously smouldering in their pockets,
happily lounging along Shaftesbury Avenue and Regent Street.

She did not need to spell out the political import: 'This is also the
summer when the country's prosperity – coming so suddenly after the
long, bleak series of governmental exhortations to cut down on spending that many citizens are inclined to pinch themselves rather sharply
– can be felt on the skin along with the sunshine.'[3]

---

The prospective Labour candidate for Grimsby was far from the
metropolis. 'So now this most gifted political problem-child, this all-
but-statesman already at 40, so outstandingly able, astringent, brave,
integral, quick, gay – such fun to have about – is on the high road up,' a
delighted, ever-admiring Hugh Dalton had written to Gaitskell in
February after the local party had chosen the undeniably gifted, undeniably arrogant Anthony Crosland, out of the Commons since 1955.
'Great success, given a flick of luck, is easily within his powers.' His
constituency was of course synonymous with fishing, and during
August the author of *The Future of Socialism* spent a fortnight on the
Grimsby trawler *Samarian's* trip to the Faro and Westerly fishing
grounds. As he docked, wearing his wartime red paratrooper beret and
an old sweater, Crosland informed the *Grimsby Evening Telegraph* that
the fishermen were 'the most hard-working and cheerful people I have
met in a long time'.

Gaitskell would have approved the sentiments. He had confided to
Richard Crossman (a fellow Wykehamist) earlier in the month, apropos
Crosland's friend and rival, Roy Jenkins,

He is very much in the social swim these days and I am sometimes
anxious about him and young Tony ... We, as middle-class Socialists,
have got to have a profound humility. Though it's a funny way of putting
it, we've got to know that we lead them because they can't do it without

us, with our abilities, and yet we must feel humble to working people. Now that's all right for us in the upper middle class, but Tony and Roy are not upper, and I sometimes feel they don't have a proper humility to ordinary working people.

It may have been around this time that Nye Bevan added his perspective. If Gaitskell won the election, someone speculated to him, there would probably be a good job for Jenkins, albeit he was said to be a little lazy. 'Lazy? *Lazy?*' reputedly exclaimed Bevan. 'How can a boy from Abersychan who acquired an accent like that be lazy?'

August bank holiday was still on the first Monday of the month, and that day questions of class were high on the agenda in a recorded conversation between Richard Hoggart and Raymond Williams, above all the increasingly vexed question of whether the new affluence was de-proletarianising the working class. Williams was inclined to be sceptical – claiming that, through for instance the universal use of the welfare state, it was as much a case of the middle class becoming working class as the other way round, and he stressed the continuing relevance of 'the high working-class tradition', defined as 'the sense of community, of equality, of genuine mutual respect'. Hoggart did not deny that tradition, but – with a nod to *Family and Kinship* – argued that whereas 'living together in a large industrial district' produced a sense of solidarity, 'if you spend some time on a new housing estate you are aware of a kind of break, of new pressures and tensions'. And he went on:

> I'm not surprised that working-class people take hold of the new goods, washing-machines, television and the rest (this is where the statement that they have become middle class is a statement of a simple truth). This is in line with working-class tradition and isn't necessarily regrettable or reprehensible – what one does question is the type of persuasion which accompanies these sales, since its assumptions are shallower than many of those people already have.
>
> A lot of the old attitudes remain, but what one wants to know is how quickly these new forces – steady prosperity, greater movement, wives going out to work – will change attitudes, especially among younger people. I've talked to a lot of working-class adolescents recently and

been struck not only by the fact that they didn't see their industrial and political situation in the way their fathers did at their age (one expected that), but by the difficulty in getting any coherent picture of their situation out of them. Everything seemed open, and they seemed almost autonomous.

But by the time they've married and settled in with commitments a great many forces encourage the picture of a decent, amiable but rather selfish, workable society – the New Elizabethan Age.

Towards the end, the conversation turned to politics. 'The emphasis the Conservatives put is quite strong and attractive,' conceded Williams.

That the competitive society is a good thing, that the acquisitive society is a good thing, that all the style of modern living is satisfying and a real aim in life. They seem to believe these things a lot more strongly than the Labour Party believes in anything. Labour seems the conservative party, in feeling, and it's bound to remain so unless it really analyses this society, not to come to terms with it, but to offer some deep and real alternative, of a new kind.[1]

As Williams and Hoggart were speaking, the Hague sisters – Frances and Gladys, unmarried, living together in Keighley – were on the third day of their week's holiday at Bridlington. 'We began with a dash for the bus, as the taxi we ordered never came, so we only just caught our train,' recorded 62-year-old Gladys about the Saturday, when public transport was its usual crowded self at the start of a bank holiday weekend.

What a crush in Leeds as all were rushing to the far end of the station for the East-coast trains. Porters need some patience as some travellers need so much reassuring about their train. We were lucky to get in a comfortable coach and sat back to enjoy the scenery . . . Bridlington station with its wooden foot bridges could do with a more modern look but at any rate we had arrived. After a good welcome and tea at our lodge we spent our first evening enjoying the air and watching the players on the putting and bowling greens. After working hard it is nice to watch others playing hard.

Sunday featured a walk on the South Sands, the afternoon on the beach, a salmon salad tea, and church in the evening ('about 300 in the congregation, very good singing'), while on bank holiday Monday itself the clerk of the weather again obliged:

> The sun was hot all morning so deck chairs were in great demand . . .
> Fathers on holiday seem to have more fun than the mothers who are left
> in chairs to keep an eye on the family's possessions, perhaps they would
> rather watch the cricket and football than take part. Races and other
> games organised by representatives of a children's comic paper attracted
> many of the younger children and there were plenty of prizes for lucky
> winners. Donkeys weren't in the mood for trotting and needed some
> coaxing.

That evening in Glasgow, Willis Hall's *The Long and the Short and the Tall*, by now on its post-London tour, opened for a week at the King's Theatre. The main actors from the original production had all left, so instead the *Glasgow Herald*'s reviewer singled out Michael Caine (26, working-class, this his first major role) as 'the remorselessly jocular cockney', Private Bamforth, with his performance 'taking (with no small success) the easy way on all occasions to raise a laugh'. The not wholly pleased Christopher Small continued: 'He does it, it must be owned, with considerable charm; nevertheless, the effect, which brings a complaisant audience almost to the point of finding funny the enforced slaughter of a prisoner, is a little odd.'

Next Saturday the Hagues set off home. 'Such large crowds at the station that it was 3 hours before we left,' noted Gladys. 'The earlier trains came in full of Butlins campers from Filey. The Boys Brigade came on the platform in very orderly style being accompanied by the band playing. Had a very restful and enjoyable holiday. All gone well.' The 18-year-old Joe Brown had been performing at Butlin's in Filey earlier in the season, but the group he was in were so wretched, and he was so fed up with being made as a gimmick to have his head shaved à la Yul Brynner, that by the start of the month he had dropped out. Meanwhile at Butlin's in Pwllheli, the 23-year-old Glenda Jackson did stick it out as a Blue Coat – 'having', she remembered rather sourly, 'to tell all the happy holidaymakers who wanted to be in York House that they were in Windsor House' – and took the opportunity to dye her hair peroxide-blonde, wear mauve and generally try to become Jeanne Moreau, in the hope of kick-starting her stagnant acting career. The ubiquitous soundtrack this August was Cliff Richard's number 1 hit 'Livin' Doll' – a single that, observes Pete Frame, 'conferred unimaginable respectability on Cliff, smoothing out all the bumps in his reputation' – and the film was *South Pacific*, on record-breaking runs all across the country. For her family, recalled Trina Beckett half a century later, it was as usual Southbourne in Dorset, even though in an old Austin Seven it was two days' drive from their Wolverhampton home. The drill was familiar – an unbendingly strict landlady ('No dinner for late arrivals'), no choice about what you had to eat, four families of four competing for the bathroom – and 'each day started with the 8.30 non-negotiable breakfast of cornflakes followed by bacon, fried egg and baked beans'. Whereupon, with no one allowed in the house after 9.30 a.m.,

Come rain or shine, we would trail down the cliff path to our beach hut, No 2,378, with a plastic beach bag stuffed with sliced white bread, margarine, meat paste, a couple of Lyons individual fruit pies and, on the last day, a pack of Kunzle cakes.

Once news got round our digs that we had a hut, other guests would often 'just happen' to pass by. 'Could we just dry our Jenny out of the wind?' A tricky one to refuse, so a cuppa would be offered, which generally extended into lunch. By the end of the week, our four-seater hut was accommodating a dozen interlopers most days.

'Look at the time!' my father would say each day at precisely 5.10 p.m., followed by a mad dash up the path to the digs, seconds after the hallowed 5.30 p.m. unbolting of the front door.

After dinner, still hungry, we would stroll out to our favourite Forte's café and tuck into vanilla slices and mugs of Horlicks.

And then, with the sky dark, the final ritual of piling into the Austin, which 'chugged along the seafront between Boscombe and Bournemouth piers, as we oohhed and aahed at fairy lights on lamp posts and the moon shimmering on the sea'.[5]

On Sunday 16 August, eight days after the Hagues left Bridlington and the day after the East Riding smallholder Dennis Dee dropped off his wife and four children for a week's caravan holiday there, the Street Offences Act 1959 came into action, immediately driving prostitutes off the street. Three days later it was the end of trolley buses on the East End's Mile End and Bow routes; two days after that, Princess Margaret's 29th birthday was marked by the release of an official portrait (photographer: Antony Armstrong-Jones); and on Saturday the 22nd (Dee fetching the family from Brid, 'all looked fit & brown, good weather') the *Manchester Guardian* announced that from Monday it would be known as the *Guardian*, reflecting the fact that two-thirds of its 183,000 circulation (72,000 behind its 'chief competitor' *The Times*) lay outside the Manchester area. The following Tuesday evening, Everton played away at Burnley and lost 5–2, bad news for the football special back to Liverpool. 'The train's return route was marked by broken glass and various missiles hurled from windows,' reported a local paper, 'and the trip was punctuated by halts as passengers pulled the communication cord.' Altogether, 20 coach windows were smashed, and many electric light bulbs removed from their fittings and smashed, but a British Railways spokesman opted for the laconic: 'Two policemen travelled with the train and they had their hands full.' Four days later the Toffeemen were at Bolton, lost again, and the home goalie Eddie Hopkinson was 'pelted with broken glass, sticks, apple cores and other missiles by hooligan fans behind the goal'.

In Liverpool itself that Saturday evening, the opening night of the Casbah Coffee Club, in the cellar of a large Victorian house in the West Derby district, starred the Quarry Men, the start of a welcome residency after treading water. They got a warm reception from almost 300 – the more troublesome Teds kept out by a bouncer – but Paul McCartney's brother Mike vomited after swallowing hair lacquer from a bottle claiming to be lemonade. The weekend's big story, though, was the mass break-out from Carlton Approved School in Bedfordshire. Over 80 boys absconded on Sunday, but by next day, after a police search with tracker dogs, only 11 were still free. 'It is not true that we are allowed too much freedom at the school – it's just the opposite,' a non-absconder told the press. 'Although we know an approved school is for punishment, the discipline is much too harsh. Our only recreation is a film show on various occasions, and otherwise we work hard in our different trades. Only the other night one member of the staff smashed our portable radio, and another took the pick-up arm from a record-player.' 'I am sorry,' he added, 'to see all this rioting happen, but some good may probably come out of it.'[6]

The weather was at last getting a little cooler, and Madge Martin on the 31st detected in Oxford even 'a real autumnal nip in the air', albeit short-lived. That Monday the British Home Stores head office in Marylebone had a telling absence. 'Frankie [a much younger colleague] not in,' noted Florence Turtle, 'her sister in law had had a baby, & Frankie had to mind the baby boy aged two. I should never have dreamed of staying from work for such a reason. Jobs are so easy to come by nowadays.' The presence of the day was Ike's, as Macmillan, only six months after the publicity coup of a summit in Moscow, now stage-managed President Dwight D. Eisenhower's visit to London, including a live television conversation – full of mutually warm bromides – between the two men, both in dinner jackets, direct from No. 10. The American's 'simplicity and directness came over rather better, most Londoners seemed to think, than the Prime Minister's urbane style, which appeared a shade uneasy', Mollie Panter-Downes informed her readers.

That same evening, 825 men reported for work at Morris Motors' first night shift at Cowley, as the company sought to boost production to meet ever-growing demand, while down the road a new revue, *Pieces of Eight*, opened at the New Theatre. Peter Cook, still at Cambridge, wrote most of the sketches ('warm, human, topical and spot on the mark', according to the *Oxford Mail*), additional material came from Harold Pinter with 'several bright sketches', and the senior member of a youthful ensemble was the 'quite irrepressible' Kenneth Williams, 'this small, cherubic bundle of high spirits'. The cherub himself recorded his mixed emotions: 'I hang above flies while cast do the opening & then descend on a wire. It was unadulterated agony. The audience was wonderful. They behaved charmingly throughout. There were quite a few vultures from London but I didn't care reely.'[7]

Two distinctive new novels were up for scrutiny in the *TLS* in early September. 'Low-life pastoral' was the reviewer's unenthusiastic tag for Colin MacInnes's *Absolute Beginners*, a novel about teenagers two years after his *City of Spades* about black immigrants. 'Sarcastic and facetious rather than humorous', an 'unsuccessful mixture of picaresque invention and knowing "copy"', a 19-year-old narrator who was not only a 'pornographic photographer' but 'an extremely sententious young man' – there was praise only for the 'vivid' London (mainly Notting Hill) descriptions, though even they were 'largely written in a sort of up-to-date Runyonese'. D. J. Enright in the *Spectator* was also unconvinced – 'Mr MacInnes himself can hardly be a teenager, and much of his "teenage *thing*" rings false' – but the *New Statesman*'s critic was far more positive. 'Although the decade is almost over, there are few novelists writing about the late nineteen-fifties,' he declared, whereas this 'sings with the vitality and restlessness that is seeping out of the glass skyscrapers and the crowded streets'. He quoted with pleasure how the novel's hero looks around him and says, 'My lord, one thing is certain, and that's that they'll make musicals one day about the glamour-studded 1950s.' Altogether, MacInnes had done 'a first-class reporting job' on 'a generation that has more money, leisure and independence than any of its predecessors', a generation instinctively impatient of class distinctions.

The reviewer was a 30-year-old *Daily Mirror* journalist, Keith Waterhouse – whose own new novel, *Billy Liar*, was the other one being appraised by the *TLS*. There, enthusiasm for the subject was muted, the reviewer calling Billy Fisher, the undertaker's clerk, 'a hapless welfare-state Yorkshire chap'; but the novel as a whole was acclaimed as 'a brilliantly funny book, rich in absurdities and beautifully edged writing'. Other critics also dished out the plaudits, with Maurice Richardson in the *Statesman* applauding how 'Billy's daydreams, with their amalgam of telly-formed consciousness and literary ideas and juke-box sex, and his dialogue, with its scriptwriter's wisecracks and puns, are contemporary right up to the minute'. A long, multimedia life lay ahead for Waterhouse's creation. But in retrospect, arguably what is most striking is not so much the contribution that *Billy Liar* made to the cultural northern drift, but more Waterhouse's delight in guying the crusty, stolid, narrow-minded northern stereotype, whether in Billy's uncomfortable encounters with Councillor Duxbury or in his fantasy conversations with the *Stradhoughton Echo*'s columnist 'Man o' the Dales'. One reviewer, John Coleman, referred to 'that humorist's playground, the grim North', but this was humour with a sardonic albeit half-affectionate twist.[8]

Yorkshire's cricketers did their bit on Tuesday the 1st by winning the county championship – 'one in the eye for J. Wardle', noted Larkin – and thereby ending Surrey's remarkable seven-year run. The following weekend included a section of the West Ham crowd starting a slow handclap and chanting 'Take him off' after the visiting goalkeeper was knocked out; *Juke Box Jury* (Murray and Stranks joined this week by Eric Sykes and Cleo Laine) in its now regular Saturday early evening slot; the death of Kay Kendall, only 32; and a one-off performance at the Royal Court of Wesker's early play, *The Kitchen*. Too many characters becoming 'People, and then Ideas', reckoned Brien, but Alvarez called it, 'without any qualifications at all, the best play of the decade'. Next day, Monday the 7th, saw the unveiling in Bethnal Green – in the new Roman Road market square adjacent to the fairly recent Greenways housing estate – of a group of modernist bronze statues. Depicting the borough's traditional 'Blind Beggar and Dog', this was the work of 29-year-old Chelsea sculptress Elisabeth Frink, who calmly told a local paper, 'I never worry about people's reactions to my work.' The mayor, Alderman Bill Hart, did the honours, but among those watching, one woman apparently spoke for most. 'It's disgusting,' she said angrily. 'I can't see how it has cost £1,000. Fancy spending money like that. The council ought to have their heads examined.' A youngster got hold of one of the blind beggar's legs, which swayed slightly before he was told to stop by a man who then said, 'It's very frail. I bet it won't be there after Saturday.' There was more vox pop next morning when the TV cameras visited. 'It looks all right,' remarked 69-year-old George Biggs, 'and if I knew what it was it would be even better.' But Councillor G. A. Hadley, chairman of the Housing Committee which had commissioned it, was adamant: 'It's typical Bethnal Green. Put a fence round to keep people away? Certainly not. People will like it when they get used to it.'[9]

These were challenging, invigorating days for Edward Thompson. During August he signed a contract to write a textbook of 60,000 words on working-class politics between 1759 and 1921 – a commission that ultimately came out in 1963 as the rather different *The Making of the English Working Class*. More pressing, though, was the organising and supporting of the New Left's only candidate in the almost certainly imminent general election. This was the highly intelligent miner

Lawrence Daly, who after leaving the Communist Party had founded the Fife Socialist League and was now about to stand in West Fife. 'Brother, I cannot produce a loudspeaker & van,' Thompson wrote from his Halifax home to Daly at the end of August. 'It is just possible we might lay hands on a speaker, but not a van. People just don't have vans to lend around.' More missives followed:

> Look. This Ernest Rodker lad is a first-class lad. He is, what a young socialist comrade ought to be, heart soul and body in the cause. He has initiative and good ideas. He is willing to listen and learn. He has proved himself as an organiser – did most of the publicity in London for the first Aldermaston. It would be good for him. The only problem? A beard. I have written to him and suggested to him he takes off his beard. If he does, I am telling you Bro. Daly, you will damn well have him for your campaign, and you will thank us all afterwards. *(2 September)*
>
> I think Ernest Rodker has been choked off with the beard business; but he might be up for a weekend . . . In my view you ought to send an address to every elector, since I think there will be arguments inside families, especially between young voters and their parents. *(8 September)*

The 8th itself was yet another warm, sunny day; Gallup put the Tories 5½ points ahead; and Macmillan at last fired the starting gun, with polling day to be exactly one month hence.[10]

---

Galaxy, Picnic, Caramac ('Smooth as chocolate . . . tasty as toffee . . . yet it's *new all through*!'), Knorr Instant Cubes, Bettaloaf, Nimble, New Zealand Cheddar ('Now I'm sure they'll grow up firm and strong'), Jacob's Rose Cream Marshmallow Biscuits, Sifta Table Salt ('Six Gay Colours'), Player's Bachelor Tipped, Rothmans King Size, wipe-clean surfaces, Sqezy ('in the easy *squeezy* pack'), coloured Lux ('four heavenly pastel shades of blue, pink, green and yellow, as well as your favourite white'), Fairy Snow, new Tide with double-action Bluinite, Persil ('washes whiter – more safely'), Nylon, Terylene, Orlon, Acrilan, Tricel, Daks skirts, Jaeger girls, 'U' bra by Silhouette ('Gives You the Look that *He* Admires'), Body Mist, Mum Rollette, Odo-ro-no, Twink ('The Home Perm that Really Lasts'), Pakamac, Hotpoint Pacemaker, Pye

Portable, Philips Philishave, 'Get Up to Date – Go Electric!'[11] Irrefutably, 1959 was the year of consumption: refrigerator sales up from 449,000 (in 1958) to 849,000; washing machine sales up from 876,000 to 1.2 million; vacuum cleaner sales up from 1.1 million to 1.5 million; radio and electrical equipment sales up by 21 per cent; motor-car sales (including exports) up from 1.05 million to 1.19 million; jewellery sales, ladies' underwear sales, money spent on eating out – all up by significant percentages. Even so, there still remained a considerable way to go in the consumer durables revolution: TV sets may have been in roughly two out of three British homes by the summer of 1959, but the ratio for telephones was one in two, for washing machines one in four and for refrigerators one in ten, while only one in three households had a car.[12]

Integral to the *FT*'s analysis in July of the 'Consumer Boom' – fuelled by the end of hire-purchase restrictions, reductions in purchase and income tax, and a 'general feeling of buoyancy and optimism' – was 'the rising trend in sales of radio and television sets, records, cameras and photographic equipment'. Soon afterwards, in late August, the National Radio and Television Exhibition at Earl's Court (heavily plugged by the BBC, including on *Saturday Club*) featured not only the technological breakthrough (and Anthony Heap's future nightmare) of the transistor radio, but also the latest TV sets, whose sales as a whole had almost doubled during the first half of 1959. Hitherto the great majority of sets had been 17-inch, but by now there were signs (noted the *FT* in its exhibition preview) that the 21-inch set was 'at last beginning to make some headway', with 'the new wide-angle cathode ray tube' making it 'possible to design a far slimmer model reducing the 21-inch set to more manageable dimensions'. Up in Liverpool, to chime in with Earl's Court, the prominent local retailer T. J. Hughes held its own Radio and Television Exhibition, with the sets on display still the smaller screen size but with plenty else to compensate, such as the Philco Slender Seventeener II:

- Takes up only a fraction of the space that older bulkier sets needed
- Biggest possible picture from 17" tube
- Finest full circuit gives perfect clarity and definition
- Finely proportioned in the contemporary style
- Rich walnut veneers with *scratch-resistant* finish

Ekco still had the largest market share among set manufacturers, but Bush, Pye, Ferguson, Murphy, Philips and Sobell were all pushing hard. 'Elegant slim cabinet covered in simulated pigskin with matching mouldings and carrying handle', promised a recent ad for the Ferguson Flight 546, while a rival made creative use of its name: 'Touch of genius! BUSH BUTTON channel change TV . . . With this exclusive Bush feature, you can change channels instantly. Once you're switched on, you have BBC or ITA at your fingertips – accurately, instantaneously!'[13]

In the kitchen – itself transformed by the mass arrival of light plastics, whether (itemises the historian Jan Boxshall) in the form of washing-up bowls or bins or laundry baskets or storage jars or tablecloths – two of the keenest marketing wars during 1959 were over soups and breakfast cereals. Heinz Tomato still accounted for one in every four tins of canned soup, and chicken and mushroom soups were still stalwarts. But, noted the *FT*, 'green pea and spinach are not what they were, and the present tendency is towards lighter or "cream" soups, and those with a meat content', while Knorr-dominated packet soups, 'almost negligible five years ago', now made up over 20 per cent of UK soup sales. As for breakfast cereals, their production some 33 per cent up since 1953, 'the latest arrivals on the market have been for the most part sugared, or pre-sweetened, cereals, almost all of which have contained some kind of free gift and have been carefully packaged to appeal to children', though the pink paper did not deny that 'brand loyalty is fairly strong among the old-established brands – Cornflakes (Kellogg Company of GB), Shredded Wheat (Nabisco Foods) and Puffed Wheat (Quaker Oats) for instance'. In terms of trends more generally, the National Food Survey carried out this year found that convenience foods (i.e. already cooked and canned, quick-frozen or dehydrated) were increasingly popular, taking around a quarter of total food expenditure on the part of younger housewives; that old-fashioned staples like potatoes, tea, herrings and kippers were being consumed less, while relatively expensive commodities like poultry, coffee (especially instant) and fresh citrus fruit were being consumed more; that housewives had lost much of their appetite for turning fat into dripping; and that, among regional variations, the people of the northwest ate the most carrots and onions, Midlanders the most canned and bottled tomatoes, and the Welsh the most pickles and sauces.[14]

If dripping's halcyon days were over, so too were tripe's. In July the *Manchester Evening News* ran a large, rather desperate, front-page ad for UCP tripe ('EVERY-NIGHT supper dish – because it is LIGHT, TASTY and NOURISHING . . . and ensures a good night's REST . . . with plenty of ZEST for tomorrow') that convinced few, just days before, in the same paper, Mary Murphy's feature 'NOW TRY THAT SALAD THE FRENCH WAY' included a recipe for French salad dressing. Other signs of Continental influence in 1959 were the popu-larity not only of Italian motor scooters but also of three-wheeler bubble cars like Isettas and Messerschmitts; the opening in Soho of the informal, modestly priced La Terrazza, 'the Trat'; and at Burton's, the arrival of the Italian suit (lighter, brighter, slimmer). The American influence had of course been spreading through the decade, but it was in 1959 that the Hungarian-born rag-trade salesman Willi Gertler won the UK distribution rights for Levi's jeans. Further straws in the wind pointing away from the rigidities of the black-and-white past and towards a more relaxed, easeful, sophisticated future included electric razors becoming increasingly available, Colston marketing its first dishwasher, sales of untipped cigarettes dropping but those of filter-tipped rising fast, and Bronco's coloured toilet paper successfully going national, with pink the most popular, followed by blue and green – perfect accompaniments for the new coloured bathroom suites.[15]

Continental influence was at work in a classic car launched in April 1959. 'The first small, affordable British car actually to look chic,' claims an obituarist of Harry Webster, designer of the Triumph Herald, whose 'sharp, sleek lines came from Italy' and which 'was available as a racy coupé and a stylish convertible, as well as a two-door saloon'. In fact, 'there was nothing else quite like it, especially at the £702 price'. Yet after only four months, in late August, the Herald was overshadowed by the launch of a car that rapidly became not only a classic but an icon. 'IT'S WIZARDRY ON WHEELS AND "QUALITY FIRST" ALL THROUGH,' proclaimed a full-page, dots-filled advertisement for the Morris Mini-Minor, made at Cowley:

> Who would have thought it possible . . . Four adults travelling in comfort in a car just 10 feet long . . . with heaps of luggage . . . at up to 70 m.p.h. and 50 miles per gallon? But today Morris make it possible! With one

stroke of genius they have turned the engine East-West *across* the car – and created the Mini-Minor, the roomiest high-performance small saloon in the whole history of motoring!

Known from almost its earliest days as the Mini, the car's origins lay in the petrol rationing caused by the Suez Crisis, prompting the BMC's Leonard Lord to demand that his chief designer, the brilliant, implacable Alec Issigonis (creator of the Morris Minor), come up with a new small car with low fuel consumption. Reaction in the national press to its unveiling was not far short of ecstatic – 'obviously destined to meet with world-wide success' (*Times*), 'the most sensational car ever made here' (*Daily Express*), 'a new era in democratic motoring' (*Daily Telegraph*) – while the bluff, handlebar-moustached John Bolster tested it for *Autosport*. 'At first sight,' he acknowledged, 'the car is not beautiful to look upon, its very short bonnet, small wheels on each corner, and lack of an overhanging nose or tail perhaps offending convention. Yet, one soon grows used to it, and the sheer good sense of its design appeals enormously.' A detailed, almost wholly positive technical appraisal followed, including a reference to how 'quite the most outstanding feature is the suspension', before Bolster ended 'on a slightly personal note':

> I have for long deplored the old-fashioned design of the typical British small car, and have had to go to the Continent for acceptable transport. Now, Britain has produced a really modern vehicle which can teach the Continentals a thing or two. I am so happy that at last patriotism may be combined with enjoyable motoring, and I have expressed my appreciation by signing an order form.

Unsurprisingly, the Mini – fatally underpriced at just under £500, including purchase tax – attracted enormous attention from the start, with an unofficial strike at Cowley in early September merely stoking up demand even more. 'No beauty to look at, certainly,' readily conceded Mollie Panter-Downes on the 3rd of the squat newcomer; but she warmed to its 'astonishing' leg room as well as parking-in-London possibilities, adding that 'every day, the BMC showrooms on Piccadilly are packed with family parties waiting their turn to hop in and out of these obliging midgets.'[16]

Even at that price, and despite their significantly enhanced disposable income (real wages up by 50 per cent since 1938, compared to 25 per cent for adults), few 'teenage consumers' could afford a Mini. The term itself was coined in July 1959 in a pamphlet by Mark Abrams, who defined the group as unmarried people aged 15–24. Clothing, footwear, drink, tobacco, sweets, soft drinks, slacks, pop records, gramophones, romantic magazines and fiction paperbacks, the cinema, the dance hall – these, according to Abrams, were the things on which *The Teenage Consumer* spent his or her money, a pattern of 'distinctive teenage spending for distinctive teenage ends in a distinctive teenage world'. Insisting that 'the teenage market' was 'almost entirely working-class', given that middle-class teenagers were 'either still at school or college or else only just beginning on their careers', Abrams offered other nuggets: fewer than 4 per cent of young women did not use cosmetics; at least two-thirds of all teenage spending was in male hands; over 60 per cent of teenagers visited the cinema at least once a week; the *Daily Mirror* was easily the most-read paper; and among young (under-25) working-class housewives, the majority used the same brands as their mother and largely stuck to traditional working-class foods (bread, potatoes, margarine), avoiding 'modern' foods like fresh milk, eggs, and fresh fruit and veg.

Around this time, interviews in Sheffield with those about to leave school, or who had just left it, revealed a little more about teenage spending habits:

> Bus fares for leisure alone take a lot of money. Dancing costs 3s od and 2s od for fares and a drink. I go to the cinema about once a week, but a boy friend pays about two out of three times. I buy two hair shampoos a week at 7d or 9d each. And I have to buy combs and hair grips. My mother buys my nylons, but they are supposed to last for two weeks. If I ladder a pair soon after getting them, I have to pay for a new pair.
>
> I go [to the cinema] with my friend three times a week. We don't go to the Ambassador, because it is full of coloured people. And we don't go to the Regent, because not many people go there, and it is usually old people who do. We like the Victoria best – it's people of your own age more, there.

'While you have the money,' fairly typically remarked a third teenager, 'you might as well spend it and enjoy yourself.'[17]

Inevitably, across the age range, not all shopping trends pointed in the same direction. Woolworth's opened in 1959 its 1,000th store (at Portslade in Sussex), though would soon be losing its way; another expanding multiple chain, Littlewoods, took over Oxford's long-established Grimbly Hughes; British Home Stores paid £140,000 for the huge Trinity Methodist Church in Scunthorpe High Street, so that it could be demolished and have a BHS store put up in its place; Edwin Jones of Southampton, one of the Debenhams group of department stores, opened what was claimed to be 'the most up-to-date store in the South', including 'high local intensity' lighting, Formica plastics 'on counters, table tops, walls and doors', and, in the large self-service food hall, 'Sweda Speeder moving belt check-out counters, designed to smooth out rush-hour peaks and eliminate queues and delays'. Self-service generally was by now reckoned to produce a 30-per-cent increase in a shop's turnover within six months of conversion, but the roughly 5,000 self-service stores still repre-sented only about 3 per cent of grocery outlets. In Northampton, the entrepreneurial Frank Brierley opened the first of his cut-price discount stores, which rapidly spread across the East Midlands, and, befitting the self-confessed 'Pirates of the High Street', adopted the skull and crossbones as their logo. At Burton's menswear shops, the tone was becoming both more upmarket and less relentlessly mascu-line, with wives actually encouraged to be present, or at least on hand, during the fitting ritual, while at another multiple tailor, John Collier (formerly known as the Fifty Shilling Tailors), the emphasis was on younger customers and new fabrics, with heavy promotion from 1959 of the John Collier 4 Star Policy, each of the stars (gold, blue, white and silver) representing a particular cash price for a range of suits, overcoats and waterproofs. Anywhere and everywhere, meanwhile, there was potentially the American-imported attraction – or threat – of Muzak, as pioneered by a company called Readitune, which by this time boasted the availability of over 5,000 'unobtrusive and relaxing' melodies, thereby creating 'in shop, store or showroom an atmosphere of goodwill and the background for better and increased business'.[18]

In prosperous Coventry, the recently built shopping centre in the city's heart was becoming particularly busy on Saturdays, as shoppers flocked there from the new estates, where local shops supplied food and essentials, to buy bigger items like furniture, radio and TV sets, kitchen equipment and larger items of clothing. 'They like to have a lie-in and then a good breakfast,' one retailer told a journalist about customers' Saturday habits, 'driving in at about 10.30 to do their shopping and make a day of it.' What did the shoppers want? 'Coventry people, say retailers, are quality and brand conscious, partly because of television advertising. Attractive prices are not enough; shoppers want selection, and the increasing popularity of the city as a shopping centre is due partly to the greater choice that shops are able to give.' Even so, and perhaps especially in rather more typical working-class areas, a strong counter-trend was towards mail-order shopping, the total sales of which virtually tripled during the 1950s. 'Slowly chipping away at the fixed-price structure', according to the *Daily Mail* in March 1959, and dominated by three major players (Littlewoods, Great Universal Stores, Grattan Warehouses), it was a type of shopping 'largely done on a friends-and-neighbours basis in industrial areas' – i.e. involving local organisers who received a commission – 'and only recently have there been signs that it is now spreading to suburbia also'. One such organiser was Mrs Isabel Stewart, a compositor's wife living in Battersea. 'I have 20 members, mostly neighbours, and with £25 in hand I can order goods worth £125,' she told the *Mail*. 'I usually manage to make enough commission for the family holiday, and enjoy meeting the friends it has brought me.' Was a possible third way, though, the development of planned shopping centres away from established town centres? Later in 1959, A. D. Spencer of Boots addressed the Multiple Shops Federation on this nascent trend. Delegates were generally sceptical, with a speaker from the British Shoe Corporation adamant that 'the women shoppers who provided the greater part of retailers' business preferred the congestion, the bright lights, the noise and the traffic of the High Street.'[19]

Television advertisements were of course on the front line of the consumer boom, but there were indications, with commercial TV almost four years old, that viewers were starting to tire. In March, shortly after Gallup had revealed 81 per cent expressing irritation about adverts *in* – as opposed to *between* – programmes, the Rev. R. G. Bliss, living near Midhurst, wrote to Geoffrey Gorer (who in a letter to *The Times* had played down the menace): 'These breaks so madden all my household that we now just cannot look at ITV even when the programme is excellent. We live deep in the countryside, without other evening entertainment, apart from what we make ourselves, which makes it all the more infuriating.' Beverley Nichols disagreed. 'During those two minutes in which the screen is filled with the rival claims of the detergent giants, one can leave the set in order to powder one's nose, replenish one's glass, and let out the cat. This is impossible during the chaste, non-commercial productions of the BBC. One must sit it out to the bitter end.' And, argued this veteran, versatile writer in his letter to the *New Statesman*, 'though some of the advertisements are admittedly idiotic, many of them – particularly the cartoons – are brilliant little cameos, worthy of Disney'. Predictably, the diarists sided with the grumblers. 'Now we are "settling down" to Television,' reflected Nella Last in July, 'I find much of the Commercial advertising irritating.' After citing the ads for two soaps, Camay and Knights Castille, as particularly 'distorted' and 'misleading', she added: 'I always take the chance of the advertisement "breaks" to let the dog out, or in, lay break-fast in the front room – any little needed job.' So too from a less house-proud perspective, that of John Fowles. 'The Roman putridness of ITV,' he declared in August during a spell of enforced television-watching at his parents' home at Leigh-on-Sea. 'Advertisements for detergent and budgerigar seed – why so many?'[20]

Plenty of activators may have worried in 1959 about the working class being swept along in a degrading consumer frenzy. The Labour politician Christopher Mayhew, for instance, launched another campaign against commercial television; *Shopper's Guide* (published by the Consumer Advisory Council) described as 'fit only for the nursery' the language of 'magic new formulas' and 'exclusive ingredients' used to sell Omo, Daz et al; and *I'm All Right, Jack* included cheerful, mind-less jingles for 'Num-Yum' and 'Detto'. But around this time two soci-ologists were uncovering salutary evidence. 'I don't need one, my wife is my washing machine' and 'My wife wouldn't have it' were frequent responses when Ferdynand Zweig asked working men in different parts of the country whether they had a washing machine. Regarding the material possessions they did have, and the general home comforts they enjoyed, gratitude and a degree of pride predominated over acquisitive greed, with remarks like 'I have many things which would be unthinkable to my father' and 'I have achieved something which I thought would have been impossible for me'. As for burgeoning automobile ownership, Zweig found that a car was prized less for status reasons than as 'a toy, a tool for pleasure', and he quoted one man: 'It is my main luxury; others spend £2 or more on beer, I spend it on a car and have something to show for my money.' Peter Willmott's relevant fieldwork was concentrated on heavily working-class Dagenham, where 'the overwhelming impression' he gained from his interviewees was that 'the improvement in material standards has generated very little tension or anxiety'. He quoted some:

> There's more pride – when you buy something now, you go out to buy the real thing. But that's not because of the green-eyed monster, or keeping up with the Joneses. It's because we're all reaching up for the same sort of thing at the same time.
>
> These things like washing machines have become necessities for working-class people. It's not a matter of copying other people. It's everybody wants them when they can get them.
>
> I was telling the young woman over the road about the Marley tiles my husband had just put down in the scullery. She seemed interested, so I said, 'Why don't you come over and look at it?' Now she's seen it she'll tell her husband about it. I gave her a sample, as a matter of fact. I expect her husband will put some down for her in their scullery. We don't mind about that. Why should we?

'There's not a bit of jealousy about these things, as far as I can see from people round here,' another wife observed to Willmott. 'People seem to be glad if someone else gets something. They don't grudge it. They say, "Good luck to them."'

As so often, it is the brief, suggestive fragment that tells the larger story. Towards the end of August 1959 the *Hampstead & Highgate Express* ran a front-page story on the 'storm of protest' that had broken out in Hampstead Village about the Tastee-Freez (i.e. ice cream) and Wimpy Bar that had opened in Heath Street a month earlier. The result was a petition to the paper, signed by over 150 residents, calling on it to mount an investigation into 'how and why this particular tasteless design complete with mock mosaic pillars of different patterns, diamond-shaped multi-coloured facia, and the lettering Tastee-Freez, was passed'. The *Ham & High* seems to have declined to do so, instead quoting the proprietors – brothers Tony and Brian Burstein – of this, the first combined Tastee-Freez and Wimpy Bar in London. 'It is our policy,' they simply stated, 'to try to please the majority.'[21]

# 14

# Beastly Things, Elections

'In my belief the Socialist Party in its present form cannot survive a third successive defeat,' declared the Conservative candidate for Southall on Saturday, 12 September at the North Hanwell Conservatives' annual garden party. 'We have,' insisted Michael Underhill, a barrister, 'the opportunity of dealing it a death blow.' It was yet another glorious day, and before everyone returned to the other attractions – a cake stall, a 'white elephant' stall, a flower display, a demonstration of square dancing by the Foot and Fiddle Dance Club – he added that he was just back from the seaside, where 'the remarkable prosperity being enjoyed at all social levels was visible on every hand'. Five days later at Grimsby Town Hall, 350 people attended Wilfrid Pearson's adoption meeting as Crosland's Conservative opponent. 'I would suggest to the working man,' said this local fish merchant, 'that he puts his faith in the Government which puts money in his pocket. Surely his loyalties lie first with his family.'

Both men were on message. The Tories had been engaged in an unprecedentedly expensive press and poster advertising campaign for the past two years, but since the spring there had been a single domi-nant slogan – 'Life's Better with the Conservatives; Don't Let Labour Ruin It' – accompanied by visuals showing either a family gathered round a well-laden table or a family washing its new small car. Now, in the campaign itself, few opportunities were lost to emphasise Labour's ruinous capacities, typified by Macmillan on radio on the 26th condemn-ing as retrogressive 'the old socialist system of controls, nationaliza-tion, extravagant expenditure and all the rest of it'. Macmillan himself – barely a year after Mollie Panter-Downes had reflected that he 'has always seemed a politician's Prime Minister', being 'popular and admired in the House but leaving the general public oddly cold' – was by this time undeniably an electoral asset. The self-confident member of the governing class, the courageous war veteran, the Keynesian sympathiser, the businessman, the loyal churchman, the unflinching patriot: altogether, notes his biographer D. R. Thorpe, he 'appealed to a remarkably broad cross-section of British society'. To which were added not only a flair for publicity (the fur hat on his Moscow trip) and remarkable phrase-making ('a little local difficulty') but that delightful, conspiratorial sense, conveyed by twinkling eye and urbane manner, that we were all in on the joke together. Doubtless there was a degree of acting involved – 'Beastly things, elections,' he muttered to one young candidate, Julian Critchley, as they toured the Medway Towns – but *The Times* got it right. 'Labour will do well to take the true measure of Mr Macmillan,' observed the paper at the start of the campaign. 'They are in the ring with a consummate politician.'[1]

Voters found it harder to warm to the more obviously cerebral Hugh Gaitskell, even though in private life it was Macmillan who was the roundhead and Gaitskell the cavalier, fond of parties, of dancing, of extramarital activity. Such was the strength and obvious appeal of the Tories' relentless focus on material gains that it proved impossible for Labour to shift the focus to an alternative central battleground. 'We hear of prosperity, but it is not what it should be if you really want a government which planned expansion in this country,' declared Gaitskell at Peterborough on the 26th, speaking on behalf of 29-year-old Betty Boothroyd. 'The fact remains that millions of our fellow citizens are still living under conditions of hardship and poverty which the rest of us ought not to tolerate any longer.' Of course, Labour tried: in a magazine-style radio broadcast the day before, in addition to Barbara Castle promising that Labour would 'protect the housewife' against 'hire-purchase ramps and shoddy goods', Harold Wilson inveighed against Tory-blessed 'City deals based purely on get-rich-quick gains for a few', Aneurin Bevan promised that a Labour government representing Britain would not be 'tainted' at a diplomatic summit 'with the poisons of the Suez adventure', and the author Compton Mackenzie flatly said of the Tories that 'as I approach advanced old age, I feel my mind cannot be at the mercy of these boneheads'. Wilson in particular

– quick-witted and starting to develop just a hint of the cheeky chappie – was emerging as a campaign star. Accusing the Tories of selling the prime minister 'like a packet of tablets' and of turning the Stock Exchange into 'a casino', his speech at Luton on the 20th was typical. 'Thirteen Old Etonian ties!' he exclaimed of the Cabinet in his homely Yorkshire accent. 'They believe they were born to rule, as the Prime Minister's favourite expression, "Masters and Men", shows. They see the country divided into first- and second-class citizens. Their only problem is to get the second-class citizens to go on voting them their privileges and their perks.'[2]

It was not an easy campaign for Wilson's one-time master. 'He looks tired and weary,' privately noted (early on) the *Daily Herald*'s Geoffrey Goodman, who was accompanying Bevan on his campaign. 'Oppressed by the scale of the problems inside the Labour movement and outside in the wider political arena. Still bitterly critical of Gaitskell whom he regards as "sincere enough in his own beliefs – but no Socialist".' Soon afterwards, Goodman described for *Herald* readers how, on 'a draughty corner in grey and smoky Blackburn', outside the gates of the Mullard radio factory and listened to 'in attentive silence' by a thousand workers, the shadow Foreign Secretary 'stood on a rickety chair beside an ageing car, speaking political poetry into a small microphone', claiming among other things that the Tories if returned to power would at last get their wish and wreck the principle of a free National Health Service. More private gloom followed in more hotel rooms, as the late-night whisky flowed. 'I am heartily sickened by the Parliamentary Labour Party,' Bevan told Goodman at Llangollen on the 24th. 'It is rotten through and through; corrupt, full of patronage, and seeking after patronage; unprincipled.' Two days later, in Coventry, he was described by Goodman as 'angry, frustrated, like a fenced tiger', yet at the last – although probably already seriously ill – refusing to yield to defeatism. 'There is always the unknown factor,' he insisted. 'You must carry on on that, if there is the chance of winning or at least doing something. If you forget that, you might as well commit suicide.'[3]

Altogether, 1,536 candidates – including 76 women, only one more than in 1955 – were contesting 636 seats. At North Devon a rising Liberal, Jeremy Thorpe, did much doffing of his brown bowler; at Epping and Falmouth two cricket-minded broadcasters, John Arlott and Alan

Gibson, also stood for the Liberals; for the Tories, Finchley of course had Margaret Thatcher ('A vote for any other person is a vote for a Socialist Government. Do not shirk this issue') and Gower had the embryonic magazine publisher and property developer Michael Heseltine ('I'm a young man looking to the future, not an old man grumbling about the past'). Labour's ranks included, at Hampstead, a charismatic black GP, Dr David Pitt; at Southampton Test the 29-year-old Shirley Williams (promising 'long-overdue provisions' for the NHS, including a plan to encourage doctors to see patients by appointment); and, at Buckingham, the 36-year-old publisher Robert Maxwell, who had only recently become a party member and spent much of the campaign fending off accusations about his business reputation, military record and even racial origins. Another Labour candidate, Anthony Crosland, made at his adoption meeting a particular pitch to the young ('They are bored by the Victorian restrictions we still maintain, by the stuffed-shirt and fuddy-duddy atmosphere of so much of life in Britain, by the lack of gaiety and opportunity open to them'), while at West Fife the Fife Socialist League's Lawrence Daly continued to receive well-meaning advice from Edward Thompson in Halifax ('You have got somehow or other to introduce more urgency and more sense of constructive politics into the campaign . . . Pit-head meetings are a "must", whatever the difficulties') and wore a full miner's outfit, including pit boots and protective helmet, when he arrived at Dunfermline Sheriff Court to lodge his nomination. In its unpleasant way the most resonant candidacy was at North Kensington, where Sir Oswald Mosley stood for the Union Movement. 'More sound and fury than anything else,' recalls Bernard Bergonzi of 'a rhetorical mode that was already becoming obsolete'. But Paul Barker remembers how, at a meeting in the Golborne Road, 'that barking voice, those clutching gestures, were impossible not to rise to' – so that eventually he 'called out in protest' at 'the drip, drip, drip of innuendo', leading to one of Mosley's henchmen turning round and inaccurately shouting, 'Go back to Jerusalem, sheenie!'[4]

In theory this was the first 'TV election', in the sense that a majority of voters now had sets, but in practice there were no interviews with party leaders (and of course no debates between them), while *Tonight* was taken off the air and *Panorama* told to ignore the contest. In any case, quite a few in the political class wished that the small screen had never been invented. A former Tory MP, Christopher Hollis, lamented in the *Spectator* that politicians were having to address the electorate in its own, debased language; Bevan claimed it was turning them into 'pure salesmen – like American politicians'; and, addressing one evening a meeting of barely 50 people in a chilly hall, Labour's candidate for North Kensington, George Rogers, lamented that 'nowadays it is hopeless for a political candidate to compete with *Wagon Train*'. It was unlikely, moreover, that the television revolution significantly enhanced or deepened political engagement – even from the comfort of voters' own homes. Audiences for the BBC's *Hustings* programmes, involving candidates in generally rather sterile, formulaic debate, were found to be 'very much less than might have been expected had the normal programme, *Tonight*, been broadcast'. Only 30 per cent of the viewing public watched party political broadcasts, 7 per cent down on 1955, and whereas normally the TV audience dropped by about one-sixth at 10 p.m., during the election (with the PPBs being broadcast simultaneously on both channels, at the parties' insistence) the drop was over a quarter. Tellingly, that precipitate fall was 'entirely due to the behaviour of ITV viewers', barely half continuing to watch, whereas 'the proportion of BBC viewers who continued to view actually rose somewhat'.

No one disputed which party took most of the PPB honours. 'When I sat down to watch the first programme, it was absolutely catastrophic – awful,' recalled the government's chief whip, Edward Heath, about the first Tory effort, broadcast on the 19th and showing (as filmed in late July) Macmillan at his country home in discussion with Butler et al:

> It was meant to be a report on our term in office, and there was Mr Macmillan sitting very comfortably in an armchair with his senior Cabinet colleagues around him. And Harold said: 'Well now, Rab, I think we've done very well, don't you?' And Rab said, 'Oh yes, I think we've done awfully well, particularly the things I've been doing.' And Iain Macleod then said, 'Yes, well, I've done awfully well and we've all done very well indeed.' After we'd had a quarter of an hour of this we were driven absolutely up the wall.

By contrast, the techno-savvy Anthony Wedgwood Benn was masterminding Labour's efforts, assisted by *Tonight*'s Alasdair Milne, and the first one was unveiled two evenings later. Fronted by Benn himself – 'a nice, intense *jeune premier*', thought a critic – it consciously adopted a topical, *Tonight*-style approach, including Gaitskell direct to camera, film profiles of several contrasting Labour MPs, a report on the inadequate level of pensions (focusing on the Kingston upon Thames constituency of the pensions minister), and an attack on government waste and inefficiency. 'Nearly every visual device was employed in a rapidly changing mélange of cartoon, diagrams, film shots, and direct interview,' praised *The Times*. Other papers largely agreed. Altogether, reflected Benn, 'we have scored a tremendous advantage'. The PM reluctantly concurred. 'The Socialists had a very successful TV last night – much better than ours,' noted Macmillan on the 22nd. 'Gaitskell is becoming very expert.'[5]

Helped also by continuing fallout from the 'Jasper Affair' (a City scandal involving takeover malpractice and the misuse of building-society funds), Labour at this point appeared surprisingly buoyant, and Gaitskell in particular a plausible prime minister. Within days of the election being called, he had given a virtuoso performance at the TUC at Blackpool, making it impossible for Cousins to cause difficulties during the rest of the campaign, while his promise – highlighted in almost all his speeches – to raise pensions by ten shillings and thereby 'once and for all abolish poverty in old age' gave him the moral high ground. 'He has suddenly become a television star, a political personality in his own right – confident, relaxed, a Leader,' reflected Crossman on the 22nd, adding two days later, as opinion polls showed the Tory lead starting to narrow, that 'the Gaitskell boom has been rapidly swelling'. On Saturday the 26th, the sage of Hull took pessimistic stock. 'I shouldn't be surprised if Labour did better than people expect,' Larkin informed Monica Jones. 'I am sure that elections go by purely irrational factors such as are we tired of having a Conservative government & w$^{\text{dn't}}$ it be more fun to have a change, rather than any considerations of record or programme, and the "innate British sense of fair play" may well give them a go, despite their farcical front line & jumbled policies.' He was also worried about the threat of a serious Liberal revival, predicting that 'Laughing Boy Grimond will get many votes by his a-plague-on-both-your-houses line.'

That evening on television was Labour's second PPB, with Gaitskell 'coming over', according to the *Spectator*'s Peter Forster, 'charming and persuasive as Older Brother rather than Big Ditto, the hysterical grace-notes of his Suez appearance on TV quite gone'. That same evening, Gaitskell predicted to Roy Jenkins that he would win. Next day, spending Sunday in bed, a temporarily exhausted Macmillan (finding comfort in 'Miss Austen's *Mansfield Park*') did not rule out the possibility. 'If everyone keeps calm, it will be all right,' he reckoned. 'If our people begin to panic, the result might be serious.' The following morning, Monday the 28th, the poll in the *Daily Mail* had the Tory lead down to 2 per cent; according to Walter Terry, the paper's political correspondent, Gaitskell had 'won hearts not with emotional gestures and cries but with economics and figures'. And although the latest jobless numbers showed a further fall (taking the unemployment rate down to only 1.9 per cent), Crossman at Labour's HQ at Transport House described the mood there as 'on top of the world'. So too Benn. 'The tightest, slickest show we have done,' he wrote in his diary that evening after his third television PPB, with John Osborne and Ted Willis (creator of *Dixon of Dock Green*) among those giving reasons for voting Labour. In short: 'We have definitely got the Tories on the run.'[6]

---

Occasionally the election seemed to pervade everything. 'Your reviewer of Miss Compton-Burnett's new novel describes its characters as "upper-middle-class",' Evelyn Waugh wrote to *The Times*. 'They are in fact large landowners, baronets, inhabiting the ancient seat that has been theirs for centuries. At this season, when we are celebrating the quinquennial recrudescence of the class war, is it not desirable to be more accurate in drawing social distinctions?' Nella Last, though, was more typical. Her diary during September kept its running preoccupation with matters televisual – even a letter back from Hattie Jacques ('such a nice one, as warm as her beautiful voice') after Last had sent her a fan letter – before this on the 27th: 'We settled to read till the Flying Doctor on ITV & then the Palladium Show. I suddenly realised today how near the General Election is – not a fortnight, & we both agree we never knew less excitement – even interest.' About this time, Mollie Panter-Downes took the pulse in a Tory marginal and found neither leaflets nor posters, nor loudspeakers from 'slowly cruising cars', managing to disturb 'the equanimity of the local inhabitants, who plod along on their daily rounds as though October 8th were no special date in their minds'. Indeed, 'the very atmosphere of Wandsworth Central sunning itself on a fine September afternoon, with the men out at work, the front doors shut tight, and only a non-political cat or two dozing on the railings, is marginally mum'. For another writer, very much an expat, these weeks were an eye-opener. 'In justice I must say that England was *marvellous* this time,' Lawrence Durrell informed Henry Miller after a lengthy autumn visit. 'You really would have been startled to see what three months of solid sun (first time in 200 years) can do to my compatriots; such humour, kindness, serviceability, exquisite manners, rugged laughter. It was uncanny! It was like a real move forward. People were sparkly, alive, forthcoming, devil may care; and all as brown as berries. Food's improved too.'[7]

It was not all sunshine, though. Scotland had its worst mining disaster for 70 years when on the 18th almost 50 miners died in Lanarkshire's Auchengeich Colliery; that day the *Romford Recorder* devoted a full page to a comprehensive round-up of the latest exam results, with no hiding place for low achievers – though surnames only for those at secondary moderns, unlike private schools and grammars; and on the 28th the musician, artist and humorist Gerard Hoffnung died at only 34 of a cerebral haemorrhage, less than a year after his 'Bricklayer's Lament' to the Oxford Union. The literary event was Alan Sillitoe's *The Loneliness of the Long-Distance Runner*, a collection of stories with a working-class setting that, according to one critic, resembled 'a war correspondent's reports from some fantastic front which although it is all round us, is only sometimes visible'. On the stage, *Pieces of Eight*'s arrival on Shaftesbury Avenue earned mixed notices ('Bernard Levin in the *Express* gives it an absolute stinker!' recorded Kenneth Williams. 'O dear o dear. I'm so depressed – this pile trouble is back again'), and on the small screen, the welcome start of *The Saga of Noggin the Nog* (created by Peter Firmin and Oliver Postgate) was offset by how Robert Robinson in *Monitor* interviewed T. H. White in his Alderney home and, according to a TV critic, 'took it upon himself to treat Mr White not merely as an equal but as an intellectual inferior, attempting to browbeat him, snub him, correct him'. Larkin meanwhile

inspected the newly released *Carry On Teacher* ('just about the unfun-
niest "comedy" I've ever seen') and read the most recent Iris Murdoch.
'*The Bells* [in fact *The Bell*] is balls,' he pronounced. 'It's dotty stuff,
with a faint whiff of the most creepy & pretentious scenes of *Women in
Love*, and I wouldn't give it room on my shelves, let alone money to
have it there.'

It was a notable Saturday the 19th in East London. That morning,
despite a waist-high metal fence having just been erected, Elisabeth
Frink's controversial 'Blind Beggar' statue was found lying horizon-
tally across its concrete base and, later in the day, was moved to a council depot for repairs and restoration. 'We are certain it is the work of
irresponsible young hoodlums,' insisted Bethnal Green's Deputy Town
Clerk, Mr E. Woolf. 'Many people said they didn't like it, but I don't
think they would stoop to this sort of thing.' A mile or two away, at
about six o'clock, All Saints' Hall, Haggerston Road saw the arrival of
the celebrity to present the prizes at the annual show of the East London
Budgerigar and Foreign Birds Society. This – at the suggestion of the
secretary's nine-year-old son, having read in a magazine that she was
fond of birds – was Jayne Mansfield, currently filming *Too Hot to
Handle* at Borehamwood Studios and who had recently switched on
the Blackpool illuminations. The hall, reported the *Hackney Gazette*,
was 'besieged by youngsters who climbed to windows to get a glimpse',
but 'smiling Jayne enjoyed every minute of it'. An organiser declared,
'She's lovely, absolutely charming, and a good sport to come here.'[8]

Elsewhere, an election campaign did nothing to halt the tide of
progress. Shell-Mex and BP launched a huge advertising campaign
('Mrs 1970') to promote the spread of oil-fired domestic central heating; the imminent demolition was announced (for the usual redevelopment reasons) of the Victorian central colonnade at Cleethorpes; 'First
Look at £1m Shopping Centre Plan for Shrewsbury' was the front-page
headline in the local *Chronicle*; Madge Martin 'on top of a dear old 13
bus' saw the new Finchley Road, 'where great blocks of flats have
replaced the small, pretty houses, many of which were destroyed in the
Blitz'; and *The Times* published a photograph of demolition in progress
at 145 Piccadilly, the Queen's childhood home. The latter's purpose was
a road-improvement scheme for Hyde Park Corner, and at the start of
October the *Architects' Journal* brought out a special issue, 'Motropolis:

A study of the Traffic Problem'. This included a lengthy analysis ('Can we get out of the jam?') by Malcolm MacEwen, advocating huge invest-ment in both public transport and the large-scale reconstruction of city centres, but not the building of roads for their own sake. 'My approach was essentially technological rather than humanistic or ecological,' he conceded many years later. 'I was looking for a top-down professional solution rather than a bottom-up democratic one.' The same issue featured a full-frontal attack by a Birmingham architect, Leslie Ginsberg, on that city's under-construction Inner Ring Road, which 'unhappily looks like being the greatest traffic and town design tragedy yet to afflict an English city'; even more damningly, he dubbed Herbert Manzoni's brainchild as the native equivalent of 'those "highwaymen" across the Atlantic who are destroying the souls of the American cities with their monstrous routes'.

Still worse perhaps was the spectre – raised a fortnight earlier at Margate at the annual conference of the Association of Public Health Inspectors – of 'a new slumdom' emerging from the housing projects that were replacing the old slums. 'The condition of common staircases, passageways and refuse disposal arrangements, not being any particular individual's responsibility, soon deteriorate and foul conditions develop,' noted Liverpool's Mr W. H. Wattleworth. 'Although it may be possible to provide a caretaker in a tower block, it may not be an economic consid-eration in the three- and four-storey flats, and in any case the attention of the attendant must be mainly concerned with any lift provided.' For William Amos, writing in the *Liverpool Daily Post*, Wattleworth's remarks raised three 'disquieting questions': 'Should it be necessary for the public to clean up after people whose accommodation is already being heavily subsidised? Is it not time that the tenement litterlouts were given a sharp administrative rap over the knuckles by the Corporation? And is Liverpool in fact building modern slums?' John Betjeman for his part was finally through with high-rise. 'Walking about in new LCC estates as I have been doing lately,' he told John Summerson, 'convinces me that the low blocks and the two-storey and single-storey houses are what we really need. I have found no large blocks I have visited either liked or inviting – they are just plot ratio buildings.'[9]

Betjeman was writing on 28 September, the day of Benn's confident diary entry – and, probably about the same time, of Gaitskell's speech at Newcastle. 'You can be assured of this,' he told the 3,000 present that evening. 'There will be no increase in the standard or other rates of income tax under the Labour Government so long as normal peace-time conditions continue.' The *Daily Herald* reported that 'a terrific cheer' greeted this unexpected tax pledge, but *The Times*'s political correspondent was immediately on the money when he called it 'extraordinary' and 'a significantly strong reaction to the massive Conservative attack that is being directed to the cost of the Labour programme'. Among politicians, two instant reactions were recorded: Hailsham's, telling a meeting in Doncaster that 'The Lord hath delivered them into our hands'; and Bevan's, turning to Geoffrey Goodman and angrily saying, 'He's thrown it away. He's lost the election.' The problem was perceived – however unfairly – as one of credibility, putting Labour firmly on the back foot, and Macmillan next evening, speaking in Glasgow, called Gaitskell's promise 'a very queer one for a professional economist and an ex-Chancellor of the Exchequer'. That same evening, 'amidst applause and cheering', Mosley was strutting his stuff in Notting Hill. Warning against 'the cheap coloured labour that is being imported into Britain', he told his white listeners that 'no matter how skilled you may be, you can't compete with a man who is prepared to live on a tin of Kit-E-Kat a day.' He added: 'In the whole of my political career I have never been so disgusted as I am now at what is happening in North Kensington. Why should English women suffer this sort of thing? Meanwhile, the police are told to look the other way.' In short: 'There is one law for the blacks and one for the whites.'[10]

On Wednesday the 30th, the opening of the much-delayed Chiswick Flyover, London's first major two-level highway to be built since the war, had a double twist: the presence – following the unavailability of Harold Watkinson (Minister of Transport), Stirling Moss and Donald Campbell – of the almost inevitable, scarlet-dressed Jayne Mansfield to cut the ribbon, as to a chorus of wolf-whistles she blew kisses to 600 admirers before announcing, 'It's a sweet little flyover'; and, a few streets away, a vehement open-air speech from the local Conservative candidate, Dudley Smith, denouncing it as 'thoroughly irresponsible to turn a fine British achievement into a stunt for a film star who is not even British'. The flyover itself stood up admirably to its first rush hour. 'A brilliant success,' claimed the AA. 'Some motorists even went back for another go.' That evening, Bevan was at a packed school in nearby Ealing, speaking on behalf of Smith's Labour opponent. Early on, a slight commotion at the back of the hall prompted Bevan to remark, 'Perhaps Jayne Mansfield has arrived,' while later, after he had called the Suez expedition 'immoral and inept', a shout of 'Why was it immoral?' prompted him to rap out to cheers: 'It was immoral because by armed might we tried to impose our will on a weaker country. We would never have done it if Nasser had had bombs to drop on London. It was the act of a coward and a bully.' The place for bullies that evening, though, was Hampstead Town Hall. There, for nearly 20 minutes, David Pitt struggled to make himself heard above shouts of 'Keep Britain white' and 'We don't want England a dump-ing ground for niggers,' before a running fight broke out between members of the White Defence League and Labour Party stewards. Chairs were broken, glass showered everywhere, even an old water-colour of Hampstead was smashed on the wall. Whatever his inner feelings, Pitt 'remained', observed the *Ham & High*, 'calm and smil-ing throughout the mêlée'.[11]

October arrived with the political outlook more uncertain than the meteorological. 'First signs of the Election – got our voting cards,' noted Nella Last on Thursday the 1st. 'I was surprised to find both Mrs Atkinson & Mrs Higham think Labour will win.' But at Transport House the mood had changed. 'We feel the Tories have now got us on the defensive,' reflected Benn, and that evening Macmillan senten-tiously if effectively declared at Nottingham that 'elections are very severe tests and Mr Gaitskell has managed to destroy in a week a repu-tation he had built up over a number of years'. Bevan meanwhile was speaking at the Co-operative Hall in Upper Tooting Road, Wandsworth – 800 inside, 500 outside listening via a loudspeaker – where most of the heckling came from League of Empire Loyalists, but a man with a large ginger beard shouted out that perhaps Bevan would join up in the next war. 'Obviously you have worn a beard to hide your weak mouth,' retorted Bevan, who later in his speech claimed that Labour had a 'moral stature' that the Tories could not possibly reach. Next morning he was conclusively down with flu and cancelled the rest of his campaign tour.

The *Spectator* now announced that it could not support the Conservatives (a party that seemed 'ready to sacrifice almost anything to stay in office') and published various voting intentions. Wolf Mankowitz and Angus Wilson were unenthusiastic backers of Labour; Evelyn Waugh hoped to see the Conservatives return 'with a substantial majority' and recalled his 'bitter memories of the Attlee-Cripps regime when the kingdom seemed to be under enemy occupation', but added that he did not personally intend to vote, since 'I do not aspire to advise my Sovereign in her choice of servants'; and Kingsley Amis, though calling Labour 'sinister as well as fatuous and revolting', conceded he would 'just about rather see a Labour Government in office than another Conservative one', given that 'Labour had an idea in its head once, even though it is now almost forgotten', whereas 'Conservatism never had an idea at all, except to hold on to its wallet'. Another novelist, Keith Waterhouse, undertook some reportage in a suburban pub on the Friday evening:

> The television lounge was populated by a crowd of youths, just touching voting age [21], who had spent a comfortable evening sipping lager and lime and watching Hancock [on BBC from 8.30 to 9, at which point they had presumably switched to ITV]. They were genuinely affronted when [at 10] the election programme came on. One minute they were singing contentedly, 'The Esso sign means happy motoring,' and the next they were on their feet shouting abuse. Four adults, sitting with their backs to the television set, turned round idly to see what the row was about, then resumed their drinking. A man came to the door carrying a glass of stout in each hand, called, 'It's only the television mention' over his shoulder, and went out again. The youths switched over to the other channel and then, seeing the same blank politician's face, pulled the plug out of its socket.

The theme of the party political broadcast was 'Britain Overseas', the main politicians featured were Alan Lennox-Boyd (Colonial Secretary) and Selwyn Lloyd (Foreign Secretary), and Waterhouse added that 'so far as those youths in the pub were concerned, the Tories might as well have put on an old film of Neville Chamberlain'.[12]

'Last day of "summer time" and light evenings,' recorded Anthony Heap on Saturday the 2nd. 'But with afternoon temperatures still soaring well up in the seventies there's no sign yet of any end to this golden summer.' Next day, speaking in Grimsby's Alexandra Hall, Anthony Crosland allowed himself a touch of exasperation. 'Who has never had it so good?' he asked. 'I am sick and tired of hearing the Tories trot out this little party piece.' Among those not having it so good, he identified not only the sick, old-age pensioners and widows but also railway workers, teachers and nurses; while those who *were* having it so good were Stock Exchange speculators (getting away tax-free) and businessmen who indulged in the 'expense account racket'. It was the last weekend before polling day, and on Sunday the psephologist David Butler – who in mid-September had privately predicted a heavy Tory victory – rang Wedgwood Benn to tell him the outcome was 'wide open'. Indeed, Gallup on Monday had the two parties level-pegging – perhaps the provocation for Lord Montgomery, hero of El Alamein, to declare publicly that anyone who voted Labour 'must be completely barmy, absolutely off his rocker' – though Richard Crossman privately reflected 'I still don't, in my inmost heart, believe in victory.' Not so Gaitskell. That evening he made his final television appeal, commending Labour's 'fine, modern, new, realistic programme', which was in tune with the British people's 'special qualities' of 'kindliness, tolerance, decency, a sense of fair play'; later, unable to sleep, he drew up a list of his Cabinet. Nella Last's preoccupation this Monday, though, was rather different. 'I was interested in & rather against character in Double Your Money – with an outstanding knowledge of Opera,' she recorded. 'When she got her £500 I sighed with relief, hoping she didn't risk it to reach out for £1,000. £500 *can* make her dream of going to New York Opera House come true. I feel Hughie Green would contact friendly people to help her. To read his life story of all his different activities and struggles, sounds like fiction rather than fact, & he seems to have a gift for making friends.'[13]

On Tuesday the 6th the election's scariest scare story turned up on the front page of the *Daily Sketch*'s later editions. 'If you vote the Socialists into power on Thursday,' it claimed entirely groundlessly, 'you can say good-bye to commercial television,' adding for good measure that abolition would take place within six months. Everywhere, the campaigning continued. 'A monstrous infringement' was the reaction of Peter Tapsell, Conservative candidate for West Nottingham, to the news that council-house tenants had been told by the Labour-run local authority to take down election posters and window bills. At lunchtime in Luton, heckled by Vauxhall workers that the Tories were the party of privilege, Charles Hill (one-time 'Radio Doctor' and now a minister) countered that his origins were 'just as humble as many of you here' and that he was 'not ashamed' he had 'made a bit of progress and worked hard'. Shirley Williams at Southampton Test put in her usual 17-hour day, driven around by her husband Bernard in a 'zippy green sports car', while in Bristol, after a similarly hectic day of loudspeakers and meetings (including at Robertson's jam factory), Wedgwood Benn privately conceded that 'there is not quite as much enthusiasm here as I had expected and the number of workers has not been as great as I had hoped', that indeed 'frankly, the campaign has lost some of its impetus'. That evening, Macmillan made his final television pitch and solemnly quoted Churchill: 'To build is the laborious task of years. To destroy can be the foolish act of a single day.' In the broadcast's immediate aftermath, the pro-Conservative members of the BBC Viewers' Panel noted that he had been 'in excellent form . . . relaxed . . . calm . . . convincing', but the anti-Conservative ones found the 'Old School Tie' atmosphere 'out of key with modern times'.

Four different opinion polls had been appearing regularly, and on Wednesday the *Telegraph* published its final throw, which unlike the others was restricted to marginal seats and now gave the Tories a 2.5-point edge. That lunchtime, Gaitskell was in Leeds (where his constituency was), speaking at an open-air meeting for factory workers. 'Don't let the telly keep you from the poll,' he urged. 'Leave the kids at home to watch *Rawhide*. They can tell you what has happened when you get back.' That evening, just as the 200th edition of *Educating Archie* on the Light Programme had Bruce Forsyth taking over from Max Bygraves as Archie's new tutor, Michael Foot, trying to wrest back Plymouth Devonport from Joan Vickers, ended his campaign at the city's newly built Guildhall. 'The Tories haven't got any dreams or ideals for the future,' he told an audience of some 1,500. 'They want the nation to stay as it is. They don't want anything better.' As ever, Kenneth Preston in Keighley was tirelessly writing up his diary. After a passing reference to how 'Spain has latterly become very popular as a Continental holiday place,' he pondered the situation: 'It has not been a very exciting election, as far as one can judge. We take things more calmly here than in other lands. The Socialists must be particularly anxious for if they do not win this time their future will be dark indeed.'[14]

'A perfect day' (Benn in Bristol), 'another glorious day' (Preston in Keighley), 'another marvellous autumn day' (Phyllis Willmott in Highgate) – the weather on polling day declined to deviate from the Tory script. 'Shares Reach New Peak on Election Hopes' was the headline in *The Times*, and indeed the three new opinion polls in that morning's papers all put the Tories ahead, by between 1.5 and 3.6 points, with Benn gloomily noting how 'the Gallup poll suggests that the enormous "don't know" group may be inclining to the right'. But for some there was no room for complacency. 'Finchley's attractive Conservative candidate, Mrs Margaret Thatcher, started canvassing at 8 a.m. in a blaze of blue,' reported a local paper. 'She wore a glamorous royal blue silk suit with matching shoes and handbag, and was driven round by her husband in a blue Jaguar.' Churchill too – wearing black overcoat, black homburg and white muffler, as well as sunglasses – was out and about, going on a 12-mile tour of his Woodford constituency in a yellow open car. 'At one of his stops,' it was reported, 'Christine Truman, the tennis star, who is helping out at the committee rooms, leant over and took Sir Winston's hand and then had a word with Lady Churchill.' The electorate largely performed its democratic duty – 'Have been & voted – wish it were for draught beer,' noted Philip Larkin, while Frank Lewis in south Wales voted despite telling himself he had 'absolutely NO interest in politics' – amidst widespread concerns about the impact of the TV set on potential evening voters. 'Let's make it the BIGGEST POLL EVER' the Labour-supporting *Daily Mirror* that morning had urged its several million working-class readers. '*Your* X Can Make The Difference Today. To Hell with the telly until we've all voted.' Indeed, the *Mirror* even declined this Thursday to list programmes before nine o'clock, when the polls closed, though presumably it was an open secret that the BBC was showing *The Black and White Minstrel Show*, and ITV not only *Rawhide* but also *Dotto* ('turns dots into pictures and pictures into pounds'). 'With The Archers, Top of the Form (sound) &

Dotto & This Wonderful World on ITV,' recorded Nella Last, 'the evening seemed to pass quickly.'[15]

Then came her inevitable wifely disappointment – 'I'd have liked to stop up awhile & listened to the Election results, but knew it was useless to suggest it' – though 59 per cent of the adult population did stay up to watch or listen. Television was overwhelmingly the medium of choice, and over twice as many watched BBC's coverage fronted by Richard Dimbleby ('the firmest base on which any such programme could rest,' noted one critic, 'and a most jolly, even skittish, jumbo he became as the night wore on') as ITV's under Ian Trethowan. Even so, 'the usual cheerful election-night crowds jammed into Piccadilly Circus and Trafalgar Square to watch the returns flashed on screens', observed Mollie Panter-Downes, including 'parties of young people bobbing along with Tory-blue balloons and shouting that they wanted Mac'.

Alma Hatt, ambitious Clerk of Basildon Council, was determined that Billericay should declare first, and through meticulous organisation and a 400-strong army of volunteers he succeeded – despite losing eight minutes after a ballot box had been left behind in a car – at almost exactly 10 p.m. This was the moment of truth, including for the Labour veteran Hugh Dalton:

> From the start the results went wrong. No. 1 Billericay, containing the New Town of Basildon, recruited by good Labour voters from West and East Ham. Surely a Labour gain. But no, held by Tories with 4,000 majority. True we held the two Salford seats but then came a stream of disappointments. Battersea South and Watford both held by Tories, and a Tory gain from Labour at Acton. And so, on and on.

In fact the first Tory gain was Holborn and St Pancras, where the handsome, personable television journalist Geoffrey Johnson Smith overcame Lena Jeger by 656 votes. Among those helping at the count was Anthony Heap, who – 'much bucked' by these 'joyous tidings' – then headed home for a 'night of gladness'. 'Election results coming in thick & fast,' recorded Kenneth Williams. 'All v. exciting. Tory gains all the time. Labour is going to be crushingly defeated.' Shortly after midnight, Crosland squeaked through in Grimsby by 101 votes; half an hour later, Thatcher swept home in Finchley ('the cheers, always more controlled from Tory than from Liberal or socialist lips, rose', she remembered); and shortly before one o'clock at Leeds Town Hall, a dignified Gaitskell conceded defeat, promising that 'the flame of democratic socialism still burns bright'. Bevan at every level was dismayed – 'I would never concede,' he told those around him at Ebbw Vale, 'I would wait until the last vote was properly counted' – while for Benn in Bristol it suddenly seemed a long time since those triumphant magazine-style PPBs. 'The count is very depressing with the crowing Tories and our people very dejected,' he noted. And, after retaining his seat with a sharply reduced majority, 'back to the Grand Hotel too depressed to watch TV'.[16]

The eventual outcome, on a 78.7 per cent turnout, was an overall Conservative majority of 100 – an astonishing triumph for a government already almost eight years old. The shares of the popular vote were 49.4 per cent for the Conservatives and 43.7 per cent for Labour, a wider margin than predicted by any of the final opinion polls, while the Liberals more than doubled their share, up to 5.9 per cent, but were still stuck on six seats. Strikingly, the Conservatives fared particularly well in newly prosperous areas like Dagenham and Coventry (where Labour lost a seat for the first time since the war) and in new working-class housing developments, such as at Borehamwood or Birmingham's outer estates, as well as (of course) at Basildon. By contrast, a mixture of unemployment and pit closures gave Labour a 3-per-cent swing in Scotland, though that country still produced plenty of Tory victors, including Sir Colin Thornton-Kemsley at Angus North and Mearns and Sir William Anstruther-Gray at Berwick and East Lothian, not to mention Lord John Hope at Edinburgh Pentlands. Elsewhere, winners included Julian Critchley, Charles Hill, Jeremy Thorpe, Dudley Smith and Peter Tapsell; losers included Michael Heseltine, Michael Underhill, Lawrence Daly (though securing almost 5,000 votes), Michael Foot, Shirley Williams, John Arlott, Alan Gibson, David Pitt and Betty Boothroyd (congratulated by her opponent Harmar Nicholls on being 'a bonny fighter'). There were two particularly outraged losers. Robert Maxwell at Buckingham declined to shake the victor's hand, claiming he would have won 'had the Tories fought cleanly'; and, in arguably the election's single most important – and heartening – result, Oswald Mosley in North Kensington simply refused to accept that he had lost his deposit.

Early reactions included frantic trading on Friday morning on the floor of the Stock Exchange, now it was clear the steel industry would not be renationalised; Graham Greene hearing about Labour's defeat while on a plane over Canada and celebrating with a slug of whisky; and Larkin in Hull observing 'some long faces in the University on Friday, haw haw', while expressing his own hope that 'the present crowd don't do anything silly in their mad flush of victory'. A quartet of female observers had their own takes. 'Now we can have Stable Government for another 4½ years,' reflected Florence Turtle; for Nella Last, notwithstanding her satisfaction with the outcome, it was 'the gallant attitude of Mr Gaitskell' that she thought would remain with her, '& his courageous smile as he spoke of the defeat as a "set-back" only'; Tom Courtenay's mother in Hull wrote to him that she felt 'very sorry for the Labour people, mainly Welsh and Scottish, and I'm sure they will hate clever buggers English mainly non-industrial South'; and Mrs B. K. of Camberwell announced in the *Daily Sketch* how glad she was, 'as a woman', that the election was finally over: 'It will be so good to have our menfolk peacefully at home again – without having to endure their arguments with neighbours over the garden fence. Or having to listen to them laying down the law to their wives and families, who apparently aren't expected to have minds of their own!'[17]

Why had the Conservatives won so conclusively? Some emphasised Gaitskell's tax-pledge blunder, some the Conservatives' much greater advertising spend during the long run-up to the election, some their greater organisational capacity in the decisive weeks. For Richard Crossman, writing up his diary on the Friday, one 'simple truth' had 'dogged' his party's efforts: 'Tory voters are far more afraid of another Labour Government than Labour voters are afraid of another Tory Government. The Tories were able to exploit fear of nationalization, inflation, flight from the pound, trade unions, and so on.' Ultimately, though, the most common – and surely correct – perception was that, whatever the attractions or otherwise of Labour's case, the electorate just did not want to change horses at a time of such welcome prosperity. 'He votes for his stomach, or not at all,' was the view of a 'furious' John Fowles about the typical voter, while the young David Owen, just starting as a medical student, was equally jaundiced. 'Can any party ever have won an election on a more immoral slogan, a positive disgrace and a sign of the moral depravity of our life?' he asked himself. 'People seem to vote solely on their bellies.' And famously, Trog drew a wonderful cartoon for the *Spectator*, showing Macmillan sitting in best Edwardian manner opposite an array of consumer durables (fridge, car, washing machine, TV set) and saying, 'Well, gentlemen, I think we all fought a good fight . . .'

There was one other dimension to this instant analysis. 'A prosperous, mainly middle-class Britain cannot be stampeded by the crude old cries of under-privilege,' declared *The Times* on Saturday the 10th. Macmillan himself fully agreed, composing that day a letter to the Queen that finished with a paragraph he must have known was destined for the history books:

> The most encouraging feature of the Election from Your Majesty's point of view, is the strong impression that I have formed that Your Majesty's subjects do not wish to allow themselves to be divided into warring classes or tribes filled with hereditary animosity against each other. There was a very significant breakdown of this structure of society which, in spite of its many material advantages, was one of the chief spiritual disadvantages of the first industrial revolution. It will be curious if the second industrial revolution, through the wide spread of its amenities of life to almost every home in the country, succeeds in destroying this unfortunate product of the first. At any rate, anything that makes Your Majesty's subjects more conscious of their unity and of their duty to each other seems to me to be a real gain.

Macmillan had probably not read (despite its address) a letter that had appeared in late August in the *Viewer*, the TV magazine covering the Tyne Tees area. 'Every time the quiz show *Concentration* comes on, it annoys me to death,' complained G. Barraclough of Lincoln Grove, Albany Estate, Stockton-on-Tees. 'I have never yet seen an ordinary working-class person on it, they are always middle-class – and most of them, no doubt, already have the prizes which they win. I might add that my friends and neighbours think the same!'[18]

# Notes

## Abbreviations

| | |
|---|---|
| Abrams | Mark Abrams Papers (Churchill Archives Centre, Churchill College, Cambridge) |
| Amis | Zachary Leader (ed), *The Letters of Kingsley Amis* (2000) |
| BBC WA | BBC Written Archives Centre (Caversham) |
| Benn | Ruth Winstone (ed), Tony Benn, *Years of Hope: Diaries, Letters and Papers, 1940–1962* (1994) |
| *Crossman* | Janet Morgan (ed), *The Backbench Diaries of Richard Crossman* (1981) |
| Crossman | Diary of Richard Crossman (Modern Records Centre, University of Warwick) |
| Daly | Lawrence Daly Papers (Modern Records Centre, University of Warwick) |
| Dee | Diary of Dennis Dee (East Riding of Yorkshire Archives, Beverley) |
| *Fowles* | Charles Drazin (ed), John Fowles, *The Journals: Volume 1* (2003) |
| Fowles | John Fowles Papers (Special Collections, University of Exeter) |
| Gorer | Geoffrey Gorer Papers (Special Collections, University of Sussex) |
| Hague | Frances and Gladys Hague Papers (Keighley Library) |
| Haines | Diary of Alice (Judy) Haines (Special Collections, University of Sussex) |
| Heap | Diary of Anthony Heap (London Metropolitan Archives) |
| Langford | Diary of Gladys Langford (Islington Local History Centre) |
| *Larkin* | Anthony Thwaite (ed), Philip Larkin, *Letters to Monica* (2010) |
| Larkin | Unpublished Letters of Philip Larkin to Monica Jones (Bodleian Library, Oxford) |
| Last | Diary of Nella Last (Mass-Observation Archive, Special Collections, University of Sussex) |
| Lewis | Diary of Frank Lewis (Glamorgan Archives, Cardiff) |
| *Macmillan* | Harold Macmillan, *Riding the Storm: 1956–1959* (1971) |
| Macmillan | Harold Macmillan Papers (Bodleian Library, Oxford) |
| Martin | Diary of Madge Martin (Oxfordshire History Centre, Oxford) |
| M-O A | Mass-Observation Archive (Special Collections, University of Sussex) |
| Preston | Diary of Kenneth Preston (Bradford Archives, Bradford Central Library) |
| Raynham | Diary of Marian Raynham (Special Collections, University of Sussex) |
| St John | Diary of Henry St John (Ealing Local History Centre) |
| Turtle | Diary of Florence Turtle (Wandsworth Heritage Service) |
| Willmott | Diary of Phyllis Willmott (Churchill Archives Centre, Churchill College, Cambridge) |

All books are published in London unless otherwise stated.

## 1 Isn' 'e Smashin'?

1. The Society of Housing Managers, *Report of Conference, Housing Management, Thursday and Friday 10th and 11th January 1957* (1957), pp 5, 18, 49; Haines, 12 Jan 1957; Preston, 12 Jan 1957; BBC WA, R9/19/2, Viewer Research Newsletters, Jan 1957 (II); Richard Webber, *Fifty Years of Hancock's Half Hour* (2004), p 214; Larkin, Ms Eng. c. 7415, 13 Jan 1957, fol 61.

2. Iverach McDonald, *The History of The Times, Volume V* (1984), p 319; Macmillan, dep.d.28, 3 Feb 1957, fol 13; Michael Cockerell, *Live from Number 10* (1988), pp 54–5; Nigel Jones, *Through a Glass Darkly* (1991), pp 354–5; Last, 18 Jan 1957; Benn, p 226; Richard Ingrams, *Muggeridge* (1995), p 187.

3. Spencer Leigh, 'Alan Sytner', *Independent*, 13 Jan 2006; *Liverpool Echo*, 17 Jan 1957; St John, 19 Jan 1957; *Listener*, 7 Feb 1957; Aurelia Schober Plath (ed), Sylvia Plath, *Letters Home* (1976), p 293; Heap, 24 Jan 1957; *Sunday Times*, 27 Jan 1957.

4. John McIlroy, '"Every Factory Our Fortress"', Pt 2, *Historical Studies in Industrial Relations* (Autumn 2001), p 75; H. A. Turner et al, *Labour Relations in the Motor Industry* (1967), p 276; Richard Etheridge Papers (Modern Records Centre, University of Warwick), 202/S/J/3/2/19, 28 Jan 1957; *Daily Mail*, 12–13 Feb 1957; Turner et al, p 277; *Barking, East Ham and Ilford Advertiser*, 16 Feb 1957.

5. Last, 30 Jan 1957; *Educating Archie*, 30 Jan 1957; Muir and Norden Archive (Special Collections, University of Sussex), Box 19, *Take It From Here*, 30 Jan 1957; *Daily Mirror*, 30–31 Jan 1957.

6. BBC WA, R9/7/26 – VR/57/66; *News Chronicle*, 5 Feb 1957; Joanna Moorhead, *New Generations* (Cambridge, 1996), pp 7–10; *Daily Sketch*, 6 Feb 1957.

7. *Picture Post*, 25 Feb 1957; *Leicester Mercury*, 4 Feb 1957, 6–7 Feb 1957; *Picture Post*, 25 Feb 1957; *News Chronicle*, 6 Feb 1957; Bill Law, 'The Boys Who Got Us Swinging', *Guardian*, 7 Mar 1997; Ray Gosling, *Personal Copy* (Five Leaves edn, 2010), pp 42–3.

8. *East London Advertiser*, 8 Feb 1957; *Architects' Journal*, 14 Feb 1957; *Glasgow Herald*, 9 Feb 1957; *East London Advertiser*, 15 Feb 1957.

9. *New Statesman*, 9 Feb 1957; *Sunday Times*, 17 Feb 1957; *Birmingham Mail*, 14 Feb 1957; Last, 11 Feb 1957.

10. Last, 11 Feb 1957; *Daily Mirror*, 11–12 Feb 1957; Heap, 15 Feb 1957; *Daily Mirror*, 18 Feb 1957; *Sunday Express*, 17 Feb 1957.

11. John Hill, 'Television and Pop', in John Corner (ed), *Popular Television in Britain* (1991), p 90; *Daily Sketch*, 11 Dec 1956; Hill, p 90; *Radio Times*, 8 Feb 1957.

12. Pete Frame, *The Restless Generation* (2007), p 219; Hill, p 93; *Sunday Times*, 17 Feb 1957; BBC WA, R9/7/26 – VR/57/95; *News Chronicle*, 18 Feb 1957; *Daily Telegraph*, 18 Feb 1957; *Daily Mail*, 18 Feb 1957.

13. *Radio Times*, 15 Feb 1957; *Daily Mirror*, 18 Feb 1957; *Sunday Times*, 24 Feb 1957; *Daily Mail*, 19 Feb 1957; *Radio Times*, 15 Feb 1957.

14. *New Statesman*, 23 Feb 1957; *Daily Mirror*, 19 Feb 1957; *Daily Telegraph*, 19 Feb 1957; *Daily Mail*, 19 Feb 1957; BBC WA, R9/7/26 – VR/57/110; Leonard Miall, 'Donald Baverstock', *Independent*, 18 Mar 1995; Alasdair Milne, *DG* (1988), p 15; Asa Briggs, *The History of Broadcasting in the United Kingdom, Volume V* (Oxford, 1995), pp 161–4; Andrew Crisell, 'Filth, Sedition and Blasphemy', in Corner, *Popular Television*, p 149.

15. http://www.televisionheaven.co.uk/ward.htm; *Sunday Times*, 24 Feb 1957.

## 2  A Lot of Mums

1. Alan Bennett, *Untold Stories* (2005), p 402; Chas Critcher, 'Sociology, Cultural Studies and the Post-war Working Class', in John Clarke et al (eds), *Working-Class Culture* (1979), p 17; *Guardian*, 7 Feb 2004; *New Statesman*, 2 Mar 1957 (Chatto & Windus advertisement); *Manchester Guardian*, 23 Feb 1957; Richard Johnson, 'Culture and the Historians', in Clarke et al, *Working-Class Culture*, p 59.
2. Peter Townsend Collection (Qualidata, University of Essex), Box 60, File B, Michael Young memorandum, 8 Jan 1956; *Star*, 23–7 Apr 1957; *Daily Herald*, 26 Apr 1957; *Daily Mirror*, 26 Apr 1957; *News Chronicle*, 27 Apr 1957; *Daily Telegraph*, 26 Apr 1957; *The Times*, 26 Apr 1957; *Daily Mail*, 30 Apr 1957; *Financial Times*, 13 May 1957.
3. *Spectator*, 1 Mar 1957, 21 Jun 1957; Nick Tiratsoo and Mark Clapson, 'The Ford Foundation and Social Planning in Britain', in Giuliana Gemelli (ed), *American Foundations and Large-Scale Research* (Bologna, 2001), p 212; *Listener*, 30 May 1957; *Encounter* (Sep 1957), p 84; *Times Literary Supplement*, 25 Oct 1957; *Case Conference* (May 1957), pp 24–5.
4. Michael Young Papers (Churchill Archives Centre, Churchill College, Cambridge), 5/23, 28 Apr 1957; Dartington Hall Trust Archives, DWE/G/11/C, 5 May 1957.
5. *Encounter*, Apr 1955, p 14; John Vaizey, *In Breach of Promise* (1983), p 119; David Marquand, *Britain since 1918* (2008), pp 246–7; Lawrence Black, *The Political Culture of the Left in Affluent Britain, 1951–64* (Basingstoke, 2003), pp 85–6; Michael Young and Peter Willmott, *Family and Kinship in East London* (Penguin edn, 1986), p xvii; Young and Willmott, *Family and Kinship* (Pelican edn, 1962), pp 197–8; Young and Willmott, *Family and Kinship* (1986), p xix.
6. *Spectator*, 20 Jan 1956; *Architects' Journal*, 31 Jan 1957.
7. Margot Jefferys, 'Londoners in Hertfordshire', in Ruth Glass et al, *London: Aspects of Change* (1964), pp 239–43; J. B. Cullingworth, 'The Social Implications of Overspill', *Sociological Review* (Jul 1960), pp 77–96; J. B. Cullingworth, 'The Swindon Social Survey', *Sociological Review* (Jul 1961), pp 151–66; *Royal Society for the Promotion of Health Journal* (Mar–Apr 1959), pp 206–8.
8. Maurice Broady Collection (Special Collections, University of Glasgow), uncatalogued red-and-green box, interview with Mrs Stewart, Craigbank, 20 Feb 1957.

## 3  Never Had It So Good

1. *Daily Mail*, 4 Mar 1957; David Jeremiah, *Architecture and Design for the Family, 1900–70* (Manchester, 2000), pp 167–8; *New Statesman*, 9 Mar 1957; Robert J. Wybrow, *Britain Speak Out, 1937–87* (Basingstoke, 1989), p 49; *Punch*, 13 Mar 1957; Anne Hardy, 'Reframing Disease', *Historical Research* (Nov 2003), p 540; Simon Berry and Hamish Whyte (eds), *Glasgow Observed* (Edinburgh, 1987), p 239; *Fowles*, p 388.
2. Deborah Geller, *The Brian Epstein Story* (2000), pp 18–21; *Guardian*, 20 Feb 2010 (David Lacey); *Daily Telegraph*, 14 Dec 2007 (Jim White); Macmillan, dep.d.29, 4 May 1957, fol 18; Anthony Thwaite (ed), *Selected Letters of Philip Larkin, 1940–1985* (1992), p 276.

3. *Economist*, 2 Mar 1957; Huw Beynon, *Working for Ford* (1984 edn), p 61; Steven Tolliday, 'Ford and "Fordism" in Postwar Britain', in Steven Tolliday and Jonathan Zeitlin (eds), *The Power to Manage?* (1991), p 88; *The Times*, 12 Apr 1957; H. A. Turner et al, *Labour Relations in the Motor Industry* (1967), p 277; John McIlroy, '"Every Factory Our Fortress"', Pt 2, *Historical Studies in Industrial Relations* (Autumn 2001), p 75.

4. Raynham, 16 Mar 1957; Heap, 20 Mar 1957; John Bright-Holmes (ed), *The Diaries of Malcolm Muggeridge* (1981), p 473; *Observer*, 24 Mar 1957; Macmillan, dep.d.28, 15 Mar 1957, fol 81; George H. Gallup, *The Gallup International Public Opinion Polls: Great Britain 1937–1975: Volume 1* (New York, 1976), p 408; Robert Shepherd, *Iain Macleod* (1994), pp 124, 126–7; *New Yorker*, 13 Apr 1957; Shepherd, *Iain Macleod*, pp 127–8. For a full account of the strikes, see Nina Fishman, '"The Most Serious Crisis since 1926"', in Alan Campbell et al (eds), *British Trade Unions and Industrial Politics, Volume One* (Aldershot, 1999), pp 242–67.

5. *Evening Standard*, 4 Apr 1957; Ferdinand Mount, *Cold Cream* (2008), p 200; *Evening Standard*, 4 Apr 1957; Jim Tomlinson, 'Inventing "Decline"', *Economic History Review*, Nov 1996, p 747; Jim Tomlinson, 'Economic Growth, Economic Decline', in Kathleen Burk (ed), *The British Isles since 1945* (Oxford, 2003), p 70; D. M. Ashford, 'Critical Comets', *Times Literary Supplement*, 18 Mar 2011; Cambridge Union Society: Record of Debates, 7 May 1957 (Cambridge University Library); Lord Moran, *Winston Churchill* (1966), p 726.

6. Colin Clark, *Younger Brother, Younger Son* (1997), p 105; Heap, 10 Apr 1957; Dominic Shellard (ed), Kenneth Tynan, *Theatre Writings* (2007), p 169; *Listener*, 2 May 1957; John Heilpern, *John Osborne* (2006), pp 215–16.

7. Richard Bradford, *Lucky Him* (2001), p 156; Kingsley Amis, *Socialism and the Intellectuals* (1957), p 13; *Universities and Left Review* (Spring 1957), pp ii, 3, 1, 32, 44–8; (Summer 1957), pp 29–34, 39–40; *New Reasoner* (Summer 1957), pp 2, 132, 141–2.

8. Alan Bold, *MacDiarmid* (1988), pp 410–11; *Daily Worker*, 22 Apr 1957; Paul Routledge, *Scargill* (1993), p 26; *Daily Worker*, 23 Apr 1957; Malcolm MacEwen, *The Greening of a Red* (1991), pp 198–9.

9. *Daily Worker*, 7 Jun 1957; Matthew Hilton, *Smoking in British Popular Culture, 1800–2000* (Manchester, 2000), p 185; Jeremy Laurance, 'Scientists Lament 40 Fatal Years of Smoking', *Independent*, 8 Mar 2002; Hilton, *Smoking*, p 229; *Manchester Guardian*, 2 Jul 1957; *Salford City Reporter*, 29 Mar 1957; Janet Frame, *The Envoy from Mirror City* (1985), pp 96–7; Martin, 24 May 1957.

10. David Bernstein, 'The Television Commercial', in Brian Henry (ed), *British Television Advertising* (1986), p 261; Adam Sisman, *Hugh Trevor-Roper* (2010), p 283; *News Chronicle*, 1 Apr 1957; Leonard Miall (ed), *Richard Dimbleby, Broadcaster* (1966), p 106; *Daily Mail*, 2 Apr 1957; Leonard Miall, 'Charles de Jaeger', *Independent*, 29 May 2000.

11. BBC WA, R9/13/142, 12 Mar 1957, 22 Mar 1957; *Financial Times*, 13 Jul 1957; Mark Lewisohn, *Radio Times Guide to TV Comedy* (2003 edn), pp 49–50; *Spectator*, 12 Apr 1957 (John Beavon); Anthony Hayward, 'Edward Evans', *Independent*, 4 Jan 2002.

12. *Radio Times*, 24 May 1957; Larkin, Ms Eng. c. 7416, 8 Jun 1957, fol 38; *Guardian*, 2 Jun 1997 (Frank Keating); C.L.R. James, *Beyond a Boundary* (Serpent's Tail edn,

1994), pp 216–17; Rupert Hart-Davis (ed), *The Lyttelton Hart-Davis Letters, Volume Two* (1979), p 120.

13. D. R. Thorpe, *Supermac* (2010), p 328; *Independent*, 30 Oct 2006 (David Prosser); Macmillan, dep.d.29, 1 Jun 1957, fol 50; Heap, 22 May 1957; Katherine Whitehorn, *Selective Memory* (2007), p 84; Francis Wheen, *Television* (1985), p 77; Vanessa Redgrave, *An Autobiography* (1991), pp 68, 76; *Sunday Pictorial* file, box 18, John Hilton Bureau Archive, News Group Newspapers Ltd Archive, News International.

14. Mark Norton, *Birmingham Past & Present* (Stroud, 2006), pp 8–9; *Yorkshire Post*, 26 Mar 1957; *Architects' Journal*, 28 Mar 1957; *Liverpool Daily Post*, 9 Apr 1957, 12 Apr 1957, 15 Apr 1957; Graeme Shankland, 'The Crisis in Town Planning', *Universities and Left Review* (Spring 1957), p 39.

15. John R. Gold, *The Practice of Modernism* (Abingdon, 2007), p 170; *Architects' Journal*, 7 Mar 1957, 14 Mar 1957; *Birmingham Mail*, 20 Mar 1957, 28 Mar 1957; *The Times*, 8 May 1957, 11 May 1957; Patrick Dunleavy, *The Politics of Mass Housing in Britain, 1945–1975* (Oxford, 1981), p 143.

16. *Manchester Guardian*, 6 Jun 1957; *Builder*, 21 Jun 1957; *Liverpool Echo*, 5 Jul 1957.

17. Ninian Johnston, 'Miracle in the Gorbals?', *Architectural Prospect* (Spring 1957), p 18; *Architects' Journal*, 18 Apr 1957; Tom Brennan, 'Gorbals: A Study in Redevelopment', *Scottish Journal of Political Economy* (Jun 1957), pp 122–6.

18. *Town and Country Planning* (May 1957), p 204; *Architects' Journal*, 4 Apr 1957; *Evening Express* (Liverpool), 22 Mar 1957; *Coventry Standard*, 17 May 1957; *Barking, East Ham & Ilford Advertiser*, 2 Mar 1957, 20 Apr 1957.

19. *Architects' Journal*, 7 Mar 1957, 13 Jun 1957; *Spectator*, 17 May 1957; *Punch*, 19 Jun 1957.

20. Haines, 6 Jul 1957; Turtle, 6 Jul 1957; Martin, 6 Jul 1957; Last, 6 Jul 1957; *Larkin*, p 223; *Liverpool Echo*, 6 Jul 1957; *Evening Express* (Liverpool), 6 Jul 1957; *Liverpool Echo*, 6 Jul 1957; Mark Lewisohn, *The Complete Beatles Chronicle* (1996 edn), p 14; Philip Norman, *John Lennon* (2008), pp 105–6; *The Beatles Press Conferences 1964–1966* (*Uncut* magazine CD, 2005), Track 21, 'John, New York City, December 8, 1980'.

21. *Vauxhall Mirror*, Jul 1957; *East Essex Gazette*, 19 Jul 1957; *Guardian*, 22 Jul 1997 (Richard Williams); Heap, 20 Jul 1957; Haines, 22 Jul 1957; *Durham Chronicle*, 26 Jul 1957.

22. *Radio Times*, 12 Jul 1957; *Bedford Record*, 16 Jul 1957, 23 Jul 1957; Macmillan, dep.c. 740; *People's Friend*, 20 Jul 1957.

## 4  Catch a Falling Sputnik

1. *Financial Times*, 14 Nov 1957; *Observer*, 23 Oct 1960 (Mark Abrams); *Never Had It So Good?*, BBC Four, 10 Dec 2007; *Liverpool Echo*, 16 Sep 1957; *Financial Times*, 6 Sep 1957; Abrams, Box 81, 'L.P.E. Merchandising Bulletin No. 3'; Lucy Ward, 'Forget Filling the Coal Shed', *Guardian*, 29 Jan 2008; *Woman's Own*, 18 Jul 1957, 30 May 1957.

2. Derek J. Oddy, *From Plain Fare to Fusion Food* (Woodbridge, 2003), p 185; Peter Bird, *The First Food Empire* (Chichester, 2000), p 226; *Woman's Own*, 18 Jul 1957;

James Obelkevich, 'Consumption', in James Obelkevich and Peter Catterall (eds), *Understanding Post-War British Society* (1994), p 148; David L. Wakefield, *The Hoover Story in Merthyr Tydfil* (Merthyr Tydfil, c. 1977), p 7; *Financial Times*, 12 Oct 1959; *Reynolds News*, 24 Feb 1957; Rhys David, 'Cyril Lord', *Dictionary of Business Biography, Volume 3* (1985), p 853; David Hunt, 'Cyril Lord', *Oxford Dictionary of National Biography* (Oxford, 2004), vol 34, p 437; Douglas Lowndes, 'Norman Parkinson', *Independent*, 20 Feb 1990; Ralph Harris and Arthur Seldon, *Advertising in Action* (1962), pp 272, 80–81.

3. Subrata Dasgupta, *Salaam Stanley Matthews* (2006), p 179; Mick Grabham, 'Low Fidelity', *Mojo* (Aug 1997).

4. Paul Levy, 'Egon Ronay', *Independent*, 14 Jun 2010; Matthew Hilton, 'The Fable of the Sheep, or, Private Virtues, Public Vices', *Past & Present* (Aug 2002), p 229; Elizabeth Dunn, 'The Quiet Man of Change', *Sunday Times*, 30 January 1977; Dartington Hall Trust Archives, LKE/G/35, Michael Young to Dorothy and Leonard Elmhurst, 10 Oct 1957.

5. Asa Briggs, *Michael Young* (Basingstoke, 2001), p 150; *The Times*, 8 Oct 1957; BBC WA, *Woman's Hour*, 11 Oct 1957; *Independent*, 3 Jul 1997 (Jack O'Sullivan); *Which?* (Winter 1957), p 20; Maurice Healy, 'Eirlys Roberts', *Guardian*, 22 Mar 2008; *Which?* (Autumn 1957), pp 3–6; Gorer, Box 103, Michael Young to Geoffrey Gorer, 14 Oct 1957; Lawrence Black, *Redefining British Politics* (Basingstoke, 2010), pp 16–25; M-O A, TC78/3/EF.

6. *Manchester Guardian*, 23 Jul 1957; Stephen Chalke, 'Peter Loader', *Independent*, 21 Mar 2011; *Larkin*, p 227; William Smethurst, *The Archers* (1996), pp 59–72; Turtle, 29 Jul 1957; Macmillan, dep.d.29, 29 Jul 1957, fol 106.

7. Elizabeth Longford, *Elizabeth R* (1983), p 182; *New Statesman*, 10 Aug 1957 (Francis Williams); Jeremy Paxman, 'Hard-pressed Royalty', *Daily Telegraph*, 19 Aug 1996; Macmillan, dep.d.29, 8 Aug 1957, fol 116; *New Statesman*, 17 Aug 1957 (Francis Williams); Robert Lacey, *Majesty* (1978 edn), p 320; *New Yorker*, 7 Sep 1957; Macmillan, dep.d.29, 1 Sep 1957, fol 137.

8. *Spectator*, 4 Oct 1957; *Sunday Dispatch*, 6 Oct 1957; Richard Ingrams, *Muggeridge* (1995), p 182; *Sunday Express*, 13 Oct 1957; Last, 13 Oct 1957; *People*, 13 Oct 1957 (Leonard Coulter); *Daily Mirror*, 15 Oct 1957; Asa Briggs, *The History of Broadcasting in the United Kingdom, Volume V* (Oxford, 1995), pp 145–6; 'Lieutenant-General Sir Ian Jacob', *The Times*, 26 Apr 1993.

9. *Financial Times*, 22 Dec 2007 (John Lloyd); Martin, 16 Aug 1957; *Liverpool Echo*, 13–14 Sep 1957.

10. Spencer Leigh, 'Alan Sytner', *Independent*, 13 Jan 2006; *Mojo* (Oct 1997), p 38 (Paul Du Noyer); *Guardian*, 20 Feb 2004 (Will Hodgkinson); Lorna Sage, *Bad Blood* (2000), p 193; Lewis, 2 Sep 1957.

11. Frank Mort, *Capital Affairs* (2010), p 194; *New Yorker*, 28 Sep 1957; *Manchester Guardian*, 5 Sep 1957; Matt Houlbrook, *Queer London* (Chicago, 2005), p 261; *Daily Mirror*, 6 Sep 1957.

12. *Daily Express*, 5 Sep 1957; Richard Davenport-Hines, *Sex, Death and Punishment* (1990), p 322; Adrian Bingham, *Family Newspapers* (Oxford, 2009), p 189; *Spectator*, 6 Sep 1957; Roger Davidson and Gayle Davis, '"A Field for Private Members"', *Twentieth Century British History*, 15/2 (2004), p 194; *Daily Mirror*, 10–11 Sep 1957; George H. Gallup, *The Gallup International Public Opinion Polls: Great*

*Britain 1937–1975, Volume One* (New York, 1976), pp 426–8; *New Yorker*, 28 Sep 1957. In general on press reaction, including for some of the quotations, see *New Statesman*, 14 Sep 1957 (Francis Williams).

13. Humphrey Carpenter, *Dennis Potter* (1998), p 67; Anthony Howard, *RAB* (1987), pp 264–5; 'Lord Denning', *The Times*, 6 Mar 1999; Ben Pimlott, *Hugh Dalton* (1985), pp 627–8; Peter Townsend, 'Professor Brian Abel-Smith', *Independent*, 9 Apr 1996; Liz Homans, 'Swinging Sixties', *History Today* (Dec 2008), pp 46–7.

14. Macmillan, dep.d.29, 17 Sep 1957, fol 153; *Evening Standard*, 19 Sep 1957; Forrest Capie, *The Bank of England: 1950s to 1979* (New York, 2010), p 93; *Crossman*, p 607; *Spectator*, 27 Sep 1957; *Financial Times*, 21 Sep 1957.

15. *Macmillan*, p 417; David Kynaston, *The City of London, Volume 4* (2001), pp 88, 98; Gary Burn, 'The State, the City and the Euromarkets', *Review of International Political Economy* (Summer 1999), pp 234–5.

16. *New Statesman*, 28 Sep 1957; *Spectator*, 11 Oct 1957, 4 Oct 1957; *New Statesman*, 5 Oct 1957; Turtle, 25 Sep 1957; Heap, 28 Sep 1957; BBC WA, R9/19/2, Nov 1957; *The Times*, 15 Jun 1998 (Tim Jones); Denis Gifford, 'Reg Smythe', *Independent*, 15 Jun 1998.

17. John Bright-Holmes (ed), *Like It Was: The Diaries of Malcolm Muggeridge* (1981), p 479; *New Yorker*, 2 Nov 1957; John Campbell, *Nye Bevan* (1997 edn), p 337; D. B. Smith, 'Michael Foot on Aneurin Bevan', *Llafur* (May 1974), p 24; Campbell, p 338; Crossman, Ms 154/8/26, 8 Feb 1961, fol 1315.

18. Haines, 4 Oct 1957; *The Times*, 8 Mar 2008 (Erica Wagner); *Financial Times*, 5 Oct 1957; Frances Partridge, *Everything to Lose* (1999 edn), p 285; Doris Lessing, *Walking in the Shade* (1997), p 277; *Evening Standard*, 7 Oct 1957; *Financial Times*, 11 Oct 1957; *New Statesman*, 12 Oct 1957; John Callaghan, 'The Left and the "Unfinished Revolution"', *Contemporary British History* (Autumn 2001), pp 74–5; Martin Gilbert, *'Never Despair'* (1988), p 1,252; *New Yorker*, 23 Nov 1957 (Panter-Downes); *Punch*, 23 Oct 1957.

19. Lewis Baston, *Reggie* (Stroud, 2004), pp 120–21; David Lowry, 'Tom Tuohy', *Guardian*, 7 May 2008; Jean McSorley, 'Contaminated Evidence', *Guardian*, 10 Oct 2007; Lord Hinton of Bankside Papers (Institution of Mechanical Engineers), 'Autobiography', chap XXIV; Last, 12 Oct 1957; *Western Daily Press*, 15 Oct 1957; *New Yorker*, 2 Nov 1957; Last, 17 Oct 1957; D. R. Thorpe, *Supermac* (2010), pp 396–7; *News Chronicle*, 9 Nov 1957; Tony Hall, *Nuclear Politics* (1986), p 63; Lorna Arnold, *Windscale* (Basingstoke, 1992), p 71; email to author from Jenny Uglow, 29 Jul 2011.

20. *Spectator*, 9 Aug 1957, 11 Oct 1957; Bevis Hillier, *John Betjeman: New Fame, New Love* (2002), pp 567–9; *Spectator*, 20 Dec 1957.

21. *Architects' Journal*, 11 Apr 1957; Peter Self, *Cities in Flood* (1957), p 166; *Architects' Journal*, 1 Aug 1957; *Listener*, 5 Sep 1957.

22. *Liverpool Daily Post*, 3 Sep 1957, 20 Sep 1957; *Liverpool Echo*, 24 Sep 1957; *Liverpool Daily Post*, 1 Oct 1957, 3 Oct 1957; John English et al, *Slum Clearance* (1976), p 156.

23. *Yorkshire Post*, 12–13 Nov 1957; *Yorkshire Evening News*, 12 Nov 1957; *Yorkshire Post*, 13 Nov 1957; Colin Ward and Dennis Hardy, *Goodnight Campers!* (1986), pp 125–7; *Bognor Regis Post*, 28 Sep 1957, 12 Oct 1957.

24. *Quarterly Bulletin of the Society of Housing Managers* (Jan 1958), p 11; *Liverpool Echo*, 13 Sep 1957; N. S. Power, *The Forgotten People* (Evesham, 1965), pp 13–14, 37–8; *Salford City Reporter*, 6 Dec 1957; John Winstone, *Bristol As It Was, 1963–1975* (Bristol, 1990), p 36; Patrick Dunleavy, *The Politics of Mass Housing in Britain, 1945–1975* (Oxford, 1981), p 312; *Architects' Journal*, 24 Oct 1957, 26 Dec 1957; *Kensington News and West London Times*, 15 Nov 1957; *Architects' Journal*, 14 Nov 1957.

25. *Architects' Journal*, 16 Jan 1958; *Sunday Times*, 1 Dec 1957, 8 Dec 1957, 15 Dec 1957; Adrian Smith, 'The Coventry Factor', *Literature & History* (Spring 1999), pp 34–5; Heap, 17 Nov 1957.

26. Haines, 12 Oct 1957; *New Statesman*, 19 Oct 1957 (Francis Williams); *New Yorker*, 2 Nov 1957; *Sunday Times*, 13 Oct 1957; *New Statesman*, 19 Oct 1957; *Macmillan*, pp 419–20; Michael Bentley, 'Maurice Cowling', *Independent*, 6 Sep 2005; *Listener*, 31 Oct 1957.

27. Tom Maschler (ed), *Declaration* (1957), pp 23, 76, 120, 155, 159, 166; *Sunday Times*, 13 Oct 1957; *Observer*, 13 Oct 1957; *Listener*, 7 Nov 1957; Humphrey Carpenter, *The Angry Young Men* (2002), p 183.

28. *Glasgow Herald*, 21 Oct 1957; *The Times*, 12 Nov 2002 (John Goodbody); Daly, Mss 302/2/1, 31 Oct 1957, 302/3/12, 8 Oct 1957.

29. 'Lawrence Daly', *Daily Telegraph*, 1 Jun 2009; Philip Norman, *John Lennon* (2008), pp 122–3; Pete Frame, *The Restless Generation* (2007), p 267; *Radio Times*, 8 Nov 1957; Owen Adams, 'The 2i's and the Birth of British Rock', *Record Collector*, Jan 2007, pp 35–6; Anne de Courcy, *Snowdon* (2008), p 52; *Yorkshire Post*, 19 Nov 1957; *News Chronicle*, 19 Nov 1957; Colin MacInnes, *England, Half English* (1986 edn), pp 11–16; Langford, 28 Nov 1957.

30. Hague, 3 Nov 1957; Macmillan, dep.d.30, 5 Nov 1957, fol 52; *New Yorker*, 23 Nov 1957; Partridge, p 290; Benn, p 251; *Yorkshire Post*, 13 Nov 1957; David Kynaston, *The Financial Times* (1988), p 261; *New Yorker*, 23 Nov 1957; *New Statesman*, 14 Dec 1957 (Francis Williams); Iona and Peter Opie, *The Lore and Language of Schoolchildren* (1959), p 106.

31. 'John Sandoe', *The Times*, 9 Jan 2008; *Yorkshire Evening News*, 12 Nov 1957; Haines, 12 Nov 1957; Derrik Mercer (ed), *20th Century Day by Day* (Dorling Kindersley edn, 1999), p 1,140; *Wisden Cricketers' Almanack, 1958* (1958), p 1,004; Mercer, *20th Century*, p 1,140; *Guardian*, 3 Sep 2011 (Fiona MacCarthy).

32. *Yorkshire Evening News*, 12 Nov 1957; Benn, p 253; *Spectator*, 29 Nov 1957; BBC WA, R9/19/2, Jan 1958; *Spectator*, 27 Dec 1957; *Daily Telegraph*, 10 Dec 1957; Lawrence Black, '"Sheep May Safely Gaze"', in idem et al, *Consensus or Coercion?* (Cheltenham, 2001), p 36; Gorer, Box 45, 'Institute of Community Studies' file, Young to Gorer, 31 Jan 1958.

33. Gorer, Box 4, file 4/A, Box 2, file 2/B, Box 4, file 4/A; *Manchester Guardian*, 20 Dec 1957; Briggs, *History of Broadcasting*, pp 222–3; *Guardian*, 9 Oct 1997 (John Dugdale); Briggs, *History of Broadcasting*, p 222; BBC WA, R9/9/21, 14 Jan 1958.

34. Haines, 30 Nov 1957; *Manchester Guardian*, 5 Dec 1957; Mercer, *20th Century*, p 1,141; Barbara Weinberger, *The Best Police in the World* (Aldershot, 1995), p 198; Brian Cathcart, 'The Police Punch that Troubled Parliament', *Independent on Sunday*, 19 Jun 1994; Olga Cannon and J.R.L. Anderson, *The Road from Wigan Pier* (1973), pp 163–8; Hansard, *House of Commons Debates*, 19 Dec 1957, cols 717–38; *Listener*, 12 Dec 1957; Sage, p 212; Cliff Goodwin, *When the Wind*

*Changed* (1999), pp 234–5; *Spectator*, 20 Dec 1957; Stephen F. Kelly, *Bill Shankly* (1996), pp 109–10.

35. Kynaston, *City*, p 90; Macmillan, dep.30, 12 Dec 1957, fol 78; Kynaston, *City*, pp 91–2; *New Yorker*, 4 Jan 1958.

36. *Listener*, 2 Jan 1958; BBC WA, R9/19/2, Feb 1958; Haines, 27 Dec 1957; Dee, 1–4 Jan 1958; Martin, 4 Jan 1958; Robert Ross, *The Complete Frankie Howerd* (Richmond, 2001), p 35; Heap, 5 Jan 1958; *Merthyr Express*, 11 Jan 1958, 18 Jan 1958.

## 5 Not a Matter of Popularity

1. Dee, 6 Jan 1958; Martin, 6 Jan 1958; Haines, 6 Jan 1958; *Daily Telegraph*, 7 Jan 1958.
2. Helpful accounts include: John Hunt, 'Much More than a "Little Local Difficulty"', *Financial Times*, 3 Jan 1989; Robert Shepherd, *Enoch Powell* (1996), pp 159–84; Simon Heffer, *Like the Roman* (1998), pp 217–41; Mark Jarvis, 'The 1958 Treasury Dispute', *Contemporary British History* (Summer 1998), pp 22–50; E.H.H. Green, 'The Treasury Resignations of 1958', *Twentieth Century British History*, 11/4 (2000), pp 409–30; D. R. Thorpe, *Supermac* (2010), pp 401–7; Chris Cooper, 'Little Local Difficulties Revisited', *Contemporary British History* (Jun 2011), pp 227–50.
3. 'Lord Thorneycroft', *The Times*, 6 Jun 1994; Cooper, 'Little Local Difficulties', p 231; David Kynaston, *Family Britain* (2009), p 447; Shepherd, *Enoch Powell*, pp 160, 194; *The Times*, 12 Feb 1998; Heffer, *Like the Roman*, p 215.
4. Cooper, 'Little Local Difficulties', p 236; Green, 'Treasury', p 416; Jarvis, '1958', p 27; Green, 'Treasury', pp 417, 420–211; Jarvis, '1958', p 31; Green, 'Treasury', p 420; Thorpe, *Supermac*, pp 400–401; Cooper, 'Little Local Difficulties', p 236.
5. Green, 'Treasury', p 419; David Kynaston, *City of London, Volume 4* (2001), pp 42–3, 77; *Listener*, 24 Nov 1957; *News Chronicle*, 18 Nov 1957; *Economist*, 21 Dec 1957; Kynaston, *City*, p 105.
6. Macmillan, dep.d.30, 22 Dec 1957, fol 95, 6 Jan 1958, fols 100–101, 104; Hunt, 'Much More'; Cooper, 'Little Local Difficulties', p 240.
7. *The Times*, 7 Jan 1958; Michael Cockerell, *Live from Number 10* (1988), pp 56–7; Macmillan, dep.d.30, 7 Jan 1958, fol 110.
8. *Daily Telegraph*, 7 Jan 1958; *Financial Times*, 8 Jan 1958; *Daily Express*, 7 Jan 1958; *Daily Sketch*, 8 Jan 1958; *Daily Mail*, 7 Jan 1958; *Spectator*, 10 Jan 1958; *Sunday Times*, 12 Jan 1958; *Economist*, 11 Jan 1958; *The Times*, 7–8 Jan 1958.
9. *Kent & Sussex Courier*, 10 Jan 1958; *Yorkshire Post*, 9 Jan 1958; *Financial Times*, 14 Jan 1958.
10. *New Statesman*, 11 Jan 1958; Preston, 7 Jan 1958; *News Chronicle*, 21 Jan 1958.
11. *News Chronicle*, 8 Jan 1958; *Spectator*, 10 Jan 1958; Hunt, 'Much More'.
12. *The Times*, 8 Jan 1958; *Daily Express*, 8 Jan 1958; Hunt, 'Much More'; *New Yorker*, 25 Jan 1958, 8 Feb 1958; *Financial Times*, 25 Jan 1958; *Daily Mirror*, 24 Jan 1958; Alan Howarth, 'Lord Thorneycroft', *Independent*, 6 Jun 1994.
13. Alan Booth, 'Inflation, Expectations and the Political Economy of Conservative Britain, 1951–1964', *Historical Journal* (Sep 2000), pp 832–4; *Independent*, 2 Jan 1989 (Anthony Bevins and Colin Hughes); *Independent*, 2 Feb 1988; 'Arthur Seldon', *Daily Telegraph*, 13 Oct 2005.

## 6 A Worried Song

1. BBC WA, R9/10/5 – VR/58/214; Turtle, 11 Jan 1958; Willmott, 14 Jan 1958; Denis Healey, *The Time of My Life* (1989), p 72; Willmott, 14 Jan 1958.

2. Sue Harper and Vincent Porter, *British Cinema of the 1950s* (Oxford, 2003), p 72; Haines, 16 Jan 1958; Denis Gifford, *Complete Catalogue of British Comics* (1985), pp 129, 191; *New Statesman*, 1 Mar 1958 (Francis Williams); *Woman's Realm*, 22 Feb 1958; Cynthia L. White, *Women's Magazines, 1693–1968* (1970), pp 170–71.

3. Langford, 18 Feb 1958; *Spectator*, 28 Mar 1958; Pat Thane, *Old Age in English History* (Oxford, 2000), pp 447–8.

4. David Kynaston, *The City of London, Volume 4* (2001), p 93; *Financial Times*, 22 Jan 1958; *New Yorker*, 8 Feb 1958 (Mollie Panter-Downes); Ben Pimlott, *Harold Wilson* (1992), pp 216–17; Kynaston, *City*, p 94; Forrest Capie, *The Bank of England: 1950s to 1979* (New York, 2010), p 99.

5. Gordon Burn, *Best and Edwards* (2006), pp 101–4; 'Peter Jackson', *Daily Telegraph*, 24 Mar 2004; *The Times*, 25 Mar 2004; *Financial Times*, 9 Sep 1995 (Christopher Dunkley); *New Statesman*, 8 Feb 1958 (Tom Driberg); Paul Ferris, *Sir Huge* (1990), p 144; BBC WA, R9/19/2, Jul 1958; *Brighton and Hove Herald*, 1 Feb 1958, 8 Mar 1958; *The Times*, 3–5 Feb 1958; *Daily Mirror*, 5 Feb 1958; Heap, 5 Feb 1958; Dee, 6 Feb 1958; Mark Lewisohn, *The Complete Beatles Chronicle* (1996 edn), p 16; *Independent*, 31 Jan 1998 (John Roberts).

6. *Guardian*, 2 Feb 2008 (Richard Williams); Preston, 6 Feb 1958; Last, 7 Feb 1958; Diary of Vincent Walmsley (Special Collections, University of Sussex), 7 Feb 1958; *Independent on Sunday*, 30 Jan 1994 (Brian Cathcart); *New Statesman*, 15 Feb 1958; *Salford City Reporter*, 14 Feb 1958; *The Times*, 1 Feb 2008 (Matt Dickinson).

7. Michael Cockerell, *Live from Number 10* (1988), pp 58–9; Bernard Sendall, *Independent Television in Britain, Volume 1* (1982), p 351; 'Sir Cyril Smith', *The Times*, 4 Sep 2010; David Steel, 'Sir Ludovic Kennedy', *Guardian*, 20 Oct 2009; BBC WA, R9/10/5 – VR/58/79; Macmillan, dep.d.30, 10 Feb 1958, fol 137; Crossman, Ms 154/8/21, 12 Feb 1958, fol 1,073; Last, 12 Feb 1958; BBC WA, *Any Questions?*, 14 Feb 1958; Cockerell, *Live*, p 59.

8. Anthony Howard, *RAB* (1987), pp 261–2; Robin Day, *Television* (1961), p 161; Sir Robin Day, *Grand Inquisitor* (1989), p 1; Sir Robin Day, *... But With Respect* (1993), p 25; Day, *Television*, pp 162–4; Macmillan, dep.d.31, 23 Feb 1958, fol 13.

9. Mark Pottle (ed), *Daring to Hope: The Diaries and Letters of Violet Bonham Carter, 1946–1969* (2000), p 196; Macmillan, dep.d.31, 13 Mar 1958, fol 33; Crossman, p 663; *The Times*, 6 Jun 1958.

10. John Campbell, *Margaret Thatcher, Volume One* (2000), pp 110–11; Pete Frame, *The Restless Generation* (2007), p 323; Derek A. J. Lister, *Bradford's Rock 'n' Roll* (Bradford, 1991), p 95; Christopher Sandford, *Mick Jagger* (1999 edn), p 29.

11. Dee, 29 Mar 1958; Archie Burnett (ed.), *The Complete Poems of Philip Larkin* (2012), p 409; Larkin, Ms Eng. c. 7418, 31 Mar 1958, fols 5–6; Simon Reynolds, 'Sorcerers of Sound', *Guardian*, 20 Sep 2008; Richard Webber, *Fifty Years of Hancock's Half Hour* (2004), pp 223–4.

12. *Punch*, 2 Apr 1958; *New Statesman*, 5 Apr 1958; David Stafford, 'Fleming's Lament for Britain', *The Times*, 18 Nov 1999; Simon Winder, *The Man Who Saved Britain* (2006), p 103.

13. Helpful accounts of CND's background and early history include: Richard Taylor and Colin Pritchard, *The Protest Makers* (Oxford, 1980), pp 5–7; Meredith Veldman, *Fantasy, the Bomb and the Greening of Britain* (Cambridge, 1994), pp 131–40; Mervyn Jones, *Michael Foot* (1994), pp 225–31; Kathleen Burk, *Troublemaker* (2000), pp 211–17.

14. *New Statesman*, 2 Nov 1957; Jones, *Foot*, pp 227–8; *The Times*, 18 Feb 1958; Day, *Respect*, p 26; Jad Adams, *Tony Benn* (1992), pp 135–6; *New Statesman*, 29 Mar 1958; BBC WA, *Any Questions?*, 4 Apr 1958.

15. *Guardian*, 10 Dec 2011 (Albert Beale); *Manchester Guardian*, 5 Apr 1958; *Observer*, 6 Apr 1958; David V. Barratt, 'John Brunner', *Independent*, 31 Aug 1995; Kathleen Tynan, *The Life of Kenneth Tynan* (1987), p 142; Veldman, *Fantasy*, pp 139–40; 'Norris McWhirter', *Daily Telegraph*, 21 Apr 2004.

16. Benn, p 272; Healey, *Time*, p 241; Julia Langdon, 'Lord Marsh', *Guardian*, 3 Aug 2011; Veldman, *Fantasy*, p 153; Peter Webb, *Portrait of David Hockney* (1988), pp 13, 18; Stephen Woodhams, *History in the Making* (2001), p 193; *Socialist Commentary* (May 1958), p 14 ('Lupus'); *New Statesman*, 21 Jun 1958; Adam Sisman, *A.J.P. Taylor* (1994), pp 276–7; *Guardian*, 30 Apr 2008 (Julie Bindel); Amis, p 521; Willmott, 9 Apr 1958; *New Yorker*, 3 May 1958; Lawrence Black, '"The Bitterest Enemies of Communism"', *Contemporary British History* (Autumn 2001), p 52; *Observer*, 6 Apr 1958.

17. *Coventry Standard*, 10 Jan 1958, 17 Jan 1958; *The Times*, 25 Oct 1957; *Observer*, 18 May 1958; Carole Newbiggin, 'The Development of Blackbird Leys', http://www.bbc.co.uk/news/england/oxford/, 'Memoryshare'; *The Times*, 9 Jun 1994 (Alan Franks); Frances Reynolds, *The Problem Housing Estate* (Aldershot, 1986), pp 15–17.

18. *Architects' Journal*, 5 Jun 1958; Andrew Homer, 'Administrative and Social Change in the Post-War British New Towns', PhD diss, University of Luton, 1999, pp 168, 170; *Architectural Review* (Jun 1958), p 422; A.G.V. Simmonds, 'Conservative Governments and the Housing Question, 1951–59', PhD diss, University of Leeds, 1995, pp 412–16; *Daily Mail*, 25 Aug 1958; *Architects' Journal*, 5 Jun 1958.

19. *Architects' Journal*, 20 Mar 1958; *Observer*, 30 Mar 1958; *New Statesman*, 21 Jun 1958; *Sunday Times*, 22 Jun 1958; *Architects' Journal*, 24 Apr 1958, 26 Jun 1958; William Whyte, 'The Modernist Moment at the University of Leeds, 1957–1977', *Historical Journal* (Mar 2008), pp 173–8.

20. *The Times*, 6 Feb 1958; Joe Moran, *On Roads* (2009), pp 23–4; Simon Jenkins, 'From Green Belt to Rust Belt: How the Queen of the Midlands Was Throttled', *Guardian*, 20 Oct 2006; John R. Gold, *The Practice of Modernism* (Abingdon, 2007), p 134; *Evening Chronicle* (Newcastle), 31 May 1958; Gordon E. Cherry, *Birmingham* (Chichester, 1994), p 213; Simmonds, 'Conservative Governments', p 206; *Architects' Journal*, 6 Feb 1968; *Independent*, 26 Feb 1992 (Lucy Musgrove); *East London Advertiser*, 28 Mar 1958, 8 Aug 1958, 15 Aug 1958; Gold, *Practice*, pp 208–9.

21. Kynaston, *City*, p 130; *Guardian*, 20 Aug 2009 (Gavin Stamp); Kynaston, *City*, p 130; Nicholas Bullock, *Building the Post-War World* (2002), pp 258–9. For suggestive accounts of why conditions were so propitious by the late 1950s for a speculative property boom, above all in offices, see: Oliver Marriott, *The Property*

*Boom* (1967), chaps 1, 3; Charles Gordon, *The Two Tycoons* (1984), chaps 2, 5; Peter Mandler, 'New Towns for Old', in Becky Conekin et al (eds), *Moments of Modernity* (1999), pp 215–20; Gold, *Practice*, pp 84–6.

22. Interview with Richard Seifert (National Life Story Collection, National Sound Archive), C467/75, p 22; 'Richard Seifert', *The Times*, 27 Oct 2001; Martin Pawley, 'Richard Seifert', *Guardian*, 29 Oct 2001; 'Richard Seifert', *Daily Telegraph*, 29 Oct 2001.

23. *Star*, 25 Mar 1958; *Listener*, 17 Apr 1958; *New Statesman*, 19 Apr 1958; Fowles, EUL MS 102/1/10, 20 Apr 1958; *Listener*, 24 Apr 1958; Heap, 23 Jun 1958; *Architectural Review*, Jul 1958, pp 7–8.

24. *News Chronicle*, 28 Jan 1958; *Western Daily Press*, 14 Feb 1958; *Salford City Reporter*, 21 Mar 1958; *Architects' Journal*, 10 Apr 1958.

25. *Architects' Journal*, 17 Apr 1958; *Kensington News and West London Times*, 11 Apr 1958; *Salford City Reporter*, 9 May 1958; Raynham, 14 Jun 1958; *Architectural Review*, Jul 1958, p 58; *Evening News*, 9 Jul 1958; N. Tiratsoo, *Reconstruction, Affluence and Labour Politics* (1990), pp 96–7; Crossman, Ms 154/8/23, 17 Oct 1958, fols 1,215–6.

26. *Salford City Reporter*, 28 Mar 1958, 4 Apr 1958; *Manchester Guardian*, 19 Jul 1958; *East London Advertiser*, 28 Mar 1958; *Reynolds News*, 20 Apr 1958; *News Chronicle*, 7 May 1958; Bryan Appleyard, *Richard Rogers* (1986), pp 87–8.

27. Gold, *Practice*, pp 212–15; *Sheffield Telegraph*, 26 Apr 1958; *Star* (Sheffield), 25 Apr 1958; *Listener*, 8 May 1958.

28. *Surveyor*, 5 Jul 1958; *Architects' Journal*, 3 Jul 1958; Brian Edwards, *Basil Spence, 1907–1976* (Edinburgh, 1995), pp 82–4; Miles Horsey, *Tenements and Towers* (Edinburgh?, 1990), p 39; *Glasgow Herald*, 28 Aug 1958; *Architects' Journal*, 4 Sep 1958; *People*, 7 Sep 1958, 31 Aug 1958, 7 Sep 1958.

## 7  Stone Me

1. *New Statesman*, 12 Apr 1958; *Accrington Observer*, 19 Apr 1958; Phil Whalley, *Accrington Stanley* (Cheltenham, 2006), pp 20–25; *Evening News* (Portsmouth), 31 May 1958.

2. John Fisher, *Tony Hancock* (2008), p 164; Robert J. Wybrow, *Britain Speaks Out, 1937–87* (Basingstoke, 1989), p 54.

3. Frank Mort, *Capital Affairs* (2010), pp 247–8, 267–70; *People*, 27 Apr 1958; Mort, *Capital Affairs*, pp 276–7; *Independent*, 6 Apr 1992 (Danny Danziger). In general on Raymond, see Paul Willetts, *Members Only* (2010).

4. Crossman, Ms 154/8/21, 6 May 1958, fol 1,109; Arnold Wesker, *As Much As I Dare* (1994), p 556; Crossman, Ms 154/8/21, 6 May 1958, fol 1,109; *Universities and Left Review* (Summer 1958), p 3; *Manchester Guardian*, 18 Aug 1958.

5. Heap, 25 Feb 1958; *Observer*, 2 Mar 1958; 'Wolf Mankowitz', *The Times*, 22 May 1998; Michael Coveney, 'Julian More', *Guardian*, 3 Mar 2010; Heap, 23 Apr 1958, 30 Apr 1958; *Financial Times*, 1 May 1958; *Sunday Times*, 4 May 1958; BBC WA, *Any Questions?*, 9 May 1958.

6. Geoffrey Wansell, *Terence Rattigan* (1995), pp 295–6; Heap, 8 May 1958; *News Chronicle*, 10 May 1958.

7. *The Times*, 20 May 1958; *Crewe Chronicle*, 24 May 1958; Heap, 19 May 1958; Michael Billington, *The Life and Work of Harold Pinter* (1996), p 74; *Daily Telegraph*, 20 May 1958; *News Chronicle*, 20 May 1958; *Daily Mail*, 20 May 1958; John Walsh, 'That Nice Mr Pinter', *Independent*, 8 Feb 1999; Billington, *Pinter*, pp 84–5; *Sunday Times*, 25 May 1958.

8. John Russell Taylor, *Anger and After* (1969 edn), p 131; *New Statesman*, 26 May 2008 (Antonia Quirke); *Daily Mail*, 27–8 May 1958; *The Times*, 28 May 1958; *Sunday Times*, 1 Jun 1958; *Observer*, 1 Jun 1958; *Spectator*, 6 Jun 1958; Wesker, *As Much*, p 667.

9. *Coventry Standard*, 4 Jul 1958; *Coventry Evening Telegraph*, 7 Jul 1958; *Coventry Standard*, 11 Jul 1958; *Coventry Evening Telegraph*, 8 Jul 1958, 11 Jul 1958; Wesker, *As Much*, p 636; *Spectator*, 18 Jul 1958; *Punch*, 23 Jul 1958; *Sunday Times*, 20 Jul 1958; Wesker, *As Much*, p 638; *Observer*, 20 Jul 1958.

10. *Punch*, 14 May 1958, 18 Jun 1958; *Spectator*, 23 May 1958; *Punch*, 11 Jun 1958; Mark Lewisohn, *Radio Times Guide to TV Comedy* (2003 edn), p 49; BBC WA, R9/19/2, May 1958; Mark Lewisohn, *Funny, Peculiar* (2002), pp 253–5; *Listener*, 29 May 1958 (Ivor Brown); *New Statesman*, 21 Jun 1958; BBC WA, R9/19/2, Sep 1958.

11. Gorer, 'Television and the English' Survey, Box 1, C(i) file, Enid Blyton to Geoffrey Gorer, 13 Apr 1958; Jeffrey Milland, 'Courting Malvolio', *Contemporary British History* (Summer 2004), pp 79–80; Gorer, 'Television and the English' Survey, Box 1, C(i) file, William Empson to Geoffrey Gorer, 14 Apr 1958.

12. Gorer, 'Television and the English' Survey, Box 1, C(i) file, Enid Blyton to Geoffrey Gorer, 5 May 1958; Hilde Himmelweit, *Television and the Child* (1958), pp 40, 49; *Sociological Review* (Dec 1959), pp 273–4 (Edward Blishen); *Spectator*, 26 Dec 1958 (Geoffrey Nicholson); *Listener*, 25 Dec 1958; Abrams, Box 88, 'Working Papers on TV, 1954–65' file, 'A Study of Children's Television', Jun 1958.

13. Haines, 1–6 Jun 1958; Dave Russell, *Looking North* (Manchester, 2004), p 253; Leo McKinstry, *Jack & Bobby* (2002), pp 105–7; Stephen Wagg, *The Football World* (Brighton, 1984), p 130; *Daily Express*, 18 Jun 1958, *Observer*, 22 Jun 1958; *Financial Times*, 26 Jun 2010 (Simon Kuper); Ian Chadband, 'Sweden, Skegness and the "First" Sven', *Evening Standard*, 27 May 2002; Matthew Taylor, *The Association Game* (Harlow, 2008), p 213.

14. Helpful accounts of the strike include: Geoffrey Goodman, *The Awkward Warrior* (1979), pp 164–99; Robert Shepherd, *Iain Macleod* (1994), pp 134–42; Nina Fishman, '"Spearhead of the Movement"?', in Alan Campbell et al (eds), *British Trade Unions and Industrial Politics, Volume One* (Aldershot, 1999), pp 268–92.

15. *Observer*, 9 Feb 1958; *Daily Mail*, 13 Jan 1958; Macmillan, dep.d.31, 29 Apr 1958, fol 90; Goodman, *Awkward Warrior*, pp 173–4; *Observer*, 4 May 1958.

16. *New Statesman*, 10 May 1958, 14 Jun 1958 (Francis Williams); Haines, 11 May 1958; Shepherd, *Iain Macleod*, p 139; Macmillan, dep.d.31, 31 May 1958, fol 135; Langford, 1 Jun 1958; *Evening News*, 3 Jun 1958; Goodman, *Awkward Warrior*, pp 187–8; Heap, 20 Jun 1958; *New Yorker*, 12 Jul 1958; Goodman, *Awkward Warrior*, p 194; BBC WA, *Any Questions?*, 14 Feb 1958; *Punch*, 14 May 1958; Turtle, 11 Jun 1958.

17. Macmillan, dep.d.31, 11 May 1958, fol 99, 10 Apr 1958, fol 69, 11 Apr 1958, fol 70; Colin Crouch, *The Politics of Industrial Relations* (1982 edn), p 40; John Campbell, *Margaret Thatcher, Volume One* (2000), p 108; Shepherd, *Iain Macleod*, p 148;

Michael Kandiah, 'Conservative Leaders, Strategy – And "Consensus"?, 1945–1964', in Harriet Jones and Michael Kandiah (eds), *The Myth of Consensus* (Basingstoke, 1996), p 62.

18. Russell Bretherton, *The Control of Demand 1958–1964* (1999), pp 6–7; *Financial Times*, 4 Jul 1958; Macmillan, dep.d.32, 31 Jul 1958, fol 91.

19. Macmillan, dep.d.32, 14 Jun 1958, fol 22; Wybrow, *Britain Speaks*, p 54; *News Chronicle*, 9 Jul 1958; *New Statesman*, 19 Jul 1958; Campbell, *Margaret Thatcher*, pp 113–15; Goodman, *Awkward Warrior*, pp 240–41; *Crossman*, pp 687–9.

20. *Independent*, 18 Jun 1999 (Robert Hanks); Alun Howkins, 'History and the *Radio Ballads*', *Oral History* (Autumn 2000), pp 89–93; Paul Leslie Long, 'The Aesthetics of Class in Post-War Britain', Phd diss, University of Warwick, 2001, p 196; *New Statesman*, 12 Jul 1958; BBC WA, R9/6/79 – LR/58/1051; *Sunday Times*, 13 Jul 1958; H. E. Bates, *The World in Ripeness* (1972), p 150; *Punch*, 20 Aug 1958 (R.G.G. Price).

21. Lawrence Black, *Redefining British Politics* (Basingstoke, 2010), p 54; idem, *The Political Culture of the Left in Affluent Britain, 1951–64* (Basingstoke, 2003), p 115; Kevin Jefferys, *Anthony Crosland* (1999 edn), p 65; *The Times*, 28 Jul 1958.

22. *Financial Times*, 14 Aug 1958; *Independent*, 29 Sep 1999 (Ian Herbert); *News Chronicle*, 19 Aug 1958; *Daily Mail*, 22 Jul 1958; Dennis Barker, 'Richard Tompkins', *Guardian*, 11 Dec 1992; 'Lawrence Batley', *Daily Telegraph*, 27 Aug 2002; Turtle, 6 Jun 1958; *Kentish Mercury*, 7 Mar 1958; *Drapers Weekly*, 1 Feb 1959; Tom Courtenay, *Dear Tom* (2000), p 133.

23. *Financial Times*, 1 Jun 1959; ITC material at British Film Institute, Audience Research boxes, 1958 box, 'Public Standing Index', Jun 1958; Ralph Harris and Arthur Seldon, *Advertising in Action* (1962), pp 317, 277–81, 82; Mark Robinson, *100 Greatest TV Ads* (2000), pp 31, 86.

24. Jan Boxshall, *Every Home Should Have One* (1997), p 72; John Orbell, 'The Development of Office Technology', in Alison Turton (ed), *Managing Business Archives* (1991), p 63; *Spectator*, 2 May 1958 (Leslie Adrian); William Osgerby, '"One For the Money, Two For the Show"', PhD diss, University of Sussex, 1992, p 265; *Independent*, 16 Jun 1997 (Nic Cicutti), 23 Nov 2002 (Howard Jacobson); Frances Woodsford, *Dear Mr Bigelow* (2009), p 279.

25. Nicholas Ind, *Terence Conran* (1995), pp 118–19; *Daily Herald*, 10 Jul 1958; *Guardian*, 4 Jan 2007 (Simon Bowers and Julia Kollewe).

26. *New Yorker*, 16 Aug 1958; *Radio Times*, 25 Jul 1958; *The Times*, 26 Mar 2009 (Valentine Low); *Daily Mirror*, 28 Jul 1958, 31 Jul 1958.

27. Patricia Greene et al, *The Book of The Archers* (1994), pp 39, 164; David Marr (ed), Patrick White, *Letters* (1994), pp 145–6; Carl Chinn, *Better Betting with a Decent Feller* (2004 edn), p 238; *The Times*, 26 Aug 1958; Martin, 27 Aug 1958; Langford, 27 Aug 1958; *Listener*, 4 Sep 1958 (Philip Henderson); Larkin, Ms Eng. c. 7418, 27 Aug 1958, fol 88.

28. http://www.theclitheroekid.org.uk; John Hudson, *Wakes Week* (Stroud, 1992), p 145; Macmillan, dep.d.33, 20 Aug 1958, fol 8; *Coventry Standard*, 25 Jul 1958; Haines, 3 Aug 1958; Sue Read, *Hallo Campers!* (1986), pp 163, 166. For a fuller version of Cliff-at-Clacton, see Pete Frame, *The Restless Generation* (2007), p 334.

29. *Sunday Times*, 1 Sep 1958; *Evening News* (Portsmouth), 23 Aug 1958, 1 Sep 1958.

## 8 Get the Nigger

1. *Guardian Journal* (Nottingham), 25 Aug 1958; *Manchester Guardian*, 25 Aug 1958; Ruth Glass, *Newcomers* (1960), p 131; *Manchester Guardian*, 26 Aug 1958; Glass, *Newcomers*, p 132; *The Times*, 1 Sep 1958; *Manchester Guardian*, 27 Aug 1958; Glass, *Newcomers*, p 135; *Kensington News and West London Times*, 29 Aug 1958, 5 Sep 1958.

2. *Daily Express*, 1 Sep 1958; Mike Phillips and Trevor Phillips, *Windrush* (1998), p 174; Glass, *Newcomers*, pp 136–7; *Kensington News and West London Times*, 5 Sep 1958; *Manchester Guardian*, 5 Sep 1958.

3. *Daily Express*, 2 Sep 1958; *Manchester Guardian*, 2 Sep 1958; *Scotsman*, 2 Sep 1958; *Kensington News and West London Times*, 5 Sep 1958; Phillips, *Windrush*, pp 175–6; *Daily Express*, 2 Sep 1958; Benn, p 286; Glass, *Newcomers*, p 140; *The Times*, 3 Sep 1958; Glass, *Newcomers*, p 141.

4. Michael Banton, *White and Coloured* (1959), p 159; *City and Suburban News* (Manchester), 11 Oct 1957; *Spectator*, 5 Sep 1958 (Eleanor Ettlinger); Glass, *Newcomers*, p 81; *Observer*, 22 Jun 1958; *Coventry Standard*, 1 Aug 1958; *Birmingham Mail*, 30 Aug 1958.

5. *Kensington News and West London Times*, 22 Aug 1958; Glass, *Newcomers*, p 60; *Manchester Guardian*, 23 Nov 1957; Sheila Patterson, *Dark Strangers* (1963), pp 179–84; Glass, *Newcomers*, p 76; *Manchester Guardian*, 4 Mar 1957.

6. Glass, *Newcomers*, p 86; *Big Issue*, 26 Apr 2004; *Radio Times*, 6 Jun 1958; *Punch*, 27 Aug 1958.

7. BBC WA, *Any Questions?*, 12 Sep 1958.

8. *The Times*, 4 Sep 1958; *Observer*, 7 Sep 1958; D. W. Dean, 'Conservative Governments and the Restriction of Commonwealth Immigration in the 1950s', *Historical Journal* (Mar 1992), p 189; *Smethwick Telephone*, 12 Sep 1958; Glass, *Newcomers*, pp 153, 155; Simon Heffer, 'What Enoch Was Really Saying', *Spectator*, 24 Nov 2001.

9. Paul Foot, *Immigration and Race in British Politics* (Harmondsworth, 1965), p 169; Arthur Marwick, *The Sixties* (Oxford, 1998), p 235; *Daily Mail*, 2 Sep 1958; *Daily Mirror*, 3 Sep 1958; Ken Lunn, 'Complex Encounters: Trade Unions, Immigration and Racism', in John McIlroy et al (eds), *British Trade Unions and Industrial Politics, Volume Two* (Aldershot, 1999), p 80; *Reynolds News*, 7 Sep 1958; Dean, 'Conservative Governments', p 192; *The Times*, 29 Sep 1958.

10. Heap, 1 Sep 1958; Maurice Edelman Papers (Modern Records Centre, University of Warwick), Ms 125/1/3/33; *News Chronicle*, 8 Sep 1958; Glass, *Newcomers*, p 123; Turtle, 17 Sep 1958; Colin MacInnes, *England, Half English* (1986 edn), p 39; BBC WA, R9/19/2, Oct–Nov 1958; Glass, *Newcomers*, p 247.

11. *Listener*, 11 Sep 1958 (Philip Henderson); *Kensington News and West London Times*, 12 Sep 1958; *Express and Star* (Wolverhampton), 4 Sep 1958, 6 Sep 1958, 8–9 Sep 1958, 11 Sep 1958; *Guardian Journal* (Nottingham), 13 Sep 1958; *The Times*, 18 Sep 1958; *North London Press*, 19 Sep 1958, 26 Sep 1958; *The Times*, 19 Sep 1958, 22 Sep 1958; *North London Press*, 3 Oct 1958; Emily Green, 'Sylvester Hughes', *Independent*, 23 Jul 1991.

12. *Evening Standard*, 4 Sep 1958; Frank Cousins Papers (Modern Records Centre, University of Warwick), Ms 282/8/3/1, Sep 1958; Olga Cannon and J.R.L.

Anderson, *The Road from Wigan Pier* (1973), pp 192–6; *Billingham Post*, 11 Sep 1958; David Kynaston, *The City of London, Volume 4* (2001), p 153.

13. Michael Hellicar, 'The First TV Set', *Daily Mail*, 14 Sep 2002; *Daily Mirror*, 15 Sep 1958, 29 Sep 1958, 6 Oct 1958, 19 Sep 1958; Morris Bright and Robert Ross, *Carry On Uncensored* (1999), pp 8, 10; Sue Harper and Vincent Porter, *British Cinema of the 1950s* (Oxford, 2003), p 193.

14. Muriel Beadle, *These Ruins Are Inhabited* (1961), pp 15–17; *Daily Mirror*, 24 Sep 1958; John Bloom, *It's No Sin to Make a Profit* (1971), pp 14–15, 21–32; T.A.B. Corley, *Domestic Electrical Appliances* (1966), p 55.

15. *Daily Mirror*, 15 Sep 1958; *The Times*, 21 Jul 2008 (Mick Hume); Joe Moran, 'Milk Bars, Starbucks and The Uses of Literacy', *Cultural Studies* (Nov 2006), p 564; Willmott, 1 Oct 1958.

16. Raymond Williams, *Politics and Letters* (1979), p 132; John Mullan, 'Rebel in a Tweed Suit', *Guardian*, 28 May 2005; Raymond Williams, *Culture and Society, 1780–1950* (1958), pp 205–6; Raphael Samuel, '"Philosophy Teaching By Example": Past and Present in Raymond Williams', *History Workshop* (Spring 1989), p 146; Williams, *Culture and Society*, pp 327–8; *New Statesman*, 27 Sep 1958; *Spectator*, 10 Oct 1958; *Times Literary Supplement*, 26 Sep 1958; *Encounter*, Jan 1959, pp 86–8; Samuel, 'Past and Present', p 142; Fred Inglis, *Raymond Williams* (1995), p 146.

17. Norman MacKenzie (ed), *Conviction* (1958), pp 92, 138, 230; *Socialist Commentary*, Nov 1958, pp 29; Noel Annan, *Our Age* (1990), p 596.

18. *Architects' Journal*, 25 Sep 1958; Turtle, 21 Sep 1958; *Daily Telegraph*, 26 Sep 1958; Benn, p 289; *Sheffield Telegraph*, 24 Sep 1958; *Architectural Review* (Oct 1958), p 282; Bevis Hillier, *Betjeman: The Bonus of Laughter* (2004), pp 167–8; *Lost City*, BBC TV, 26 Oct 1958 (TV Heaven at National Media Museum, Bradford); Dan Smith, *An Autobiography* (Newcastle upon Tyne, 1970), pp 48, 61–5.

19. Spencer Leigh, 'Halfway to Paradise', *Record Collector* (Feb 2008), p 59; *Observer Music Monthly* (May 2004), p 25 (Simon Napier-Bell); Spencer Leigh, 'Ian Samwell', *Independent*, 17 Mar 2003; *Guardian*, 26 Sep 2008 (John Pidgeon); *The Times*, 25 Jun 2004 (Lisa Verrico).

20. *The Times*, 4 Oct 2008 (David Robertson); *Guardian*, 23 Jun 2007 (Ian Jack); Ronald Miller and David Sawers, *The Technical Development of Modern Aviation* (1968), pp 179–82; Clive Jenkins, 'BOAC: The Anatomy of a Strike', *Universities and Left Review* (Spring 1959), pp 30–34.

21. Peter Weiler, 'The Rise and Fall of the Conservatives' "Grand Design for Housing", 1951–64', *Contemporary British History* (Spring 2000), p 132; Hilary Spurling, *Secrets of a Woman's Heart* (1984), p 245; Richard Davenport-Hines, 'Peter Rachman', in *Oxford Dictionary of National Biography*, vol 45 (Oxford, 2004), p 716. In general on the Rent Act's background and implementation, see (in addition to Weiler's 'Rise and Fall'): John Davis, 'Rent and Race in 1960s London: New Light on Rachmanism', *Twentieth Century British History*, 12/1 (2001), pp 69–92; Alan G. V. Simmonds, 'Raising Rachman: The Origins of the Rent Act, 1957', *Historical Journal* (Dec 2002), pp 843–68.

22. *Guardian*, 11 Oct 2008 (Bobby Smith); Garry Whannel, '"Grandstand", the Sports Fan and the Family Audience', in John Corner (ed), *Popular Television in Britain* (1991), p 188; *Radio Times*, 3 Oct 1958; Larkin, Ms Eng. c.7418, 16 Oct 1958, fol 120; Martin Bauml Duberman, *Paul Robeson* (1989), p 471.

23. Alan Sillitoe, *Saturday Night and Sunday Morning* (Pan edn, 1960), p 5; Richard Bradford, *The Life of a Long-Distance Writer* (2008), p 152; *New Statesman*, 25 Oct 1958.

24. Turtle, 16 Oct 1958; *Radio Times*, 10 Oct 1958; Biddy Baxter, 'Christopher Trace', *Independent*, 8 Sep 1992; Lawrence Black, *Redefining British Politics* (Basingstoke, 2010), p 87; BBC WA, R9/7/36 – VR/58/558; *Guardian*, 28 Oct 2008 (Frank Keating), 15 Sep 2009 (Richard Williams); *News Chronicle*, 21 Oct 1958; *New Yorker*, 1 Nov 1958; *Daily Mirror*, 20 Oct 1958, 22 Oct 1958.

25. Macmillan, dep.d.33, 4 Oct 1958, fol 60, 18 Oct 1958, fol 74; Neil Rollings, 'Butskellism, the Postwar Consensus and the Managed Economy', in Harriet Jones and Michael Kandiah (eds), *The Myth of Consensus* (Basingstoke, 1996), p 111; Macmillan, dep.d.33, 22 Oct 1958, fols 80–81; *Manchester Guardian*, 28 Oct 1958; George H. Gallup, *The Gallup International Public Opinion Polls: Great Britain 1937–1975, Volume One* (New York, 1976), p 482.

26. Jonathan Dimbleby, *Richard Dimbleby* (1975), p 342; Langford, 28 Oct 1958; Heap, 28 Oct 1958; *TV Times*, 26 Oct 1958; Tony Jasper, *The Top Twenty Book* (1994 edn), p 42; *Radio Times*, 24 Oct 1958, 31 Oct 1958; *Oldie*, Sep 2000, p 59 (Frank Keating); Jim White, 'And Coleman is 70', *Independent*, 26 Apr 1996; Dennis Barker, 'Bryan Cowgill', *Guardian*, 18 Jul 2008.

## 9 Parity of Esteem

1. *Socialist Commentary* (May 1956), p 13; Michael Young, *The Rise of the Meritocracy, 1870–2033* (Penguin edn, 1961), pp 94, 169.

2. Paul Barker, 'A Tract for the Times', in Geoff Dench (ed), *The Rise and Rise of Meritocracy* (Oxford, 2006), pp 44, 40; *Spectator*, 21 Nov 1958; *The Times*, 30 Oct 1958; Barker, 'Tract', p 39; *Encounter*, Feb 1959, pp 68–72.

3. Harry Ritchie, *Success Stories* (1988), p 79; Humphrey Carpenter, *The Angry Young Men* (2002), p 153; *Crossman*, p 598; *Daily Sketch*, 25 Jan 1958; David Edgerton, *Warfare State* (Cambridge, 2006), p 180; Joe Moran, *On Roads* (2009), pp 20, 34; 'Sir Denis Rooke, OM', *Daily Telegraph*, 6 Sep 2008; Tam Dalyell, 'Sir Denis Rooke', *Independent*, 8 Sep 2008.

4. Nicholas Faith, 'Lord Weinstock', *Independent*, 24 Jul 2002; D. C. Coleman, *Courtauld's: III* (Oxford, 1980), pp 141–2, 327; David Kynaston, *The City of London, Volume 4* (2001), p 78.

5. Michael Leapman, 'Robert Robinson', *Independent*, 15 Aug 2011; Michael Leapman, 'Brian Redhead', *Independent*, 24 Jan 1994; Harold Evans, *My Paper Chase* (2009), p 208; 'Jean Rook', *Daily Telegraph*, 6 Sep 1991; Michael Leapman, 'Keith Waterhouse', *Independent*, 8 Sep 2009; Peter Guttridge, 'Professor Sir Malcolm Bradbury', *Independent*, 29 Nov 2000; Jonathan Coe, *Like a Fiery Elephant* (2004), p 82; Lucasta Miller, 'John Carey', *Guardian*, 4 Jun 2005; *Ian Hamilton in Conversation with Dan Jacobson* (2002), pp 13, 113; Tony Richardson, *Long Distance Runner* (1993); Stephen Fay, *Power Play* (1995); 'John Thaw', *Daily Telegraph*, 23 Feb 2002; Peter Stead, *Film and the Working Class* (1989), pp 190–91; Val Williams, 'Terence Donovan', *Independent*, 25 Nov 1996; Tim Cumming, 'Shooting Stars', *Independent*, 7 Aug 2002; Pierre Perrone,

'Brian Duffy', *Independent*, 17 Jun 2010; *Financial Times*, 3 Nov 2007 (Julian Flanagan); Natalie Rudd, *Peter Blake* (2003), pp 7, 25; Tim Marlow, 'Bryan Robertson', *Independent*, 26 Nov 2002; Wikipedia, 'Zandra Rhodes'; *Independent*, 9 Jan 2009 (Michael Coveney); John Repsch, *The Legendary Joe Meek* (1989), pp 52, 63.

6. *Encounter*, Feb 1958, p 60, Apr 1958, p 70; Humphrey Carpenter, *Dennis Potter* (1998), pp 55–98; Margaret Forster, *Hidden Lives* (1995), pp 244–9; *Daily Telegraph*, 31 May 2003; *Guardian*, 10 Oct 1998.

7. *Sunday Times*, 11 Oct 1959; Anton Rippon, *A Derby Boy* (Stroud, 2007), chap 6; Mary Evans, *A Good School* (1991), pp 91, 9, 83–5, 101, 4, 10–11, 41, 120; Roy Greenslade, *Goodbye to the Working Class* (1976), pp 23, 151–9; *The Ashbeian*, 1957–8, pp 28–9.

8. *Spectator*, 28 Jun 1957; Jacqueline Wilson, *Jacky Daydream* (2007), pp 285–7; Haines, 24 Jan 1958; Wilson, *Jacky*, pp 287–90; Haines, 24–5 Apr 1958; Ken Blakemore, *Sunnyside Down* (Stroud, 2005), pp 145–6; Greenslade, *Goodbye*, pp 20–21; Kevin Cann, *Any Day Now* (2010), p 18.

9. Peter Willmott, 'Some Social Trends', in J. B. Cullingworth (ed), *Problems of an Urban Society, Volume III* (1973), p 96; *News Chronicle*, 21–3 Apr 1958; *Listener*, 24 Oct 1957; Roy Lewis and Rosemary Stewart, *The Boss* (1958), p 99.

10. J. E. Floud et al, *Social Class and Educational Opportunity* (1956), p 42; William Taylor, *The Secondary Modern School* (1963), pp 51, 156, 47; Michael Sanderson, *Educational Opportunity and Social Change in England* (1987), p 56; William Liversidge, 'Life Chances', *Sociological Review* (Mar 1962), pp 21–2, 33; M. P. Carter, *Home, School and Work* (Oxford, 1962), pp 71, 79.

11. Sanderson, *Educational Opportunity*, p 52; Alan Little and John Westergaard, 'The Trend of Class Differentials in Educational Opportunity in England and Wales', *British Journal of Sociology* (Dec 1964), p 303; Eva Bene, 'Some Differences between Middle-Class and Working-Class Grammar School Boys in their Attitudes towards Education', *British Journal of Sociology* (Jun 1959), p 151.

12. Sanderson, *Educational Opportunity*, p 71; Brian Simon, *Education and the Social Order, 1940–1990* (1991), pp 201–2; *Observer*, 4 Sep 1960; Willmott, 'Social Trends', p 96; *New Statesman*, 30 Aug 1958 (K. W. Wedderburn); *Sunday Times*, 29 Dec 1957; *Observer*, 4 Sep 1960.

13. Floud et al, *Social Class*, p 81; Abrams, Box 85, file '1 of 3', Research Services Ltd, 'A Pilot Enquiry into Some Aspects of Working-Class Life in London' (1957); Peter Willmott, *The Evolution of a Community* (1963), pp 115–16; Brian Jackson and Dennis Marsden, *Education and the Working Class* (1962), pp 103–23, 237; Carter, *Home*, pp 118–19.

14. *Daily Mail*, 1 Aug 1958, 4–5 Aug 1958; *Wisden Cricketers' Almanack, 1958* (1958), pp 111–12; Michael Marshall, *Gentlemen and Players* (1987), pp 253–4.

15. Gerald Aylmer, 'Lord James of Rusholm', *Independent*, 21 May 1992; George Perry, *The Great British Picture Show* (1985 edn), pp 200–201; Basil Bernstein, *Class, Codes and Control, Volume 1* (1971), pp 43–61; Anne de Courcy, *Snowdon* (2008), p 57; John Moynihan, 'Sunday Soccer', in Ian Hamilton (ed), *The Faber Book of Soccer* (1992), pp 76–86.

16. *Radio Times*, 15 Aug 1958; BBC WA, R9/2/10, week 17–23 Aug 1958; Kynaston, *City*, p 212.

17. Turtle, 15 Sep 1958; *New Statesman*, 23 Aug 1958; Anthony Crosland, *The Future of Socialism* (2006 edn), p 218; *Spectator*, 4 Jan 1957; Dennis Dean, 'Preservation or Renovation? The Dilemmas of Conservative Educational Policy 1955–1960', *Twentieth Century British History*, 3/1 (1992), pp 28–9; *Daily Mail*, 20 May 1958.

18. *New Statesman*, 30 Aug 1958, 20 Sep 1958, 27 Sep 1958, 11 Oct 1958; *Socialist Commentary*, Oct 1958, p 26; Muriel Beadle, *These Ruins are Inhabited* (1961), pp 148–51; Crosland, *Future*, p 218; BBC WA, R9/7/26 – VR/57/66.

19. Sanderson, *Educational Opportunity*, p 47; Robin Pedley, *Comprehensive Education* (1956), p 41; Simon, *Education*, p 209; P. E. Vernon, *Secondary School Selection* (1957), pp 169, 177; Harry Judge, *A Generation of Schooling* (Oxford, 1984), pp 47–8; *New Statesman*, 25 May 1957; *News Chronicle*, 5 Feb 1957; *Daily Express*, 8 May 1957.

20. Taylor, *Secondary Modern*, p 34; *Sunday Times*, 21 Apr 1957; *Spectator*, 14 Jun 1957; Carter, *Home*, p 5; Gary McCulloch, *Failing the Ordinary Child?* (Buckingham, 1998), p 89; Taylor, *Secondary Modern*, p 50.

21. Taylor, *Secondary Modern*, p 37; *New Statesman*, 21 Sep 1957; H. C. Dent, *Secondary Modern School* (1958), pp 14, 42, 152; Melissa Benn, *School Wars* (2011), pp 45–7; John Lanchester, *Family Romance* (2007), pp 234–5.

22. Taylor, *Secondary Modern*, pp 106–7, 110; Rhodes Boyson, *Speaking My Mind* (1995), p 52; Taylor, *Secondary Modern*, p 118; Brian Simon, 'The Tory Government and Education, 1951–60', *History of Education* (Dec 1985), p 293; *Economist*, 6 Dec 1958.

23. George H. Gallup, *The Gallup International Public Opinon Polls: Great Britain, 1937–1975*, Volume One (New York, 1976), p 470; Melissa Benn, 'Allen Clarke', *Guardian*, 25 Aug 2007; *Economist*, 6 Dec 1958.

24. *Sunday Times*, 27 Jan 1957; *Times Educational Supplement*, 15 Feb 1957; *Economist*, 22 Jun 1957; *Spectator*, 12 Dec 1958; Brian Simon, 'Harry Rée', *Independent*, 21 May 1991; Simon, *Education*, p 210; *New Statesman*, 12 Oct 1957, 18 Oct 1958; *Listener*, 11 Jul 1957; *New Statesman*, 21 Feb 1959, 25 May 1957; Vernon, *Secondary School Selection*, p 50; Raymond Williams, *Culture and Society, 1780–1950* (1958), pp 331–2.

25. David Crook, 'The Disputed Origins of the Leicestershire Two-Tier Comprehensive Schools Plan', *History of Education Society Bulletin* (Autumn 1992), pp 55–8; *Observer*, 19 Oct 1958; *Times Educational Supplement*, 12 Apr 1957; Leicestershire RO, DE 3627/207, Oadby Gartree School minutes, 23 Sep 1957, 21 Jan 1958; Gerald T. Rimmington, *The Comprehensive Issue in Leicester 1945–1974 and Other Essays* (Peterborough, 1984), pp 8–9.

26. *Western Daily Press*, 12 Oct 1957; Simon, *Education*, pp 206, 219; *Western Daily Press*, 14 Oct 1957, 18 Oct 1957; *Northern Despatch*, 3 Oct 1958, 8 Nov 1958, 23 Oct 1958; Richard Batley et al, *Going Comprehensive* (1970), pp 36–9, 98.

27. City of Bradford, *Official Records of Council Meetings, 1957–8* (Bradford, 1958), pp 148, 151, *1958–9* (Bradford, 1959), pp 142–5.

28. *Socialist Commentary*, Apr 1957, p 9; Labour Party Archives (People's History Museum, Manchester), 'Study Group on Education: Minutes and Papers: 27 March 1957–8 Jan 1958', 'Study Group on Education: Minutes and Papers: 20 Jan 1958–4 Feb 1959'; Crossman, Ms 154/8/21, 10 Feb 1958, fols 1,070–72.

29. *Spectator*, 20 Jun 1958; Robin Pedley, *The Comprehensive School* (Penguin edn, 1969), p 180; *New Yorker*, 6 Sep 1958; Beverley Shaw, *Comprehensive Schooling* (Oxford, 1983), pp 56–7; *New Statesman*, 28 Jun 1958, 5 Jul 1958.
30. *The Times*, 30 Sep 1958; *Journal* (Newcastle), 30 Sep 1958; *New Statesman*, 4 Oct 1958; Philip M. Williams, *Hugh Gaitskell* (1979), pp 468, 896; *Sociological Review* (Dec 1959), pp 269–70.

## 10 Unnatural Practices

1. *TV Times*, 31 Oct 1958; *Spectator*, 21 Nov 1958 (Peter Forster); *Radio Times*, 7 Nov 1958; Tony Jasper, *The Top Twenty Book* (1994 edn), p 42; *New Statesman*, 8 Nov 1958, 22 Nov 1958; Charles Marowitz et al (eds), *The Encore Reader* (Methuen pbk edn, 1970), pp 96–103; *Larkin*, p 244; Fowles, EUL Ms 102/1/10, 9 Nov 1958; *News Chronicle*, 17 Nov 1958; Raynham, 8 Nov 1958; Haines, 17 Nov 1958; Heap, 28 Nov 1958.
2. Ian Harvey, *To Fall like Lucifer* (1971), pp 105–13; *The Times*, 21 Nov 1958, 25 Nov 1958; Macmillan, dep.d.33, 21 Nov 1958, fol 106; *The Times*, 30 Jul 2002.
3. *The Times*, 19 Oct 1995 (William Rees-Mogg); *New Yorker*, 13 Dec 1958 (Mollie Panter-Downes); *Hansard*, House of Commons Debates, 26 Nov 1958, cols 417, 428–9, 465; Trevor Fisher, 'Permissiveness and the Politics of Morality', *Contemporary Record* (Summer 1993), p 161; George H. Gallup, *The Gallup International Public Opinon Polls: Great Britain, 1937–1975, Volume One* (New York, 1976), p 487; *Encounter* (Feb 1959), p 62 (Peter Wildeblood); *Spectator*, 26 Dec 1958 (letters); Gordon Westwood, *A Minority* (1960), pp ix, 182–90.
4. Fisher, 'Permissiveness', pp 159, 161–2; Tanya Evans, 'The Other Woman and Her Child', seminar at Institute of Historical Research, London, 20 Feb 2008.
5. Peter Pagnamenta and Richard Overy, *All Our Working Lives* (1984), pp 93–4; Stephen Wilks, *Industrial Policy and the Motor Industry* (Manchester, 1984), p 77; Peter Scott, 'The Worst of Both Worlds', *Business History* (Oct 1996), p 54; Michael P. Jackson, *The Price of Coal* (1974), pp 100–101; *Listener*, 13 Nov 1958; *The Times*, 4 Dec 1958; Geoffrey Owen, *From Empire to Europe* (1999), pp 66–7; John Singleton, *Lancashire on the Scrapheap*, (Oxford, 1991), p 160.
6. A.G.V. Simmonds, 'Conservative Governments and the Housing Question', PhD diss, University of Leeds, 1995, p 41; Chris Maume, 'Sir Lawrie Barratt', *Independent*, 21 December 2012; John Turner, 'A Land Fit for Tories to Live In', *Contemporary European History* (Jul 1995), p 201; *Hansard*, House of Commons Debates, 15 Dec 1958, col 892.
7. *New Statesman*, 6 Nov 1958; Geoffrey Goodman, *The Awkward Warrior* (1979), pp 205–6; *Crossman*, p 726; Anthony Howard, *Crossman* (1990), p 214; *Financial Times*, 14 Nov 1958; *Evening Standard*, 21 Jan 1959; *Crossman*, p 726.
8. Benn, pp 294–5; *Universities and Left Review* (Autumn 1958), p 66; Eric Hobsbawm, *Interesting Times* (2002), pp 212–14; Willmott, 3 Jan 1959, 29 Jan 1959.
9. Joe Moran, *On Roads* (2009), p 20; *The Times*, 6 Dec 1958; Michael Bond, *A Bear Called Paddington* (Young Lions edn, 1971), p 9; *The Times*, 6 Apr 1998 (Dalya Alberge); *Times Literary Supplement*, 21 Nov 1958; Michael Bond, *Bears & Forebears* (1996), p 159; Bevis Hillier, *John Betjeman: New Fame, New Love* (2002),

pp 605–11; *New Statesman*, 6 Dec 1958; *Listener*, 11 Dec 1958; Rupert Hart-Davis (ed), *The Lyttelton Hart-Davis Letters: Volume Three* (1981), p 176.

10. *New Statesman*, 13 Dec 1958; *New Musical Express*, 19 Dec 1958; Spencer Leigh, 'Tito Burns', *Independent*, 17 Sep 2010; 'John Koon', *Daily Telegraph*, 12 Feb 1997; Heap, 18 Dec 1958; *Spectator*, 2 Jan 1959; *TV Times*, 26 Dec 1958; BBC WA, R9/7/38 – VR/59/6.

11. *News Chronicle*, 17 Nov 1958; *Financial Times*, 24 Dec 1958; *New Statesman*, 3 Jan 1959 (Francis Williams); *Financial Times*, 1 Jan 1959; *Economist*, 3 Jan 1959; Gerold Krozewski, *Money and the End of Empire* (Basingstoke, 2001), p 150; *Listener*, 12 Feb 1959.

12. For the fullest recent account of the Aluminium War, see Niall Ferguson, *High Financier* (2010), pp 183–99, though see also Tim Congdon's review in *Times Literary Supplement*, 30 Jul 2010.

13. David Kynaston, *The City of London, Volume 4* (2001), pp 107–14.

14. Larkin, Ms Eng. c.7419, 27 Dec 1958, fol 43; *News of the World*, 4 Jan 1959; *Sunday Express*, 4 Jan 1959; Jim Laker, *Over To Me* (1960), p 53.

11  Morbid Sentimentality

1. *The Times*, 3 Jan 1959, 7 Jan 1959; *Sunday Express*, 4 Jan 1959; Heap, 6 Jan 1959; 'Edwin Brock', *The Times*, 26 Sep 1997; Anthony Thwaite, 'Edwin Brock', *Independent*, 10 Sep 1997; Larkin, Ms Eng. c. 7419, 12 Jan 1959, fol 51; *The Times*, 13 Jan 1959; D. R. Thorpe, *Supermac* (2010), p 424; *Spectator*, 24 May 1963; *The Times*, 16 Jan 1959.

2. *New Yorker*, 7 Mar 1959; *Birmingham Post*, 25 Feb 1959; Michael Frostick and Mark Pottle, 'Michael Hawthorn', *Oxford Dictionary of National Biography*, vol 25 (Oxford, 2004), p 977; Preston, 23 Jan 1959; Haines, 29–30 Jan 1959; *Radio Times*, 23 Jan 1959; *Guardian Weekend*, 17 Aug 2002 (Gary Younge); Colin Prescod, 'Carnival', in Marika Sherwood (ed), *Claudia Jones* (1999), pp 151–8.

3. *Spectator*, 6 Feb 1959; *Daily Mirror*, 6 Feb 1959; *New Statesman*, 7 Feb 1959; Benn, p 298; Macmillan, dep.d.34, 6 Feb 1959, fol 76; Brian McHugh, 'The Saturday after Buddy Holly Died', *Guardian*, 8 Jan 2011; BBC WA, R9/7/38 – VR/59/68.

4. *Vogue* (Feb 1959), p 98; David Hendy, 'Bad Language and BBC Radio Four in the 1960s and 1970s', *Twentieth Century British History*, 17/1 (2006), p 76; *Spectator*, 30 Jan 1959; *New Statesman*, 31 Jan 1959; John Hill, *Sex, Class and Realism* (1986), p 191; Paddy Whannel, 'Room at the Top', *Universities and Left Review* (Spring 1959), p 24; Dave Russell, *Looking North* (Manchester, 2004), pp 184–5; *Birmingham Mail*, 27 Feb 1959.

5. http://www.youtube.com/watch?v=Dictn9woAve; Dave Rolinson, '"If They Want Culture, They Pay"', in Ian MacKillop and Neil Sinyard (eds), *British Cinema of the 1950s* (Manchester, 2003), p 91; Vincent Porter, 'The Hegemonic Turn', *Journal of Popular British Cinema* (2001), p 91; Hill, *Sex*, pp 192–3; Heap, 26 Mar 1959; Dennis Barker, 'Peter Rogers', *Guardian*, 16 Apr 2009.

6. Alan Strachan, 'Willis Hall', *Independent*, 12 Mar 2005; Dennis Barker, 'Willis Hall', *Guardian*, 12 Mar 2005; *Spectator*, 16 Jan 1959; *Birmingham Mail*, 8 Jan 1959; Michael Billington, *The Life and Work of Harold Pinter* (1996), p 106;

*Birmingham Mail*, 13 Jan 1959; *Birmingham Post*, 13 Jan 1959; Stuart Laing, *Representations of Working-Class Life, 1957–1964* (Basingstoke, 1986), p 106; *Spectator*, 27 Feb 1959.

7. *News Chronicle*, 11 Feb 1959; Heap, 10 Feb 1959; *News Chronicle*, 11 Feb 1959, 13–14 Feb 1959; *Sunday Times*, 15 Feb 1959; *Observer*, 15 Feb 1959; *Sunday Express*, 15 Feb 1959; *News Chronicle*, 16 Feb 1959, 19 Feb 1959; *New Statesman*, 21 Feb 1959, 28 Feb 1959; Graham Payn and Sheridan Morley (eds), *The Noël Coward Diaries* (1982), p 408.

8. *TV Times*, 12 Sep 1958; Leonard Miall, 'Sydney Newman', *Independent*, 4 Nov 1997; *Spectator*, 27 Mar 1959; Derrik Mercer (ed), *20th Century Day by Day* (Dorling Kindersley edn, 1999), p 1,144; 'The Army Game' (TV Heaven fact sheet); BBC WA, R9/7/38 – VR/59/52; Richard Webber, *Fifty Years of Hancock's Half Hour* (2004), p 267; Geoff Phillips, *Memories of Tyne Tees Television* (Durham City, 1998), pp 116–17; Dave Nicholson, *Bobby Thompson* (1996 edn), pp 19–20, 27–8, 43, 109–10, 118–19, 130–31, 139–40.

9. BBC WA, R9/7/39 – VR/59/145; *Listener*, 19 Mar 1959; *Radio Times*, 27 Feb 1959; *New Statesman*, 21 Mar 1959; *Punch*, 11 Feb 1959, 18 Mar 1959; Leo McKinstry, *Jack & Bobby* (2002), pp 159–60; *Oxford Mail*, 6 Mar 1959.

10. *Neath Guardian*, 27 Feb 1959; Cy Young, 'The Rise and Fall of the News Theatres', *Journal of British Cinema and Television*, 2/2 (2005), p 238; Holbeck Working Men's Club Centenary Brochure (Leeds Central Library, Local Studies, PLH69 (367)); *Romford Times*, 4 Mar 1959; *Oxford Mail*, 9 Mar 1959; Turtle, 11 Mar 1959; *Scunthorpe and Frodingham Star*, 13 Mar 1959; Wikipedia, 'Eurovision Song Contest 1959'.

11. *TV Times*, 6 Mar 1959; Larkin, Ms Eng. c. 7419, 15 Mar 1959, fols 93–4; *Herts Advertiser*, 20 Mar 1959; *The Times*, 26 Aug 2003 (Roger de Mercado); Martin, 20 Mar 1959; *Daily Mirror*, 23 Mar 1959.

12. *New Yorker*, 4 Apr 1959; Crossman, p 742; Steven Fielding, 'Activists Against "Affluence"', *Journal of British Studies* (Apr 2001), p 251; *Socialist Commentary* (Mar 1959), pp 15–17; *New Statesman*, 21 Mar 1959 (Francis Williams); *Woman*, 14 Mar 1959.

13. *Woman's Mirror*, 3 Apr 1959, 10 Apr 1959, 17 Apr 1959, 24 Apr 1959, 1 May 1959; Abrams, Box 54, Industrial Welfare Society, 'What I Expect from Work', May 1959.

14. *Observer*, 22 Mar 1959; http://garydexter.blogspot.com, 7 Oct 2009; Wikipedia, 'Ernö Goldfinger'; *Hampstead & Highgate Express*, 14 Nov 1958; *Architects' Journal*, 12 Mar 1959; Nigel Warburton, *Ernö Goldfinger* (2004), p 142.

15. *Architects' Journal*, 12 Mar 1959; *East London Advertiser*, 19 Dec 1958; Paul Barker, 'London Witness', *Prospect* (Apr 2005), p 44; *The Times*, 10 Apr 1959; David Kynaston, *The City of London, Volume 4* (2001), pp 131–2; *New Yorker*, 4 Apr 1959.

16. *Independent*, 21 Feb 1990 (James Dunnett); *Vogue* (Feb 1959), pp 100–101; 'David Pearce', *The Times*, 17 Oct 2001; *Architects' Journal*, 22 Jan 1959; *New Yorker*, 4 Apr 1959.

17. *Birmingham Mail*, 25 Feb 1959, 5 Mar 1959; Anthony Sutcliffe and Roger Smith, *Birmingham, 1939–1970* (1974), p 445; *Birmingham Mail*, 26–7 Feb 1959, 5 Mar 1959, 27 Feb 1959, 5 Mar 1959, 19 Feb 1959, 25 Feb 1959; David Harvey, *Birmingham Past and Present: The City Centre: Volume 2* (Kettering, 2003), p 69;

*Radio Times*, 20 Feb 1959; *Who Cares?* ('Never Had It So Good' evening, BBC Parliament, 10 Oct 2009).

18. *Radio Times*, 30 Jan 1959; *Listener*, 12 Feb 1959 (K. W. Gransden); BBC WA, R9/7/38 – VR/59/77; Miles Glendinning and Stefan Muthesius, *Tower Block* (1994), pp 220–24; *Times Literary Supplement*, 4 Sep 1959; T. Brennan, *Reshaping a City* (Glasgow, 1959), p 200; Alec Cairncross, *Living with the Century* (1998), pp 178–9.

19. *Liverpool Echo*, 14 Nov 1958, 24 Nov 1958; Benn, pp 299–300.

20. *Architectural Review* (Jan 1959), pp 71–2; Benwell Community Project, Final Report Series no 4, 'Slums on the Drawing Board' (Newcastle upon Tyne, 1978), pp 8–10; *Proceedings of the Council of the City and County of Newcastle upon Tyne for 1958–1959* (Newcastle upon Tyne, 1959), pp 743–9; *Architects' Journal*, 23 Apr 1959; Clare Hartwell, *Manchester* (2001), pp 35–6, 240–41, 189–90; *Manchester Evening News*, 28 Nov 1958; *Salford City Reporter*, 3 Apr 1959, 10 Apr 1959.

21. *Derbyshire Times*, 30 Jan 1959, 6 Feb 1959; *Oxford Mail*, 5 Mar 1959; *Wigan Examiner*, 20 Mar 1959.

22. *Journal of the Royal Institute of British Architects* (Dec 1958), p 48; *Architects' Journal*, 6 Nov 1958; David Watkin, 'Quinlan Terry', *Standpoint* (Jul 2008), p 81; *Listener*, 12 Feb 1959; Kenneth Powell, 'Geoffrey Powell', *Independent*, 7 Feb 2000; *Architects' Journal*, 19 Mar 1959; *Encounter* (Feb 1959), pp 54–6.

23. N. Tiratsoo, *Reconstruction, Affluence and Labour Politics* (1990), pp 86, 97; *Birmingham Mail*, 16 Feb 1959; *Socialist Commentary* (Apr 1959), pp 12–14; *Spectator*, 1 May 1959.

24. St John, 30 Mar 1959; *Guardian*, 10 Dec 2011 (Albert Beale); *Architects' Journal*, 9 Apr 1959; Simon Gunn and Rachel Bell, *Middle Classes* (2002), p 111; *New Statesman*, 4 Apr 1959; *Ayr Advertiser*, 2 Apr 1959.

25. Last, 4 Apr 1959; *Radio Times*, 27 Mar 1959; *Listener*, 9 Apr 1959; Anthony Thwaite (ed), *Selected Letters of Philip Larkin, 1940–1985* (1992), p 301; Joanna Moorhead, *New Generations* (Cambridge, 1996), p 23.

26. Macmillan, dep.d.35, 7 Apr 1959, fol 71; Heap, 7 Apr 1959; *Financial Times*, 8 Apr 1959; *The Times*, 8 Apr 1959; *Hansard*, House of Commons Debates, 8 Apr 1959, cols 233–4; *Crossman*, pp 744–5; Macmillan, dep.d.35, 9 Apr 1959, fol 72.

27. Peter Willmott and Michael Young, *Family and Class in a London Suburb* (1960), pp 1, 13–14, 112–13, 117–22; *Hansard*, House of Lords Debates, 8 Apr 1959, col 490; *Woman's Mirror*, 3 Apr 1959; *Weekly News*, 4 Apr 1959, 18 Apr 1959.

28. 'Russ Conway', *The Times*, 17 Nov 2000; Spencer Leigh, 'Russ Conway', *Independent*, 18 Nov 2000; Pete Frame, *The Restless Generation* (2007), p 309; *Daily Mirror*, 28 Mar 1959; *New Musical Express*, 24 Apr 1959; *Derby Evening Telegraph*, 20 Apr 1959; Frame, *Restless*, p 373; *Hansard*, House of Commons Debates, 22 Apr 1959, cols 381–2; *Derby Evening Telegraph*, 23–4 Apr 1959, 27 Apr 1959; *New Musical Express*, 1 May 1959; Frame, *Restless*, pp 360–61.

29. Heap, 26 Apr 1959; Gyles Brandreth, *Something Sensational to Read in the Train* (2009), p 4; *Accrington Observer*, 21 Apr 1959, 2 May 1959; Haines, 30 Apr 1959; *South London Press*, 5 May 1959; *Hants and Berks Gazette*, 8 May 1959; Last, 1 May 1959; *Crossman*, Ms 154/8/24, 6 May 1959, fol 1304; *The Times*, 4 May 1959.

30. Raynham, 4 May 1959; *Crossman*, Ms 154/8/24, 6 May 1959, fols 1304–5; *The Times*, 4 May 1959; *Neath Guardian*, 8 May 1959; *Aldershot News*, 8 May 1959.

31. *Sunday Express*, 3 May 1959; *Radio Times*, 24 Apr 1959; *TV Times*, 24 Apr 1959; *The Times*, 4 May 1959; Crossman, Ms 154/8/24, 6 May 1959, fol 1,305; *Nottingham Evening News*, 4–5 May 1959. In general on Forest's triumph, see Gary Imlach, *My Father and Other Working-Class Football Heroes* (2005), pp 110–34, 224–31.

## 12   A Merry Song of Spring

1. *Daily Sketch*, 5 May 1959; Peter Willmott and Michael Young, *Family and Class in a London Suburb* (1960), p 113; Haines, 5 May 1959; Tom Courtenay, *Dear Tom* (2000), pp 196–8; John Heilpern, *John Osborne* (2006), p 252; Graham Payn and Sheridan Morley (eds), *The Noël Coward Diaries* (1982), p 409; *Larkin*, p 249; *New Yorker*, 20 Jun 1959; Michael Billington, *State of the Nation* (2007), p 122.
2. *New Statesman*, 6 Oct 1956; Labour Party Archives (People's History Museum, Manchester), 'Study Group on Education Minutes and Papers: 27 Mar 1957–8 Jan 1958'; Guy Ortolano, 'Two Cultures, One University', *Albion* (Spring 2003), pp 607–9; C. P. Snow, *The Two Cultures* (Cambridge University Press pbk edn, 1969), pp 11, 14, 36–7, 50.
3. *Economist*, 16 May 1959; Russell Davies (ed), *The Kenneth Williams Diaries* (1993), p 150; Lawrence Black, '"Sheep May Safely Gaze"', in Lawrence Black et al, *Consensus or Coercion?* (Cheltenham, 2001), p 37; *Daily Mirror*, 5 May 1959; *The Times*, 2 May 1959; *Daily Express*, 10 Jun 1959; *Punch*, 13 May 1959; Robert Ross, *The Complete Frankie Howerd* (Richmond, 2001), p 166; Graham McCann, *Frankie Howerd* (2004), p 164; Courtenay, *Dear Tom*, pp 198–9.
4. *The Times*, 8 May 1959, 11 May 1959; Richard Bradford, *The Life of a Long-Distance Writer* (2008), p 169; *Kensington News and West London Times*, 22 May 1959; Jerry White, 'Evening All', *Times Literary Supplement*, 13 Nov 2009; *Observer*, 24 May 1959. See also: Mark Olden, *Murder in Notting Hill* (Alresford, 2011).
5. *Observer*, 24 May 1959; *The Times*, 25 May 1959; Mike Phillips and Trevor Phillips, *Windrush* (1998), pp 184–5; *Kensington News and West London Times*, 12 Jun 1959; Yasmin Alibhai-Brown, '50 Years of Race', *Independent*, 11 May 2000; Anthony Sutcliffe and Roger Smith, *Birmingham 1939–1970* (1974), pp 375–6; *Birmingham Mail*, 16 May 1959.
6. Stephen Wagg, *The Football World* (Brighton, 1984), pp 90–91; *Aldershot News*, 29 May 1959; *The Times*, 25 May 1959; *New Statesman*, 6 Jun 1959; Langford, 31 May 1959; David Clutterbuck and Marion Devine, *Clore* (1987), pp 81-3; *Punch*, 10 Jun 1959; E. P. Thompson 'The New Left', *New Reasoner*, Summer 1959, p 16; *Observer*, 31 May 1959.
7. *Listener*, 21 May 1959; John Hill, *Sex, Class and Realism* (1986), p 196; Peter Stead, *Film and the Working Class* (1989), pp 188–9; *Guardian*, 26 Sep 2008 (John Pidgeon); John Hill, 'Television and Pop', in John Corner (ed), *Popular Television in Britain* (1991), pp 101–3; *Radio Times*, 29 May 1959; *Star* (Sheffield), 1 Jun 1959; *Daily Sketch*, 29 May 1959; *Daily Mirror*, 29–30 May 1959, 2–3 Jun 1959.
8. John Hudson, *Wakes Week* (Stroud, 1992), pp 65–6; Aubrey Jones, *Britain's Economy* (Cambridge, 1985), p 80; *New Statesman*, 13 Jun 1959; Martin, 19 Jun

1959, 24 Jun 1959; Patricia Greene et al, *The Book of The Archers* (1994), p 227; Rupert Hart-Davis, *The Lyttelton Hart-Davis Letters: Volume Four* (1982), p 78; Heap, 9 Jun 1959; Macmillan, dep.d.36, 13 Jun 1959, fol 8; *Daily Mirror*, 18 Jun 1959; Paul Bailey, 'Hokum Writ Large', *Times Literary Supplement*, 5 Mar 2004; Richard Roberts, 'Regulatory Responses to the Rise of the Market for Corporate Control in Britain in the 1950s', *Business History* (Jan 1992), pp 193–4; *The Times*, 25 Jun 1959; R. A. Leeson, *Strike* (1973), p 189.

9. Gordon Bowker, *Through the Dark Labyrinth* (1996), p 274; *Daily Express*, 9 Jun 1959; *Crossman*, pp 764, 759; Macmillan, dep.d.36, 25 Jun 1959, fol 32; Geoffrey Goodman, *The Awkward Warrior* (1979), pp 217, 219–21.

10. Arnold Wesker, *Roots* (Harmondsworth, 1959), p 16; Heap, 30 Jun 1959; *Spectator*, 10 Jul 1959; Willmott, 15 Jul 1959; Paul Leslie Long, 'The Aesthetics of Class in Post-War Britain', PhD diss, University of Warwick, 2001, pp 205–6; *Noël Coward Diaries*, p 412.

11. *The Times*, 7 Jul 1959; *Architects' Journal*, 4 Jun 1959; Graeme Shankland, 'Barbican and the Elephant', *Architectural Design* (Oct 1959), p 416; *Architects' Journal*, 17 Sep 1959, 27 Aug 1959; Maxwell Hutchinson, 'Back in the High Life Again', *Independent*, 23 Feb 1994; *Architects' Journal*, 13 Aug 1959; Nigel Warburton, *Ernö Goldfinger* (2004), p 147; *East London Advertiser*, 4 Sep 1959; *Architectural Review* (Apr 1962), p 236.

12. Elain Harwood, 'White Light/White Heat', *Twentieth Century Architecture* (2002), p 61; *Guardian*, 26 Aug 1959; *Birmingham Mail*, 19 Aug 1959; Andrew Motion, *Philip Larkin* (1993), pp 293–4; *Larkin*, p 252.

13. Candida Lycett Green (ed), John Betjeman, *Coming Home* (1997), p 333; *East London Advertiser*, 19 Jun 1959; *Observer*, 14 Jun 1959; *Architects' Journal*, 21 May 1959; Rodney Gordon, 'Modern Architecture for the Masses', *Twentieth Century Architecture* (2002), pp 73–4; Nikolaus Pevsner, 'Roehampton LCC Housing and the Picturesque Tradition', *Architectural Review* (Jul 1959), pp 21–35.

14. *Shrewsbury Chronicle*, 11 Sep 1959; *Hampstead & Highgate Record*, 28 Aug 1959; *Hampstead & Highgate Express*, 4 Sep 1959, 18 Sep 1959, 25 Sep 1959.

15. *Manchester Guardian*, 17 Jun 1959; *New Statesman*, 8 Aug 1959; *Sheffield Telegraph*, 9 Jun 1959; *Birmingham Post*, 20 May 1959.

## 13 We're All Reaching Up

1. Last, 3 Jul 1959; Tim McDonald, 'Cliff Adams', *Guardian*, 1 Nov 2001; Last, 7 Jul 1959, 10 Jul 1959; Frances Partridge, *Everything to Lose* (1985), p 332; BBC WA, R9/41 - VR/59/428, T16/439/1.

2. Geoffrey Goodman, *The Awkward Warrior* (1979), p 224; Brian Brivati, *Hugh Gaitskell* (1996), pp 320–21; George Cyriax and Robert Oakeshott, *The Bargainers* (1960), p 129; *Courier and Advertiser*, 4 Jul 1959; *Oxford Mail*, 21 Jul 1959, 12 Aug 1959; Alan Thornett, *From Militancy to Marxism* (1987), p 26; *News Chronicle*, 7 Sep 1959; Peter Stead, 'A Paradoxical Turning Point', in Sheila Rowbotham and Huw Beynon (eds), *Looking at Class* (2001), p 48; Alexander Walker, *Peter Sellers* (1981), pp 87–9, 92; Geoffrey Macnab, 'Strikes . . . Camera, Action', *Independent*,

17 Sep 2010; Tony Shaw, *British Cinema and the Cold War* (2001), p 160; *Daily Mirror*, 14 Aug 1959; Shaw, *British Cinema*, p 159; D. R. Thorpe, *Supermac* (2010), pp 441, 767.

3. Macmillan, dep.d.36, 30 Jul 1959, fol 103, 5–6 Aug 1959, fols 112–14; Nigel Nicolson (ed), Harold Nicolson, *Diaries and Letters, Volume III* (1968), p 369; *New Yorker*, 29 Aug 1959.

4. Ben Pimlott, *Hugh Dalton* (1985), pp 630–31; *Grimsby Evening Telegraph*, 22 Aug 1959; *Crossman*, pp 769–70; *New Statesman*, 27 Mar 1998 (Peter Hennessy); Richard Hoggart and Raymond Williams, 'Working Class Attitudes', *New Left Review* (Jan–Feb 1960), pp 28–30.

5. Hague, Box 2 (green notebook), Bridlington diary, 1–3 Aug 1959; *Glasgow Herald*, 4 Aug 1959; Hague, Box 2 (green notebook), Bridlington diary, 8 Aug 1959; Pete Frame, *The Restless Generation* (2007), p 399; Chris Bryant, *Glenda Jackson* (1999), pp 39–40; Frame, *Restless*, p 429; *Evening Sentinel* (Stoke), 7 Sep 1959; Trina Beckett, 'Our Beach Hut on the South Coast', *Guardian*, 26 Nov 2011.

6. Dee, 15 Aug 1959; Jerry White, *London in the Twentieth Century* (2001), p 323; *East London Advertiser*, 14 Aug 1959; *Evening Sentinel* (Stoke), 21 Aug 1959; Dee, 22 Aug 1959; *Manchester Guardian*, 22 Aug 1959; *Liverpool Echo*, 26 Aug 1959, 31 Aug 1959; Mark Lewisohn, *The Complete Beatles Chronicle* (1996 edn), p 13; Chris Salewicz, *McCartney* (1986), p 79; *Liverpool Echo*, 31 Aug 1959.

7. Martin, 31 Aug 1959; Turtle, 31 Aug 1959; Michael Cockerell, *Live from Number 10* (1988), p 67; *New Yorker*, 12 Sep 1959; *Oxford Mail*, 1 Sep 1959; Russell Davies (ed), *The Kenneth Williams Diaries* (1993), p 154.

8. *Times Literary Supplement*, 4 Sep 1959; *Spectator*, 4 Sep 1959; *New Statesman*, 5 Sep 1959; *Times Literary Supplement*, 4 Sep 1959; *New Statesman*, 12 Sep 1959; Dave Russell, *Looking North* (Manchester, 2004), p 105; *Spectator*, 11 Sep 1959.

9. Larkin, Ms Eng. c. 7420, 2 Sep 1959, fol 34; *Sunday Pictorial*, 6 Sep 1959; *Radio Times*, 28 Aug 1959; *Spectator*, 18 Sep 1959; *New Statesman*, 12 Sep 1959; *Hackney Gazette*, 11 Sep 1959; *East London Advertiser*, 4 Sep 1959, 11 Sep 1959.

10. David Goodway, seminar at Institute of Historical Research, London, 1 Feb 1994; Daly, Ms 302/3/13, 31 Aug 1959, 2 Sep 1959, 8 Sep 1959; *News Chronicle*, 8 Sep 1959.

11. Sources for this collage include: *Liverpool Echo*, 27 Aug 1959; *Woman*, 20 Jun 1959; *Stores and Shops*, Jul 1959; *TV Times*, 20 Jun 1959, 5 Sep 1959.

12. *Daily Mail*, 25 Jun 1960; *Daily Express*, 4 Sep 1959.

13. *Financial Times*, 25 Jul 1959; *New Statesman*, 5 Sep 1959 (Tom Driberg); *Financial Times*, 29 Aug 1959; *Liverpool Echo*, 24 Aug 1959; *Financial Times*, 29 Aug 1959; *Manchester Evening News*, 1 Jul 1959; *Essex & Thurrock Gazette*, 8 May 1959.

14. Jan Boxshall, *Every Home Should Have One* (1997), p 73; *Financial Times*, 31 Jul 1959, 15 May 1959, 2 Feb 1960; *Guardian*, 14 Jun 1961.

15. *Manchester Evening News*, 15 Jul 1959, 21 Jul 1959; Ian Allan, *abc Scooters & Light Cars* (1959); Peter Evans, 'Mario Cassandro', *Guardian*, 10 Aug 2011; Frank Mort, 'Retailing, Commercial Culture and Masculinity in 1950s Britain', *History Workshop* (Autumn 1994), p 122; Roger Tredre, 'Willie Gertler', *Independent*, 21 Aug 1991; *Spectator*, 13 Feb 1959 (Leslie Adrian); Susan Bowden, 'Sir Charles Colston', *Dictionary of Business Biography, Volume 1* (1984), p 757; *Daily Mirror*, 28 May 1959; Ralph Harris and Arthur Seldon, *Advertising in Action* (1962), p 82.

16. Giles Chapman, 'Harry Webster', *Independent*, 17 Feb 2007; *Daily Mirror*, 26 Aug 1959; Simon Garfield, *Mini* (2009), p 40; *The Times*, 26 Aug 1959; Garfield, *Mini*, pp 78–9; *Autosport*, 28 Aug 1959; Garfield, *Mini*, p 84; *New Yorker*, 12 Sep 1959.

17. Catherine Ellis, 'The Younger Generation', *Journal of British Studies* (Apr 2002), p 211; Mark Abrams, *The Teenage Consumer* (1959), pp 10–22; M. P. Carter, *Home, School and Work* (Oxford, 1962), pp 284–5, 298–9.

18. Maggie Urry, 'Woolies Gets into Shape for the 1990s', *Financial Times*, 6 Nov 1989; *Oxford Mail*, 19 Aug 1959; *Scunthorpe and Frodingham Star*, 2 Oct 1959; *Stores and Shops*, May 1959, p 47; *The Times*, 9 Mar 1959; 'Frank Brierley', *Daily Telegraph*, 28 Jul 1999; Mort, 'Retailing', pp 122–3; Harris and Seldon, *Advertising*, pp 304–6; *Stores and Shops*, May 1959, p 17.

19. *Coventry Evening Telegraph*, 11 Aug 1959; *Daily Mail*, 11 Mar 1959; *Retail News Letter*, Sep 1959, p 9.

20. *News Chronicle*, 10 Mar 1959; *The Times*, 11 Mar 1959; Gorer, 'Television and the English', Box 1, file 1/C1; *New Statesman*, 21 Mar 1959; Last, 11 Jul 1959; Fowles, EUL Ms 102/1/11, 14–22 Aug 1959, fol 35.

21. Lawrence Black, *The Political Culture of the Left in Affluent Britain, 1951–64* (Basingstoke, 2003), p 100; Stefan Schwarzkopf, 'They Do It with Mirrors', *Contemporary British History* (Jun 2005), p 136; Dave Rolinson, '"If They Want Culture, They Pay"', in Ian MacKillop and Neil Sinyard (eds), *British Cinema of the 1950s* (Manchester, 2003), p 94; Ferdynand Zweig, *The Worker in an Affluent Society* (1961), pp 9–10, 105–6; Peter Willmott, *The Evolution of a Community* (1963), pp 99–100; *Hampstead & Highgate Express*, 21 Aug 1959.

## 14 Beastly Things, Elections

1. *Middlesex County Times and West Middlesex Gazette*, 19 Sep 1959; *Grimsby Evening Telegraph*, 18 Sep 1959; D. E. Butler and Richard Rose, *The British General Election of 1959* (1960), p 24; *Listener*, 1 Oct 1959; *New Yorker*, 2 Aug 1958; D. R. Thorpe, *Supermac* (2010), p 447; Julian Critchley, *A Bag of Boiled Sweets* (1994), p 67; *The Times*, 9 Sep 1959.

2. Paul Routledge, *Madam Speaker* (1995), p 77; *Listener*, 1 Oct 1959; *Luton News*, 24 Sep 1959.

3. Michael Foot, *Aneurin Bevan: Volume 2* (1973), p 622; *Daily Herald*, 24 Sep 1959; Geoffrey Goodman, *From Bevan to Blair* (2003), pp 81–2; Foot, *Bevan*, pp 624–6.

4. Butler and Rose, *General Election*, pp 124, 126, 138; John Campbell, *Margaret Thatcher: Volume One* (2000), pp 119–20; Michael Crick, *Michael Heseltine* (1997), p 89; Joan Lestor, 'Lord Pitt of Hampstead', *Independent*, 20 Dec 1994; *Southampton Evening Echo*, 25 Sep 1959; Tom Bower, *Maxwell* (1988), pp 89–93; *Grimsby Evening Telegraph*, 17 Sep 1959; Daly, Ms 302/3/13, c 22 Sep 1959; *Evening Times* (Glasgow), 25 Sep 1959; Bernard Bergonzi, *No Lewisham Concerto* (privately published, 1997; University of Warwick Library), p 240; *New Statesman*, 13 Feb 1998.

5. Butler and Rose, *General Election*, p 81; *Spectator*, 11 Sep 1959; John Campbell, *Nye Bevan* (1997 edn), p 358; *Kensington News and West London Times*, 2 Oct 1959; Asa Briggs, *The History of Broadcasting in the United Kingdom, Volume 5*

(Oxford, 1995), p 249; BBC WA, R9/13/182; Lawrence Black, *The Political Culture of the Left in Affluent Britain, 1951–64* (Basingstoke, 2003), p 181; BBC WA, R9/9/23 – LR/59/1597; Michael Cockerell, *Live from Number 10* (1988), p 70; *Spectator*, 9 Oct 1959 (Peter Forster); 'Never Had It So Good' evening, BBC Parliament, 10 Oct 2009; *The Times*, 22 Sep 1959; Benn, p 313; Harold Macmillan, *Pointing the Way, 1959–1961* (1972), p 8.

6. David Kynaston, *The City of London, Volume 4* (2001), p 243; Butler and Rose, *General Election*, p 55; *Crossman*, pp 779-80; Larkin, Ms Eng. c. 7420, 26 Sep 1959, fos 49-50; *Spectator*, 9 Oct 1959; Philip M. Williams, *Hugh Gaitskell* (1979), p 526; Macmillan, *Pointing*, pp 9-10; Williams, *Gaitskell*, p 526; Butler and Rose, *General Election*, p 63; *Crossman*, p 780; Benn, p 314; Butler and Rose, *General Election*, p 85.

7. *The Times*, 19 Sep 1959; Last, 18 Sep 1959, 27 Sep 1959; *New Yorker*, 10 Oct 1959; Ian S. MacNiven (ed), *The Durrell–Miller Letters 1935–80* (1988), p 360.

8. *The Times*, 19 Sep 1959; *Romford Recorder*, 18 Sep 1959; Wikipedia, 'Gerard Hoffnung'; *The Times*, 8 Oct 1959; Russell Davies (ed), *The Kenneth Williams Diaries* (1993), p 155; *Radio Times*, 4 Sep 1959; *Listener*, 24 Sep 1959; Larkin, Ms Eng. c. 7420, 10 Sep 1959, fol 36, 23 Sep 1959, fol 46; *Hackney Gazette*, 18 Sep 1959, 22 Sep 1959, 25 Sep 1959.

9. Ralph Harris and Arthur Seldon, *Advertising in Action* (1962), pp 67–70; *Grimsby Evening Telegraph*, 24 Sep 1959; *Shrewsbury Chronicle*, 25 Sep 1959; Martin, 1 Oct 1959; *The Times*, 7 Oct 1959; *Architects' Journal*, 1 Oct 1959; Malcolm MacEwen, *The Greening of a Red* (1991), pp 213–14; *Architects' Journal*, 1 Oct 1959; *Liverpool Daily Post*, 16 Sep 1959; Candida Lycett Green (ed), John Betjeman, *Letters: Volume Two* (1995), p 177.

10. *Daily Herald*, 29 Sep 1959; *The Times*, 29 Sep 1959; Ian Gilmour and Mark Garnett, *Whatever Happened to the Tories?* (1997), p 151; Geoffrey Goodman, *The Awkward Warrior* (1979), p 237; *The Times*, 30 Sep 1959; *Kensington News and West London Times*, 2 Oct 1959.

11. *Northern Echo*, 1 Oct 1959; Harry Mount, *How England Made the English* (2012), p 190; *Daily Sketch*, 1 Oct 1959; *The Times*, 1 Oct 1959; *Daily Herald*, 1 Oct 1959; *Middlesex Independent*, 9 Oct 1959; *Hampstead & Highgate Express*, 2 Oct 1959.

12. Last, 1 Oct 1959; Benn, p 314; Butler and Rose, *General Election*, p 62; *Daily Herald*, 2–3 Oct 1959; *Spectator*, 2 Oct 1959; *New Statesman*, 10 Oct 1959.

13. Heap, 3 Oct 1959; *Grimsby Evening Telegraph*, 5 Oct 1959; Benn, pp 312, 314; *News Chronicle*, 5 Oct 1959; Butler and Rose, *General Election*, p 66; *Crossman*, p 785; Butler and Rose, *General Election*, p 66; *Crossman*, p 788; Last, 5 Oct 1959.

14. *Daily Sketch*, 6 Oct 1959; *The Times*, 7 Oct 1959; *Luton News*, 8 Oct 1959; *Southampton Evening Echo*, 7 Oct 1959; Benn, p 316; Butler and Rose, *General Election*, p 67; BBC WA, R9/13/182; *Daily Telegraph*, 7 Oct 1959; *Daily Sketch*, 8 Oct 1959; *Radio Times*, 2 Oct 1959; Mervyn Jones, *Michael Foot* (1994), p 240; Preston, 7 Oct 1959.

15. Benn, p 316; Preston, 8 Oct 1959; Willmott, 8 Oct 1959; *The Times*, 8 Oct 1959; Butler and Rose, *General Election*, p 105; Benn, p 316; *Hampstead & Highgate Express*, 9 Oct 1959; *Grimsby Evening Telegraph*, 8 Oct 1959; Larkin, Ms

Eng. c. 7420, 7–8 Oct 1959, fol 60; Lewis, 8 Oct 1959; *Daily Mirror*, 8 Oct 1959; Roy Greenslade, *Press Gang* (2003), p 117; Last, 8 Oct 1959.

16. Last, 8 Oct 1959; George H. Gallup, *The Gallup International Public Opinion Polls: Great Britain 1937–1975, Volume One* (New York, 1976), p 543; Briggs, *History of Broadcasting*, p 253; *Spectator*, 16 Oct 1959 (Peter Forster); *New Yorker*, 24 Oct 1959; *Billericay Times*, 7 Oct 1959, 14 Oct 1959; Ben Pimlott (ed), *The Political Diary of Hugh Dalton* (1986), p 693; David Childs, 'Geoffrey Johnson Smith', *Independent*, 26 Aug 2010; Heap, 8 Oct 1959; *Kenneth Williams Diaries*, p 156; *Grimsby Evening Telegraph*, 9 Oct 1959; Margaret Thatcher, *The Path to Power* (1995), pp 100–101; Roy Hattersley, *Who Goes Home?* (1995), p 23; Foot, *Bevan*, p 627; Benn, p 316.

17. Butler and Rose, *General Election*, pp 189–90; Kevin Jefferys, *Retreat from New Jerusalem* (Basingstoke, 1997), p 81; N. Tiratsoo, *Reconstruction, Affluence and Labour Politics* (1990), p 99; Lewis Baston, *Reggie* (Stroud, 2004), p 135; Roy Jenkins, *A Life at the Center* (New York, 1991), p 122; Butler and Rose, *General Election*, p 216; Routledge, *Madam Speaker*, p 79; Bower, *Outsider*, p 93; Butler and Rose, *General Election*, pp 184–5 (Keith Kyle); Kynaston, *City*, p 244; Norman Sherry, *The Life of Graham Greene, Volume 3* (2004), p 215; *Larkin*, p 260; Larkin, Ms Eng. c. 7420, 9 Oct 1959, fol 62; Turtle, 9 Oct 1959; Last, 10 Oct 1959; Tom Courtenay, *Dear Tom* (2000), p 244; *Daily Sketch*, 10 Oct 1959.

18. *Crossman*, p 786; *Fowles*, p 431; David Owen, *Time to Declare* (1991), p 54; Butler and Rose, *General Election*, p 201; *The Times*, 10 Oct 1959; Macmillan, *Pointing*, p 15; *Viewer*, 29 Aug 1959.

# Acknowledgements

The following kindly gave me permission to reproduce copyright material: Evelyn Abrams (Mark Abrams); The Agency (London) Ltd (extracts from the writing of Arnold Wesker; extract from *As Much As I Dare* © Arnold Wesker, 1994; extract from Wesker's piece in Charles Marowitz et al, *The Encore Reader* © Arnold Wesker 1970; letter to New Statesman © Arnold Wesker, 1959; letter to Charles Parker © Arnold Wesker, 2001, as quoted in Paul Leslie Long, 'The Aesthetics of Class in Post-War Britain'. All rights reserved); Aitken Alexander Associates (extracts from the diaries of John Fowles © J. R. Fowles Ltd); Lady Diana Baer (Mollie Panter-Downes); BBC Written Archives Centre; Ken Blakemore (*Sunnyside Down*); Alan Brodie Representation Ltd (extracts from *The Noël Coward Diaries* copyright © NC Aventales AG 1982); Jonathan Clowes Ltd (extract from *Walking in the Shade* © Doris Lessing 1997; extract from 'The Small Personal Voice' by Doris Lessing in *Declaration*, ed Tom Maschler 1957; extract from *The Four-Gated City* copyright © Doris Lessing 1969); John Cousins (Frank Cousins); Virginia Crossman (Richard Crossman); Curtis Brown Group Ltd, London (on behalf of the Trustees of the Mass-Observation Archive, copyright © Trustees of the Mass-Observation Archive); The Dartington Hall Trust Archive; Mary Evans, Centennial Professor, London School of Economics (*A Good School*); Ray Galton and Alan Simpson (extract from the opening sequence from *Hancock's Half Hour*, 'Sunday Afternoon at Home'); Roy Greenslade (*Goodbye to the Working Class*); Rachel Gross (Geoffrey Gorer); Pamela Hendicott (Judy Haines); Islington Local History Centre (Gladys Langford); the *Liverpool Echo*; The Trustees of the Harold Macmillan Book Trust (extracts from the late Harold Macmillan's diaries); Jamie Muir and Denis Norden (Frank Muir and Denis Norden Archive); News Group Newspapers Ltd Archive (John Hilton Bureau); Allan Preston (Kenneth Preston); The Random House Group Limited (extracts from *Years of Hope: Diaries, Letters and Papers 1940–1962* by Tony Benn, published by Hutchinson; extracts from *Dear Tom: Letters from Home* by Tom Courtenay, published by Doubleday; extracts from *Culture and Society 1780–1950* by Raymond Williams, published by Chatto & Windus); Marian Ray and Robin Raynham (Marian Raynham); Rogers, Coleridge and White Ltd (*Diaries 1939–1972* by Frances Partridge Copyright © Frances Partridge 1985); The Society of Authors as the Literary Representative of the Estate of Philip Larkin (extracts from the unpublished letters of Philip Larkin); Roxana and Matthew Tynan (*Theatre Writings* by Kenneth Tynan); United Agents LLP (extracts from *The Kenneth Williams Diaries* © The Estate of Kenneth Williams); Phyllis Willmott; The Wylie Agency (UK) Ltd (extracts from reviews published in the *Spectator* of *The Uses of Literacy* and *Family and Kinship in East London*, and extracts from *Socialism and the Intellectuals* and *The Letters of Kingsley Amis*, all © Kingsley Amis); Toby Young (Michael Young).

Many people have helped to make this book happen, and (with apologies to anyone inadvertently omitted) I am grateful to: Mark Aston; Joe Bailey; Michael Banton; Sophie Bridges; Mike Burns; Nigel Cochrane; James Codd; Nick Corbo-Stuart; Fiona Courage; Helen Ford; John Gold; Adam Harwood; Sir Antony Jay; Helen Langley; Rose Lock; Sandy Macmillan; Duncan Marlor; Nick Mays; Louise North; Jonathan Oates; Stanley Page; Jessica Scantlebury; John Symons; Sue Taylor; Richard Thorpe; Lisa Towner; Jenny Uglow; Karen Watson; Annalisa Zisman (Back to Balance).

In addition, a special 'thank you' goes to Amanda Howard (Superscript Editorial Services) for her meticulous transcribing of my tapes, and to four fellow-historians for their generosity and encouragement: Richard Davenport-Hines, Juliet Gardiner, Dil Porter and Andy Ward.

The endgame of any book has its challenges, and I would like to thank: Harry Ricketts (for making helpful stylistic suggestions); David Milner (for running a sympathetic but dispassionate eye over a draft at a particularly valuable moment); Andrea Belloli (for her copy-editing skills); Catherine Best, Patric Dickinson and David Warren (for their careful and constructive proof-reading); Christopher Phipps (for his excellent index). Between them they have done much to improve this book's quality.

Bloomsbury remains a fine publishing house, combining professionalism with a human touch, and I am especially grateful to my editor Bill Swainson and his colleagues Nick Humphrey and Anna Simpson.

I am fortunate to have Deborah Rogers as my agent, and my heartfelt thanks go to her and her colleague Mohsen Shah.

My deepest debt is twofold: to my family (Lucy, Laurie, George and Michael) for their unfailing practical as well as emotional support; and to the doctors, nurses and staff of the Trevor Howell Ward at St George's, Tooting, for their care and kindness after my life took an unexpected turn around the time of the Olympics.

New Malden
January 2013

# Picture Credits

The Bradford Empire just before demolition, 1957 (*Picture courtesy of Telegraph & Argus, Bradford*)

Birmingham, May 1957: Aston Villa players and mascot parade the FA Cup at Villa Park (*photographer unknown*)

Unrationed sweets: London, 1957 (*Popperfoto/Getty Images*)

Clarendon Crescent, Paddington, 1957 (*Mary Evans Picture Library ROGER MAYNE*)

Notting Hill at night, 1958 (*Getty Images*)

Fishermen carry coracles to the River Teifi in Cardiganshire, March 1958 (*Getty Images*)

Cherry-picking: West Malling, Kent, July 1958 (*The Times/NI Syndication*)

Redevelopment in Everton Heights, Liverpool, 1959 (*Courtesy of the Liverpool Echo*)

Youth club float, New Malden, Surrey, July 1959 (*Courtesy of the Kingston Heritage Service Picture Collection*)

St George's Day parade, St Helier Estate, South London, 1959 (*Photo taken by a photographer from the Croydon Times, now incorporated in the Croydon Advertiser. Image courtesy of Sutton Local Studies & Archives Service*)

Harold Macmillan in the north-east, January 1959 (*Jim Pringle/AP/Press Association Images*)

Hugh Gaitskell at the Midland Area Miners' Gala, June 1959 (*Mirrorpix*)

Election night, October 1959 (*Copyright BBC Photo Library*)

# Index